C000172279

HIGHLAND SOLDIER

A Social Study of the Highland Regiments, 1820 - 1920

DIANA M. HENDERSON

JOHN DONALD PUBLISHERS LTD
EDINBURGH

ISBN 0 85976 217 3

Distributed in the United States of America and Canada by Humanities Press Inc., Atlantic Highlands, NJ07716, U.S.A.

Phototypeset by Print Origination (NW) Limited, Formby, Liverpool L37 8EG
Printed in Great Britain by Bell & Bain Ltd., Glasgow

Foreword

by Brigadier James A. Oliver, CB, CBE, DSO, TD, DL, LL.D

I read *Highland Soldier* with very great interest and enjoyment, and to anyone who has the interest of the Highland Regiments at heart I am quite sure that it will prove fascinating reading. It covers not only one hundred years of the social and domestic history of the Highland Regiments, but also gives an excellent account of life throughout the Highland area during that period.

Dr. Henderson's book shows how important both the regimental system and morale have always been in the Highland Regiments and the steps that were taken to support morale even when no actual fighting was involved. For some considerable time there has been a threat to the regimental system and I understand that this threat is again very real today. No doubt warfare methods of the past are now completely out of date and the regimental system would cause difficulties in modern war, but I feel sure that morale at the sharp end, which has always been so important in the past, is likely to be equally important and probably more so in the future. War at the sharp end has always been, and no doubt always will be, a very unpleasant and frightening experience and anything which helps to achieve a satisfactory result should not be interfered with lightly.

Some years ago, correspondence about a threat to the regimental system appeared in *The Times* and Field Marshal Sir Gerald Templer, one of the great soldiers of the last war and the immediate post-war period, wrote, 'Do you not realise that the regimental system of the British Army is and always has been the envy of the world? I know what it is that makes an infantry man ready if necessary to die for his country at the sharp end of battle. . . I trust that this long proven national asset of the regimental system will never be thrown away for administrative convenience.'

The people of the United Kingdom are not, unlike some other nations, warlike by nature. There was a time when Highlanders, owing to instinct, tradition and necessity, were warlike but this time is long past now. Field Marshal Lord Montgomery however, who commanded Highland soldiers from Alamein in 1942 to VE Day in 1945, repeatedly said that he fully realised that the clan instincts and regimental pride of his Highland soldiers required and justified very special attention.

Every aspect of the social and domestic side of soldiering in the Highland Regiments has been examined and explored most thoroughly and is clearly explained in *Highland Soldier*. Recruitment, living conditions and family life, discipline, religion, music, financial arrangements, trooping and food and drink are all dealt with in detail; drink during the period covered by this book presenting a considerable problem in a soldier's life as, in fact, it did in many other walks of life at that time.

As I have said, I am sure *Highland Soldier* will give much pleasure to readers who have the interest of the Highland Regiments at heart. If, in addition to providing an excellent record and review of a very important period in military history, this book also helps to persuade people that the regimental system should, if at all possible, be preserved it will have served a very useful further purpose.

James A. Oliver, West Newton, Arbroath.

Preface and Acknowledgements

A serious attempt has been made in this study to seek out hitherto under-researched archival sources in the various Regimental Museums and other locations, and the search has not been in vain. The Regimental Museums have yielded in particular a considerable amount of valuable information and unpublished material, but none of this research would have been possible without the entirely free hand which was accorded to me, to dig in dim and distant files, cupboards and cellars, by the Regimental Secretaries; Lieutenant Colonel G.P. Wood MC of the Argyll and Sutherland Highlanders, Lieutenant Colonel Angus Fairrie of the Queen's Own Highlanders, Colonel the Hon. David Arbuthnott MBE of the Black Watch, Major Donald Mack of the Royal Highland Fusiliers and Major Ian Martineau of the Gordon Highlanders.

Wherever possible Regimental Museum reference numbers have been given to archive sources, and while these are complete and comprehensive in the Queen's Own Highlanders Museum and the Black Watch Museum, few items are referenced in the Gordon Highlanders Museum and a new system of index is presently being introduced at the Argyll and Sutherland Highlanders Museum. While the study was in progress the archives of the Royal Highland Fusiliers were destroyed by fire and many of the sources for the 74th Highlanders are now, sadly, unobtainable.

The Regimental Secretaries, while allowing me unrestricted access to archives, also very generously and frankly gave me most valuable advice and support, and in this respect I am particularly grateful to Lieutenant Colonel Angus Fairrie and Lieutenant Colonel G.P. Wood MC, who together with my good friends Mr. William Boag of the Scottish United Services Museum, Lieutenant Colonel David Murray, Queen's Own Cameron Highlanders (retd.), Lieutenant Colonel Brian Mackenzie (retd.), Mr. Douglas Anderson, Dr. Donald Galbraith of the Scottish Record Office, Mr. Eddie MacMillan and Major John Allan, Queen's Own Highlanders, were always ready to put up with my many questions, discuss contentious areas and advise me from the depths of their considerable and irreplaceable experience.

As a result of very good fortune I was able also to speak to two remarkable men, Private Reginald Lobban of the 1st Battalion Queen's Own Cameron Highlanders and Corporal Frank MacFarlane MSM of the 1st Battalion Black Watch. Both these men served before 1914 in the Regular Army and through their efforts and generosity they gave me a first-hand picture of the pre-First World War Highland Battalions that could be gained from no other source. Private Lobban died in 1984 as the last known pre-1914 Cameron Highlander, and I can only hope that in the writing I have done justice to both of these gentlemen.

While doing the research I was disappointed with the scarcity of Gaelic sources, although there was compensation particularly in the War Office material at the Public Record Office, Kew, London, whose staff, like that of the Imperial War Museum, the National Army Museum, the Scottish United Services Museum, the Scottish Record Office and the National Museums of Scotland, were always helpful. My thanks too go to the Royal Commission on the Ancient and Historical Monuments of Scotland, the National Library of Scotland, the Central Library Edinburgh, the librarians of the Universities of Edinburgh and Glasgow, Sergeant Major Mullen of the Corps of Commissionaires Edinburgh, Brigadier Miles Marston MC of Queen Victoria School, Dunblane, the Chief Constable of Tayside Police and Heart of Midlothian Football Club.

Having assembled the various sources, it is clear that some important primary source material has come to light, particularly the Diaries of Colonel J.W. Wedderburn and Private A.W. McIntosh of the 42nd, the letters and papers of Lt. Colonel the Hon. Lauderdale Maule of the 79th, the diaries of Spencer Ewart of the Queen's Own Cameron Highlanders, the diary of Lt. William Parke of the 72nd, the Descriptive Roll Book of the 93rd and the books and papers of Lt. Colonel Bertie Gordon of the 91st. All these sources and others provided an interesting chronological spread but were nevertheless not continuous as far as individual Regiments were concerned, and in many cases these sources, or gaps in the sources, reflect not only the strength of individual personalities, but also the interest of the Regiment in their history and archives at the critical period in the 1840s when many Regimental records were destroyed, and at the beginning of the twentieth century when many records must have been discarded in the absence of Regimental museums. Thus, the quotation of sources may not always appear Regimentally even, but I took the view that a competent, relevant source was worth noting no matter what the Regiment, and therefore the material used does not reflect any Regimental prejudice or favouritism.

Finally I have to express my appreciation to Dr. William Ferguson of the Department of Scottish History, University of Edinburgh, who patiently and with good humour advised and encouraged my work and directed me to valuable material.

Contents

Abbreviations

SRO	Scottish Record Office
PRO	Public Record Office
NLS	National Library of Scotland
CL	Central Library, Edinburgh
SUSM	Scottish United Services Museum
ASHRM	Argyll and Sutherland Highlanders Regimental Museum, Stirling Castle
BWRM	Black Watch Regimental Museum, Balhousie Castle, Perth
GHRM	Gordon Highlanders Regimental Museum, Viewfield Road, Aberdeen
QOHRM	Queen's Own Highlanders Regimental Museum, Cameron Barracks and Fort George, Inverness
RHFRM	Royal Highland Fusiliers Regimental Museum, Glasgow
WO	War Office
HO	Home Office
AD	Lord Advocate's Department
MW	Ministry of Works
JC	Justiciary Court Registers, West Register House, Edinburgh
RHP	Register House Plans
PP	Parliamentary Paper

CHAPTER 1
Historical Introduction

The maintenance of a Regular Standing Army is a relatively recent innovation in British history.[1] Unless there was a specific cause to fight, regiments were raised and disbanded as required. Standing armies cost a great deal of money and were traditionally opposed by Parliament and taxpayers alike. In 1638 Charles I's 'Regular' army comprised Gentlemen Pensioners,[2] the equivalent of one troop of horse, the Yeomen of the Guard,[3] about the size of an Infantry company, the Garrisons of the various Royal Castles and Forts and the Board of Ordnance in charge of cannon, stores and ammunition, with its headquarters at the Tower of London.[4]

At the same time however there was a tradition of English and Scottish service in Continental armies, particularly in Dutch, Swedish and French service, and many of these men provided the military background and experience that was to lay the foundation of a British Regular Army.[5] Many of the men who volunteered as mercenaries came from the Highlands.[6]

With the Union of the Crowns in 1603, the English and Scottish armies came under one King but maintained separate establishments. England was principally defended by the Militia, there being no Militia Act in Scotland until 1797, but the muster and embodiment of trained bands was inefficient and unreliable. There was no territorial recruiting in the seventeenth century, and although Scots did serve both Charles I and the Commonwealth, the raising of Scots regiments for defence or internal security was contrary to the view of Scotland as a somewhat dangerous appendage to the English mainland. Within Scotland too, a deep rift was developing between Highlands and Lowlands as patterns of trade, agriculture and social structure changed, threatening the fabric of Highland society and culture.

After the Civil War the Army clearly became the responsibility and charge of Parliament not the Monarch, and after the battles of Dunbar and Worcester (1650-1651), Monck, commanding the Cromwellian forces in Scotland, carried out the first serious attempt to garrison and pacify the Highlands on a permanent basis.

In 1661, as a result of a complex transition, and from the remnants of the New Model Army, arose the basis of regular forces in Britain, the Coldstream Guards and the Life Guards.[7] However, some Scottish troops in French service, claiming origins as far back as the Scottish Archer Guard of France[8] and the Garde du Corps Ecossais, having been recalled and claimed by Charles II in 1678, claimed precedence over all other regiments and the title, 'First or Scots Regiment of Foot' (The Royal Scots):

> Even at this early stage there ran high in the new army an esprit-de-corps, a mutual jealousy and a struggle for precedence. The Royals asserted that their Corps was far senior to the Guards or the Coldstreamers and showed that they were nettled at not having precedence of these; and the others retorted by bestowing upon the sticklers for antiquity, whose origin was indeed placed so far back as to become somewhat mythical, the nickname of 'Pontius Pilate's Guards'[9]

Thus, although regiments were still commonly known by the name of their Colonel, claims of precedence and numbering developed. The use of a number alone by which to differentiate one Regiment from another was an eighteenth-century innovation and the standardisation of the numbers themselves was not finalised until the nineteenth century, many regiments changing their numbers during their history; for example the 43rd Highland Regiment became 42nd in order of precedence in 1749.[10] Thus precedence and numerical designation were two different things. Precedence, too, implied position in the line of battle, the right of the line being the coveted place as formalised field tactics developed in the eighteenth century.

As distinctive as the numbers of precedence at this time were the colours of the 'Facings' or linings of the jackets, which are actually older therefore than the fixed numbers of a later date. The cuffs, lapels and collars were turned back and the Drummers usually wore jackets in the facing colour of the Regiment. Thus the buff facings of the 78th Highland Regiment gave them the nickname and later the formal title of the 'Ross-shire Buffs'. These facing colours survived in the uniform of the Number 1 Dress jackets of Highland Regiments until they were allowed to lapse in 1984.

After the Restoration a separate Scottish military establishment was formed which lasted until 1707.[11] Scottish Regiments and individuals continued to serve as mercenaries, employed in English and European service, but distrust of a standing army continued. Scots units and Regiments served in the Dutch Wars, the Thirty Years War, the Revolution of 1689, the war in Ireland and the War of the Spanish Succession. During the last-named conflict, Union of the Parliaments of Scotland and England had been completed, which, coupled with the question of Succession and religion, created deep internal conflicts in Scotland. After the disbandment of large sections of Marlborough's successful army in 1714, following the Treaty of Utrecht, and urged on by the French, rebellion broke out in Scotland in 1715.

By 1715 the importance of trade and the acquisition of foreign garrisons and colonies such as Nova Scotia, Newfoundland, Gibraltar and Minorca meant that internal rebellion was viewed with great concern. European armies were becoming organised and professional, while in Britain there was still only a skeleton of a Standing Army and an undrilled Militia. The successes of the Highlanders in the 1715 Rebellion severely shook the establishment in England and in Scotland, and the powers of endurance and fighting qualities of these men became all too apparent.

Early Highland social structure was based on a system of kinship or 'clann' (children), linking groups by blood or marriage, younger sons or grandsons forming cadet branches of the group. The Chief, originally the man considered the wisest and best able to lead, came to be chosen from amongst a particular line, but the position was not always passed direct from father to son. The clan structure was not unique to the Highlands and as a social system still survives in Papua New Guinea.

The area in which the clans lived covered one fifth of the total land area of Britain and half of Scotland. It was, and in many cases still is, remote and inaccessible. Geography and climate added to the isolation from the more easily farmed and managed lower lands on the coastal fringes and in the South.

With the geographical limitations on movement, clans became associated with particular areas, as clan territories. The introduction of the feudal system however took little account of these territories and the Charter holder might have living on his lands, as vassals or tenants, men who owed allegiance, by clan, to someone entirely different. Law and order was therefore not the simple matter of exerting pressure on feudal superiors to control their vassals on pain of forfeiture.

Chiefs could raise from amongst their supporters large numbers of armed men, who could be used for defence, attack, clan feud or in the service of the king. Disputes were common and successive Scottish kings, from James I in 1424, tried hard to control restless and truculent chiefs.

The chiefs and their clans were no more warlike than the comparable great houses of England, but they were geographically more difficult to control and they did continue to challenge the established law and order for a longer period of time. Devices for their control included commissions of 'fire and sword', as against Clan Chattan in 1528, castle building, the appointment of 'Lieutenants', such as Argyll and Huntly, making chiefs responsible for the arrest of offenders amongst their own kinsmen and a system of rewards and punishments.

James VI of Scotland made the most determined and systematic efforts to end the internal feuds and unrest. Insisting upon the divine right of his kingship, he acknowledged the difference between the feudal superior and the clan chief and enacted that where the latter held power, he was responsible for his offending clansmen. Titles of lands claimed were ordered to be produced in 1598 on pain of forfeiture and 'broken' clans, that is those with no specific land areas associated with their names, such as the MacGregors, were placed under considerable pressure to conform to the law or ally with another clan.

The Isles were seen by James VI as a particular problem and after imprisoning the Island Chiefs, they agreed to the Statutes of Iona in 1609.

A select group of large and powerful families began to emerge, who held in the main both feudal title and chieftainship: Gordons, Mackenzies, Campbells and Macintoshes for example.

Thus the Highland area had, since the Wars of Independence, posed a particularly difficult problem both geographically and militarily. Its isolation and social structure conflicted with that of the remainder of the Kingdom and the Highlands were in a sense 'left out' in the social, economic and cultural developments of the period. The clan as a social group survived, providing both obligations and mutual support, and in the wild country and equally wild climate a tough, self-reliant and warlike people survived, who were accustomed to battle and skilled in arms.

The first Earl of Breadalbane is credited with the suggestion, in 1690, of a Highland force for internal security, in the form of Independent Highland Companies commanded by Highland Chiefs.[12] A similar recommendation was made by Lord Lovat in 1724 and General Wade in 1725, but as early as 1667 the second Earl of Atholl had held a Commission to raise independent companies to 'keep watch upon the braes'. Other corps followed but all were disbanded in 1717.[13]

On 12th May 1725 four Independent Companies of Highland men were re-established followed by two others in 1729. The Companies were collectively known as 'the Watch, the Highland Watch or am Freiceadan Dubh'.[14] In 1739, these six Companies, with four additional Companies, were formed into a Highland Regiment of Foot, 43rd in precedence.[15]

Thus, under extraordinary circumstances of rebellion and internal unrest, the first regular Highland Regiment in British service was formed. In 1749 their order of precedence was 42nd and this Regiment survives today as the 1st Battalion the Black Watch (Royal Highland Regiment).

Their history was not a long string of glorious military successes however, such as would inspire great confidence in raising further Highland corps. In 1743 the 43rd (Black Watch) mutinied at Finchley Common amidst a feeling of distrust and Highland suspicion, largely based on the fear that they were to be sent to serve in the American plantations.[16] In 1745 a further Jacobite Rebellion in the midst of a major European war determined the Government on a policy of permanently garrisoning the Highlands, proscription of the Highland dress and carrying arms except in Government service, and the dispossession of disloyal chieftains.[17] These measures affected the very fabric of Highland society and further emphasised the gulf between Highlands and Lowlands. The bearing of arms was an important part of Highland social structure and the Disarming Act tried to ensure that the only legitimate outlet was in Government service.

From the first, the men in Highland Battalions retained their national language and music, an adaptation of their form of dress became their uniform and they were officered in the main by men of their own lands and origins.[18] Their fighting abilities were proven at Fontenoy in 1745, a campaign which marked the abandoning of the original principle of 'Highland Watch'.

These fighting qualities were not however always appreciated. At Fontenoy the 43rd (Black Watch) had loaded their muskets and awaited the enemy's command of 'present'. The Highlanders then fell down on the ground just as the enemy fired, rose quickly to their feet, fired a volley and then with wild abandon threw their muskets away and charged with the broadsword.[19] Wolfe was known to be infuriated by the Highlanders' indiscipline and recklessness in the field and their insistence on the Highland charge.[20]

Between 1725 and 1800, thirty-seven units of Highlanders were raised (exclusive of Fencibles and Militia) for British service. Of these, twenty-six were reformed, disbanded or drafted. Two serve today as part of a Lowland Regiment and nine as parts of Highland Regiments.[21]

In a period of seventy-five years, between 1725 and 1800, the numbers of men involved were considerable.[22] There appear to be two distinct views on this use of Highland manpower. Firstly, that it was a deliberate Government policy not only to disarm the Highlands but to depopulate them, draining the manpower permanently to an army destined for foreign stations and wars, where it would inevitably be ravaged by disease and battles; that the men so recruited were frequently abused, abandoned and betrayed by a distant and unfeeling Government, who made no attempt to understand their Highland culture and motivation. Secondly, and alternatively, that it was unrealistic for the old clan structure to continue any longer. There was serious Highland overpopulation: recruiting to the Army saved many from starvation and restored the credibility of the Highlander as a loyal fighting man. In the international situation during these seventy-five years Britain could not afford to have a rebellious and potentially open Northern flank, a view supported by English, Lowland Scots and even Highlanders. The Army provided a realistic outlet for the Highlander's natural fighting abilities,[23] and no other regiments in the British Army, recruited from within the Islands, were allowed such privileges as the retention of national dress in uniform. Fighting under their own officers to whom many men had a personal relationship, the Highland Regiments formed an élite, proud of their service, second to none and would have greeted any suggestion of abuse with anger and disdain.

Both points of view have merit. What is clear is that in the nine Highland Regiments that survived, there developed an extraordinary esprit-de-corps, loyalty, courage and pride. The best qualities of Highland men had been brought to their full potential in these Regiments. It is difficult to understand how this could have been done if the Highlanders had not had their hearts in the business.[24]

By 1777 the principle of raising Highland Regiments was well established, and of the twenty regiments raised between 1777 and 1800, no less than half were still on the establishment in 1820.[25] Lord Seaforth's Highlanders, raised 1778 (78th and later 72nd); the Perthshire Highlanders, raised 1780 (73rd); The Highland Regiment of Foot, raised in 1787 (74th); the Stirlingshire Regiment, known as Abercromby's, raised 1787 (75th); the Highland Regiment of Foot, later known as the Ross-shire Buffs, raised 1793 (78th); the Cameronian Volunteers or Cameron Highlanders, raised 1793 (79th); the Argyllshire Highlanders, raised 1794 (98th and later 91st); the Gordon Highlanders, raised 1794 (100th and later 92nd); and finally the Sutherland Highlanders, raised 1800 (93rd). These were all raised by eminent Highland men, drawing upon the loyalties and discipline of the clan system. Initially, these Regiments served in the Carnatic, Mysore and Mahratta campaigns and in the Netherlands, Egypt, Peninsular and Cape of Good Hope.

The method of 'raising' these Regiments was to have important repercussions on their subsequent character when compared with Lowland and English Regiments. Although the mechanics were roughly equivalent, the motivation of the officers and men and the territorial nature of the recruiting were unique.

To raise any regiment the prime mover had to have influence, ambition and financial backing. Application was made to the King for authority to raise a regiment of foot soldiers, and after receiving approval the officer destined to command received his Commission, signed by the Secretary of State for War. It is suggested that the King himself prompted Argyll to raise his Regiment, although George II had previously vetoed the raising of regular Highland regiments.

Thereafter, the Order and Warrant for raising a Regiment of Foot was signed by the King and the Secretary for War. Known as 'the Beating Order', that of the 79th (Cameronian Volunteers later Cameron Highlanders) read:

> . . . to our Trusty and Well Beloved Alan Cameron Esqr, Major Commd't of a Regiment of Foot to be forthwith raised or to the Officer appointed by him to raise men for Our Kingdom of Great Britain, as shall be wanted to Complete the said Regiment . . . .[26]

Then, a Letter of Service was issued, laying down the terms of the contract between the prime mover and the Government. These were not always standard and it is interesting to compare those of the 79th (Cameron) Highlanders and the 93rd (Sutherland) Highlanders.[27] Thereafter recruiting began. Once completed to the allotted number of men, the Regiment was inspected by a General Officer and established as 'effective'.

The Commanding Officer (or the prime mover if he did not actually command), having expended considerable sums in this process, was then able to claim his outgoings from the Paymaster General which he did through the intermediary of Regimental Agents, acting in the capacity of brokers. The whole arrangement had considerable similarities to the standard method of investment in any company enterprise. The man raising the Regiment, for an outlay of approximately £15,000, gathered, paid, clothed and fed recruits and on 'establishment' of the regiment obtained his return on capital by way of public funds, through the Regimental Agents. He, in turn, paid Captains of Companies, who paid their men. All down the chain everyone expected to make a profit. In addition, in time of war, a Commanding Officer could expect considerable prize money and always additional funds through a complex system of allowances, and of course power and prestige as commander of a regiment.

It is in the area of recruiting that the Highland Regiments were unique. Firstly, as regards the senior officers, by far the majority were Highland gentlemen and, with the exception of Alan Cameron of Erracht, all had considerable resources and connections with estates in the Highland area from which they drew their recruits.[28] Some of these men had lived in exile, such as Alan

Cameron, or had only recently had their forfeited estates returned to them, such as the Earl of Seaforth. Perhaps some were motivated by greed or personal aggrandisement but certainly not all, for the financial rewards were decidely precarious. Some, with a real fear of Republican France, acted from motives of genuine loyalty and patriotism.

For their officers, these men turned to friends, relatives or at least acquaintances. Some Letters of Service limited the recruitment of officers to men already on the Half Pay list, but ways were frequently found to get round this. Nearly all these early officers were Highlanders or had Highland associations and they, in their turn, went to recruit for the rank and file in areas of the Highlands where they held sway and influence, often to their own estates or kinsmen.

In 1778, Lord Seaforth recruited 500 men from his own estates and obtained a further 400 through his chosen officers from other Mackenzie lands at Scatwell, Kilcoy, Applecross and Recastle; the remaining 130 were Lowlanders, English and Irish.[29] Francis Humberston Mackenzie raised his 78th Highland Regiment from his own estates in Ross-shire and Lewis. The 93rd (Sutherland) Highlanders were built around a nucleus of 269 men disbanded from the Sutherland Fencibles: most of the remaining 394 were raised not by recruiting but by levy and ballot.

Alan Cameron, desperate to complete the 79th (Cameron) Highlanders in the given time of three months and short of money, but not energy or influence, sought men in Inverness, Aberdeen, Paisley and Stirling. The greater part of the 79th were however freely recruited in Lochaber, Appin, Mull and North Argyll, where despite opposition from the influential Gordon family he was greeted as a hero at the Martinmas Fair at Maryburgh in 1793. There, taking advantage of his reputation and the local celebrations, he completed the Regiment.[30] The financial records of the Regiment of this period show that although enlistment may have been voluntary, it was assisted by liquid refreshment:

> 7 November 1793 . . . to 66 gallons of whisky £12.8.3.[31]

Men from Gordon lands are romantically said to have been encouraged to enlist by a 'kiss and a guinea' from the Duchess herself.[32]

The wide service of these various Highland Regiments meant heavy losses in killed, wounded and sick, and a considerable drain on Highland manpower. Between 1794 and 1809 the 79th (Cameron) Highlanders alone lost 737 officers and men, killed in action and died of wounds, disease or accident.[33] By 1809, it was found difficult to keep all these nine regiments, together with the 42nd (Royal Highland) (and the 71st and 94th), filled up with Highland men. It was argued that Lowlanders and others were reluctant to join because of the Highland dress and in 1809, six regiments lost Highland status (72nd, 73rd, 74th, 75th, 91st and 94th).[34] Whether or not this was true is difficult to say, but the action does not seem to have been taken with any malicious intent against the Highland Regiments. The motivation may well have been cost consciousness and the real loss of manpower due to emigration.

However, such was the draw of tradition in these Regiments that the Highland association was not permitted to lapse. There is evidence that tartan continued to be worn where it had been officially abolished,[35] pipers were retained, [36] and some Regiments continued to be designated 'Highland'.[37]

In 1820, the 91st took the title 'Argyllshire'. The 72nd regained tartan in the form of trews in 1823. The 74th regained their 'Highland' title and trews in 1845. The 73rd assumed the title the 73rd (Perthshire) Regiment in 1862, and the 75th became the 'Stirlingshire' Regiment in 1862 also. The 91st (Argyllshire), went into tartan trews in 1864 and took the title 'Argyllshire Highlanders'.[38]

Thus, in 1809, five Regiments wore the kilt: the 42nd (Royal Highland), the 78th (Ross-shire Buffs), 79th (Cameron) Highlanders, the 92nd (Gordon) Highlanders, and the 93rd (Sutherland) Highlanders.

The 72nd, 73rd, 74th, 75th and 91st wore the uniform of Regiments of the line, but all were destined to regain their full Highland status and dress by 1881.[39]

By 1815, all ten Regiments had seen considerable action and service, and if ever there had been doubts about their fidelity, these doubts were completely dispelled. Their coveted Battle Honours, particularly 'Waterloo', spoke for themselves.[40]

In place of doubt there grew up, particularly around the kilted regiments, an aura of heroism and romance. In the popular interest and enthusiasm surrounding Wellington's army, and especially the Battle of Waterloo, the Highlanders assumed in the eyes of the British public an entirely new status. *The Times* of Wednesday 21st June 1815, reporting on the fighting of the 17th June, referred to 'the brave Highlanders' and the following day gave an account of the bitter fighting in which the 42nd (Royal Highland), the 79th (Cameron) Highlanders and the 92nd (Gordon) Highlanders had been involved.[41] Along with the 73rd, these three kilted Regiments won the coveted Battle Honour, 'Waterloo', which in itself gave great prestige. Poetry and music were composed around them and the Regiments were feted and honoured. A Commission in such a Regiment became a desirable acquisition for an officer. Thomas Creevey MP wrote in his diary on 26th March 1828:

> We have an event in our family. Fergy [Sir Ronald Ferguson] has got a regiment—a tip top crack one—one of those beautiful Highland Regiments that were at Brussels, Quatre Bras and Waterloo.[42]

The conduct of all the Regiments which are the subject of this study must have contributed in bringing about this volte-face in public and Government opinion, with regards to the Highland Regiments and the Highlands in general.

In less than 100 years the repressive attitude towards the 'rebellious' and 'uncivilised' North changed to at least one of romantic curiosity frequently tinged with a jealous respect. Sergeant Thomas Campbell of the Grenadier Company of the 79th (Cameron) Highlanders, recalls his summons to the presence of Alexander, Emperor of Russia, on 17th August 1815:

> In the month of August 1815 I was ordered to proceed, with Private John Fraser and Piper Kenneth Mackay, to the Palace Elysee in Paris, then the residence of the Emperor of Russia, where we were joined by Sergeant M'Gregor, Private Munro, and Piper M'Kenzie of the 42nd Highlanders, and Sergeant Grant, Private Logan and Piper Cameron of the 92nd Highlanders. About half an hour after our arrival at the Palace, Lord Cathcart sent a valet to conduct us to the grand hall, where we met his lordship, whom I immediately recognised. He was pleased to order me to take charge of the party while he went to the Emperor to acquaint him of our arrival, and in about ten minutes after the Emperor entered the hall accompanied by his two brothers, as well as Prince Blucher, Count Platoff, and several other distinguished personages. The Emperor made a very minute inspection of us, and his curiosity led him to call upon me, as being the most robust of the party, to step to the front, when he ordered the rest to sit down. As soon as I stepped to the front I was surrounded by the astonished nobility, and the Emperor commenced his inspection and questions as follows:
>
> First, he examined my appointments and drew my sword; inquired if I could perform any exercise with that weapon, which I told him I could not, and at the same time Lord Cathcart made a remark that it was a deficiency in the British Army which he had never taken into consideration before.
>
> Second, he examined my hose, gaiters, legs, and pinched my skin, thinking I wore something under my kilt, and had the curiosity to lift my kilt up to my navel, so that he might not be deceived. The questions were: If I was present at the actions of the 16th, 17th, and 18th of June? Whether I was in Egypt? If I wore the kilt in winter, or, if I did not feel cold in that season? If I was married? If my parents were alive?
>
> The Emperor then requested Lord Cathcart to order me to put John Fraser through the 'manual and platoon' exercise, at which performance he was highly pleased. He then requested the pipers to play up, and Lord Cathcart desired them to play the Highland tune 'Cogue na Shee' (*sic*) which he explained to the Emperor, who seemed highly delighted with the music.
>
> After the Emperor had done with me, the veteran Count Platoff came up to me and, taking me by the hand, told me in broken English that I was a good and brave soldier, as all my countrymen were. He then pressed my hand to his breast, and gave me his to press to mine. After all this was over I was ordered to take the party to Lord Cathcart's quarters, where we had refreshments, and received a piece of money each from his lordship, and also his approbation for our appearance.[43]

After Waterloo, all ten Regiments which are the subject of this book were reduced in strength and had an actual recruited strength of between 818 and 385 all ranks. In the Monthly Returns of January 1820 it is interesting to study the breakdown of nationalities and see the encroachment of English and Irish recruiting in the 72nd, 73rd, 74th and 75th Regiments. The 91st (Argyllshire) Regiment, although a regiment of the line, still had a large majority of Scots (there is no distinction between Scots and Highlanders in the returns, but at the time the 91st were recruiting in Glasgow, Edinburgh, Perth and Aberdeen).

Table of Nationalities of the Kilted and Highland based regiments January 1820[45]

Regiment	Nationality	Off'rs	Sgts.	Cpls.	Drum's	Priv'ts	Totals
42nd (Royal)	English	1		1		12	
Highland)	Scotch	34	32	26	22	552	
	Irish	4	3	3	2	26	
(Dublin)	Foreigners					1	
		39	35	30	24	591	719
72nd	English	15	3	4	2	81	
	Scotch	13	33	23	7	462	
	Irish	10	3	6	6	143	
(Cape Town)	Foreigners	1		1		5	
		39	39	33	16	691	818
73rd	English	17	7	14	8	358	
	Scotch	7	12	7	7	35	
	Irish	13	16	6	2	137	
(India)	Foreigners	1	2			3	
		41	35	27	19	533	655
74th	English	5	3	4	6	138	
	Scotch	12	17	11	4	128	
(New Brunswick	Irish	12	11	14	8	322	
Canada)	Foreigners						
		29	31	29	18	588	695
75th	English	7	3	5	1	130	
	Scotch	11	24	18	10	291	
	Irish	6	3	3	3	160	
(Malta/Corfu)	Foreigners		1	1		5	
		24	31	26	15	586	682
78th (Ross-	English	6		8	1	8	
shire Buffs)	Scotch	33	33	30	20	605	
	Irish	2	2		1	1	
(Athlone)	Foreigners					4	
		41	35	38	22	618	754
79th (Cameron	English	4	3	2	1	39	
Highlanders)	Scotch	32	32	28	20	493	
	Irish	3			1	46	
(Jersey)	Foreigners						
		39	35	30	22	578	704
91st (Argyll-	English	5	2		1	49	
shire) Regiment	Scotch	29	26	26	13	452	
	Irish	5	7	3	2	71	
(Dublin)	Foreigners			1	1		
		39	35	30	17	572	693
92nd (Gordon)	English	1			4	8	
Highlanders	Scotch	14	26	24	16	234	
	Irish	1	1	1		54	
(Jamaica)	Foreigners					1	
		16	27	25	20	297	385
93rd (Suther-	English	12			4	14	
land) Highlan-	Scotch	19	34	28	15	540	
ders)	Irish	8	1	2	3	47	
(Naas)	Foreigners						
		39	35	30	22	601	727

The 42nd (Royal Highland), 78th (Ross-shire Buffs), 79th (Cameron) Highlanders, 92nd (Gordon) Highlanders and 93rd (Sutherland) Highlanders were all predominantly Scots, with the 93rd (Sutherland) Highlanders having the greatest proportion of English officers. There is good reason to believe, taking into acount the surnames on the Muster Rolls of the period, that of the Scots a majority were of Highland origin.[44]

There were seven vacant Commissions in the 92nd (Gordon) Highlanders, stationed at Up Park Jamaica, caused by deaths between 17th September 1819 and 19th November 1819. The Foreigners were probably coloured men who had been recruited for the band or men from Continental armies who had joined near the end of the Napoleonic period. In addition the 72nd and the 92nd (Gordon) Highlanders had 24 and 59 Black Pioneers respectively, not included in the effective strength. The 75th had three Drummer Boys under 15 years old, the 79th (Cameron) Highlanders had three, the 91st (Argyllshire) had four and the 93rd had two.

Our study therefore opens in 1820 with five 'Highland' Regiments and five 'Line' Regiments with Highland origins, all firmly established, with battle experience and excellent reputations behind them. Before examining recruiting and training in detail, however, it is important to place military matters in the context of the social and economic condition of Scotland of the period, in order to appreciate the soldier's lifestyle, motivation and expectations.

NOTES

1. Correlli Barnet, *Britain and Her Army* (London: 1970), pp. 59-78.
2. The Band of Gentlemen Pensioners was instituted by Henry VIII about 1509.
3. The Yeomen of the Guard were formed by Henry VII in 1485.
4. Colonel Clifford Walton CB, *History of the British Standing Army 1660-1700* (London: 1884), pp. 8-10.
5. The Hon. J.W. Fortesque, *A History of the British Army*, Vol.I (London: 1910), pp. 141, 168-169, 173 (Scots in Swedish service), 190 (Scots in French service).
6. *Register of the Privy Council of Scotland II*, 235, 237, 238, 256, 257, 641. John Mackay, *An Old Scots Brigade—Being the History of Mackay's Regiment* (Edinburgh: 1885), p. 5. Leask and McCance, *The Regimental Records of the Royal Scots* (Dublin: 1915), Vol. 1, pp. 1-20. James Ferguson (ed.), *Papers Illustrating the History of the Scots Brigade in the Service of the United Netherlands 1572-1782* (Edinburgh: Scottish History Society, 1901), Vols. I and II.
7. Julian Paget, *The Story of the Guards* (London 1976), p. 34, and Lois G. Schwoerer *No Standing Armies* (Baltimore and London: 1974), pp. 72-81.
8. The Scottish Archer Guard of France are said to date from the eighth Crusade, 1249-1270.
9. Walton, *History of the British Standing Army 1660-1700* (London: 1884), p. 11.
10. A clothing regulation of 1747 ordered numbers of precedence to be placed on regimental colours, and by Royal Warrant of 1751 each regiment was ordered to be referred to by its number.

11. S.H.F. Johnston, 'The Scots Army in the Reign of Anne', *Transactions of the Royal Historical Society*, 1953, p. 3.
12. 'Proposals concerning the Highlands', GD/112/52.
13. 'An Authentic Narrative of Marshal Wade's Proceedings in the Highlands of Scotland', quoted in Captain Burt, *Letters from a Gentleman in the North of Scotland to His Friend in London* (London: 1818), Vol.2, pp. 268-337; James MacVeigh, *Historical Record of the 42nd Royal Highlanders (Royal Highland Regiment, the Black Watch)*, (Edinburgh: edited and annotated by Major I.H. Mackay Scobie, copy held in SUSM, Edinburgh Castle), Vol. 1, pp. 4-6.
14. Literally, 'the Black Watch'.
15. James MacVeigh, *op. cit.*, p. 7.
16. The leaders of this mutiny, Corporal Samuel Macpherson, Corporal Malcolm Macpherson and Private Farquhar Shaw, were shot at the Tower of London on 18th July 1743; of the remaining 100 or so who survived the pursuit and trials, 26 were sent to the Mediterranean, 38 to the West Indies and 38 to Georgia as drafts to Regiments in Station. John Prebble, *Mutiny* (London: 1975), pp. 40-87.
17. Act of Attainder 1746. 2 Geo 19 C XXVI. Act for Disarming the Highlands 1746. 2 Geo 19 CXXXIX. Vesting Act 1747. 2 Geo 20 C XLI. Heritable Jurisdictions Act 1747. 2 Geo C XLIII. Act for the Annexation and Administration of Forfeited Estates 1752. 2 Geo 25 C XLI.
18. *The McLagan Collection*, Glasgow University MS 1042/11. Selection from the King's Regulations in Gaelic. James McLagan was Minister at Amulree and Chaplain to the 42nd (Royal Highland) *c.* 1776.

    The most distinctive feature which marked out the Highland soldier in the 18th century, as it does today, was the wearing of the kilt. The Black Watch Companies appear to have worn the belted plaid, a full length of material gathered around the body and secured in the centre with a belt, allowing the upper half of the material to be used either as a cloak shoulder and head covering or alternately hanging in folds below the waist. The pattern or tartan of the early 42nd dress seems to have varied according to the Companies and was locally woven. 'The Knock Note-Book of 1731-1733', Kenneth B. Fraser, a private research paper.

    Of the examples of Highland Regimental Dress that survive from about 1820, it appears that the belted plaid had entirely fallen from use and the little kilt was substituted, worn on the waist with the pleats stitched in and held by three pins on either side of the unpleated front apron. These pins, resembling hat pins, were still in use in the 1st Battalion Black Watch in 1914 where buckles were never used. Examples of early kilts can be seen in SUSM and GHRM.
19. Major R.M. Barnes, *The Uniforms and History of the Scottish Regiments* (London: 1972), p. 54.
20. Katherine Tomasson and Francis Buist, *Battles of the '45* (London: 1962), p. 174.
21. See Appendix I.
22. The numbers between 1793 and 1808 are estimated at 70,000 men. R.P. Dunn-Pattison, *History of the 91st Argyllshire Highlanders* (Edinburgh: 1910), p. 41.
23. Speech of William Pitt, 1766: 'I have no local attachments: it is indifferent to me, whether a man was rocked in his cradle on this side or that side of the Tweed. I sought for merit wherever it was to be found. It is my boast, that I was the first minister who looked for it, and I found it in the mountains of the north. I called it forth, and drew it into your service, an hardy and intrepid race of men! men, who, when left by your jealousy, became prey to the artifices of your enemies and had gone nigh to have overturned the state, in the war before last. These men, in the last war, were brought to combat on your side: they served with fidelity, as they fought with valour, and conquered for you in every part of the world: detested be the national reflections against them! they are unjust, groundless, illiberal, unmanly'. *Hansard*'s Parliamentary History 1766 (London: 1813), Vol. xvi, p.98.

24. William Drummond-Norrie, *Loyal Lochaber* (Glasgow: 1898), pp. 336-339.
25. Macleod's Highlanders raised in 1777 (73rd and later 71st) were designated as Light Infantry before 1820 and do not form part of this study although where appropriate evidence concerning the 71st has been included. See Lt. Colonel L.B. Oatts DSO, *Proud Heritage, The Story of the Highland Light Infantry* (Edinburgh: 1952), Vol. 1. Also excluded are the 90th raised in 1794 as The Perthshire Volunteers (Light Infantry).
26. *Order and Warrant for the 79th*, 15 August 1793. WO/26/35.
27. Ibid. and WO/4/173/481.
28. 42nd (Royal Highland), John, 20th Earl of Crawford (a Lowlander, to prevent objections of partiality among the Clansmen).
    72nd (Highland) Regt., Kenneth Earl of Seaforth.
    73rd (Highland) Regt., Norman MacLeod of MacLeod, first Lt. Colonel (from 2nd Battalion 42nd).
    74th (Highland) Regt., Major General Sir Archibald Campbell of Inverneil. (First Colonel Commandant Gordon Forbes).
    75th (Highland) Regt, Robert Abercromby of Tullibody.
    78th (Highland) Regt. (to be the Ross-shire Buffs), Francis Humberston Mackenzie of Seaforth.
    79th (Cameronian Volunteers later Cameron) Highland Regt., Alan Cameron of Erracht.
    91st (Argyllshire) Highlanders, The Duke of Argyll. (First Lt. Colonel Commandant, Duncan Campbell of Lochnell).
    92nd (Gordon) Highlanders, The Duke of Gordon (first Lt. Colonel Commandant was the Duke of Gordon's son George, Marquis of Huntly).
    93rd (Sutherland) Highlanders, Major General William Wemyss of Wemyss (cousin of the Countess of Sutherland).
    Note: the 74th and 75th were specifically raised for service in India.
29. MacKerlie (published Anon.), *An Account of the Scottish Regiments with the Statistics of Each, from 1808 to March 1861* (Edinburgh: 1862), p. 12.
30. An excellent study of the raising of the 79th (Cameron) Highlanders can be found in the *Queen's Own Highlander*, Regimental Magazine of the Queen's Own Highlanders (Seaforth and Camerons), by Lt. Colonel A.A. Fairrie under the title, 'Erracht's Regiment', in eight parts, May 1976-Winter 1980.
31. Alan Cameron's Accounts, QOHRM.
32. Lt. Colonel C. Greenhill Gardyne, *The Life of a Regiment* (London: 1929), Vol. 1, p. 13.
33. *Historical Records of the Queen's Own Cameron Highlanders* (Edinburgh: 1909), Vol. II, p. 350.
34. Adjutant General's Memorandum 7 April 1809: 'As the population of the Highlands of Scotland is found insufficient to supply recruits for the whole of the Highland Corps on the establishment of His Majesty's Army, and as some of these Corps, laying aside their distinguishing dress, which is objectionable to the natives of South Britain, would in a great measure tend to the facilitating the completing of the establishment, as it would be an inducement to the men of the English Militia to extend their service in greater numbers to these regiments: it is in consequence most humbly submitted for the approbation of His Majesty, that His Majesty's 72nd, 73rd, 74th, 75th, 91st and 94th Regiments should discontinue to wear in future the dress by which His Majesty's Regiments of Highlanders are distinguished; and that the above Corps should no longer be considered as on that establishment'. The 94th (The Scots Brigade) was disbanded at Dublin in 1818, the last Highland Regiment to be completely disbanded. The 94th was regarded as the oldest Regiment in the British Army. It was raised in 1572 for service in the United Provinces, the officers and men being predominantly Scottish. It served in the pay of Holland until 1782 when the Dutch favoured the American colonies and the Dutch government

demanded that the officers renounce their allegiance to George III. Sixty-one refused, left Dutch service and were put on the British half pay list. In 1793 and 1794 these officers were brought back on to full pay and four battalions were raised as 'the Scotch Brigade'. These four battalions eventually shrank to one and that was sent to India in 1797 where it fought at Seringapatam and Argaum. In 1802 the battalion were renamed the 94th (Scotch Brigade). In 1807 they returned to Britain and adopted the kilt, which they lost in 1809. They were disbanded at Dublin in 1818 but the 94th Regiment of Foot was reformed in 1823 and in 1881 became 2nd Battalion Connaught Rangers, who finally ceased to exist in 1922 when the Southern Irish units were disbanded. Ed. Michael Glover, *A Gentleman Volunteer—Letters of George Hennell from the Peninsular War 1812-13* (London: 1979).

35. Letter from the Quartermaster (2nd Bn.) 72nd to William Wilson and Son, Bannockburn, tartan manufacturers, 16 Feb. 1810. SUSM.
36. On July 8th 1850 the 91st were inspected at Dover by the Adjutant General; when he saw the pipers on parade he ordered their immediate disbandment. G.L. Goff, *Historical Records of the 91st Argyllshire Highlanders* (London: 1891), p. 215.
37. Army List 1816.
38. WO Letter 3 May 1864.
39. Appendix I.
40. Army Lists.
41. *The Times*, London, 21st and 22nd June 1815. There is little doubt that before 1815 Highland Regiments largely because of their unique dress were viewed with some suspicion and curiosity; the time they spent abroad meant that when they did appear in England many of the general public were not really sure who they were. When Allan Macpherson of Cluny returned with the 42nd from America in 1762 he recorded:

> . . . I arrived from America in the year of 1762 (at Bristol). I was dressed in the uniform of the 42nd or Royal Highlanders, to which I then belonged; a great crowd of people came round me and a respectable looking man asked me, 'Pray sir, forgive me for asking whether you be with us or against— for I never saw such a dress before'.

The Red Hackle, No. 213, August 1985, p. 2.

42. *Historical Records of the Queen's Own Cameron Highlanders, op. cit.*, Vol. 1, p. 134 (footnote).
43. GD/45/26/85, SRO.
44. WO/12.

CHAPTER 2

Recruiting

The recruitment of men to the Regular Army was one of the most vexed and complex questions throughout the period 1820 to 1920. In relation to the Highland Regiments, recruiting had particular and unique characteristics which had their roots in the land and culture. The availability of men was to be affected by the considerable changes in population in the Highlands, both geographically and numerically, the clearances, emigration and agricultural improvements.

Military recruiting requirements fluctuated too, so that at times the demand was less than the supply, while at other times the supply fell far short of the requirement, causing the Highland Regiments to turn away from their traditional areas for recruits. While recruiting pre-1815 was largely a reflection of the Highland landholding system, between 1820 and 1920 the system of recruiting changed very little.[1] Until the introduction of conscription in 1916[2] all were volunteers; some however were probably more voluntary than others as there is no reason to suppose that the Highland Regiments did not employ some of the less orthodox methods of recruiting as well as appealing to national characteristics and clan loyalty. It is important therefore to look at some of the background to recruiting: firstly, the Highland population and the available pool of manpower, secondly, attitudes, motivation and historical factors, and thirdly, the factors affecting those attitudes in relation to the Highlands.

Sutherland, Ross, most of Inverness, Cromarty and Argyll, including Skye and the Inner Hebrides and Lewis and the Outer Hebrides, are considered as the traditional Highland counties,[3] which, together with further areas of Inverness, parts of Moray, Banff, Aberdeen, Angus, Perth, Stirling and Dumbarton fell within the geographical limitation of the Highland Line. The line was however a geographical boundary, not a social or cultural one and Orkney, Shetland, Caithness, Cromarty, Nairn, Kincardine, Fife, Kinross and Clackmannan were all considered as legitimate areas from which Highland soldiers could be recruited, together with Edinburgh, Glasgow and the Clyde ports.

Who in the Highland Counties was available for the recruiting parties? The statistics of Highland population are marked, firstly, by a period of overpopulation linked with agricultural improvement and the first series of emigrations, and secondly, by clearances for sheep farming resulting in migration to the coastal areas and to the South, and a further period of emigration. These factors affected the numbers available for recruiting and the attitude and approach of potential recruits.[4]

Overpopulation in the Highlands was not related to the land area as a whole,

The Scottish Mainland and the Western Isles

1:2500000

but to the area that could provide sufficient to support the people on a subsistence basis. The end of the requirement for large numbers of men on the land as a military necessity coincided with an era of unprecedented interest in agricultural improvement. The traditional agricultural economy based on cattle was highly labour-intensive, but worked well and in sympathy with the land, its geography and climate, and the social structure. Tenant farmers, some of whom were substantial, existed alongside joint tenants, sub-tenants, cottars and squatters, and their farming standards were by no means always primitive.[5]

Measured against the Lowlands and the South, however, the Highland economy, agriculture and standard of living in the 1750s fell far short of the rest of the country.[6] Between 1750 and 1780, agricultural improvements in housing, crops and field fencing which were taking place in the Highlands resulted in increased rents, and farmers and tenants at all levels were faced with the choice of a reduced income or leaving their land. This period of agricultural change brought about considerable voluntary emigration in the middle classes of Highland Society: tacksmen, men who could pay their way, organise their move themselves and go largely in family groups.

After 1780 came the second and major factor in upsetting the balance of Highland life: enclosures and sheep farming. Men were no longer required, nor were small cottars and sub-tenants and especially not squatters on a large sheep unit, and the population gradually moved, or was removed, to the coastal areas where they were generally unable to support themselves and their families, with fishing, the kelp industry and small plots.[7]

Individual areas therefore became overpopulated as opposed to the area of the Highlands in general. There were still plenty of people, but their distribution and social structure had changed and the emigrations which took place after 1820 were essentially of poor and in many cases desperate cottars who, despite considerable assistance from landlords and government in food and job creation, simply did not have enough room to live in their traditional manner and were unable, or unwilling, to adapt to another.[8]

In the Napoleonic and particularly the pre-Napoleonic period the army had been very successful in recruiting in the tacksman and tenant farmer bracket, both for officers and men. These tenants and their sons had status in their own communities and they displayed a pride and individuality rare among soldiers of the period. The removal of the more substantial tenant farmers, the middle classes of Highland society, meant that men were gradually no longer tied to the land and each other as formerly and the chain of kinship and landholding was broken.[9]

Not only was there emigration, but there was also migration. The energy and zeal of the improvers and 'civilisers' of the Highland area was of an almost missionary nature, to be compared with the 'civilisation' of remote areas of Africa and South America, and the young were anxious to learn English and dress in modern Southern dress, as opposed to homespun materials.[10]

The Minister of Assynt noted that the young were especially keen to learn

English for 'personal advancement',[11] while people moved to the towns and cities, particularly the Glasgow area, for the prospect of increased income and perhaps trade training. A study of Highland migration to Greenock shows that the movement commenced as early as 1750 and it continued until the latter part of the nineteenth century. In 1851, it is estimated that 11% of the population of Greenock were Highlanders, and Greenock cannot be alone in this population pattern.[12]

Therefore, by recruiting in areas in Scotland to which Highlanders migrated, it does not necessarily follow that the 'Scots' on the Muster Rolls are Lowlanders. The pattern of migration continued for such an extended period that even in the 1900s recruiters may well have been taking second or even third-generation Highland men from the Lowlands, and particularly from the Clyde area.

A restricting factor on the figures of population available for recruiting was the persistent preponderance in numbers of females over males, in Scotland in general, and the Highlands in particular. The trend was noted by several Ministers in the *New Statistical Account*, for example in Inverness, where it was stated:

> . . . from emigration of males abroad in quest of occupations, and their fondness for a military life, there is, and it is thought there always has been a considerable excess of females.[13]

Population censuses confirm the trend.[14] The recruitable population was therefore limited not only in numbers but also by the fact that in rural agrarian and fishing communities men were required to stay to do the heavy labour and support womenfolk and families.

R.D. Lobban's study of Greenock not only illustrates the migration of Highlanders, but also the intermixing of the Highland, Lowland and Irish populations. While the Irish had long historical associations with the west coast of Scotland, their numbers increased in Scotland around 1830 when Irishmen began to take over the seasonal and harvest labour which had been the preserve of Highland workers until that time. They migrated to the West of Scotland and adjacent areas during the depression, bad harvests and potato blight in Ireland and they became part of the Scottish social structure. Many of their number were to join Scottish and Highland Regiments.[15]

By 1820 the first period of agricultural improvements and emigration was over and the clearance and removal of the population either to the coast, planned villages or overseas was under way. The process was marked by a general slackness of trade following the war boom, the loss of the kelp industry, and a series of bad harvests and potato disease in 1839/40. Emigration continued, many discharged soldiers trying their hand in Australia as late as 1918.[16] The overall effect during the century 1820-1920 was to restrict the pool of truly resident Highland manpower available to the Army. There were quite simply fewer people in Argyll, Inverness, Perth and Sutherland, while Ross and

Cromarty, after reaching a peak in 1851 was, in 1921, only some 2000 above the 1821 figure.

Between 1820 and 1916 recruitment to the British Regular Army remained voluntary. Historically, in relation to the Highland Regiments, this statement must be qualified, not for the well-worn reason of unorthodox recruiting methods, but because of the very nature of Highland society. Before 1745 the power of a clan and their chief was measured by the numbers of men they could raise. Therefore, regardless of land area or productive capabilities, chieftains, holding landlord status, encouraged men to stay on their land with the implied if not written contract of military service in return. Overpopulation was not considered a problem, but within reason was a source of status and mutual support, and landholding therefore came to mean more than the mere words of a legal lease as it was inseparable from clan, loyalty, protection and service. While these factors remained undisturbed the whole system retained an integrated balance providing population remained at a reasonable level to avoid serious food shortages.

After 1745 it became clear that men were no longer a landlord's primary requirement. While cultural, ecclesiastical, domestic, linguistic and transport 'improvements' were carried out, it was agricultural reforms which struck not only at the system of landholding but also at Highland society and related military service.

At the beginning of the French Wars loyalties of service were coming under considerable strain, but they were no less real and important. This was a time of twilight transition between compulsion and request. Much of the compulsion was implied, but William Wemyss was able to carry out his levy of men in Kildonan and on the Sutherland Estates, while on the other hand on 26th February 1794 Maclaine of Lochbuie could write an open letter to his tenants in the following terms:

> Major Maclaine of Lochbuy wish to intemate to his tennants that in obedience to His Majesty's orders and in duty to his country he is in Honour Bound to be concerned in a military line and sho (*sic*) he wishes for some men from his own estate his intention is not to trouble any posessor of land but only men that can be spared from the country for some little time such as Tennants sons & etc.
>
> He will give such as enlist with him ample encouragement, such as Five Guineas Bounty or if . . . . they hold lands on his property he will give them a deduction of thirty shillings p^{r}. year for five years of his rent which in place of five pounds five will make his reward in money seven pounds ten shillings together with the good treatment he may expect after the Regiment is Reduced.[17]

The arguments concerning the military characteristics of Highland men were embroiled in the agricultural upheaval, for it was used as part of the claim for pressing agricultural improvements. The pattern of landholding and military service seems to have worked well and to the satisfaction of both parties, but the system ran into trouble when 'rights' could not be maintained and promises appeared to be, or were, broken. Sir G. Stewart Mackenzie, an ardent agricultural reformer, presented his 'General view of the agriculture of

Ross and Cromarty with observations on the means of their improvement', in 1810. He wrote:

> The arguements which have been raised on the supposition that the people must be kept to supply the Army and Navy are worse than absurd . . . . The highlands are trumpeted forth as our only resource for soldiers, while it is notorious that the inhabitants have a strong aversion to a military life.

Mackenzie was an advocate of emigration to remove the population which had formed such an important part of the landholding and military service 'contract':

> The present race of tennentry is universally allowed to have an aversion to active employment, and therefore it is neither for the interest of the proprietors, nor of the public, to retain it . . . . A great part of the superfluous population has been removed and very beneficial effects have followed.[19]

It was therefore in the interests of the agricultural improvers, firstly, to show the population to be idle and unproductive, secondly, to encourage removal of the people and, thirdly, to detract from any martial characteristics which the people might have to fend off any argument for their retention on the land. If however a characteristic can be defined as a consistent and repetitive trait, it would seem from the evidence of Highland history that martial endeavours were fairly well established.

In replying to Mackenzie, Colonel David Stewart of Garth, an Officer of the 78th, commented:

> In my battalion . . . . 240 men, as good soldiers as ever left the Highlands, enlisted from the Island of Lewes (Lewis), one portion of Lord Seaforth's estate on the Long Island. If these men, and many thousands of Highlanders who enlisted in the Mackenzie regiments were notoriously averse to a military life, their conduct displayed an inconsistency not easily accounted for in any common principles of action. If the young men who engaged with me had the same feelings, they so completely concealed their aversion that I could discover nothing but the best spirit and desire to learn and discharge their duty.[20]

It is clear however that not all observers, commentators and improvers were ardent advocates of removal and emigration or retention of the population for military service, and that there were alternative reasons for emigration and a strong case for the injection of capital to keep the people where they were. Thomas Telford, while appreciating that 'the inhabitants are strongly attached to their native country', deplored the hardship and injustice of eviction and emigration and urged the establishment of fishing communities and the improvement of the country by public works. The 5th Earl of Selkirk however took the view that the land and its working and possession was so important to the Highland structure that men simply could not be separated from it and placed in convenient communities or work at alternative labour. Accordingly emigration to new landholdings in America, maintaining the Highlanders' way of life, skills, pride and social structure was the only reasonable alternative for a people who he considered had no place in industrial centres, or as day or casual labourers.[21]

Four factors were however at work influencing Highland attitudes: over-recruiting, social change, alterations in military organisation and war reaction. Firstly, over-recruiting. Particularly during the French and Napoleonic wars there was competition for recruits for the Regular Army, the Volunteers, the Fencibles and the Militia. Men became more cautious about offering their services to the first bidder with a bounty. Sir Robert Sinclair, the Duke of Gordon's son-in-law, wrote to the Duke's factor on 19th March 1794 regarding drummers he had enlisted for the 100th Regiment (later 92nd) at Fort George:

> Do let me know if the Marquis raises his Bounty when he comes, as very fine lads laugh at 12 guineas.[22]

There was competition too with the Navy, particularly in Argyll and the West, and there was a resentment not only in the Highlands but all over Scotland at the compulsion of the Ballot of the Militia and the Army of Reserve of 1803.[23] The anti-militia disturbances in Scotland must have affected in some way attitudes to the Regular Army although it is clear that despite Mackenzie's assertions thousands of men volunteered for the regular service and did so freely.

Although therefore the compulsion of service through landholding was, or appears to have been, acceptable as a two-sided bargain, the compulsion of the Militia Ballot was not. It had no alternatives or choices and nothing was given in return.

Secondly, Highland attitudes were affected by the great social change that was taking place during the French and Napoleonic Wars. A society which rightly or wrongly feels threatened will react defensively. The Highlanders' grievance was

> not that their poverty had been increased: it had not. It was that they had been evicted from land occupied from time immemorial. It passed their comprehension that the landowner could turn off men to make way for animals.[24]

Seeing or being the subject of removals made men suspicious and bitter. An 'us' and 'them' attitude grew up fed by contemporary ideas emanating from Republican feelings and Paine's *Rights of Man*. Yet, in spite of social upheaval and the spread of Republican ideas there only seems to have been one incident involving recruiting to the Regular Army, that of the gathering of the tenants at Uig, Lewis, to oppose the recruiting of Seaforth's Highlanders, the 78th Regiment, by Francis Humberstone Mackenzie in the Spring of 1793:

> Three hundred or so Lewismen had taken to a hill, where they had taken an oath to stand by each other and vow death to any Sergeant, Drummer or other Recruitor who dares enter the Parish and also threaten with death whosoever dares Inlist.[25]

Opposition to the recruiting parties had been stirred up, firstly, by discharged men of the 72nd who alleged that men of the Regiment had been left in India without any means of getting home:

> The publick had broken faith with the late 78th Regiment [which was re-numbered 72nd in 1786], there was no saying but they might do the same by this regiment.[26]

Secondly, the opposition came from Republican and radical ideas circulating in the area in the form of handbills and copies of Paine's *Rights of Man* then available in Stornoway. It was believed too that the men in Uig had been incited by men from Greenock and Inverness but the latter influence, coupled with suspicion founded on social upheaval, was probably the prime factor. Men of the 'old 78th' (i.e. 72nd in 1786), had engaged in 1778 to serve for three years or until the end of the rebellion, and when the war in America was finished therefore, in 1783, they were due to be disbanded. They had arrived in India in 1782 after a disastrous ten-month voyage, losing nearly 250 men, the Earl of Seaforth himself dying on board, but because the Regiment was needed in India it was decided not to disband but to give all those entitled to discharge a choice of continued service with a bounty of £10, or discharge and return home. There probably was pressure to take the bounty and 300 did so; the remainder may well have had to pay their passage home.[27]

Social change and its effect on attitudes was linked with the fear of breach of trust on behalf of the landowners, some of whom were of course recruitors. During the clearances at Kildonan, Sutherland, in 1813, Houston, the Sheriff Substitute, Sellar and Young were recieved by tenants who rejected plans for resettlement on the coast and claimed that they were entitled to the land because of promises and letters given after the tenants had furnished men for the 93rd Regiment:[28]

> . . . a good many of us has our children serving in the 93rd and was promised to continue their parents in their possessions during paying regularly the yearly rents.[29]

Their petition stating their claims was taken to London by William McDonald, a retired Sergeant of the 93rd.[30]

By 1854 the appeal of the traditional contract had, for many, lost all credibility:

> It seems that the Secretary of War has corresponded with all our Highland proprietors, to raise as many men as they could for the Crimean War, and ordered so many officers of rank to the Highlands to assist the proprietors in doing so—but it was a complete failure as yet. The nobles advertised by placards, meetings of the people; these proclamations were attended to, but when they came to understand what they were about, in most cases the recruiting proprietors and staff were saluted with the ominous cry of Maa! maa! boo! boo! imitating sheep and bullocks and, send your deer, your roes, dogs, shepherds and gamekeepers to fight the Russians they never done us any harm. The success of his Grace the Duke of Sutherland was deplorable. I believe you would have pitied the poor old man had you seen him.[31]

While this may be a highly coloured account of recruiting in 1854, the fact remains that due to failures in recruiting the Highland Brigade bound for the Crimea had to be brought up to strength by drafts.

Perhaps because of the publicity which the Sutherland clearances provoked many of the instances of 'breach of trust' are linked with the 93rd. For example evictions were taking place at Greenyards, Strathcarron, Easter Ross in March and April of 1854 by the proprietor, Major Robertson of Kindeace, and it was alleged that some of the menfolk of Greenyards were serving in the 93rd Regiment in the campaign against Russia,[32] although there is no record of any repercussions from amongst the men serving with this Regiment at the time. In the light of this link between recruiting, landholding, tenancy and social change, the achievement of Alan Cameron appears all the more remarkable, and this aspect could shed some light on the different characteristics which developed and marked each Highland Regiment in subsequent years.

Thirdly, the whole character of the Army was changing in the period of the French and Napoleonic wars, a factor which Highlanders cannot have been slow to appreciate. While men enlisted in 'Seaforth's Highlanders' or 'Erracht's Regiment', each individual regiment was part of a large army, centrally controlled and operating worldwide. Little account could be taken of the individual prejudices and likes and dislikes of soldiers. They had to go where they were sent and stay for however long the duty took. Men had enlisted to serve particular officers, but these officers themselves had to go where they were told to go even though they did find it easier to get out of duty in unhealthy climates.

The Highlanders, deeply suspicious and superstitious, consistently expected special treatment which they sincerely felt they deserved, and when the fighting was over they considered that they had a perfect right to leave and go home. But armies no longer operated in this way and a good deal of the feeling of breach of trust is based in this area. Returning to Glasgow in 1802 from Egypt, for example, the men of the 92nd waited to be discharged after the Peace of Amiens. When it became clear that their discharges were not forthcoming they prepared a petition demanding disbandment which was refused:

> . . . they had expected to be discharged at the end of the war, as had been the case after former wars with several of the Highland Regiments; many of those enlisted on the estates of the officers so understood the terms of their enlistment. Their experience of soldiering had been of the roughest; they had the old Highland idea of a fight, and then home again to tend the cattle, and they demanded their discharge in fulfilment of what they believed to be their engagement.[33]

Finally, after the euphoria of victory in 1815 there must have been by 1820 a psychological reaction against war and military service. After previous wars it had been the practice not only to reduce the establishment of battalions, i.e. have fewer men per battalion, but to carry out wholesale disbandments. In 1815 this was not the case. The war had resulted in Colonial obligations, and garrison duty was not nearly such an attractive proposition as campaigning, with the possibility of prize money, bounty and victory.

Something which may well have played a positive part in recruiting was the opportunity to serve with men of similar background and origins. Eviction or removal was a particularly painful separation for a Highland man who believed firmly in his links with the land. Highland Regiments were close and élite societies which seemed in many ways to mirror the society from which they originated. Their cohesiveness provided an alternative to social disintegration and Highlanders had a particular aversion to being drafted into other regiments, a factor which had resulted in several mutinies.[34] Both officers and men strongly disliked the Brigade Depot System established in 1872, whereby for example the 93rd and the 92nd were linked and recruits going to the Depot at Aberdeen could be sent to either Battalion.[35] While men would volunteer for service with another Battalion, as for example the two officers and 130 men of the 79th who volunteered for the 42nd in the Ashanti War, compulsion was another matter.

It must not be overlooked either that some men just simply wanted to join. Youth, adventure, crime, boredom, unemployment and poverty all played their part, and it was not uncommon for men and boys to volunteer eagerly for service by letter, as for example the unknown boy from Leeds who wrote to the Cameron Highlanders in 1903:

> Colanil General Royal Cammeran Highlanders.
> G.C.P. Taylar Cammeran Highlander
> Inverness Scotland
> Sir, I want to no if are in want of any drumers. if so send me a papar to sign willing to join the army.
> Yours truely. J.W.M.[36]

Between 1820 and 1854, however, joining with the prospect of long garrison duties in Ireland, the Mediterranean or the West Indies can have had little appeal, but what may have been attractive was the possibility of service in Canada and South Africa with opportunities of discharge or desertion and a chance to make a new life in a new and much publicised land.

While too there was reaction after a war, patriotism immediately before or during a war cannot be ignored. Private Alexander Robb, who enlisted in the 42nd on 13th February 1854, was a Dundee weaver:

> 'I am sure,' he recalled in 1887, 'there was not a town in the country more full of a martial spirit than Dundee, and in particular among the handloom weavers, for I along with other eight left our looms in Belmont Factory in one day . . . . A hundred and twenty five enlisted in the 93rd in one month and were all handloom weavers.'[37]

Similar popular enthusiasm was exhibited in 1899 and 1914 as a result of the special national popular appeal of service with the colours.

It is important too when examining recruiting to look at political aspects, establishments, the competition for recruits and recruiting areas.

The consistent feature, in relation to the Army, which runs through the first half of the nineteenth century and beyond is what can only be politely termed penny pinching on the part of the politicians. In the Infantry, the establishments, that is, the number of men per battalion, were regularly altered and there were persistent attempts to cut back at every opportunity, not only on the Half Pay list but also on the numbers of regular serving soldiers, both officers and men. The result on a already hard-pressed recruiting service was to subject any system there was to considerable strain when recruits were suddenly urgently required, to force disruptive transfers between battalions to make up numbers and to make potential recruits wary of the Army as a long-term employer.

In 1824 six new regiments were raised and numbered 94th to 99th. Two of these had Scottish connections, the 94th and the 99th, adding to the competitive element of recruiting in Scotland. No particular account, at any time, seems to have been taken of the peculiar historical background of the Highland Regiments, and in the major Royal Commissions on recruiting which took place in 1861 and 1867 no serving officer of a kilted Highland Battalion gave evidence.[38]

While the information presented to these Commissions was lengthy, it was not always as detailed and accurate as it might have been, and they show a lack of coherent policy in respect of recruiting, recruiting methods and recruiting difficulties. While Lt. General Wetherall, Adjutant General stated, 'We cannot recruit from Scotland for Highland Regiments',[39] the records show that the 78th for example contained in their ranks in 1861 73% Scots, with even higher proportions in the 42nd (79%), the 79th (78%), the 92nd (81%) and the 93rd (83%).[40]

The lack of overall policy was a reflection of more pressing political and domestic issues as well as being almost a policy in itself as it allowed figures to fluctuate regularly without having to acknowledge the necessity of a large standing army.[41] The variations in the figures of establishments must have caused hardship to those peremptorily discharged and also must have placed pressure on the recruiting parties, who were either desperate for recruits and accepting anybody they could find, or were highly selective and rejecting men who would have made perfectly good soldiers. In 1833 for example it was decided to reduce the Army strength to the 1830 establishment. Staff Officers of the recruiting districts were placed on half-pay, Staff Sergeants reverted to their out-pension and parties were withdrawn. In 1834 recruiting was resumed.[42]

Establishments of Infantry Battalions could fluctuate between 1000 plus to below 600 and were not always standard in every battalion. To complicate matters battalions were often below establishment in strength either by design or failure to recruit. They could also be above establishment by about 20 or 30 men, particularly before being sent to an overseas station.[43] Because there was no concept of a permanent reserve on Prussian lines until the reforms of the 1860s, 1870s and 1880s, sudden recruiting influxes were of little use until the men were trained, and transfers between battalions were the only solution.

Between 1820 and 1854 there were twenty-one wars, campaigns or expeditions in which British European troops took part, besides the continual demands on the Army due to Ireland and Chartist, industrial and political disturbances in the United Kingdom, but it was not until 1854 and the Crimean War that there was a large-scale demand that necessitated widespread recruiting and transfers. Before this the Highland Battalions had achieved a high degree of integration and continuity which bred a particular loyalty to their own Battalions. Deaths, mainly from disease in foreign stations, and men volunteering to remain abroad at the end of a foreign tour, did not generally upset this continuity, but the demands of the Crimean War and the absence of a viable reserve caused a big shake-up. The 92nd was reduced to a Staff and Band in the effort to make other battalions up to war strength in 1854 when 234 non-commissioned officers and men volunteered from the service companies in Gibraltar for the 30th, 55th and 44th Regiments out of a Battalion strength of 538 NCO's and men, and most of the trained men at the 92nd Depot volunteered for the 79th and the 42nd.[44]

In 1872 when localisation established minimum strengths at home and abroad on a rotational basis, the problem of short-term emergencies in recruiting and establishments was not entirely solved, and even with the two-battalion system of 1881 it took some time to create an effective reserve without having to resort to pulling men out of whichever battalion happened to be at home.[45]

Set against the background of increasing Scottish industrialisation and emigration, and removal of the Highland population, the continued existence of the Highland Battalions as distinct units with a highly developed sense of pride and individuality is a remarkable achievement which can only be attributed to the officers and men who served in them, for they received little encouragement from official quarters in the way of cohesive policy for recruitment or planning.[46]

By 1820 the country was divided into recruiting districts with inspecting officers, paymasters and surgeons superintending each district. Scotland comprised one district, the 'North British', which was for example in 1839 run from the centres of Edinburgh, Glasgow, Perth, Inverness and Aberdeen, with Field Officers at Glasgow and Edinburgh, the relevant depots of the battalions being situated anywhere in the United Kingdom. It is notable that not one of the superintending officers at that date was of a Highland Regiment.[47]

As a result of recruiting problems, the inefficiency of the existing peripatetic depot system, whereby each Regiment maintained their own depot for recruiting and training somewhere in the United Kingdom (for the Highland Regiments usually in Ireland and seldom in Scotland), and the difficulties of mass recruiting demonstrated during the Crimean War, the Depot Companies of several Regiments were grouped together in large towns in 1856 to form Depot Battalions. In 1870 this system was replaced by the pairing of Depots of Regiments overseas with a regiment at home: the 78th for example in Canada had their Depot with the 93rd Regiment then at home in Aberdeen.

In 1872 localisation set down permanent recruiting areas, dividing the country into sub-districts which were intended to support the recruiting of two line battalions who shared a Brigade Depot situated within the sub-district. The Highland Regiments under this localisation and Brigade Depot system were divided as follows:[48]

Localisation: The Brigade Depot System 1872

Brigade	Regiments	Depot	Male Population of Sub-District
55	78th/71st	Ft. George	161,368
56	92nd/93rd	Aberdeen	162,000
57	42nd/79th	Perth	241,515
58	72nd/91st	Stirling	240,001
59	26th/74th	Hamilton	377,739
60	73rd/90th	Hamilton	377,739
39	39th/75th	Dorchester	95,590

This scheme was replaced in 1881 by the abolition of the old regiment numbers, the re-linking and re-naming of Battalions to form the 1st and 2nd Battalions of one Regiment and the establishment of permanent individual depots for each Regiment, with specific geographical recruiting areas attached to be known as Regimental districts. Under this scheme the Queen's Own Cameron Highlanders remained the only single Battalion in the British Army and the Highland Regiments were divided as follows:[49]

Re-Linking and Territorialisation 1881
Regimental Districts and Depots: Kilted Regiments only

Regtl. Dist.	Regiments	Old Numbers	Depot
72	Seaforth Hdrs.	72/78	Ft George
75	Gordon Hdrs.	75/92	Aberdeen
79	Q.O. Cameron Hdrs	79	Cameron Bks
91	Argyll and Sutherland Hdrs	91/93	Stirling
42	Black Watch	42/73	Perth

Localisation in 1872 was a major long-term boost for these Battalions but it was not viewed as such at the time.[50] From the nature of their history and historical associations Highland Regiments were in fact localised in their recruitment from the start. The assigned areas with local headquarters and depots did not altogether reflect the true origins and links of the Regiments which were based on estate and landholdings of clan, not merely on geography and population, but the system did go a long way to retain the unique qualities of Highland Battalions, providing them with a firm and known base to which they could associate themselves when the system of clan and landholding was no longer appropriate.

Even when localised, though, the geographical areas were seldom sufficient to supply recruits, and when for example the 2nd Battalion The Queen's Own Cameron Highlanders was eventually raised in 1897, the whole of Scotland was allowed as the recruiting area, not merely the Regimental District.[51]

While localisation did not end competition for recruits from the Navy, it did go a long way to stop the intense activity of indiscriminate recruiting in the Highland area. Prior to 1872, providing authority was obtained, any regiment could send a recruiting party into the District to recruit, and there seems to have been no restriction to Scottish let alone Highland Corps. In addition regiments, Cavalry, Infantry and Artillery, based at the garrisons at Dumbarton

Localization 1872: The Brigade Depot System

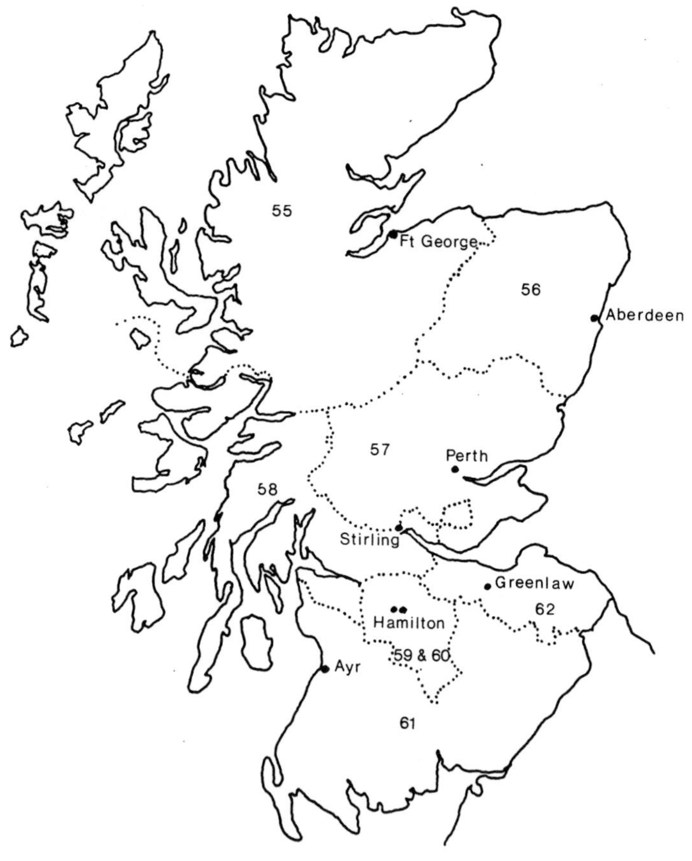

Re-linking and Territorialization 1881:

Regimental Districts & Depots: Kilted Regts. only.

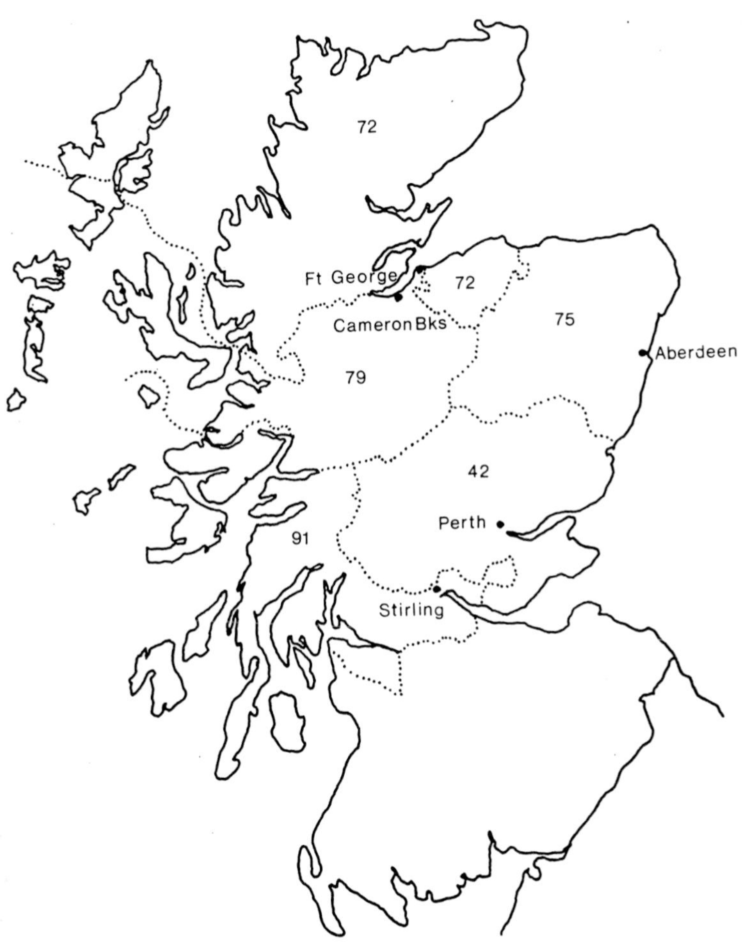

1:2500000

Castle, Edinburgh Castle, Fort George, Stirling Castle and Fort William, and at the barracks at Aberdeen, Perth, Glasgow, Paisley, Dundee, Piershill (Edinburgh), Hamilton, Leith Fort, Blackness and Fort Augustus were all able to recruit whether they had Scottish or Highland origins or not.[52]

Thus Colonel A.C. Pole, Superintending Officer in Glasgow commented in 1861:

> The 2nd Battalion 12th Foot quartered here, is about 200 below its proper strength and appears the favourite Corps and this of course much affects the recruiting into other Regiments. The band and drums of that Regiment constantly marching to and fro between the barrack and parade ground no doubt attracts men . . . . I have 23 parties here. In my opinion so many are standing in each others way.[53]

The Royal Artillery and the Royal Engineers had recruiting representatives in Edinburgh and there was always a Cavalry Regiment at Piershill and Hamilton. The length of time the Highland Regiments spent abroad during the period 1820-1920 was no help at all in keeping them in the public eye, while prior to 1857 the Honourable East India Company also competed in the recruiting field, having an officer at Edinburgh.

Competition for recruits was severe, and while there are no separate records of how many Highlanders enlisted in English and Irish Regiments, in the Navy, the Honourable East India Company, the Royal Engineers or the Royal Artillery, this must have had a serious and detrimental effect on the numbers and quality of Highland recruits who actually joined Highland Regiments.[54]

It is interesting too to study, in relation to the Highland Regiments 1820-1920, the relationship of regular recruiting to the Militia and Volunteers, the operation of Pensioners and recruiting parties, the alternative sources and the wider base of recruiting, the enlistment of boys and the treatment of recruits.

The Militia in Scotland, originally conceived as an army of the people for home defence and internal security raised by ballot on a county basis, originated in 1797, with the Scotch Militia Act of 1802 delegating responsibility for the provision of officers and the raising of men to the counties. The Militia in Scotland was the subject of bitter opposition largely because of the fact that recruitment by the Navy, Regular Army, Fencibles, Volunteers and Yeomanry had already taken the more willing recruits, and the compulsion of the ballot pressed heavily on those who remained and were unable to pay for substitutes.[55] During the French and Napoleonic Wars, however, by allowing the Militia to volunteer for service with the Regular Army abroad, the original concept of the Militia had changed although it still remained a balloted 'constitutional force'. In 1815 volunteering from the Militia to the Regular Army was discontinued, the Militia was disembodied, annual training was suspended and a reduced permanent staff only was maintained.[56]

Between 1815 and 1852 the ballot was only effected twice, in 1830 and 1831, and during this period it can only have been a matter of chance that the Militia attracted men to regular service.[57] The Militia Act of 1852, prompted by the actions of Louis Napoleon in France, established voluntary militia enlistment, with the ballot kept in reserve only, and men had to complete twenty-one days' training each year. During the Crimean War hundreds of Militiamen again volunteered for regular service,[58] but in 1860 such volunteering was prohibited in an attempt to prevent disruption of Militia strengths, although in 1875 volunteers were accepted for service in Malta and Gibraltar. In the reforms of 1881 the Militia finally lost their civic, although not their local character, and became formally the reserve of the Regular Army, with each regular Regiment of two battalions having a permanent depot and recruiting area with Militia and Volunteer units integrated with the parent Regiment, the regular depot also being the Militia headquarters and the Militia battalion being numbered the 3rd Battalion of the parent Regiment (or 4th battalion where appropriate).

In 1908 the Haldane reforms converted the Militia finally into the Special Reserve, and in the event of war both officers and men were liable to be drafted to the Regular Army. The character, nature and roles of the Militia were not therefore conducive to their being used as a major source of recruiting to the Regular Army, although in 1906 the 3rd Militia Battalion of the Queen's Own Cameron Highlanders was chosen as one of twenty selected battalions to operate an extended training scheme to improve Militia standards and encourage recruitment to the Regular Battalions.[59] Recruits were trained for six months under their own officers at Telford Road, Inverness, together with extended annual training, and as a result the strength of the Militia Battalion was brought up to almost 1000 men. The Militia Battalions were popular and in general were respected in the Highland area after 1856, and these Militiamen, always considering themselves far superior to the Volunteers formed in 1859, may well have influenced many a young man to join the colours.

The Volunteers of 1859,[60] formed as a result of French ambitions and the growth of continental armies, were initially merely voluntary, uniformed rifle clubs under the direction of Lords Lieutenant of Counties, and it was not until 1871 that responsibility for their administration came under the Secretary of State for War and they became subject to military discipline. In 1872 they were placed under the command of the Brigade Depots, thus linking them for the first time with the Regular Army. The Volunteer movement was popular and widely supported in Scotland and became an important part of Scottish and Highland social life in the second half of the nineteenth century. In 1881 these Volunteer Battalions were linked with the Regimental Districts and parent Regular Regiments and gradually they adopted the title and uniform of their associated Regular Regiment. Their role was limited to home defence, but in 1908 they became the Territorial Battalions with a reserve field force role, taking the numbers 4th, 5th and 6th in the Battalion numbering as appropriate.

The physical proximity, the linking and the shared training of the Militia (Special Reserve) and the Volunteeer (Territorial) Battalions, with the Regular Army, were attempts not only to improve training, but also recruiting; however, from the Regular Army recruiting point of view the results were frequently disappointing.[61] Probably more important was the fact that the number and variety of these Militia and Volunteer units in the Highland area showed a martial enthusiasm which must have prompted some young men to join the Regular Army. Private Reginald Lobban is an excellent example, for, while working as a footman in 1913 he found himself unemployed when Lord Lovat cut his staff at Beauly Castle. He had seen the Lovat Scouts at annual training camp nearby in the summer of 1912 and, having visited them and made a few friends amongst their number, determined upon joining the Army, and although he had never served in their ranks he was attracted by their presence.[62]

A further influence and source of recruits may well have been the large number of Army Pensioners resident in the Highlands.[63] In a culture where story, song and legend still play a prominent part, soldier pensioners held a special position. They seem to have been looked upon with respect in the Highland communities. They would have been able to tell tales of wars, service and life in distant lands and may well have encouraged their friends or acquaintances to follow their military example.

A pension of any kind was a rare commodity prior to 1908 and most were extremely proud of their service and the experiences they had had,[64] although without doubt some were disillusioned, particularly those who had enlisted with promises of security of tenure prior to the clearances.

Pensioners held status in isolated communities; for example, the petition of the Kildonan tenants of 1813 was entrusted to Sgt. William MacDonald.[65] Pensioners acted not only as an informal influence on recruiting, they were also actively employed in the recruiting service. Sergeants were taken from the pension list and placed on duty as Staff Sergeants attached to every recruiting district. They acted as Sergeant Majors, Paymaster Sergeants and conducting Sergeants.[66] They were also used experimentally in direct recruiting,[67] but this was not a success. Colonel W.A. McCheveley, AAG, Edinburgh, reported in 1861:

> . . . the Pensioner force in this district only obtained one recruit during March and April.[68]

The numbers of pensioners so employed was reduced in 1870[69] and perhaps their influence was indirect, but no less worthy of consideration.

Beggar pensioners and those soldiers discharged unfit or as bad characters without a pension may well have had a detrimental effect on recruiting. In 1861, it was noted, the discharge of men after the war without pensions and in search of employment

> . . . has the effect of bringing great unpopularity on the Army as a profession, and of deterring many, whom it would be most desirable to enlist . . .[70]

Many of these men lived in semi-destitution, particularly in the cities, begging where they could, often homeless and without employment or trade, resorting to alcohol and charity. They certainly were not the best advertisement the Army could provide, and they reinforced the image of the Army as a bad employer with poor pay, long and thankless service, an inadequate pension system and the old soldier syndrome of 'boose and begging', but on the other hand in an age where the welfare state was inconceivable and beggars were a common sight, their situation perhaps did not assume the significance that it would today.

While several men in Highland Regiments left detailed and carefully written diaries of their service, few actually give details of how, where and under what circumstances they were recruited. Private A.W. McIntosh, for example, merely records:

> January 1858 4th Monday. Enlisted in the 42nd ROYAL HIGHLAND REGt. at Edinburgh,[71]

while Angus Cameron, born in Strontian, Argyll, and working in Glasgow in 1853, remembers that he went to Edinburgh specifically to join up. There, he was 'caught' by a recruiting Sergeant of the 79th in the High Street who

> . . . kindly gave me a billet upon Mrs Dixon, a motherly old woman who at that time kept a cookshop and beds for recruits, the house being well patronised by the military . . .[72]

By 1820 there is scant evidence of any compulsion or call to arms on the part of Highland landlords to their tenantry, and the pattern of Highland recruiting had lost many of its traditional aspects. Recruiting was carried out by small parties, sometimes under an officer, but usually under a Sergeant in all seasons of the year, operating in a wide area of Scotland and billeted on the local population or in a public house. On 1st January 1850 the numbers of men detached on the recruiting service were:

Regiment	Sgts.	Cpls.	Privates[73]
42nd 1st Bn.		2	4
Reserve Bn.		2	4
72nd	2		4
73rd			
74th	2		4
75th	2	1	6
78th			
79th	1	1	5
91st 1st Bn.	3		6
Reserve Bn.	3		6
92nd	2		4
93rd	2		5

These were fairly typical figures. The parties are known to have operated at Fairs and on Market Days and at Feeing Fairs right up to before the First World War, when Corporal Frank MacFarlane of the 1st Battalion Black Watch remembers that at 'Forfar Mart you could usually find the Scots Guards and perhaps the Black Watch'.[74] Parties either singly or in groups hung about street corners in the major cities and greeted the passenger boats at Greenock and Leith. Sometimes they might be accompanied by a Piper or a Drummer of the Regiment, which would have guaranteed that they attracted attention.

The men themselves would have been a draw in their regimentals, frequently trimmed with ribbons. It would seem that recruiters were often chosen for their looks as well as their trustworthiness, and many were known in their own counties in the Highlands or became familiar figures, frequenting certain areas or public houses:[75]

> There is a particular stamp of man that makes a good recruiter. It is not always the smartest or the best men that make the best recruiters. The man who can raise recruits is the man who can tell a good story, or sing a good song, that is the sort of man to raise recruits.[76]

It was in fact in the recruiter's own interests to be outgoing and successful, for while the recruit received his bounty (until 1870), the recruiter received 'bringing money'.[77]

Not that it was always easy for the recruiting parties living in Scotland and billeted on the local population. In Edinburgh in particular there was opposition to this practice which came to a head in 1827, when the proprietors and inhabitants of eight southern districts of the City presented a memorial regarding the billeting of troops. They asked why the men could not be accommodated in the Castle, but this was strongly opposed by the military authorities and the garrison on the grounds that these men did not form part of the resident battalion, many were recruits and there was a strong possibility that they might transmit disease to the soldiers if admitted to the barracks. Further complaints ensued in 1838 when the City claimed exemption from billeting under an act of 1689 on the grounds that they had a town guard to maintain and were therefore exempt from further taxation. When it was suggested, in 1839, that Queensbury House, the Edinburgh house of refuge, be given up to the barrack master for the use of recruiters and recruits, the Provost, Magistrates and Sheriff rose in protest and it seems the matter was left unresolved.[78]

While recruiters were urged to be smart and clean in their appearance, it can hardly have been easy in some of the billets that were allotted them. Sergeant Major William Rammage of the 72nd, writing from Edinburgh on 6th June 1839 reported:

> . . . and so till Mondey when quartered Mr McFarlen Leith Street who accepted of us, although quarters that I could not live in, and on maney other occasions we have been Billet on People who had more need of Charity than People Billet on them.[79]

Similarly Sergeant Ferguson of the 79th, also recruiting in Edinburgh in 1839, complained of his billet

> . . . the bed he housed me [in] was not fit for any human being to sleep in it.[80]

While it is often thought that soldiers lived in squalid conditions at that time, both Sergeants Rammage and Ferguson were obviously dissatisfied with the standards of civilian accommodation in comparison with that which they had come to expect from their rank and position.

In isolated rural areas where the men were probably known or had relations locally, there must have been a strong temptation to revert to the country ways. There were for example complaints regarding a party of the 92nd in the Elgin area about 1825:

> Sergeant Fraser superintends his brother's farm, Private Thom works at his trade as a weaver, Donald McDonald as a shoemaker, Corporal Renton keeps a shop in Elgin, and Private Cheyne drives a carriers cart from Elgin to Fochabers and they only wear uniform on market days and Sundays.[81]

If both the Regiment and the Depot were stationed outwith Scotland, the recruiting parties would have no actual base from which to work, and parties travelling to the Highlands had long and sometimes dangerous journeys by sea, by overland coach and on foot to reach their destinations and return to the Depot with their recruits. The isolation of many of these parties is reflected in Lance Sergeant Cameron's report (of the 79th) dated 18th July 1822 from Fort William:

> Sir, Although the men of the party and I have been as attentive as possible in the execution of our duty ever since we came here I find it out of my power to succeed and as you are acquainted in this country and aware of the remoteness of the situation of this village I hope that you will have the goodness to represent that disadvantage to the Inspecting Field Officer, with view of changing the party to some other place.[82]

But recruiting was much more widely based than mere recruiting parties, pensioners, and the Militia and the Volunteers. Men in the Regiment or men at the Depot were encouraged to bring potential recruits, and this was not restricted to Scotland but applied also in England and Ireland. While late Victorian prejudice did much to cover it up, there is evidence too of recruitment of foreigners and coloured men for the band and as pioneers, for example Thomas P. Mamparang, a black Madagascan of the 93rd, and it is believed that the 42nd had several negroes on the Regimental strength into the 1830's.[83] While English, Irish and foreigners do feature in the recruiting figures, it is clear that in the kilted Regiments there was a strong emphasis on recruiting in Scotland with a decided preference for Highlanders,[84] which was not wholly attributable to official policy but to a series of 'Highland minded' and frequently outstanding Commanding Officers, such as Lieutenant Colonel Duncan MacGregor of the 93rd, Lieutenant Colonel 'Jock' Fordyce of the 74th, Lieutenant Colonel Lauderdale Maule of the 79th and Lieutenant Colonel Bertie Gordon of the 91st.

Losses through disease or wartime emergencies could overthrow all these good intentions, such as the loss of 535 officers and men of the 78th in India in 1844-45 from cholera. This loss was made good by recruiting in England and Ireland and by accepting 100 volunteers from the 2nd (The Queen's Royal) Regiment, resulting in the composition of the Regiment being 47% Scots, 30% English and 23% Irish.[85]

One reason Highlanders seem to have been particularly favoured as recruits was their better behaviour; also their height and physique, which were important attributes in an army which, through necessity, depended on display and 'steadiness' as opposed to firepower.

While various height limits were imposed throughout the period 1820-1920, Highland Regiments sometimes placed their own height limits which were above the standard.[86] The recruiting parties too were looking for 'growing lads' who with exercise and regular feeding would make the required height.[87] The ability to read and write came second to the physical requirements of freedom from rupture and disease. Men who spoke only Gaelic gradually became more unusual but it was no bar to enlistment in the Highland Regiments; although Private Lobban remembers that when a man was discovered in the 1st Battalion Queen's Own Cameron Highlanders, in France in 1914, who could not speak English, he was returned home.[88]

There was no prohibition against married recruits but only a limited number of couples were permitted to be married on the strength, and only six or eight out of every hundred were allowed to travel with the regiment overseas. Some men may well have enlisted to absent themselves deliberately from wives and families and avoid the burden of maintaining them.[89]

No doubt sharp practice of plying men with drink and tall stories was used by recruiters of the Highland Regiments, as in other regiments of the British Army, but when these men were recruiting in Scotland they were often known to the inhabitants. Scotland is a large and sometimes wild country, but in other ways it is a notoriously 'small' one, and carrying off a young man against his or his family's will might have been a fairly difficult task. Spencer Ewart, an officer of the 1st Battalion Queen's Own Cameron Highlanders, wrote in his diary of recruiting in the Highlands in 1889.

> In March 1889 I and Captain Malcolm went on a recruiting trip for the 79th to Lochaber. I personally travelled with Piper James Macdonald by Oban to Fort William (supported by a Roman Catholic Priest and Presbyterian Ministers) . . . At Fort William we got three recruits, but we had to release one of them named Dougal MacLachlan because his mother kicked up such a dust.[90]

There was no doubt who these men were or what they were about, and even those operating in the cities were identifiable by their dress alone. Perhaps, too, the potential recruits were well able to cope with the sales pitch and gave as good as they got.

Often the simple presence of a recruiting party would attract men, and from his own account it seems that it was Donald Cameron himself who approached the recruiting party of the 79th at Dunfermline in 1847 and bought the drinks before enlisting:

> . . . I was . . . working at Dunfermline [on] the Railway 1847 a recruiting party of the 79th Regt. came to the town passed through us and going from my work one wet day I thought that I would like to be one of their number went home took my dinner went out again met two of them asked one of them if he would have a drink he con-

sented we went into a public house and I was enlisted by Private Semple went back to my lodgings packed up my clothes and sent them home to Braeside and then went to Edinburgh Glasgow Dublin and then on the march to Castlebar . . .[91]

The contact between recruiter and recruit was thus essentially a personal one, for although handbills had been used in 1775 and 1776 and particularly at the outbreak of the French wars, they seem to have been uncommon until 1881, when the Annual Report of the Inspector General of Recruiting suggested advertising by placards and posters the advantages of the Army and he also supplied Postmasters throughout the country with forms of Application to Enlist. The result in the Highland Regiments was a series of high-quality posters embodying what was then considered as the ingredients of appeal: a smart uniform, regular employment and pay, travel, training, and belonging to a local and national regiment with a history and tradition.[92]

One source of recruiting was however internal. Every regiment had a certain number of boys in their ranks and the Highland Regiments were no exception. These boys were under the age of 18, some were as young as 7 on joining, but most were 13 to 14. They came from two sources. Firstly, from the regiments themselves, being the sons, brothers or orphans of serving soldiers and, secondly, they came from special establishments which were set up to educate soldiers' children: The Royal Hibernian Military School, The Duke of York's School, Queen Victoria School and the Lawrence Schools in India.

In 1875 there were 3031 boys under 18 serving in the British Army.[93] The Highland Regiments had an average of twelve boys each, and with wives and families living in barracks it is not surprising that boys should enlist and follow their fathers, for many of them had lived abroad for most of their lives, had been educated at the Regimental School and had known little of any other way of life. While on the face of it this may carry the taint of introversion and nepotism, it must be remembered that such recruiting kept families together, gave the regiments family characteristics, and provided employment and opportunities of trade for boys who became tailors, shoemakers, saddlers and musicians.

Whoever the recruits were or however they were recruited, they were recognised as a valuable commodity and their treatment seems to have been considerate and careful. Standing Orders of the 93rd instructed that men employed on recruiting

. . . are to state fairly and honestly the advantages enjoyed by soldiers, which ought to operate with most young men of spirit and enterprise, as sufficient inducement to enlist without the aid of exaggeration.[94]

Lt. Colonel Duncan MacGregor, who devised these orders and was noted for his humanity, further ordered that recruits were to be treated on parade with 'moderation'.

The Standing Orders of the 79th similarly instructed that

the recruit must be treated with the greatest kindness.[95]

How much this care was a reflection of contemporary political tension or of the social and economic conditions of the Highlands, it is difficult to tell.

The question must be asked, therefore, how successful was recruiting in the Highland Regiments? There are two aspects of success in recruiting, quantity and quality. The Recruiting Department memorandum of 12th December 1833 shows no hint of misgivings as regards the quantity of recruits coming forward:

> Every result anticipated from the adoption of the existing system has been fully realised, and it is now settled down into a well organised establishment; yet at the same time contracted to the limited scale suited to a period of peace. In 1824 six new regiments were raised in less than 4 months through the exertions of the district staff and the parties of other regiments not then recruiting for their own Corps . . . In 1825 upwards of 15,000 men were recruited in the districts and the total number of men enlisted in that year, including the recruiting at the Head Quarters of regiments, amounted to 23,000; a number unprecedented in the annals of recruiting.[96]

There is no mention in this memorandum of any particular difficulties being encountered in the North British district as regards numbers. Even in 1835, after losses in the Regiment as a result of diseases in the West Indies, Colonel MacGregor of the 93rd, who had had to resort to recruiting in 'the large manufacturing towns of Scotland', expressed no reservations that he would not be able to recruit the numbers of Highland men required, now that the Regiment had returned home.[97]

Between 1845 and 1849 the North British district was producing an average of 1482 recruits per annum, but this figure is deceptive as it excludes Artillery, Guards and Engineers and includes recruitment to all regiments, not just Scottish or Highland,[98] and from the example of the 78th in 1844-45 it is clear that Highland Regiments could no longer attract large numbers of men suddenly in peacetime, particularly when the regiment was abroad. (The 78th did not embark for home until 1859.) In time of war the recruiting system and the lack of adequate reserves resulted in severe deficiencies of numbers and Sir George Brown admitted as early as 1850 that insufficient men were coming forward to keep the Highland Regiments solely restricted to Highlanders, but the implication is that his classification of a Highlander is limited to Gaelic speakers, which by 1850 is an unrealistic qualification and impossible to define.[99]

The introduction of limited service in 1847, as opposed to enlistment for life (which effectively meant 21 years), did not materially alter the quantity of recruits required until these men began to be discharged after their service of ten years had expired, when the system increased the overall turnover of manpower. The ten-year service period could be extended by two years if the regiment was abroad, and as a result of this provision men serving in the Indian Mutiny had their service extended, thus delaying the manpower problem by two years.

By 1861 the difficulty of recruitment in relation to turnover was an acknowledged fact,[100] but the particular problems of geography and history of the

Highland Regiments seem just to have been written off as difficult and incomprehensible, a situation in which nobody wished to dabble seriously. 'We cannot recruit from Scotland for Highland Regiments'[101] was a statement that was neither accurate nor constructive, and so long as the intense competition from other regiments continued in Scotland, it is hardly surprising that the Highland Regiments had difficulties with numbers.

Immediately prior to the establishment of the Brigade Depot system in 1872 the composition of the kilted Highland Regiments in NCO's, Corporals and Privates was:[102]

Regiment	English	Scots	Irish
42nd	30	611	13
78th	21	509	25
79th	51	611	31
92nd	105	810	48
93rd	30	642	16

and of those Regiments with Highland designations wearing trews or line uniform:

Regiment	English	Scots	Irish	
72nd	242	646	67	Trews 1823
73rd	616	86	231	Perthshire Regt. 1862
74th	84	576	71	Trews 1845
75th	512	85	322	Stirlingshire Regt. 1862
91st	218	299	113	Trews 1864

The total figures per regiment are not necessarily a reflection of failure to recruit, but an indication, in part, of the station of the regiment and the length of time spent abroad. These figures do clearly show the considerable and mostly successful efforts that were being made by the kilted regiments and also by the 72nd, 74th and 91st to retain their national identity in spite of the pressure of competitive recruiting.

Between 1873 and 1880 recruits raised in the appropriate sub-districts show the difficulties that were arising in the numbers of recruits:[103]

Sub-District	Regiments and Depot Location	1873	1874	1875	1876	1877	1878	1879	1880	Male Pop.
55	78/71 Ft. George	24	29	23	34	28	38	53	48	161,368
56	92/93 Aberdeen	77	64	34	82	69	128	97	108	162,000
57	42/79 Perth	23	83	83	110	108	123	153	200	241,515
58	72/91 Stirling	60	246	101	178	165	298	189	83	240,041
59	26/74 Hamilton	137	322	209	309	244	297	235	210	377,739
60	73/90 Hamilton	124	363	347	352	205	227	173	124	377,739
39	39/75 Dorchester	120	23	14	64	76	73	81	89	95,590

Keeping in mind short-service increased manpower turnover and the fact that these sub-districts had to supply two battalions, recruiting was certainly not keeping pace.

The figures in relation to the Highland Regiments must be viewed however in the light of the fact that the Brigade Depot system was not popular.[104] It was the first time depots had been fixed in one position with a set recruiting area.

Recruits were being sent from other sub-districts, not only in England but other areas of Scotland, and many men were particularly anxious not to conform to the sub-districts, but to join specific regiments.

In addition, the Depots took some time to establish themselves, and in the case of the 74th, while favoured with an area of high population, they had no associations with their linked Battalion and hated the Lowland base assigned to them. (Their Depot did not in fact take station at Hamilton until 1877.)[105]

After 1882 the percentage of Scots in the Army as a whole remained remarkably constant despite a falling percentage of the UK population,[106] and the re-linking of the Battalions the year before, in 1881, really had nothing to do with recruiting figures or population per territorial areas, as much of the argument about which Regiment would be linked with another centred on historical attachment and who would agree to wear which tartan.[107]

The final report of 1881 was produced,

> .... framed after careful consultation with the Commanding Officers of the Scotch Regiments and special regard ... to the strong feelings entertained by the men of various clans for their special tartans.[108]

The problem was a source of deep frustration to the War Office officials, but it was a subject as close to the hearts of these regiments then, as it is now, regardless of policy, statistics, recruiting figures or percentages of the population.

In 1881, when the territorial system was introduced, recruiting figures settled down into a fairly steady pattern, interrupted only by the effects of the Egyptian Campaign and more especially the South African War. In the period 1881-1889 recruiting in the relative districts was:[109]

Date	PERTH 1 and 2 B.W. 42nd/73rd	FT. GEORGE 1 and 2 Seaforth Hdrs. 72nd/78th	ABERDEEN 1 and 2 Gordon Hdrs. 75th/92nd	INVERNESS 1 QO Cameron Hdrs. 79th	STIRLING 1 and 2 A. and S Hdrs. 91st/93rd
1881	225	83	109		88
1882	331	111	100		191
1883	299	162	123		225
1884	347	302	117		318
1885	407	149	195	46	354(see detail below)
1886	293	125	191	70	268
1887	278	102	143	83	234
1888	225	72	143	51	192
1889	226	73	141	67	101

While this return shows good recruiting figures, particularly in Perth and Stirling, it does indicate the problems that were being experienced in Inverness, Ross, Caithness and Sutherland and the Northern and Western Isles. But again the statistics cannot be looked at without qualifications. Taking 1885 as an example, a further breakdown shows the detailed recruitment of Cavalry, Artillery, Engineers and Guards, and most noticeably recruits going to other Infantry Battalions.[110]

1885

District	INFANTRY Recruits joining Territorial Regt.	Other Inf Bns.	OTHERS Cav.	Arty.	RE	Guards	Depot	TOTAL RECRUITS PER DISTRICT
PERTH - Black Watch	200	128	31	30	5	13	-	407
FORT GEORGE Seaforth	106	12	2	17	6	2	4	149
ABERDEEN- Gordon	94	55	6	12	6	12	10	195
INVERNESS -Q.O. Cameron	28	10	3	4	-	1	-	46
STIRLING- A. and SH	230	72	26	17	1	4	4	354

The trend reaffirms the recruit's preference to choose his own Regiment and the fact that the Territorial system was by no means fixed and static. The Seaforths and the Argylls were particularly successful in retaining recruits in their own districts. Overall the recruiting figures for this year, 1885, were considered by the Inspector General as good results.

The intermixing is also seen in the returns of recruits joining the Regular Army from the Militia (1885):[111]

	Militia Recruits joining Linked Battalion	Militia Recruits joining Other Bns.	Total
Royal Hdrs. 3rd Bn.	77	91	168
Seaforth Hdrs. 3rd Bn.	14	11	25
Gordon Hdrs. 3rd Bn.	32	31	63
Q O Cameron Hdrs. 2nd Bn.	3	10	13
A and S Hdrs. 2nd Bn.	72	58	130
4th Bn.	8	31	39

The figures for 1909 (1.10.08 – 30.9.09, below)[112] show town-based recruiting as particularly successful, favouring the Black Watch and the Gordon Highlanders. The Argylls are losing just over half of their recruits to other battalions and corps, while the Seaforths and Camerons, although with low figures, retain most of their men in their Territorial Regiment (Seaforths 90.19%, Camerons 94.44%).

1.10.08 - 30.9.09 Regular Army Recruiting

	Recruits joining Terri-torial Regt.	Other Infantry	Other Corps	Total	% joining Territorial Regt. from Territorial Area	% discharged medically within 3 months
PERTH - Black Watch	113	61	58	232	64.94	3.01
FORT GEORGE -Seaforth Hdrs.	46	5	12	63	90.19	6.34
INVERNESS- Q O. Cameron Hdrs.	51	3	5	69	94.44	2.89
ABERDEEN - Gordon Hdrs.	112	30	52	194	78.87	4.12
STIRLING- A and S Hdrs.	92	65	62	219	58.59	0.91

N.B.: The cities of Glasgow, Edinburgh and Dundee were separate districts used as "feeder" areas.

The overall poor results in Scotland in 1909 were attributed to emigration but the Territorial areas were clearly not supporting their Battalions in respect of recruitment, and in time of peace they would never do so again.

Quality was an entirely different matter. Highland recruits were much sought after for their stature, looks, bearing and behaviour. When they embarked for the Crimea in 1854, the 42nd, the 79th and the 93rd (the 'Old Highland Brigade') were all commended for their appearance, the Grenadier Companies being picked men seldom under 5 foot 8 inches;[113] but the concept of appearance and physical health, of increasing urbanisation and above all of changes and developments in medical science, altered the meaning of the word 'quality'.

Rejection of recruits on medical grounds in the whole of the British Army was 298 per 1000 between 1832 and 1841; 335 per 1000 between 1842 and 1851 and in 1860 was 250 per 1000. In the last year the returns from Edinburgh and Glasgow show very high rates of rejection in Glasgow:

	Number of recruits inspected 1860	**Rejections**		
		1st Inspection	2nd Army Doctor	2nd Civilian Doctor
Edinburgh	1172	292	19	156
Glasgow	2099	432	143	282

Overall in Scotland in 1860 the ratio of rejections on medical grounds was the highest in the Kingdom at 318 per 1000, compared with 243, 233 and 258 per 1000 in England, Wales and Ireland respectively. In the Recruiting report these figures were attributed to the fact that '. . . the greater proportion of the recruits in that country (i.e. Scotland) . . . . [are] drawn from large manufacturing towns', but the report was astute enough to realise the thinking behind the standards set for the health of recruits:

> In the British Army, kept up as it is by voluntary enlistment, the proportions of rejections must vary considerably with reference to the demand and supply. When men are not required . . . none but the most eligible recruits will be taken, while during a pressure for men those only quite unfit are refused.[114]

In the last quarter of the nineteenth century there was considerable concern about the quality of recruits, not only in education and conduct, but more especially in health. In Scotland, as recruiting became concentrated and centred on the towns and cities, the proportion of recruits from rural and agricultural backgrounds fell. Scottish housing was notoriously bad, the national diet was little better, and alcoholism was a serious problem. Physical standards undoubtedly fell but at the same time medical standards rose and the recruit of 1820 who was readily accepted, albeit 'marked with smallpox', 'of weak intellect', or 'having the itch',[115] would almost certainly have been rejected seventy years later. In many ways the later Victorians required their soldiers to look the part, with photography and rising standards of morality and cleanliness contributing to this expectation. In addition, training standards and requirements rose dramatically and placed new demands on intellect and physique.

What is clear throughout the period 1820-1920 is the high standard achieved by the Senior Non commissioned officers in the Highland Battalions. In the words of Private Lobban on his joining the 1st Battalion The Queen's Own Cameron Highlanders in the Spring of 1914:

> The Regimental Sergeant Major was Geordie Burt. He was a smart soldier. Yes oh! I admired these people. I went on fatigue in the Sergeant's Mess the first week I was there . . . I never saw such a body of people. Everyone a wee bit better at something than somebody else. Each was second to none in his class, whether it was musketry or gymnastics or fieldcraft or machine gun . . . the drill sergeants . . . could prove a rank better than the guards . . . You know it was something to belong to . . . .[116]

The mechanics of enlistment and attestation, while simplified in 1862,[117] changed very little between 1820 and 1914 and they were standard in the British Infantry. The recruit made contact with the recruiter either at his own initiative or of that of the recruiter. He received enlistment money (which was held to constitute consent to enlistment), and then had a medical examination, which became more searching as time progressed. He was taken before a Justice of the Peace, within 96 hours but not sooner than 24 hours after enlistment, and here he was questioned, read two Articles of War on mutiny and desertion and took the Oath of Allegiance. He received his Bounty in stages, but before 1870 could not guarantee to retain much of it for long as it was used for the purchase of 'necessaries'.

In 1870 enlistment Bounties were abolished and any recruit who could prove that he had been duped into enlisting was given a free discharge. The recruit was finally medically examined and joined his regiment or depot. The recruit could be rejected at several stages in the procedure, the most normal cause of rejection being medical, but the Commanding Officer could also turn a man away.[118] Particularly common before 1870 were recruits who enlisted, took the Bounty and promptly deserted, only to enlist in another regiment for another Bounty.[119]

The pure mechanics of enlistment however say little about the long distances travelled by the recruiting parties operating in the North and the Islands, bringing young men to the Regiments who had never been away from their native place; or how the questions and the oath were administered to Gaelic-speaking recruits presumably using the Recruiting Sergeant as interpreter, all the forms being in English.

One final factor contributed to this picture of Highland recruiting as in Scotland in general, and in the Highlands in particular 'gone for a soldier' simply did not have the same connotations as in England and Ireland. As a result of history, literature and culture, soldiering was widely looked upon as a respectable profession in Scotland. The close links with bagpipe music, whose development in the nineteenth century was largely fostered through Army pipers, the Gaelic bardic tradition of an heroic romantic culture, the works of Walter Scott, the influence of the Highland Societies and the active support of a Monarch who came to associate herself with Scotland and in particular with the Highland Regiments,[120] all affected Scottish attitudes to the Army and recruiting.

Scottish newspapers such as the *Caledonian Mercury*, the *Edinburgh Courant*, the *Glasgow Herald* and the *Scotsman* regularly carried reports on Army matters, promotions, movements of troops, inspections and letters from Scots in foreign stations. The arrival of a battalion from abroad was the signal for hundreds of ordinary people to turn out to see them march from the quayside.[121]

Through clearances, migration, emigration, industrialisation, famine and political unrest this attitude to soldiering was never lost sight of in Scotland, a fact that was reflected in the ability to recruit for, and maintain as primarily Scottish, nine 'Highland' Battalions of Foot to 1881 and that allowed these Regiments to survive and increase to a total of ten kilted Highland-based Battalions by 1897.

The well-documented recruiting problems of the British Army in the nineteenth century concerning numbers, standards and methods were just as applicable in Scotland as they were in England, Wales and Ireland, yet in spite of these problems being compounded by additional and often severe historical, political and economic difficulties, a feeling still persisted that 'a soldier's life is viewed with favour by all classes in Scotland'.[122] Even Donald McLeod was not anti-Army:

> There is not a man in the civilised world who does not admire the energy, daring, perseverance and bravery of the glorious 78th, in their victorious march against the Indian mutineers.[123]

McLeod in fact uses the bravery and reputation of the Highland Regiments to support his argument, which was in fact anti-landlord, anti-deer forest and above all anti-Sutherland family.

This is not to deny however that there were recruiting problems and opposition to recruiting in the Highland area. In a paper entitled 'A District Command', probably written about 1909, Colonel R.B. Urmston of the Argyll and Sutherland Highlanders wrote:

> Why the barrack gate is not perpetually besieged by a crowd of would-be soldiers can only be explained by the innate aversion of the modern British youth to exchange what he imagines to be the perfect independence of civil life for the comparative discipline and restraint incidental to the military one, or by the aversion of his parents to see him wander far from home, an aversion not altogether unnatural among the working class relying much as they do or have done before the days of old age pensions and an Insurance Act on the support of their children in old age and sickness.[124]

These explanations were an echo of the difficulties expressed to the Wantage Committee in 1891 when Captain Stewart of the Argyll and Sutherland Highlanders reported his lack of recruiting success in Argyll as the

> . . . strong prejudice against and mistaken views as to the conditions and advantages of service in the army, mostly among the older people who bring strong family influence to bear on such of the young men who are disposed to enlist.[125]

Lieutenant Colonel Leslie of the 1st Battalion Queen's Own Cameron Highlanders summed up his Regimental recruiting problems to the Wantage Committee, stating:

> Inverness-shire as a regimental district is miserable in its unproductiveness; the districts are congested, the men are addicted to slothfulness and have a stay-at-home inclination, moreover the teaching of the Free Church and the political agitators interfere with our recruiting efforts in those districts; as a matter of fact there are too many men for the districts, and yet they will not enlist.[126]

In spite of all these problems, in August 1914 the Regular Battalions were brought up to war strength by the Special Reserve Battalions, and they prepared for war. Initially, it was not appreciated that these Battalions would be so finally altered by what was to happen.

Being 'home' Battalions, the 1st Battalion The Black Watch, 1st Battalion The Queen's Own Cameron Highlanders, the 1st Battalion The Gordon Highlanders, the 2nd Battalion The Argyll and Sutherland Highlanders and the 2nd Battalion Seaforth Highlanders took part in the earliest and most vital battles in which, despite desperate tiredness and inequality of numbers, the British Expeditionary Force held off and finally stopped the German advance.

As a result of a command controversy 500 men of the 1st Battalion The Gordon Highlanders were captured at the little village of Clary, near Le Cateau, in the early hours of 27th August 1914. Of the original 1007 men who left Aldershot with the 1st Battalion The Black Watch in August 1914, only 29 remained still serving with the Battalion in 1918. A similar figure applied to the 1st Battalion Camerons and probably the other Battalions too. Lance Corporal Frank MacFarlane and Private Reginald Lobban, to whom the author has had the privilege of speaking and of recording their experiences, were in 1983 the only two known survivors of these pre-1914 Battalions. When the remaining 1st or 2nd Battalions of the linked Regiments were involved in the conflict they suffered the same fate. Most of the Territorial Battalions were quickly committed and casualties were again high.

In 1914, Kitchener, forseeing a war of at least three years' duration, raised by dint of personal enthusiasm and an appeal to popular patriotism the New Armies, K1, 2, 3 and 4.

Voluntary recruiting prior to 1916 was conducted on a vast scale; the Seaforths, for example, had three Service Battalions in the New Army and the Camerons had four, exclusive of Reserve, Garrison and Labour Battalions.

Because many of the Battalions of kilted Regiments were allowed to keep men of certain areas, villages and communities together, when those Battalions were committed to battle, particularly in France and Belgium, significant numbers of young men from small Highland communities, who could ill afford their loss, were all killed or wounded together, as the many War Memorials in Highland villages and parishes testify.

By 1919, therefore, the rebuilding and reconstruction of the Regular Army was a major task. Firstly, the Regular Battalions, envisaged by Haldane as the base upon which the whole system was founded, had all but disappeared. Most of the old Regulars who remained were due for discharge, the remainder for demobilisation.

Secondly, as a result of the heavy commitment of the Territorial Battalions large numbers of Highland men were either dead or unfit for further Regular or Territorial service. And thirdly, because the New Armies and Conscription had drawn on the remaining fit and eligible manpower, recruiting for the long term posed a serious problem. It had after all been the war to end all wars. Men like Reginald Lobban and Frank MacFarlane were tempted by promotion to remain with their Battalions, but both had girlfriends and felt that they had pushed their luck quite far enough. The Camerons, like other Battalions who were warned for India, were in desperate need of older and more experienced NCO's, and there is no doubt that it took several years before all the kilted Highland Battalions were returned to anything like the service efficiency and depth of experience they had enjoyed prior to 1914.

In conclusion, therefore, recruiting to the Highland Regiments in the period 1820-1920 must, firstly, be placed in its historical context of the nature of Highland society and landholding and the effects of agricultural improvements on the numbers, location and composition of the population. There was, secondly, a lack of central policy and planning and above all an apparent lack of any understanding in official circles of the special nature of these Regiments and the particular difficulties they faced in recruiting. Thirdly, recruiters operating in small parties in their own areas and already having local associations before 1872, were a feature in Scotland, and official interference with the Highland Regiments, their names and tartans was strongly resented. Fourthly, despite urbanisation, public attitudes, affected by history, culture and contemporary writings, were generally favourable towards the Scottish soldier. Fifthly, Highland recruiting is principally a study in contradictions, for there is no single distinct reason why these Highland regiments should have survived at all, their national language dying and their particular dress falling from general civilian use. They faced the same problems of numbers and quality of recruits as other regiments of the British Army, but the little leaven of Highlanders to which Sir Douglas Haig referred, coupled with a stubborn Celtic pride and a curious sense of romance, meant that although the whole base of Highland recruiting shifted in less than one hundred years, the man who enlisted to a Highland Regiment at Glasgow in 1920 felt himself no less Highland than his Inverness contemporary or native Gaelic-speaking predecessor.

NOTES

1. The system of recruiting by the use of recruiting parties of Non-commissioned officers and Private men was adopted in 1813 at the suggestion of the Duke of York in a letter of 13.1.1813. PP1850 X c662, Appendix No.52 p. 895.
2. The Military Service Act 27.1.1916
3. Not to be confused with the Crofting Counties, see The Crofters Act 1886 49 and 50 Vict c29.
4. R.H. Campbell and J.B.A. Dow, *Source Book of Scottish Economic and Social History* (Oxford , 1968), p.8.
5. Marianne McLean, *Peopling Glengarry County—The Scottish Origins of a Canadian Community*. Canadian Historical Association, June 1982.
6. Captain Burt, *Letters from a Gentleman in the North of Scotland to his friend in London, op. cit.*
7. Eric Richards, *A History of the Highland Clearances* (London and Canberra: 1982), pp. 126-136. Vol.I.
8. The problem of social dislocation was compounded by a series of bad harvests and a recession in trade. Many landlords found themselves in an economically impossible position, drawing on capital to support their tenants whose arrears of rent they had no hope of collecting; Clanranald for example went bankrupt in the process. Although the Sutherland Estates carried out some of the most ruthless evictions between 1811 and 1820, they also spent some £60,000 in relief measures and schemes between 1811 and 1833. Several landlords wrote off rent arrears, bought cattle at independent valuations from tenants and sub-tenants and provided free passages to Canada, America and Australia.
9. Stewart of Garth estimated that '... three fourths of the old respectable race of Gentlemen tacksmen have dissappeared.' General Stewart of Garth, *Sketches of the Character, Manners and Present State of the Highlands of Scotland with details of the Military Services of the Highland Regiments* (Edinburgh:1822), Vol. II, Appendix p. xxxiii.
10. *New Statistical Account* (Edinburgh: 1845), Vol. XV, p.96.

11. *Ibid.*, p. 112.
12. R.D Lobban, The Migration of Highlanders into Lowland Scotland (1750-1890) with particular reference to Greenock. Edinburgh University Ph.D. thesis 1969-70.
13. *New Statistical Account, op. cit.*, Vol. XIV, p. 18.
14. B.R. Mitchell and Phyllis Deane, *Abstract of British Historical Statistics* (Cambridge: 1971), Population and Vital Statistics 2-B Scotland, p. 6.
15. The overall recruiting policy of the British Army was to obtain two thirds of the men required from England and Scotland and one third from Ireland. Glasgow however was so busy with North Irish recruits that in 1850 one Inspecting Field Officer was specially employed to deal with them. MacKerlie (published Anon.), *An Account of the Scottish Regiments with the Statistics of Each* (Edinburgh: 1862), p.38, and PP 1850 X c662 p.206 Para 2636, Evidence of Lt. Gen. Sir J. Macdonald.
16. *Edinburgh Evening News*, 30.3.1934.
17. GD 174/2217.
18. Sir G. Stewart Mackenzie Bart., *A General view of the Agriculture of the Counties of Ross and Cromarty with observations on the means of their improvement* (London: 1810), pp. 297-298.
19. *Ibid.*, p. 296.
20. General Stewart of Garth, *Sketches of the Character, Manners and Present State of the Highlands of Scotland, op. cit.*, p. 445.
21. Thomas Telford, Survey and Reports of the Coasts and Central Highlands of Scotland in the Autumn of 1802, PP 1802-03. Reports of the Select Committee on the Study of the Central Highlands of Scotland, and the 5th Earl of Selkirk, *Observations on the Present State of the Highlands of Scotland with a view of the causes and probable consequences of Emigration* (London: 1805).
22. Sir Robert Sinclair to Menzies 19.3.1794. Quoted J.M. Bulloch, *The Gordon Highlanders. The History of their Origin together with a Transcript of their First Official Muster.* Banffshire Field Club, 1913, p. 16.
23. Kenneth J. Logue, *Popular Disturbances in Scotland 1780-1815* (Edinburgh: 1979), and Gen. Stewart of Garth, *op. cit.*, pp, 499-500.
24. T.C. Smout, *A History of the Scottish People 1560-1830* (London: 1973), p. 334.
25. HO (Suppl) RH 2/4/207, p. 465. F.H. Mackenzie of Seaforth to Lord Adam Gordon 27.4.1793.
26. HO RH 2/4/71, f.238v. Donald McLeod, Sheriff Depute of Ross to Robert Blair, Solicitor General 23.5.1793.
27. Lt. Colonel A.A. Fairrie, *A History of the Queen's Own Highlanders* (Inverness: 1983), p.5.
28. K.J. Logue, *Popular Disturbances in Scotland 1780-1815, op. cit.*, p.69.
29. AD 14/13/9 Precognition, the Kildonan Riots. Declaration of John Bannerman 3.2.1813.
30. K.J. Logue, *Popular Disturbances in Scotland 1780-1815, op. cit.*, p.71.
31. Donald McLeod, *Donald McLeod's Gloomy Memories* (Glasgow: 1892), p. 165.
32. *The Scotsman*, 8.4.1854.
33. Returns and States 92nd Regiment 1799-1805, GHRM. Lt. Colonel C. Greenhill Gardyne, *The Life of a Regiment* (London: 1929), Vol. 1, p. 111 and Journal by a Private Soldier in the Ranks of the 92nd 1794-1805, GHRM.
34. See John Prebble, *Mutiny, op. cit.*
35. See, Map.
36. *79th News*, No. 69, October 1903, p. 1.
37. Private Alexander Robb, *Reminiscences of a Veteran*, BWRM 933/Ac. No. 4440. 3001 Alexander Robb aged 17, enlisted 13.2.1854 at Dundee into 42nd. Weaver. Discharged Private 1.8.1865. Pension 8d per day for 30 months.
38. PP 1861 XV c 2762; PP 1867 XV c 3752.
39. PP 1861 XV c 2762 Evidence of the Adjutant General Para 73.

40. MacKerlie (pub. Anon.), *An Account of the Scottish Regiments, op. cit.*, pp. 34-36.
41. Lord Hill to the Secretary at War 21.12.1833, PP 1850 X c 662 Appendix 52 p. 895.
42. PP 1850, ibid.
43. For example, the 92nd in March 1838 were permitted to recruit 30 men above establishment. Lt. Colonel C. Greenhill Gardyne, *The Life of a Regiment, op. cit.*, Vol. 2, p. 30.
44. Lt. Colonel C. Greenhill Gardyne, *The Life of a Regiment, op. cit.*, Vol. 2, p. 55.
45. See B.J. Bond, The Introduction and Operation of Short Service and Localisation in the British Army 1868-1892, London University M.A. Thesis, 1962, pp. 198-204.
46. The Highland Regiments were regarded in some official circles as something of unfathomable nuisance value. In an acrimonious exchange between Major General George Brown and the Commissioners, only Brown seems to have been clear as to how many kilted regiments there were in 1850 and who exactly wore the kilt and who wore 'trousers'. PP 1850 X c 772 pp. 253-254.
47. Army List 1839.
48. PP 1873 XVIII c 712.
49. PP 1881 XX c 2793. The Regimental District numbers were derived from the lowest number of the two Battalions linked to that district. The 72nd District was split north and south of the Moray Firth. In 1887 the 72nd district acquired the County of Nairn and gave up the Isle of Skye to the 79th District. The 72nd District included Orkney and Shetland. The 74th (2nd Battalion HLI) were, much to their disgust, placed in the Lowland area and they fought a long but unsuccessful battle to regain their place in a Highland Depot within the Highland area.
50. Lt. Colonel A.A Fairrie, '100 Years of the Local Regiment', Part 3, *The Queen's Own Highlander*, 1982, Vol. 22 No. 62, p. 31.
51. *Historical Records of the Cameron Highlanders, op. cit.*, Vol. 1, p. 299. This was the first Regular Highland Battalion to be raised since 1800.
52. See Map, Forts, Garrisons and Barracks in Scotland 1820-1920. p. 169.
53. PP 1861 XV c 2762. Evidence of Colonel A.C. Pole, Inspecting Field Officer, Glasgow, p. 154.
54. Recruits raised in Scotland between 1.1.1845 and 31.12.1849 totalled 8210 (excluding Artillery, Engineers and Guards). PP 1850 X c 662, p. 903.
55. Colonel George Jackson Hay, *The Constitutional Force* (London: 1905), pp. 148-155.
56. Harold Baker, *The Territorial Force* (London 1909), pp. 38-39.
57. The impression created by the Militia during this period may not always have been a favourable one. Major Robert Winchester 92nd Highlanders, reporting on the permanent Staff of the Inverness-shire Militia, found that of the 25 Sergeants and Drummers, none was under the age of 36, only 4 were considered 'efficient for active service' and none had performed any military duty for 2 years and 8 months. The Royal Perthshire Militia and the Ross, Sutherland and Cromarty Militia were slightly better, but most of the Permanent Staff were still over 50 years old and had not performed military duty for 2 to 3 years. PP 1835 XXXVIII c 171, pp. 73-77.
58. For example, 5 officers and 270 men volunteered for the Regular Army from the Stirlingshire Militia, 229 of them joining the 42nd. *Records of the Stirlingshire, Dumbarton, Clackmannan and Kinross Militia, Highland Borderers Light Infantry,* compiled by Colonel A.H. Middleton (Stirling: 1904), pp. 15-16.
59. Army Order 186 of 1906.
60. See Major General J.M. Grierson, *Records of the Scottish Volunteer Force 1859-1908* (Edinburgh: 1909).
61. PP 1877 XVIII c 1654. p. 96 para.2459, and p. 98 para.2518.
62. Private Reginald Lobban, 1st Bn Queen's Own Cameron Highlanders. Oral history archive in possession of the author.
63. It is estimated in the 1830s some £2000 in pensions were paid in a day in the Kingussie area alone. Colonel C. Greenhill Gardyne, *Life of a Regiment, op. cit.*, Vol. 2, p. 29.

64. See, for example, *Scotsman*, 3.11.1909. The Reminiscences of C/Sergeant Bertram (aged 90) of the 2nd (Queen's Royal) Regt. and the 78th Highlanders; or *Inverness Courier,* 14.7.1830, the Story of William Cameron of Croy, who served in the 73rd and whose son, two grandsons and son-in-law served in the 42nd.
65. Eric Richards, *A History of the Highland Clearances, op. cit.*, p.380.
66. PP 1850 X c 662, p. 269 para 3728-9. Evidence of Lt. Colonel A.M. Tulloch.
67. WO Circular 194 of 28.12.1857.
68. PP 1861 XV c 2762, p. 154.
69. PP 1870 XLII c 57, pp. 3-4.
70. PP 1861 XV c 2762, p xvii.
71. Diary of Private A.W. McIntosh, 42nd BWRM 421 (3591(1)).
72. *79th News*, 1.11.1896. Vol. 2, No. 28.
73. PP 1850 X c 662, p. 796 Appendix 21.
74. Cpl. Frank MacFarlane, 1st Bn Black Watch 1912-1919. Oral history archive in the possession of the author.
75. Such as C/Sergeant James McPherson of the 79th, 1846-67. McPherson was born in Glasgow in 1828. He enlisted on 16.5.1846 aged 18 and served in Gibraltar, Quebec, Scotland, Lancashire (during the disturbances), Crimea and the Indian Mutiny. He held the GC medal with £10 gratuity. Discharged to pension 1867. C/Sgt. Royal Lanark Militia for 9 years. Worked on the Recruiting Staff at Glasgow Cross for 6 years. After 30 years as a Pensioner he received £10 annuity and a silver medal. He had two brothers, one in the 60th and one in the 79th. His four sons joined the 90th, the 93rd, the 79th and the Argyll and Sutherland Hdrs. 'This man was recruiting at Glasgow Cross for many years and gets the credit for enlisting several thousand men'. *79th News*, 1905-06, No. 77, p. 11.

Sergeant George P. Miller of the 71st (HLI), recruiting in Stirling in 1868, recalled wearing a 'pair of officer's tartan trews, a new diced Forage cap with, a snoot, a cunning wee silver bugle (a wee 71 in the centre) a braw new tunic, white gloves, a smart cane with a silver tip. A bonny bit lassie—a daughter of the house—made a nice rosette and ribbons—red, white and blue, fully a foot long...' *HLI Chronicle,* Vol. VII, No. 1, January 1907, p. 24.

76. PP 1850 X c 662, p. 246 para 3296. Evidence of Major General George Brown.
77. GO 71 of 3.2.1858. Levy Money (Infantry).

		£	s	d
To the Recruit	On being attested in cash		2	6
	On final approval by the IFO in cash		7	6
	On joining his Corps in cash	2	10	0
	Amount of Bounty	£3	0	0
	And a free kit of necessaries			
	On final approval by the IFO to cover the expenses of posts etc.		5	0
To the Officer	For attesting		1	0
	Surgical examination		4	0
To the party incl. bringer	On final approval of the IFO including 7s 6d. to be paid to the bringer		15	0
	For conducting the recruit to his Corps		2	6
	Total levy money	£4	7	6

N.B. An additional Bounty was given in Highland Regiments to pay for feather bonnets. PP 1850 X c 662, p.252 para 3395. I.F.O. - Inspecting Field Officer.

78. WO/43/422.
79. WO/43/422/54039.
80. Ibid.

81. Colonel C. Greenhill Gardyne, *The Life of a Regiment, op. cit.*, Vol. 2, p. 12.
82. In 1825 Depots to which recruits were sent were formed for each Battalion. No buildings were provided for them and they were stationed or billeted anywhere in England, Ireland or Scotland as convenient. They could be used as military units, particularly in Ireland in aid of the civil power, or amalgamated with the Regiment when it was at home. GD/364/1/1287. Horse Guards Memo. 25.4.1825. In 1856 Depot 'Battalions' were formed by amalgamating the Depots of several Battalions, but again they were given no set accommodation; the 'Battalions' merely moved around together. They did not include Battalions serving in the East Indies. HG Order 9.9.1856. In 1870 Depot 'Battalions' were replaced by pairing the Depots of Regiments overseas with a Battalion stationed at home. In 1872 the Localisation Scheme gave Depots permanent 'homes' and set recruiting areas. In 1881 the Territorial Scheme re-linked some of the Regiments and again set down permanent locations for Depots. QOHRM. MS/646.
83. See Chapter 3 and Farmer Collection, Glasgow University Library. MS 118.
84. PP 1881 XX c 2832. Annual Report of the Inspector General of Recruiting, p.20. 57th District Report (Perth – 42nd/79th). 'The recruits enlisted in the 57th Sub-district are very good in every respect. But some of those sent from other districts, especially from Brigades in England, although physically good, are in many instances of bad character and introduce crime. When recruiting was opened in England some weeks ago several disreputable characters were sent to the 56th Brigade Depot (Aberdeen – 92nd/93rd) and their conduct became known from newspaper reports of their conduct in the town. [The Inspecting Officer] . . . is convinced that this has deterred many good recruits from joining 57th Brigade.
85. Lt. Colonel A.A. Fairrie, *A History of the Queen's Own Highlanders, op. cit,*.p. 18.
86. The 92nd in 1824 were permitted by the C-in-C to restrict their enlistments to men of 5′ 8″ and over. Colonel Greenhill Gardyne. *The Life of a Regiment, op. cit.*, Vol.2, p.11.
87. There were sixteen alterations in the minimum height requirement between 1820 and 1859. Edward M. Spiers, *The Army and Society* (London: 1980), p. 40.
88. Private Reginald Lobban. Oral history archive in possession of the author.
89. In 1837 the Mutiny Act was amended to protect soldiers from the liability of imprisonment for failure to maintain their families. WO/43/666.
90. Diary of General Sir Spencer Ewart. 79th, RH/4/84/1.
91. Donald Cameron, 79th and 93rd. RH/4/141.
92. See recruiting poster of the Black Watch c.1902, BWRM. PP1881 XX c 2832, p. 7.
93. PP 1877 XVIII c1677.
94. Standing Orders of the 93rd, 1835. ASHRM, R/226.
95. Standing Orders of the 79th 1835. QOHRM, 143/79.
96. PP1850 X c662 Appendix 53.
97. PP 1835 VI c473, p.97 para 1755.
98. PP 1850 X c662, p.903.
99. *Ibid.*, p.254 para 3431.
100. PP 1861 XV c2762 para 73.
101. *Ibid.*
102. PP 1872 c171.
103. PP 1872 XXXVIII c 493 and pp 1881 XX c 2832.
104. *79th News*, May 1908, p. 199.
105. Lt. Colonel L.B. Oatts, *Proud Heritage* (Edinburgh: 1959), Vol. II, p.340.
106. Edward Speirs, *The Army and Society, op. cit.*, p. 50.
107. On 28th January 1881 the Adjutant General enquired of the 79th by telegram, 'If 79th is linked to 42nd will your Regiment adopt tartan of 42nd Regiment. Linked regiments must wear the same tartan. Wire reply'. The reply, 'No—The Cameron Highlanders will not adopt 42nd tartan'. *Historical Records of the Cameron Highlanders, op. cit.*, Vol. 1, p. 234.

108. PP 1881 XX c 2793 p. 9 para 24.
109. PP 1886 XIII c 4677 and PP 1890 XIX c 5953.
110. PP 1886 XIII c 4677 Appendix N.
111. PP 1886 XIII c 4677 Appendix B.
112. PP 1910 LX c 5016 Section 2 Pt.3.
113. WO/17/627.
114. PP 1862 XXXIII c 3051, pp. 34-40.
115. Register of Deserters 92nd Regiment. GHRM.
116. Private Reginald Lobban, Oral history archive in possession of the author.
117. New forms of enlistment and attestation were introduced in 1862. PP 1861 XV c 2762.
118. PP 1850 X c 662, p.903.
119. PP 1877 XVIII c 1655, p.2.
120. The Queen, who hated both Childers (the Secretary of State for War) and the linking of Battalions, brought her influence to bear in 1881 and refused to allow 'Her' Highlanders, i.e. The Queen's Own Cameron Highlanders, to be linked with another Battalion. This left them as the only single Battalion in the whole of the British Army. E.S.E. Childers, *The Life of Childers* (London:1901), Vol. 2, p.38, and B.J. Bond, *The Introduction and Operation of Short Service in the British Army, op. cit.*, p. 201. Diary of General Sir Spencer Ewart 79th, RH/4/54.
121. The arrival of the 42nd at Greenock on 19th June 1852. 'The whole people of Greenock turned out to see us, and cheered us like fun the whole way to the Rail Station'. Diary of Colonel J.W. Wedderburn. BWRM, 28/714/1, p. 404.
122. MacKerlie (published Anon.), *An Account of the Scottish Regiments with the Statistics of Each, op. cit.*, p.39.
123. Donald McLeon, *Donald McLeod's Gloomy Memories, op. cit.*, pp. 202-204.
124. Colonel R.B. Urmston, 'A District Command'. An unpublished paper c.1909. ASHRM.
125. PP 1892 XIX c 6582, p. 302.
126. Ibid., p. 416.

CHAPTER 3

Recruiting: The 93rd Sutherland Highlanders, 1799-1831[1]

In the light of the historical background to recruiting in the Highland Regiments before 1820 it is fascinating to study one of the few Roll Books which is available, that of the 93rd Sutherland Highlanders. The book is incomplete, but provides a good guide to trends and recruiting patterns. Most of these volumes have been lost, as they were carried around with the Regiments and carefully kept up to date until they were full and then were discarded, fell into private hands or were destroyed. They provide a much more complete and detailed picture than any of the Muster Rolls or War Office Records, and initially I believed that this book was the original roll book of the 93rd, but upon examination it is clear that this is not the case.

In the major investigation into soldiers' services which took place between 1828 and 1833 the books of the 93rd were examined, and it seems this Roll Book was the subject of scrutiny:

> The Description Book of the Depot 93rd . . . is stated to have been well kept and the court give it as their opinion that the Books of this Regiment will be found free from the system of fraudulent alterations of service which has extensively prevailed.

The report, however, continues:

> Many vouchers having been ascertained to be forgeries is I fear conclusive proof of fraud on behalf of the Acting Quarter Master Sergeant [Frazer].[2]

The forged vouchers amounted to £21. 14. 9d. Alexander Frazer from Kiltern in Inverness was a weaver who enlisted aged 19 in 1805. He was discharged at Chatham in 1830 'worn out', and there is no reference in the Descriptive Roll Book to his having been tried by court-martial regarding these frauds.

In every other Highland Regiment frauds, sometimes on a large scale, were discovered, but the Report does give an indication that up to about 1830 the Descriptive Roll Book of the 93rd may be considered reliable.

'The Descriptive Roll Book of the XCIII Sutherland Highlanders, commenced 1799, concluded 1831' is a handwritten ledger ten inches by sixteen inches. The watermark on the pages is 1809, but from the content it would seem that the book was commenced much later, probably around 1820, when the Regiment was in Ireland. While some of the details are written in various hands, all the name entries of enlistments to 1824 have been written by one person, who was possibly Sergeant James Beveridge, a labourer from Kirkcaldy, who enlisted on 28th August 1820.[3]

The volume contains details of enlistment, former service, promotion, casualties and observations. The Roll Book therefore gives a fairly clear picture of the members of the 93rd Sutherland Highlanders in the early 1820s, during their service in Ireland and the West Indies. There is no full list of enlistments after 1828 and the book has not been kept up after 1831, to provide details of the service pensions etc. of those serving at that time. Only soldiers are listed, not officers.

The 93rd Highlanders were, in 1820, serving in Ireland, mainly broken up into small detachments at Cork, Birr, Athlone, Limerick, Ennis, Naas and Mulligan.[4] The following Table shows the counties of birth of those serving in the 93rd c.1820 who had enlisted between 1799 and 1819.

Date	1799	1800	1801	1802	1803	1804	1805	1806	1807	1808	1809	1810	1811	1812	1813	1814	1815	1816	1817	1818	1819	Total by Counties
Sutherland	65	12	5	7	10	6	17	2	6	12	4	5	9	11	17	2			14	9	7	220
Caithness	2	1		1	1		10	1						1	3	2	1			1		24
Ross	1	2	3			2	8		3	4		6		5	11		1		1			47
Argyll		1			2																	3
Inverness				1		1	3		4		3		2	5	23	6	1			1		50
Cromarty							1															1
Stirling		1			1															1	1	4
Aberdeen		1	4	1	5		1		1						1	2						16
Orkney		2																				2
Shetland				5	4																	9
Perth			2		1		3	1			1		2	3	18	1			1	1	3	37
Moray							1	1													1	3
Nairn									2			2		4	2	1	2					13
Banff		1			1		1							1	1							5
Forfar				1			5								1					1	1	9
Fife		2	4	1	2	1	24	1	1		4		4	4	35	1				5	9	98
Angus		2	1		4		4							2	4						1	18
Kinross																				1	1	2
Bute																					1	1
Midlothian		1					1		3				1	1	6					2	2	17
Lanark		1			1		2		1		2		3	1	4	1					9	25
Renfrew							2				1		1									4
Haddington															1	1						2
Ayr															1						1	2
East Lothian							1	1				1										3
Dumfries			1		1																	2
Roxburgh		1	1												2							4
Jersey								1														1
England					1				1		1				4		1			4	1	13
Ireland					2		1	1				1					10	1		18	19	53
Totals by yr. of enlistment	68	28	21	17	36	10	85	9	22	16	16	15	22	38	134	17	16	1	16	44	57	688

A hard core of the Battalion were Highlanders from Sutherland and these men provided the nucleus of NCO's and Sergeants. Sixty-eight men still remained of those who had enlisted in 1799, 65 of whom were born in Sutherland, 2 in Caithness and 1 in Ross. These 68 men alone provided 4 Corporals, 18 Sergeants and the Quarter Master of the Battalion,[5] and they must have played a major part in shaping the character of the corps in 1820. Ten of these men who enlisted in 1799, while being born in Caithness, Sutherland or Ross, were attested at Ayr, which would imply that they were men from the Sutherland Fencibles, the remainder of the 1799 men being attested at Dunrobin, Golspie, Assint (*sic*), Farr, Achnahiglish, Ardevan, Kintradwell, Clyne, Kildonan, Loath, Bettyhill, Lairg, Dornoch and Craicag.

By 1820 the average age of these men who had enlisted in 1799 was, however, 41 years, and 65 were discharged between 1820 and November 1823. Two of them, Alexander Macpherson from Golspie and Angus Mackay from Sutherland, died at Cork in the spring of 1821, and Sergeant Robertson Gordon from Kildonan served on until 24th January, 1828. Excepting Quarter Master Dallas, the two men who died and Sergeant Major William Mackay from Loath, for whom there is no record, every one of these 1799 men received a pension from Kilmainham Hospital of between 7d and 1/11½d per day. They were discharged as 'worn out', as 'supernumaries to the establishment' and with ophthalmia, wounds, rheumatism and pulmonary disease. George Grant was 'blind in the right eye and worn out', while George Ross from Golspie still carried a musket ball in his left arm from the Battle of New Orleans in 1815 and was 'unable to march'.

While the preceding Table essentially shows 'survivors' as opposed to enlistments, it would appear to indicate that in 1799 the Regiment was primarily composed of men from Sutherland and that a recruiting drive took place in 1805, prior to embarcation for the Cape of Good Hope, primarily in the counties of Sutherland, Caithness, Ross and Fife.

From the Sutherland Estate Management papers it would seem that in 1805 Lady Stafford maintained strict control of recruiting parties operating in the estate area through her factor, Colonel David Campbell. It is known that two Regiments had been recommended to the tenants, the 78th and one other unnamed Regiment. The unnamed Regiment was certainly not the 79th Cameron Highlanders:

> Colonel Campbell is directed to inform the Kildonan Tennants who furnished Recruits to Captain Cameron of the 79th in preference to the 78th recommended by Lady Stafford that they are not to expect to be continued in their possessions, and this notice to be given at the ensuing Martinmas.[6]

The Sutherland recruits of 1805 came from the parishes of Kildonan (1), Dornoch (1), Clyne (2), Farr (3), Loath (2), Durness (2), Rogart (3), Creech (*sic*) (2) and Golspie (1), and it is by no means conclusive that the recruiting parties of the 93rd had the sanction of the estate or that the 93rd was the other named Regiment, for in all those parishes, with the exception of Kildonan and Loth, there were other landowners, apart from the Sutherland Estates, who could have provided recruits.[7]

What is certainly clear is that even as early as 1805, if not before, the estates had seen the dangers and the impossibility of using promises of security of tenure to attract recruits and that the idea of having an 'estate' Regiment had been abandoned, for large numbers of men were coming in that year from Fife, Caithness, Ross and Forfar. As far as the Estate was concerned,

> In 1804 and 1805 nothing more was done than to recommend Regiments, and to threaten not to give new leases to tennants who gave recruits to other formations. It was the final withdrawal from the attempt to raise and maintain a regiment from the Sutherland estate alone.[8]

There appears to have been another recruiting drive in 1813, but those men remaining in the Battalion in 1820 who enlisted in 1813 were probably not originally 1st Battalion 93rd men. A second Battalion of the 93rd Highlanders was raised in 1813 for service in France: when peace was declared in 1814 the Second Battalion were sent to Newfoundland, returning the following year to be disbanded on 24th December 1815 when a large draft of men from the Second Battalion joined the First Battalion. The peaks in figures in 1813 show that Inverness, Perth and Fife were productive sources of recruits, but of course these numbers are 'survivors', *not* all recruits. What is interesting is that recruiting is taking place in Sutherland in 1813 and the parishes where the men came from:

Recruits from the County of Sutherland 1813	
Golspie	2
Assint (*sic*)	3
Dornoch	3
Rogart	5
Loth	1
Farr	3
	17

Between 1811 and 1816 William Young held the position of Sutherland Estates Factor, and his factoring is marked primarily by the re-arrangement of estate tenancies, which resulted in the removal of small tenants and the creation of sheep farms and muir settlements. In all the parishes where men were recruited in 1813, with the exception of Farr (Strathnaver) where the resetting did not commence until 1814, Young was altering the tenancy arrangement and effecting removals. In theory there should have been ample numbers of young men from the estate available for the recruiting parties. That so few appear to have joined may indicate the hostility of the tenants or former tenants to the Army, whom they identified with the Estate, or that the estate was no longer encouraging recruiting by promises of security of tenure. The tenants in addition saw that these promises were essentially temporary and were held by the Estate to expire like any other lease, and therefore gave no long-term protection or security. It is noticeable that if there were any recruits from Kildonan in 1813, the scene of riots in that year, none of these recruits was still serving in the 93rd in 1820.

In general in 1820 from the figures in the Roll Book men from Sutherland predominate, the second largest group being Fifers. The connection here is through General Wemyss who was not only a cousin of the Countess of Sutherland but also 'of Wemyss', south of Cupar in Fife, where he held large estates.[9] Of the twenty-four men, however, who enlisted in 1805 for example from the county of Fife, only David Todd, a weaver, was born in Wemyss. The remainder are mainly 'labourers' and 'weavers'. Perhaps some were sub-tenants or cottar handloom weavers, but there is no indication that these men were ever subject to the kind of pressures or promises that had applied to the Sutherland recruits.

Even allowing for the discrepancy in the age of enlistment caused by men not knowing their age or lying about it to obtain adult pay and reckoning of service, the 93rd was in 1820 essentially an 'old' Regiment, ninety-six men having over twenty years' service. Of the remainder, men like John Rollo, a flax dresser from Dundee who enlisted in 1801, had already served for a year, in Rollo's case in the 'Princess Royal's Light Dragoons'. Others had seen service in the 72nd, 73rd, 21st, the Elgin Fencibles, the Ross and Cromarty Rangers, the Inverness Fencibles and the Caithness Highlanders. The enlistments of 1803 also included ten men from the Aberdeen Fencibles.

Until 1809, all the men had enlisted for 'unlimited service'. The exception in that year is David Currie, a Renfrew weaver, who is stated as having enlisted for 21 years.[10]

In 1810, men, taking advantage of the limited service option introduced in 1806, began to enlist for shorter periods, mainly 10 and 11 years, but sometimes less. For example 16-year-old private John Sutherland from Clyne, Sutherland, enlisted in 1811 for 9 years. He was duly discharged at Birr in 1820, the term of his service having expired and, although of good character, he was not recommended for a pension.

Most men re-engaged for an 'unlimited period' when their short service had expired. James Ross from Nigg, for example, only 9 years old and four feet high enlisted for 16 years in 1813 and re-engaged for unlimited service in Antigua on 22nd December 1828 when he was a Sergeant and 25 years old.[11] By 1813 the short service period is being used by men over 18 years old, with 7 years being a popular term of service. Approximately half the short service men re-engaged.[12]

There was thus a wide spectrum of age in the Regiment, and amongst the boys were five Drummer Boys enlisted into the Regiment as volunteers from the Royal Hibernian Military School in 1818. Probably with a view to looking after and teaching the young lads of the Battalion, Lt. Colonel Creagh enlisted 35-year-old Thomas Fuller, an Edinburgh teacher, who had formerly served with the 84th Regiment, and he served as School Master Sergeant until 8th September 1830.

In 1819 the 93rd was taking men with former service in other regular battalions, three of the eight men coming from the 94th Regiment (The Scots Brigade), which was disbanded in Dublin in 1818. Transfers were, however, uncommon and all of these eight men had been discharged and re-enlisted as of new.

It is interesting therefore to speculate on the demeanour and appearance of the Regiment in 1820 as gleaned from the information in the Roll Book. As far as health and presentation is concerned the 93rd cannot be said to be in good heart, for many men were quite simply old and ill. A sample of the causes of discharge of men enlisted before 1820 is interesting:

Rheumatism 16
Pulmonary Disease 10
Ingurial (*sic*) hernia 3
Ulcerated legs 1
Wounds 18
Chronic dysentery 2
Chronic hepatitis 6
Bad feet 1
Mental derangement 2
Defect of vision 3
Disease of the spleen 1
Disease of the testicle 1
Disease of the anus 1
Ophthalmia 1

Some men had a combination of complaints, as for example John Sutherland, enlisted in 1800 and discharged in 1820 as a result of 'length of service, wounded in the left thigh, fistuluous ulcer and worn out'. Other men were worn out, unable to march, insane or sickly and the Regiment can hardly have presented an imposing sight or been militarily effective with such high numbers of ineffectives in relation to their overall strength, and such a high proportion of older men in the ranks.

In the light of the events in Sutherland during the period 1799 to 1820 and the fact that the Regiment had once reflected a part of the land policy of the estate, it might be expected that either recruiting would have died out altogether in Sutherland as a logical corollary to tenant/estate hostility, or, alternatively, that recruiting would have expanded in Sutherland when tenants and their families found themselves landless and in search of employment. In fact neither of these things seem to have happened. Recruiting in Sutherland was reduced but continued; on the other hand, perhaps as a result of the association in people's minds between the estate and the Regiment, the 93rd had no influx of landless Sutherland recruits and preferred to broaden the base of their recruiting to other Highland counties and the developing Lowland towns and cities.

Had the Regiment not been required for duties in Ireland, it seems possible that they might have been completely disbanded in 1815, taking into account their losses, health, combat potential and recruiting circumstances. In retrospect the whole situation on the estate and the link with the recruiting to the 93rd has all the ingredients of possible mutiny, but there was no mutiny and the Regiment was probably reprieved by Wemyss himself who did not die until 1822, by which time British Colonial obligations required more not less regiments.

The Roll Book also betrays nothing of the kind of tension and concern that must have existed in the Regiment, particularly amongst the men from Sutherland, at the time of their return from America in 1815 when they must have learned of some of the clearances and removals that had taken place. However, there is no indication of any increase in desertion, or of men being punished or dismissed for mutinous conduct.

Finally, how many of the men from Sutherland who enlisted prior to 1820 and who returned to their homes or home area is unknown. The Rent roll of small tenants on the Reay Estate at Martinmas 1822[13] lists one 'soldier', William Gunn, five 'Pensioners', Hugh Mackay, Donald McLeod, Donald Calder, Donald Mackay and Robert Mackay, and three 'Pipers', Angus Campbell, John McLeod and George McLeod. While the pipers may not have been military pipers, the pensioners were almost certainly discharged soldiers. Unfortunately, because of the persistent recurrence of certain surnames and christian names it is not possible to connect clearly any of these tenants with soldiers' names in the Descriptive Roll Book of the 93rd.

One man who certainly did return to Sutherland was Private Alexander Murray, son of George Murray of Creach (*sic*). Alexander Murray enlisted on 9th November 1805 aged 21, having been born at Rogart on 8th November 1784. While his service details are in the Descriptive Roll Book, in the back cover of the Roll Book is Murray's Soldier's Small Book or Account Book, which gives additional information on him. Murray was born in Rogart but in 1827 gives his next of kin as his father who was then residing in Creach (*sic*). Alexander was attested in Inverness in 1805 and was finally approved on reaching the Battalion in the Isle of Wight when he received the remaining half of his bounty which totalled sixteen guineas. He presumably served in the Cape of Good Hope and at the Battle of New Orleans although there is no record of this. He was certainly in St. Kitts in the West Indies in 1827 where the account book was issued to him on 24th November. Murray was in hospital in Barbados in June 1828, and with sixteen shillings and nine pence standing at the credit of his account he was sent home and discharged from the Invalid Depot at Chatham on 13th August 1828. Because of his good character he received an out pension, and he returned to Sutherland sometime before 1832. His account book must have been a treasured possession because he used it along with his discharge certificate to obtain his pension, but he carefully wrote in it as might be written in a family bible:

> Margaret Murray was born on the 6th of November
> 1812 and Married to Alex^r Murray on the 14th
> December 1832 in the church of Creich
> John her brother Married on the 23rd of August 1833
> George was born on the 14 December 1833
> Donald on the 11th August 1835
> Jennet (*sic*) on the 2nd October 1837
> Anne on the 14th of October 1839 (this is scored
> out so presumably Anne died) Christy 11th August 1841
> Alex^r on the 20th May 1848.[14]

Murray's case illustrates the length of service of these soldiers and the fact that many remained private soldiers and were also unmarried. It is unlikely that Murray returned to Sutherland between 1805 and 1828, and his return must have been a difficult and emotional experience. He probably received about 1/- per day as a pension but it would not have been easy for him to support himself, his young wife and family on this sum especially as it seems he was 54 when their last child was born. In view of his age and 23 years' service mostly spent overseas, it seems unlikely that he would have been able to work at anything more than a very small holding.

The figures from 1820 to 1828 provide a more detailed look at recruiting, as opposed to those already serving in the Regiment. Because there is no recorded death or discharge earlier than 1820 the book was probably made up about this time, and the total figures of 688 from the book (in Table) and 688 in War Office Records correspond.[15]

The following Table, however, shows an interesting change of emphasis in recruiting. The Sutherland men are not being replaced in the Regiment, but Highland men in general are still the mainstay of recruitment, Caithness, Inverness and Perth dominating. The Fife connection provides the second-largest single group and Lanark is dominant amongst the Lowland counties. Englishmen are few until the intake of General Service men from the 4th (The King's Own Royal) Regiment on 25th February 1826 in Antigua. This draft included six Canadians and four Irishmen, a total of twenty-five. Twenty-one of these men were deserters from a variety of other regiments, none of them Scottish or Highland. Four were 'commuted' men. They can have had very little in common with the men of the 93rd and were without doubt reluctant soldiers. Although they were comparatively small in numbers, their influence caused endless problems of discipline, as witnessed by Lt. Colonel Duncan MacGregor in his evidence to the Commission on Military Punishment:

> From what we suffered in the West Indies, I am quite sure that the great increase of crime there was caused by the union, to all the Corps in those islands, of a number of military convicts, men of most abandoned habits, whose punishment in their own regiments, in different parts of the world, had been commuted for service in the West Indies. A certain number of these culprits were attached to the 93rd, and remained incorporated with it during the time we were in that country. Although the intention was without doubt that we should be the means of reforming them, yet the consequence was, that their presence and example were most destructive to us.[16]

This system of drafting was contrary to the whole ethos of the Highland Regiments. In the 93rd, the men had initially been organised in platoons and companies by parish of origin, bringing about considerable social control which had the effect of nullifying the most severe aspects of contemporary military punishment. Not a single man of the Light Company of the 93rd was reputed to have been punished between 1799 and 1819.

The combination of the wider spread of recruiting, the lessening of the more personal aspects of recruiting, the alcoholic temptations of garrison service,

Counties of Birth of those Enlisted in the 93rd 1820-1828 (1831 figures incomplete)

Date	Sutherland	Caithness	Ross	Argyll	Inverness	Cromarty	Stirling	Aberdeen	Orkney	Shetland	Perth	Moray	Nairn	Banff	Forfar	Fife	Angus	Kinross	Bute	Kincardine	Midlothian	Lanark	Renfrew	Dumbarton	Linlithgow	Haddington	Ayr	East Lothian	Dumfries	Berwickshire	Roxburgh	Peebles	?	England	Ireland	Cape of Good Hope	Madagascar	Canada	Totals by year
1820	4		6		6			2			2	6	5			26	1	1			2	1	1	1	1									1	3	1			70
1821	7	9	2		10	1		1			2					5						1			1							1			8	1			49
1822	5	18	3		6	1		1			10	1	1		4	1				1		2												1	4	2	1		62
1823	11	10	5		4						7	1	2	1	1	5				1											1		2	1	1	2			55
1824	4	6	5		5						6	5		1	1	5						1								1				1	7				48
1825	2	9	1								9				2	1	1					2	1									1		1					30
1826	11	2	2	1	2		4	5			28	3			13	9	5				2	4	1			1	1				1			18	7	1		6	127
1827	4	4	2	2	3		1	10			11				7	10				1		23	5	4	1		1		2					2	1				94
1828	2	2		1	2			2			2	1	1			2					3	16	2	1										1					38
1831																																		1	1 (incomplete)				2
Total by County	50	60	26	4	38	2	5	21			77	17	9	2	28	64	7	1		3	7	50	10	6	3	1	2		2	1	2	2	2	27	32	7	1	6	575

particularly in the West Indies, the discharge of all the remaining original recruits and the intake of unconnected and unenthusiastic general service men, all combined to change the character of the Regiment and the original very close relationship between recruiting, the land, personal service and mutual acquaintance.

The War Office, while they accepted that 'a Highland Corps' recruited mainly in the Highlands, looked, it would seem, at figures, costs and establishments. Recruiting in the Highlands was without doubt slow, competing against other regiments, migration, emigration and a peacetime lack of enthusiasm. Regiments, however, whoever they were, had to be filled up to establishment to be effective for duty.

These transfers and drafting continued therefore to cause problems of cohesion and discipline, and it is to the great credit of the Highland Regiments that the spirit created by the original men lived on. Colonel Douglas Haig (later Field Marshal Sir Douglas Haig) commented as follows in his evidence to the Royal Commission on the South African War on the subject of *esprit de corps*:

> Question: Take the Highland Regiments; do you know whether the men of those regiments are entirely Highlanders?
>
> Col. Haig: I fancy that there are a good many Highlanders in them; anyhow they have got the traditions, and Englishmen joining get to believe they are Scotsmen. There is a little leaven of Highlanders that leavens the lot.[17]

One of the reasons why recruiting in the 93rd in the 1820s became so urgent was losses through death, which reached serious proportions after the 93rd arrived in the West Indies in three transports on 14th, 17th and 21st December 1823. A further two Companies arrived on 9th January 1824 and the Battalion remained stationed here until the spring of 1834.

As can be seen from the following Table, prior to leaving the Battalion had prepared itself for foreign service and there are obvious indications of a weeding-out process before embarcation, older men and those unfit and unable to march being discharged, together with those undersize or otherwise unacceptable in the ranks. Discharges thereafter remained fairly constant, although they too were probably affected by West Indian service, as chronically sick men who were unable to recover their health, even in a more moderate climate, were discharged. In 1823 many of the older men with long service and good character transferred into the 1st Royal Veteran Battalion.

After 1824, however, it was not long before deaths began to increase to a total recorded in the Roll Book of 61 in 1830. With the West Indies' reputation for sickness, it is hardly surprising that recruiting was affected, particularly in terms of the standard and age of men accepted.

Some interesting information is available with regard to the service of the 93rd in the West Indies in a Report of 1837-1838 by Captain Alexander M. Tulloch, 45th Regiment,[18] and, combined with the details from the Roll Book, a much more informed picture can be obtained of the kind of life a recruit or serving soldier could expect to find in the West Indies between 1823 and 1834.

Recorded Casualties of the 93rd from The Sutherland Highlanders Descriptive Roll Book, 1820-1833

	1820	1821	1822	1823	1824	1825	1826	1827	1828	1829	1830	1831 (figures unreliable)	1832 (figures unreliable)	1833	Serving or unknown	No date
Discharges Receiving 1½ yrs pay												2				
Worn out, length of service, time expired unfit, supernumerary	75	82	56	75	10	27	28	38	28	21	10	1		1	390	
Deaths	3	10	11	6	20	21	27	22	24	39	61	25	1			57
Transfers	2	8	9	17	1	5		1	1	2	4	1				1
Buying Out		1	4	2	2	1		2		2		3				1
Deserters Not Returned			5	1					1							
Drummed Out	1	2	1					2								
Dismissed					1											
Shot by Sentence of Court Martial								1								
Claimed by Militia					1											
Promoted to Officer	1			1			1		1			1				1 (1835)
Totals by Year	82	103	86	102	35	54	56	66	55	64	75	33	1	1	390	60
Comparative recruiting figures by year	70	49	62	55	48	30	127	94	38			2				

Summary

Total from recruitment figures 1799-1831 1263
Total casualties recorded 1263

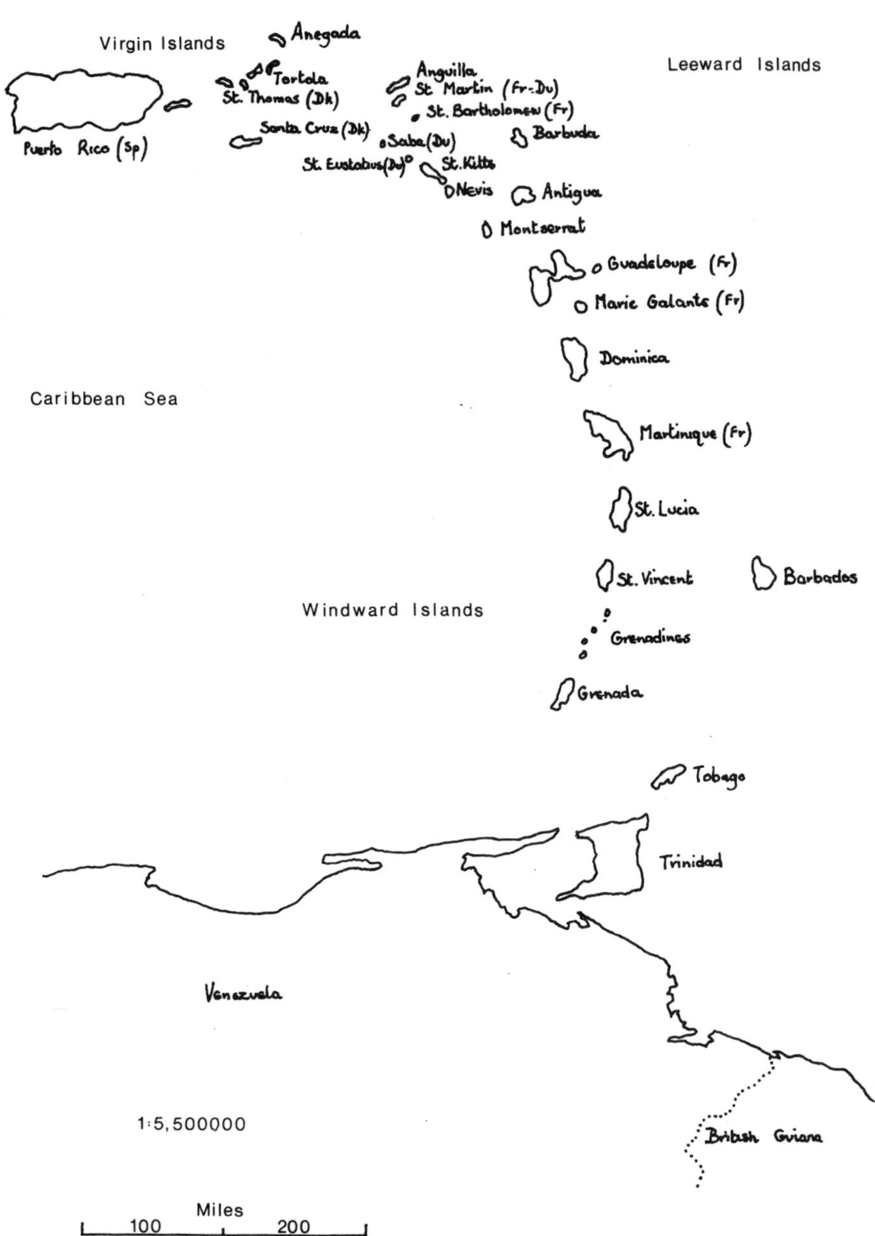
The Windward & Leeward Command
Virgin Islands
Anegada
Leeward Islands
Tortola
St. Thomas (Dk)
Anguilla
St Martin (Fr-Du)
St. Bartholomew (Fr)
Puerto Rico (Sp)
Santa Cruz (Dk)
Saba (Du)
Barbuda
St. Eustatius (Du)
St. Kitts
Nevis
Antigua
Montserrat
Guadeloupe (Fr)
Marie Galante (Fr)
Dominica
Caribbean Sea
Martinique (Fr)
St. Lucia
St. Vincent
Barbados
Windward Islands
Grenadines
Grenada
Tobago
Trinidad
Venezuela
1:5,500000
British Guiana
Miles
100
200

The West Indies was divided into four commands, the Windward and Leeward Islands, Jamaica, Bahamas and Honduras. The 93rd were stationed in the Windward and Leeward command which included British Guiana, Trinidad, Tobago, Grenada, St. Vincent, Barbados, St. Lucia with the small nearby Pigeon Island, Dominica, Antigua, Monserrat, and St. Kitts with Nevis and Tortola.[19] Geographically Trinidad, Tobago, St. Lucia and Dominica are mountainous, while Antigua and Barbados are low, barren and rocky. The temperature ranges between 82°F and 79°F with a rainfall of between 60 and 70 inches per annum. Hurricanes can occur between August and the end of October and there are basically two wet and two dry seasons. In 1831 a hurricane in Barbados killed 36, injured 253 and damaged practically every building on the island.

There is some conflict as to where exactly the 93rd were in the Windward and Leeward Islands. The Report of 1837-1838 gives certain stations, but from the Roll Book lists of the re-engagements, discharges and deaths it is obvious that there were many small detachments and that the Regiment were only really all together at the beginning and end of their service in the command. Movement between the islands was by Garrison or Regimental Canoe or hired transport sailing ships,[20] but it is not the method of transport which is notable but the distances between islands and the isolation of the small detatchments.

Localities of the 93rd Sutherland Highlanders 1823-1833

Date	1837-1838 Report	Roll Book Additions
1823	Barbados	
1824	Barbados	
1825	Barbados	
1826	Barbados	Montserrat
	Antigua	St. Kitts
1827	Antigua	Montserrat
		St. Kitts
1828	Antigua	St. Kitts
		Barbados
1829	Antigua	St. Kitts
1830	Antigua	Dominica
	St. Lucia	Pigeon Island
		St. Kitts
1831	St. Lucia	Pigeon Island
		Dominica
1832	St. Lucia	
	Barbados	
1833	Barbados	
1834	Barbados	

The 93rd shared their stations with negroes, planters, black troops of the West Indian Regiment, convicts and other British Regiments. The barracks were mainly stone or brick buildings of large apartments with an attached hospital built high on a hill and above the sea as it was commonly believed that the prevalent fevers and diseases were caused by the 'influence of miasma from the

South American continent'.[21] Sometimes the barracks were situated in forts or bomb-proof casemates.

Prior to 1827, 22 to 23 inches were allowed per man in these barrack rooms, and hammocks were used until the introduction of iron bedsteads in that year.[22] The barracks were generally 'in a great state of dillapidation before 1830' when improvements of a sort were commenced using largely military labour.[23] As regards food:

> In most of the Corps the soldier has two meals; breakfast consisting of a pint of cocoa and his ration bread and dinner consisting either of fresh meat made into broth, with vegetables or the salt meat boiled into soup with the peas and eaten with yams or potatoes.[24]

The soldier was issued with a gill of rum daily but he could always acquire native spirits. The men were not permitted to work in the heat of the day and Tulloch reported:

> . . . black troops take most of the guards as are most likely to prove prejudicial to health of the whites.[25]

Musters of the wings and detachments of the Regiment together with local pensioners took place at the end of every month and the men were marched to church parade every Sunday, but in general activity and work during the heat of the day were actively discouraged. There were however numerous guards, work parties and artillery duties[26] to perform.

There was apparently no understanding of aspects of sanitation, clean water and the transmission of diseases, and the death ratios were high. Both officers and men added to these ratios by excessive drinking and indiscriminate sexual relations with negro and mulatto women.

The recorded deaths in the 93rd Regiment (from War Office monthly returns) are given in the 1837-1838 Report (on page 67).

The fluctuations in strength reflect incoming or outgoing drafts of men, desertion and death. The causes of death are not broken down by individual Regiments but include:

Fevers
Diseases of the Lungs
Diseases of the stomach and Bowels
Diseases of the Brain i.e. delirium tremens
Dropsies
Rheumatic affections
Venereal disease
Abscesses and ulcers
Wounds and injuries
Diseases of the eyes
Diseases of the skin
All other fevers.[28]

Recorded Deaths Of The 93rd Regiment, By Year And Month
With The Regimental Strength. Windward And Leeward
Islands 1823-1834[27]

		JAN	FEB	MAR	APR	MAY	JUN	JUL	AUG	SEP	OCT	NOV	DEC	Total Deaths
1823	Strength												508	
	Deaths													
1824	S	507	506	505	502	499	497	487	485	484	481	478	478	
	D	1			2	2	1	3	1	2	2	2		16
1825	S	478	507	496	515	513	517	502	500	493	491	489	489	
	D		4	5		1	1	3			2	2		18
1826	S	497	504	501	504	502	497	497	463	462	463	461	459	
	D	2	1	3	2	3	5			1		2	2	21
1827	S	516	512	512	510	507	475	472	451	449	449	448	520	
	D	1	4		1	1	3	3	2	2		1	2	20
1828	S	519	518	515	512	511	480	478	476	475	473	526	523	
	D		1	2	3	1	2	1	1	2	2	4	3	22
1829	S	519	513	511	510	504	478	475	474	471	467	466	462	
	D	2	4	2	2	5	3	3	1	3	3	1	4	33
1830	S	511	508	505	498	491	485	469	466	459	456	451	445	
	D	2	3	3	5	7	6	10	3	7	3	4	6	59
1831	S	481	478	476	473	472	462	457	452	448	444	442	439	
	D	3	3		3	1	3	5	5	3	4	3	2	35
1832	S	431	492	483	478	475	437	430	426	417	409	406	405	
	D	8	3	6	3	4	7	5	3	6	5	3	1	54
1833	S	402	403	400	397	395	537	503	503	502	383	380	378	
	D	2	2		2	1	2	1	1	1	2	3	1	18
1834	S	376	377	258										
	D	1		2										3
														299

Unfortunately the Roll Book does not record cause of death, except in a few cases, especially incidents of drowning such as Hugh Chisholm from Urquhart, Inverness who was drowned at Pigeon Island on 24th November 1830.

Comparing, therefore, the 'casualty' figures from the Roll Book with those deaths recorded in the War Office Returns, the Roll Book does show the trend but there are discrepancies in the numbers. It is interesting that the figures in the Roll Book of deaths between 1824 and 1830 are consistently higher than the numbers in the War Office returns, but why this should be is not clear.

The two sets of death figures and the location details do bring out, however, the fact that Antigua, St. Kitts, Dominica, St. Lucia and Pigeon Island were particularly unhealthy stations while Barbados was a station where fewer deaths occurred. There are 14 recorded deaths of men of the 93rd on Pigeon Island alone where the garrison can only have comprised 15 to 20 soldiers, and in addition it would seem that the 93rd were only on the island in 1830 and 1831.

Transfers on the table of recorded casualties in the Descriptive Roll Book reflect the preparation of the Regiment for foreign service in 1821, 1822 and 1823. Thereafter transfers out are few although it is noticeable that men are obviously transferring to another regiment in order to stay in the West Indies. Perhaps they had married or alternatively had no wish, for whatever reason, to return to Scotland. An example is William Henderson from Halkirk in

Caithness, who enlisted in 1822 and transferred to the 1st West Indian Regiment on Christmas Day 1829.

Men were permitted to buy out at a cost set on a sliding scale, and those men who are recorded as buying out between 1824 and 1831 presumably remained in the West Indies. Sergeant George Gunn from Kildonan who enlisted in 1822, purchased his discharge at St. Lucia on 10th March 1831 for £18. Even a sergeant was unlikely to have this sum of money and it is possible that Gunn was either given or borrowed money from a potential employer.

Higher numbers of deserters not returned would be expected particularly in Ireland and the figures here may well be inaccurate. It is clear, however, that desertion in the Windward and Leeward Islands was virtually impossible. The low numbers of losses by punishment, i.e. drumming out, dismissal or execution, say a great deal about the character of the Regiment who, in spite of heavy losses in America, unique circumstances in their recruiting area and unsavoury duties in Ireland and the West Indies, maintained a remarkable discipline. In 1826 Lt. Colonel Duncan MacGregor assumed command and he is known to have been against the contemporary harsh discipline, particularly flogging.[29]

One man is claimed by the Militia, and six men who enlisted as private soldiers are recorded in the Roll Book as becoming commissioned officers. The most notable of these is William Macdonald from Lairg, Sutherland, who enlisted aged 16 in 1812 for 9 years' service. At Birr in 1820 he re-engaged for unlimited service, having risen in 1817 to the rank of Corporal and in 1819 to the rank of Sergeant. He was appointed Sergeant Major in 1824, commissioned Quarter Master in 1826 and held the post of Lieutenant and Adjutant of the 93rd between 1827 and 1847.

Two men were discharged, receiving 1½ years' pay and, although there is no further explanation of this in the Roll Book, these men probably were permitted to commute their pay and pension as men wishing to become settlers in the Colonies in terms of the War Office Memorandum of 1831.[30]

The Table of recorded casualties brings out the relative importance of such incidents as buying out, deserters not returned and men drummed out, aspects which often attract a lot of biased attention.

The indications are that in the 93rd drumming out was used as an absolute last resort, the process not only bringing disgrace on the individual, but also discredit to the Regiment. In 1820, Donald Baillie from Clyne in Sutherland, who enlisted in 1809 as a 14-year-old drummer boy, was drummed out, 'bearing the marks of punishment and being a notorious thief'. He received only a protecting certificate.

William Smith of Reay in Sutherland was shot by sentence of a General Court Martial on 25th May 1827. He had probably committed murder, but the surviving Judge Advocate's records do not state the nature of his crime.[31] Francis McNamara and Patrick Irwin were drummed out of the 93rd in April 1827. These two men were 'considered no longer fit to remain in His Majesty's Service having been guilty of unnatural and polluted crimes when on detachment at St. Kitts . . . .' This wording from the Descriptive Roll Book implies that these men were tried by court martial for sodomy, but again no case papers survive. These dramatic and interesting cases detract from the record of the 660 men or so in the Battalion who served without incident of this kind.

There is plenty of evidence in the Roll Book, too, of the opportunities for social advancement which the Army provided. While a great majority of men were content (or perhaps only able) to serve as private soldiers, when men showed responsibility and trustworthiness there were opportunities open to them as Drummers, NCO's, Sergeants and Officers, with combatant and non-combatant Commissions.

William Holme and David Holme, both from Kirkmichael, Ross (possibly brothers), were aged 18 and 13 respectively in 1810 when they enlisted, and were 'labourers'. They became Corporals in 1825 and subsequently Sergeants. George McDonald assumed the position of Paymaster Sergeant on 26th October 1826; he too was a 'labourer'. To be appointed to the post he would have to have been able to write (in a hand few could emulate today), read and add. He would have had to prove his responsibility and trustworthiness, for although the whole pay system was riddled with 'perks' and inconsistencies, outright fraud or incompetence was not tolerated.

When Alexander Dallas from Clyne enlisted in 1799, he was already 23. He was appointed Sergeant on 30th March 1806 and was probably made Drum Major at this time. The Roll records that he was appointed Sergeant Major on 21st October 1817 and was finally appointed 'Quarter Master with the Regiment' on 31st August 1820. He went on to the Half Pay List in 1824. As a 'labourer', enlisted by Major General Wemyss himself, this man had advanced materially and socially beyond any reasonable expectations he may have had, had he remained in Sutherland.

From the Descriptive Roll Book it is possible to build up a picture not only of who was in the Regiment in 1820 but who was recruiting from that date, where they were recruiting and where the recruits were born and where attested.

The principal recruiters are primarily Highland and five are from Sutherland, but while recruiting seems to have been supervised by an officer, the groundwork of actually getting the recruits was done by the Sergeants, Corporals and private soldiers. The biographical notes on the main recruiters indicate and emphasise their local origins, their stature and their background and military career. They were primarily local men recruiting in an area known to them, and as regards the Highland, and in particular the Sutherland, recruits this might reflect Highland suspicion of unknown soldiers recruiting in their areas. In Kildonan, with the exception of one man recruited in 1823 by Lt. Sutherland, recruits between 1821 and 1823 were obtained by Sergeant Bruce, a native of Kildonan parish. Bruce worked on until 1827 when he was discharged in Thurso, but despite his efforts no men are listed in the Roll Book as having been recruited from Kildonan after 1823.

Recruiters, Places of Attestation and Birthplace of Relative Recruits in the 93rd Highlanders 1820-1828 taken from the 93rd Descriptive Roll Book

Date	Recruiter	Place where their Recruits were Attested	Birthplace of relative recruits
1820	Ensign Sutherland	Nairn, Forres, Miltoun	Nairn, Inverness, Sutherland, Moray, Ross
	Sgt. Wardlaw	Dunfermline	Fife, Angus, Perth, Dumbarton, Linlithgow, Midlothian
	Sgt. F. Macdonald	Glasgow	Lanark, Aberdeen, Renfrew, Dunfermline
	Sgt. Todd	Kirkcaldy	Moray, Fife, Perth, Durham, Aberdeen
	Lt. Col. Creagh	Naas	Cape of Good Hope, Dublin, Cork, Ross, Sutherland
	Sgt. Bruce	Thurso	Sutherland
1821	Ensign Sutherland	Nairn, Forres, Swardale, Aldearn	Ross, Moray, Sutherland. Cromarty Inverness
	Sgt. Wardlaw	Dunfermline	Fife, Perth, Peebles
	Sgt. F. Macdonald	Edinburgh	Linlithgow, Lanark
	Sgt. Todd	Kirkcaldy	Fife
	Sgt. Wm. Bruce	Thurso	Sutherland, Caithness
	Sgt. Macbeth	Inverness	Inverness
	Sgt. Gilchrist	Turriff	Aberdeen
	Sgt. Sutherland	Kyleakin	Inverness
1822	Lt. Sutherland	Thurso	Sutherland, Caithness
	Sgt. Bruce	Thurso	Caithness
	Sgt. Gilchrist	Perth	Cromarty, Perth, Inverness, Moray, Forfar
	Sgt. H. Sutherland	Tain, Portree, Kyleakin	Ross, Inverness
	Sgt. R.N.(?) Gordon	Nairn, Aberdeen, Inverness	Forfar, Perth, Angus, Galloway, Nairn, Ross, Kincardine, Inverness
1823	Lt. Sutherland	Thurso	Caithness, Sutherland
	Sgt. Bruce	Thurso	Sutherland, Caithness
	Sgt. Gilchrist	Perth	Forfar, Fife, Essex, Perth
	Sgt. Sutherland	Dornoch	Nairn
	Sgt. R. Gordon	Inverness, Aberdeen	Ross, Kincardine, Inverness, Sutherland
	Cpl. Murray	Nairn	Moray
	Pte. D. Ross	Banff	Banff
	Pte. John Fraser	Glasgow, Perth	Fife, Perth
	Pte. H. Mackay	Thurso	Sutherland
	L/Cpl. McDonald	Perth	Perth
	Cpl. McPherson	Thurso	Sutherland
1824	Lt. Gordon	Thurso	Caithness
	Sgt. W. Bruce	Thurso, Brora	Sutherland, Caithness, Ross
	Sgt. Gilchrist	Perth, Edinburgh	Perth, Lanark, Somerset
	Sgt. Sutherland	Portree	Inverness
	Sgt. R. Gordon	Inverness, Campbeltown	Inverness, Ross
	Cpl. Murray	Nairn	Moray
	Pte John Fraser	Perth	Banff
	Pte. H. Mackay	Thurso	Caithness
	L/Cpl. McDonald	Dunkeld, Perth, Falkland, Edinburgh	Berwick, Perth, Fife
	Cpl. McPherson	Thurso	Caithness
	Pte. Geo. McDonald	Thurso	Sutherland

Date	Recruiter	Place where their Recruits were Attested	Birthplace of relative recruits	
1824 (ctd.)	Sgt. A. Fraser	Perth	Perth, Fife	
	Cpl. I. Grant	Forres	Moray	
	Pte. Neil McLeod	Inverness	Inverness	
	L/Cpl, McKenzie	Dundee, Perth	Fife, Perth	
	Drummer Jas. McKay	Inverness	Sutherland	
	Pte. Jas. Shaw	Forres	Moray	
	Lt. Brownings (Rifle Brigade)	Limerick	Limerick	
	Cpl. Blair (21st Foot)	Nenagh	Tipperary	Recruiters from
	Sgt. Russell " "	Nenagh	Clare	other Regiments
	Sgt. Aughey " "	Adart	Limerick	
	Cpl. Breen " "	Adart	Limerick, Longford	
1825	Sgt. Wm. Bruce	Thurso	Caithness, Sutherland	
	Sgt. Gilchrist	Edinburgh	Midlothian	
	Sgt. Gordon	Dingwall	Ross	
	Cpl. H. Mackay	Thurso	Sutherland	
	Cpl. W. McDonald	Perth	Perth, Angus	
	Sgt. H. McPherson	Edinburgh	Perth, Peebles, Lanark, Donn, Aberdeen	
	Acting Cp. McDonald	Perth	Perth	
	Sgt. Fraser	Perth	Perth	
	Cpl. McKenzie	Edinburgh	Lanarkshire	
	Drummer Jas. Mackay	Inverness	Sutherland	
	Sgt. W. Brown	Thurso	Caithness	
	Pte. Hugh Watson 72nd	Edinburgh	Lanark	Recruiters from
	Sgt. Major Best	Loudon	Renfrew	other Regiments
1826	Sgt. Bruce	Thurso	Sutherland, Caithness	
	Sgt. Rt. Gordon	Inverness	Moray	
	Cpl. Mackay	Thurso	Sutherland	
	Sgt. McDonald (F or J)	Perth	Perth, Sutherland, Argyll	
	Sgt. McPherson	Edinburgh, Cupar	Fife, Perth	
	Cpl. McDonald	Perth	Forfar, Perth	
	Drummer J. Mackay	Dingwall	Sutherland	
	Cpl.-L/Sgt. Murray	Tain	Stirling, Sutherland	
	Acting Sgt. Maj. Wardlaw	Perth	Perth, Forfar, Fife, Donegal, Manchester, Dorset, Haddington	
	Cpl. Grant	Cupar, Edinburgh	Fife, Edinburgh, Lanark	
	Acting Cpl. - Cpl. Peddle	Perth	Fife, Perth	
	Cpl. Morgan	Aberdeen	Cape of Good Hope	
	Pte. McLeod	Tain	Ross	
	Pte. Anthony Simpson	Perth	Perth, Lanark	
	Pte. John Ferguson	Perth	Perth	
	Pte. John Smith	Perth	Perth, Angus	
	Pte. Jas. Scot	Perth	Forfar	
	Cpl. Gunn	Perth	Fife, Forfar	
	Pte. D. Yeaman	Perth	Forfar	
	Pte. J. Robertson	Perth	Perth	
	Pte. T. Wilson	Perth	Forfar	
	Pte. Alex. Grant	Perth	Forfar	
	Pte. R. Scott	Perth	Forfar	
	Pte. J. Stevenson	Perth	Forfar, Lanark, Fife	
	Cpl. Malcolm	Aberdeen	Kincardine	

Date	Recruiter	Place where their Recruits were Attested	Birthplace of relative recruits
1826 (ctd.)	Pte. G. Fraser	Thurso, Tain	Sutherland, Ross
	Pte. W. Munro	Aberdeen	Aberdeen
	Pte. A. Noble	Aberdeen	Aberdeen
	Pte. A. Spence	Perth	Fife
	Acting Cpl. A. Smith	Perth	Angus
	Pte. Alexr. Rose	Perth	Sutherland
	Pte. Neasmith	Perth	Stirling
	H. Sutherland (Piper 78th)	Edinburgh	Sutherland } Recruiters from other Regiments
	Sgt. J. Mackay 25th	Edinburgh	Roxburgh }
	In this year the Depot Companies were probably formed at Perth, moving sometime in 1827 to Glasgow.		
1827	Sgt. Bruce	Thurso	Caithness
	Sgt. Mackay	Golspie	Sutherland
	Sgt. (J?) McDonald	Glasgow	Inverness, Lanark
	Sgt. McPherson	Edinburgh	Lanark
	Cpl. I. McDonald	Perth	Kent
	Sgt. Wardlaw	Perth	Lanark, Forfar, Renfrew, Fife, Lancaster, Kings, Aberdeen, Dumbarton, Galloway, Stirling
	Acting Sgt. Morgan	Aberdeen	Aberdeen, Kincardine, Forfar
	Sgt. A. Gunn	Wick, Thurso	Sutherland, Caithness
	Pte. J. Robertson	Perth	Moray, Perth
	Pte. Jas. Stevenson	Perth	Perth
	Cpl. Munro	Glasgow	Ayr, Lanark
	Cpl. A. Rose	Dingwall	Ross
	Sgt. Munro	Edinburgh, Glasgow, Paisley	Fife, Ayr, Donn, Inverness
	Pte. R. Peters	Perth	Perth
	Pte. W. Hutcheson	Glasgow	Dumbarton, Lanark
	Cpl. Gowans (?)	Perth	Fife
	Pte. A. McIntosh	Perth	Perth
	Pte. H. Davidson	Perth	Stirling
	Pte. A. Cameron	Perth	Fife
	Pte. W. Morrison	Perth	Perth
	Cpl. Johnstone	Glasgow	Hants
	Pte. James Nelson	Glasgow	Lanark
	Pte. N. McLeod	Dingwall	Ross
	Pte. Wm. Rogers	Perth	Angus, Perth
	Pte. Gilmore	Glasgow	Renfrew
	Pte. Jas. Grant	Perth	Perth
	Pte. D. Black	Glasgow	Lanark
	Pte. W. Christie	Perth	Fife
	Recruit Jas. Gunn	Thurso	Caithness
	Cpl. I. Grieve	Edinburgh	Linlithgow, Galloway
	Pte. A. Douglas	Perth	Forfar
	Pte. W. Campbell	Thurso	Sutherland
	Pte. M. Shannon	Glasgow	Lanark
	Pte. D. M. McMillan	Glasgow	Dumbarton
	Pte. W. Peacock	Glasgow	Lanark
	Pte. W. Taylor	Glasgow	Lanark
	Pte. G. Gilchrist	Glasgow	Argyll
	Pte. A. McLennan	Glasgow	Argyll
	Pte. J or I (?) Wood	Glasgow	Lanark
	Pte. D. Fraser	Glasgow	Inverness

Officers of the 1st Battalion Black Watch August 1914. 12 of these men were killed or died of wounds.

The 79th Highlanders preparing to move from Edinburgh Castle 1852, painted by R.R. McIan. The group in the foreground, some of whom are dressed in civilian clothes are from right to left, Lieutenant Colonel the Hon. Lauderdale Maule, Quarter Master Robert Jameson, Lieutenant and Adjutant Henry MacKay, a Private Soldier, possibly Colonel Maule's servant. Surgeon John Grant and Quarter Master Sergeant David Paton, "Foxy" so nicknamed because of "his having been so cute". QOHRM.

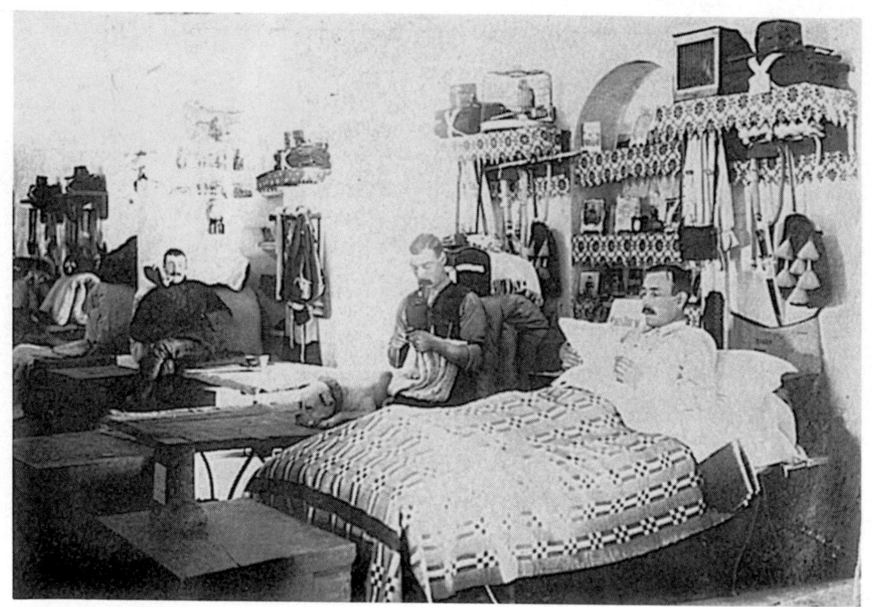

2nd BN. Argyll and Sutherland Highlanders Barrack Room, Dagshai India c.1890. ASHRM.

Men's First Meal Call – "Come to the Cook House Door Boys!" Orderly men queue for rations in Edinburgh Castle in 1882: 2nd Battalion Gordon Highlanders. GHRM.

1st Battalion Queen's Own Cameron Highlanders. A Company New Year Celebration in a barrack room at Aldershot about 1912. QOHRM/RHQ/20/2.

1st Battalion Argyll and Sutherland Highlanders Officers Mess Servants, Cape Town, March 1882. ASHRM.

The Sergeants Mess of the 2nd Battalion Argyll and Sutherland Highlanders, Poona India, 1904. ASHRM.

Duties in aid of the Civil Power, August 1911. Men of the 1st Battalion Gordon Highlanders march through Sheffield to guard the railway stations, wearing khaki tunics and feather bonnets. GHRM.

72nd Drummers Room, Edinburgh Castle c.1886. SUSM.

The Cricket Team of the 42nd India c.1858. BWRM.

The Football Team of the 1st Battalion Black Watch Simla, India 1899. Winners of the Durand Football Cup 1897, 1898 and 1899. BWRM.

Private Reginald Lobban, 1st Battalion Queen's Own Cameron Highlanders. Photograph from the author's collection.

Corporal Frank MacFarlane MSM 1st Battalion Black Watch with his sisters in 1919. Photograph from the author's collection.

The Pipes and Drums of the 2nd Battalion Gordon Highlanders Beat Retreat at Fort William, Calcutta, 1909. GHRM.

Date	Recruiter	Place where their Recruits were Attested	Birthplace of relative recruits
1827 (ctd.)	Cpl. Cunningham	Glasgow	Dumbarton
	Pte. J. Provan	Glasgow	Lanark
	Pte. George Mackay	Glasgow	Lanark
	Pte. Douglas Skigh	Glasgow	Lanark
1828	Sgt. I or J McDonald	Glasgow	Lanark, Renfrew, Edinburgh
	Sgt. Gunn	Wick	Caithness
	Sgt. Munro	Inverness	Inverness
	Pte. Donald Black	Glasgow	Renfrew
	Pte. G. Gordon	Inverness	Nairn
	Pte. J. Mackay	Aberdeen	Aberdeen
	Pte. J. Malcolm	Aberdeen	Fife
	Pte. J. McLeod	Glasgow	Edinburgh, Midlothian
	Acting Sgt. Mackay	Inverness	Inverness
	Pte. Alex. Mackenzie	Wick	Sutherland
	Pte. W. Murray	Tain	Sutherland
	Sgt. Geo. Mackay	Glasgow	Lanark
	Sgt. Peddie	Perth	Perth
	Pte. Jas. Moncur	Perth	Argyll
	Sgt. W. Morgan	?	Aberdeen
	Pte. Jas. McFarlane	Perth	Fife
	C/Sgt. Sutherland	St. Lucia	Dublin

Thereafter "By Whom Enlisted" column not filled up.

Biographical Notes on various Recruiters

Ensign Sutherland
George Mackay Sutherland
b. Udale, Ross-shire
Ensign 2.8.1815
Lt. 14.10.1824 (?) This date does not correspond with the Roll.
Capt. 5.6.1828. To 23rd Lt. Dragoons 21.11.1828.
died 1847

Sgt. F. Macdonald
Finlay Macdonald 5′ 7½″
b. Golspie, Sutherland, attested Dunrobin 1799 aged 18. Labourer.
Cpl. 29.3.1806
Sgt. 24.4.1813
Discharged 16.8.1821 Cork
Kilmainham Pension 1/10½ per day
'Character very good'.

Sgt. Wardlaw
John Wardlaw 6′ 0¼″
b. Culross, Perth: attested Beccles 1805 aged 18 Weaver
Cpl. 27.11.1808
Sgt. 25.7.1811
Discharged Chatham 4.10.1828

Sgt. Todd
John Todd 5′10½″
b. Cupar, Fife: attested Inverness 1813 aged 24 Weaver
Cpl. 8.12.1813
Sgt. 25.10.1814
Quarter Master Sgt. 29.4.1823
died 10.7.1825 Barbados

Sgt. Bruce
William Bruce 5′7″
b. Kildonan, Sutherland: attested Golspie 1800 aged 22 Labourer
Cpl. 11.11.1806
Sgt. 24.4.1813
Discharged Thurso 24.5.1827 worn out

Sgt. Gilchrist
John Gilchrist 5′9″
b. Kildonan, Sutherland: attested Inverness 1812 aged 18 Labourer
Cpl. 4.2.1815
Sgt. 25.5.1822 'Depot'

Sgt. H. Sutherland
Hugh Sutherland 5′7½″
b. Golspie, Sutherland attested Dornoch 1802 aged 19 Labourer
Cpl. 1.11.1815
Sgt. 25.11.1820
'Was taken on the strength of the Depot
Companies at the time of their formation'
Discharged 16.4.1826 worn out

Sgt. R. Gordon
Robertson Gordon 6′0″
b. Farr, Sutherland attested Inverness 1813 aged 16 Labourer
Cpl. 11.2.1819
Sgt. 20.9.1820
QM Sgt. 10.7.1826
Quarter Master 24.4.1828 Antigua

Sgt. A. Gunn
Alexander Gunn 6′0″
b. Reay, Caithness: attested Fort George 1814 aged 18 Labourer
Cpl. 1.1.1824
Sgt. 15.11.1824
died St Lucia 18.11.1830

Drummer Jas. Mackay
James Mackay 4′10″ (1820)
b. Bantry, Cork: attested Birr 1820 enlisted by Lt. Colonel Creagh aged 15, Labourer 9.8.1820
Drummer from 9.8.1820 to 24.12.1826
'Depot'

In the early 1820s men were being recruited to the 93rd by small parties of recruiters in Scotland. How they operated is not exactly clear, but in 1820 for example there would seem to have been one party, under Ensign Sutherland, based in the Inverness, Moray, Nairn and Forres areas, a party under Sergeant Finlay Macdonald in Glasgow and two parties under Sergeants Wardlaw and Todd in Dunfermline and Kirkcaldy respectively. The locations are not exactly certain, as the Roll Book does not actually state where the recruit was *enlisted*, only where he was *attested*.

Sergeant Wardlaw, for example, enlisted John Macleod from Skye who was attested at Dunfermline. It is unclear therefore if, in the winter of 1820, Wardlaw was in Skye recruiting, or if Macleod had found his way to the Fife area for the two men to meet.

Along with Sergeant Bruce these are the only recruiters' names mentioned in 1820. From the communications point of view they cannot have operated as one party, and yet it seems unlikely that they would have worked individually.[32] In addition, of course, it is not known exactly where these recruiters lived or moved, only where, roughly, their recruiting was successful.

If parishes of birth of the recruits were also their places of residence when recruited, it may be assumed that Ensign Sutherland was working around or near his own home area, as were Sergeants Todd and Wardlaw. By 1820, Sergeant Finlay Macdonald was, at 39, coming to the end of his service, having served 21 years. His 'very good' character and service as Sergeant since 1813 may have guaranteed him a sheltered position as the Glasgow Recruiting Sergeant.

In the winter of 1820 Sergeant William Bruce from Kildonan is enlisting men in the Sutherland and Caithness area. He would almost certainly have been a Gaelic speaker and brought to the Regiment several men from Kildonan. Sergeant Hector Macbeath, also from Kildonan, is working in Ross and Inverness and is joined by Sergeant Hugh Sutherland (from Golspie) in 1822.

These men are working amongst their own people, their kinsmen, family, relatives, friends and acquaintances, and it is difficult to see how in these circumstances they could use unscrupulous recruiting methods. They might well have been sent to their respective areas because they knew the country, the people and the language. They were all senior and long-serving soldiers; they must have cut imposing figures in their uniforms, and it is noticeable that none are under 5′ 7″. To dupe recruits by drink or trickery into enlisting seems unrealistic, although there may have been elaborate promises of 'black servants' and rapid promotion.

Taking the year 1824, it would seem that early summer and autumn were the best time for recruiting, but overall it is difficult to see that there was a recruiting 'season' as such.

Recruiting figures by months, 1824

Month	**Number of Recruits**
January	4
February	3
March	1
April	2
May	4
June	5
July	8
August	3
September	3
October	7
November	3
December	5
	48

The pattern was more probably set by the weather, the 'terms' of Whitsunday and Martinmas, and the incidence of local fairs and markets, which recruiting parties usually attended.

In 1824, for example, Sergeant William Bruce attested two Sutherland men, Gordon Fraser and Hugh Sutherland, at Brora on 15th October. The Brora Fair had taken place on the second Wednesday of October. Again, in 1826, Corporal Grant and Sergeant McPherson attested two men, William Campbell and Durham Gordon, at Cupar, Fife, on the 10th and 14th of February, an 'old style' Fair being held annually at Cupar on the first Wednesday of February. The only man to be attested at Campbeltown in the entire Roll was George Munro, who had been born in Alness. He was attested on 12th August 1824, a few days after the 'old style' Fair which was held in the town on the first Tuesday of the month.[33]

The trades, or declared trades, of the serving men to 1819, and the recruits from 1820 to 1831, show remarkable variety and would have meant that there was in the Regiment a wide range of skills, tailors, shoemakers, saddlers, butchers and bakers being particularly useful.

Declared Trades of Recruits from the Descriptive Roll Book

1. Men Serving 1799-1819:

Unknown (MS torn)	1
Labourer	448
Tailor	29
Shoemaker	33
Weaver	102
Printer	1
Flaxdresser	6
Miner	1
Miller	1
Saddler	1
Butcher	2
Baker	6
Woolcomber	1
Hairdresser	1
Nailer	3
Carpenter	6
Coalhewer	8
Bookbinder	2
Wright	4
Chandler	2
Brickmaker	1
Saddle tree maker	1
Cabinet maker	2
Bottlemaker	1
Watchmaker	1
Gardener	2
Smith	2
Blacksmith	1
Mason	4
Cooper	3
Painter	1
Stocking Weaver	1
Glazier	1

Declared Trades of Recruits from the Descriptive Roll Book

Men Serving 1799-1819: (Continued)

Teacher	1
Armourer	1
Cotton Spinner	1
Plasterer	1
Joiner	1
Glassmaker	1
Carrier	1
Sawyer	1
Mater	1
	688

Recruits 1820-1831

Labourer	344
Tailor	10
Shoemaker	19
Weaver	94
Flaxdresser	14
Baker	6
Hairdresser	1
Carpenter	5
Coalhewer	2
Miner	1
Wright	6
Gardener	3
Smith	1
Blacksmith	5
Mason	5
Armourer	1
Plasterer	1
Slater	3
Founder	2
Joiner	2
Cartwright	1
Sawyer	1
None (Boys)	11
Gunsmith	1
Carrier	1
Papermaker	1
'Tipe Caster'	1
Compositor	1
Engineer	1
Confectioner	1
Clerk	1
Servant	1
Collier	2
Printer	1
Upholsterer	1
Dyer	1
'Callander'	1
Gilder	1
Calico Printer	1
Carder	1
Basket Maker	1
Rope Maker	1
Cutler	1
Clothier	1
Unknown	15
	575

The Majority of the Highland men were labourers, that is, general farm workers, crofters, cottars and tenants. From Fife came labourers, weavers and coalhewers; and flax-dressers from the Dundee and Aberdeen area. In theory, apprentices were not taken and many of the young men would therefore have completed their trade training. How many lied about this it is impossible to say. The basket maker, rope maker, cutler and clothier were part of the 1826 draft and were all from England. Overall the majority of the men were unskilled or semi-skilled. Eleven of the boys were too young to have a trade, while others were designated 'labourers'.

On joining, recruits from the Highlands, and especially from Sutherland, had a greater chance of promotion to NCO and Sergeant. This may not be a reflection of their practical or educational skills, but the fact that many were well-built and fine-looking men, handsome by the standards of the day. Because of the numbers of Highland recruits, Gaelic-speaking NCO's were a necessity. Some of the Fife men would have had greater educational opportunities, and they form the second-largest group from which NCO's and Sergeants were drawn.

Counties of Origin of Non Commissioned Officers recorded in 93rd Descriptive Roll (including those who were later reduced)

Sutherland	102
Caithness	21
Ross	12
Argyll	4
Inverness	18
Aberdeen	6
Perth	16
Moray	2
Nairn	3
Banff	2
Forfar	8
Fife	32
Angus	4
Kinross	2
Kincardine	1
Midlothian	6
Linlithgow	2
Renfrew	4
Ayr	1
Lanark	5
East Lothian	1
Ireland	8
England	3
	262

In general, of the details of the age of recruits, for example, it is difficult to know whether or not they are correct. It was common practice for men to claim they were 18 years old, and if they could get away with it, well and good, they would receive man's pay and service reckoning. In two cases there is a marginal note in the Roll, 'this man was under age on enlistment'. The average age in the Book overall on enlistment is 19, but this must be read in the light of the above. Some of the names, too, may be fictitious, although there is no direct evidence of this in the Roll itself.

The Roll not only provides statistics and bare facts, or the basis of reasonable supposition, it also shows a human and personal side of life in the 93rd. The Clerk, commenting on the death of Jedburgh weaver John Hume in 1826, wrote, 'Got a blow from Private Dugal McLennan supposed to have caused his death'. McLennan, from Inverness, returned to the Depot at Liverpool in 1829, where he died a few months later. The cause is not recorded.

On the death of Private John McIntosh from Perth, in Antigua on 14th August 1829, the Clerk notes:

> This unfortunate man by some inadvertant means took the liberty of going with the intention of seeing one of his comrades who had arrived from Barbados in the 'Joseph Green' transport for the purpose of proceeding to England his term of service having expired, and it would appear that in the event as he was coming home to his quarters being intoxicated he had fallen asleep and whether he was actually murdered or torn by beasts is a matter of doubt, but under all the circumstances of the case it is natural to form the conclusion that he actually died in a state of intoxication occasioned probably by suffocation.

One man, Alexander Mackay, committed suicide in 1825 by putting 'an end to his existance by gunshot through the head', and Owen O'Neil was dismissed the service in 1824, 'on suspicion of having wilfully maimed himself'.

One very interesting recruit is Thomas P. Mamperang, born in Madagascar, who was attested at Ennis in 1822 aged 25. He was certainly a negro with his 'black' complexion, eyes and hair. Although he is not designated as a drummer, he was probably enlisted for this purpose, or perhaps to march in front of the band and carry the 'Jingling Johnnie', formerly carried by the Sutherland Fencibles and now in Stirling Castle.

Several of the younger boys were 'raised at Head Quarters'. James Sutherland (14) 1822, Neil Graham (15) 1822 and Simon Mackay (13) 1822 are good examples. All three of these boys were born in the Cape of Good Hope, where the Battalion served from 1806 to 1814. These and others would seem to be examples of internal recruiting, where children were born and grew up in the Regiment. They would enlist as Drummer Boys aged 14 or younger when they were no longer classified as 'children' allowed to live in barracks or married quarters with their parents.

Recorded in pencil only are the Regimental numbers of some of the men. The fact that these numbers are written in pencil, and very roughly at that, indicates that numbers might not have been of such importance at this time and that the men were known and identified primarily by their names and nicknames.[34]

The Descriptive Roll Book of the 93rd, therefore, provides a most interesting insight into recruiting and the composition of the 93rd in the 1820s. It shows firstly at this time, the changing composition of the Regiment in age and background, while retaining a hardcore of Highland and Sutherland men. Secondly, the spread and location of the net of recruiting and the change from personal and land-based recruiting to recruiting parties of soldiers themselves, who often came from the area in which they recruited. Thirdly, the nature of casualties and their relative proportions, in particular the losses through death in the West Indies and the fact that recruiting does not keep pace with casualties although the shortfall is not as serious as in other Regiments. Fourthly, it shows the type of men who were joining and would serve on through the 1830s and 1840s, their trades, ages and birthplaces. It shows in the main they were young, unskilled or semi-skilled and broadly Highland in origin, although not necessarily from the County of Sutherland. In particular the Roll illustrates the gulf between what Regimental histories would like to believe, and what was actually the case, and the serious disservice that was done to the Highland Regiments by creating a distorted 'Balmoralised' image, when such an image was not really necessary at all. To say that at this time (1823-1854) the men of the Regiment were 'nearly all Gaelic speakers' is obviously not possible.[35] Gaelic was already dying out, particularly amongst the young in the Highland mainland counties, and was not spoken in the Lowland areas and Fife.

Fifthly, it shows the preference for Sutherland men in positions of responsibility, the possibility of personal advancement within the Regiment from young and presumably humble beginnings; and finally, the Roll gives a frequently touching personal insight into the lives of individuals about whom so little is known and who are frequently used merely as a statistic in Regimental history.

NOTES

1. MS Roll Book of the 93rd Sutherland Highlanders, ASHRM. Few of these early books and Rolls survive in Highland Regiments because in 1822 the War Office called for the Compilation of Records of Service for each Regiment (WO/3/72/391) and from these Records of Service Richard Cannon drew up the various records of Regiments and Regimental histories after which many of the original and irreplaceable books and records were destroyed in the interests of economy in respect of baggage space (PP 1833 VII c 650 p. 196 Q.2319). As the Regiments had no fixed or permanent museums or Regimental Headquarters, it was, apart from essential or current books, purely a matter of chance and individual interest if documents survived, while Cannon's Georgian/Victorian romanticism and literary approach did considerable harm to Regimental historical credibility in the long term (H.G. Order of 1.1.1836).
2. WO/25/1137 Vol. 6-156.
3. Beveridge deserted in Antigua between 26.7.1828 and 6.4.1829, losing his rank in his absence on 27.7.1828. Another hand has written in the observations column 'was clerk of the orderly Room'.

4. See map of principal stations in Ireland. p. 171.
5. Q.M. Alexander Dallas, born Clyne, Sutherland, enlisted 1799 aged 23. Drum Major 1814. Q.M. 1820-1824.
6. R.J. Adam (ed.), *Papers on Sutherland Estate Management 1802-1816* (Edinburgh: Scottish History Society, 1972), vol. 1, pp. 3, 9.
7. R.J. Adam (ed), *Papers on Sutherland Estate Management 1802-1816*, vol. 1, p. xii.
8. *Ibid.*, p. xxviii.
9. William Wemyss of Wemyss, Fife, Born 9.4.1760. Ensign 2nd Foot Guards 25.6.1777. Colonel 2nd Sutherland Fencibles 8.2.1779. Colonel 93rd Highlanders 25.8.1800. Died 4.2.1822.
10. Currie was promoted Corporal 4.4.1809, the day of his enlistment, and Sergeant on 24.7.1815. He transferred to the 2nd West India Regiment on 25.5.1823 where he died as Lieutenant and Adjutant in 1824, aged 35.
11. Ross was eventually discharged on 2nd May 1848 'to reside and receive pension in Quebec', Canada. At the time he was suffering from chronic rheumatism but his condition had 'not been aggravated by vice or intemperence'. His discharge papers noted: ' His character is good. He was tried on 3rd March 1829 (Regimental Court) for embezzlement of £69. 16. 9d sterling public money given to him to pay his Company. Sentenced to be reduced and to solitary confinement'. WO/97/1020 James Ross 93rd.
12. While the evidence from the 93rd Roll Book is far from conclusive, it would be wrong to say that limited service 'had little appeal'. As far as the 93rd are concerned, it was popular. See Edward Spiers, *The Army and Society 1815-1914*, *op. cit.*, p. 52.
13. Sutherland Estate Papers, NLS/313/3478.
14. Soldiers Small Book or Account Book of Alexr Murray Number 1 Company Service Battalion 93rd Regiment, ASHRM.
15. WO/17/346.
16. PP 1836 XXii c59 p.101, para. 1806.
17. PP 1904 XL c 1789.
18. PP 1837-38 XL c596.
19. See map of Windward and Leeward command.
20. Regimental Order Book Left Wing 93rd Highlanders Morne Bruce, Dominica, 1830-1832. ASHRM, Sb 17.
21. PP 1937-1838 XL c596 p.102.
22. Ibid., p.4.
23. Ibid., p.5
24. Ibid.
25. Ibid., p.4.
26. Regimental Order Book Left Wing 93rd Highlanders 1830-1832. *op. cit.*
27. PP 1836-1837 XL c596 p.33.
28. Ibid., pp.39-40
29. PP 1836 XXII c 59 p. 98 para. 1764.
30. WO/43/542.
31. WO/81/69.
32. That there were groups or parties of recruiters as opposed to individuals is supported by the presence of Private George Kinnaird in or about 1822. He is not credited with any recruits, but it seems he was injured while on duty.
    George Kinnaird 5′8½″
    b. Leslie, Fife: attested Perth 1812 aged 17. Weaver
    Discharged Ennis 24.5.1822
    Out pension 6d per day.
    'Disslocation and fracture of the elbow joint while
    recruiting in Scotland'.

33. *The Edinburgh Almanac or Universal Scots and Imperial Register for 1826* (Edinburgh: 1825).
34. In 1829 there was a major administrative reform of the documentation of soldiers. A survey and enquiry was carried out about 1828 to 'ascertain and balance the services of every serving soldier'. 'Thereafter the soldier with the longest service in the Regiment will be registered No. 1, the next No. 2 and so on to the Recruit who last joined the Regiment'. 'Instructions for keeping the Records of Soldiers' Services', 25.11.1829 GD/225/Box 42 BL XI.
35. Lt. Colonel G.I. Malcolm, *The History of the Argyll and Sutherland Highlanders* (Stirling: 1972), p. 22.

CHAPTER 4

Officers

Any study of officers in the nineteenth and early twentieth centuries is today bedevilled by myth, prejudice and the image of the aristocratic, incompetent, lisping, Anglicised and aloof men so frequently projected by the media. Alternatively, the words 'Highland officer' can conjure up a romantic heroic image of an undoubtedly brave handsome figure, in kilt and scarlet tunic, with broadsword in hand fighting the Empire's battles, preferably on the North-West Frontier. Somewhere between the two lie the majority of Highland officers of the period 1820 to 1920. It is important to try to set aside modern misconceptions of class and to attempt to see these men for what they were in their own time, without immediately prejudging them incompetent simply because they fell into a category of 'landed gentry', or alternatively noble and good because they rose from the ranks or humble beginnings.

The number of officers in an infantry battalion varied according to the number of NCOs and private soldiers and the establishment set at any one time. The number actually with the battalion could vary as much as between 15 and 50, and the kilted Highland battalions were no exception to this, with leave seasons, alternative employment as ADCs or instructors, illness and attendance at courses all affecting the figures. A Highland battalion had no fewer and no more officers than any other infantry battalion because of its Highland status, as the numbers were a matter of central policy.

Before 1881, when the ratio of Captains and Majors changed, largely as a result of the abolition of purchase,[1] the battalion comprised ten companies and was officered accordingly. The Colonel was the senior officer of the regiment, and while seldom present with it, except perhaps at official parades such as the presentation of colours, his patronage and interest were important, especially in the first half of the nineteenth century. Some important and influential men were Colonels of the kilted Highland battalions such as Lt. General Sir George Murray of the 72nd and the 42nd (1817-1823 and 1823-1846), Lt. General Sir Alan Cameron of Erracht of the 79th (1793-1828), General Sir Colin Campbell, Lord Clyde of the 93rd (1858-1860), and Lt. General Sir John Spencer Ewart of the 79th (1914-1929). The influence and patronage of these men could not only result in their own personal advancement, but could also affect the standard of dress of the regiment, the appointment of officers and even the location of the corps in foreign stations.[2]

With changes in War Office structure, and particularly in clothing supply, the direct financial involvement of these men became less and less[3] and by 1920 the Colonel could find his financial obligations by way of subscriptions, uniform and so on far greater than any income he might receive from the position. Nevertheless a good Colonel fulfilled an important function. He was usually an experienced officer although he had not necessarily served in, or in association with, the regiment, but in his capacity as adviser and patron he could guide the regiment through internal difficulties and bring his influence to bear when regimental interests were at stake.

A Lieutenant Colonel actually commanded the regiment, his title 'Lieu-tenant' literally meaning what it says, that is in command of the regiment on the ground. In his hands was placed the responsibility for some 400 to 1000 officers and men, their training, discipline and welfare, together with the funds, equipment and records of the regiment. His personality, qualities and interests shaped the whole character of the regiment in a way which would be impossible in the contemporary army. Until 1881, when it was limited to five years, the period of command was unrestricted and a man obtaining command, usually by purchase, could hold it for as long as he wished or was able. Lt. Colonel Duncan MacGregor, the benevolent reforming commanding officer of the 93rd, held command for twelve years, while Lt. Colonel F.W. Burroughs, later to be famous as the evicting landlord of Rousay in Orkney, commanded the same regiment for nine years (1864-1873).

Responsible to the commanding Lieutenant Colonel were the remaining officers of the battalion. Until 1881 the battle tactics and contemporary drill, which were closely related, divided a battalion into two wings, left and right, commanded by the two Majors, the senior one of whom would command the regiment in the absence of the Commanding Lt. Colonel. As there were only two Majors per battalion, the position was much sought after and held considerable responsibility. One of these Majors might also command the Depot when the battalion was overseas, but when Depot Battalions were formed, unattached Majors tended to fill the Depot commands.

The Companies, 1 to 8 with the Grenadier and Light Companies, were commanded by Captains.[4] Lieutenants acted as second-in-command of the Companies and one of their number might also be Adjutant, the position being one of the busiest and most responsible in the Battalion:

> In the morning the Adjutant is obliged to raise at an untimely hour to superintend the drilling of recruits, which probably keeps him occupied till breakfast time. Then comes guard mounting, at which he must be present, being responsible not only for the accuracy of the details but for the sobriety and fitness of the guards for their duty, which generally occupies him till twelve o'clock, when he waits on the commanding officer with the delinquents of the preceeding day. Their cases being discussed, he has to remain in the orderly-room preparing the Regimental orders as directed by the Commanding Officer, and arranging for the details of duty for the following day. After which a considerable portion of his time must necessarily be occupied superintending the various returns required to be forwarded in the course of the month as for the accuracy of which his commission is responsible. If there is a Court Martial sitting,—his presence is indispensable to give evidence as to the character and service of the prisoner. Should there however be no duty of this kind to attend to—no skeleton drill or exercise for officers—no afternoon drill for recruits to detain him,—it is

> possible that about once a week he may enjoy the privilege of breathing the air beyond the precincts of the barracks for an hour or two, when he is summoned to the evening parade, at which he remains till the bugle warns him to prepare for the more pleasant duties of the Mess Table. These over he probably closes the evening by writing such official letters as the commanding officer has instructed him to prepare in the course of the day.[5]

The Adjutant was therefore carefully chosen by the Commanding Officer from amongst the officers of the Battalion according to his personal preference or the station and circumstances in which the Battalion found themselves. He might either be chosen from amongst the veteran soldiers who had seen the relationship between drill and tactics in action, from the literate and experienced ex-NCOs such as Lieutenant and Adjutant Henry Mackay of the 79th, or when stationed in important garrisons such as Dublin and Cape Town when turnout, drill, reviews and parades together with social attributes were required, from amongst the bright and socially acceptable young officers of the battalion. In garrisons such as Gibraltar and when the regiment was detached in Ireland for example, the remaining Captains and Lieutenants were occupied with the numerous, but not necessarily mentally demanding duties, of guards, drills, inspections, keeping the Company books, Boards of Examination or Inquiry, Courts Martial and the like.

The Ensigns, Sub or Second Lieutenants, were considered to be under training learning their drill or, having passed that, learning the ins and outs of the battalion, its life and organisation.

The abolition of purchase in 1871, while hailed as a democratic reform by some, caused considerable problems with regard to promotion to those *in situ*. In 1881 the period of command of a Lt. Colonel was reduced to five years, and to ease the problem of stagnation in promotion Captains were obliged to retire if not promoted by the age of forty, or after twenty years. In 1881 there were a large number of Captains in this category. As Majors retired after twenty-seven years a solution was found to the discontent by increasing the number of Field Officers per battalion to six, while reducing the Captains to five.[6]

On 1st July 1881, 137 Majors were gazetted Lt. Colonel and 613 Captains gazetted Major. Majors now commanded Companies, and in the opinion of many the rank of Captain was thus devalued. The newly gazetted Majors did not receive Major's pay until they had held the rank for three years and, as they were not permitted to be mounted, were quickly dubbed 'Running Majors' or 'Mud Majors'. The position of commanders of Companies was further complicated by the advent of double companies in 1913, whereby the eight service Companies were doubled up to form four large Companies, A,B,C and D.

Of the specialist officers the Quarter Master held a position of trust and responsibility and also a position that was potentially very lucrative. As the man in charge of the clothing, stores and equipment of the regiment he held a non-combatant Commission with honorary rank. The position was reserved for responsible, literate, numerate long-serving, meritorious or deserving senior Non-commissioned officers. They were men of considerable experience and no little ability, and as they held their positions for many years they comprised a special élite. Many of the Quarter Masters of the Highland Regiments became legends in their own time and provided an important personal link in the regiment by way of regimental history, tradition and organisation. Robertson Gordon, the recruiting Sergeant of the 93rd, was one of their number,[7] as were John Simpson VC of the 42nd and Alexander Cruikshanks and Alexander Preston Yeadon of the 79th.

Also holding honorary non-combatant rank was the Paymaster. The majority of these men were again commissioned from the ranks of the regiment, until the position was abolished in 1878 and the Army Pay Department formed. The appointment carried great responsibility and required no small amount of skill in keeping complex and detailed accounts, sometimes in two currencies, requisitioning funds and disbursing the same to the Captains of Companies. Fraud was not however unknown amongst Paymasters, as for example John McArthur, Paymaster of the 1st Battalion 79th, who between 1811 and 1819 amassed a deficiency in his accounts of £2650-10-3d none of which was recovered in 1822, and before being accepted for their appointments therefore Paymasters were required to lodge caution and supply the names of guarantors.[8]

Specialist officers included the Surgeon and Assistant Surgeon. Until 1873 these were Regimental Officers, wearing a black hackle in their bonnets in Highland Regiments. Many of these Surgeons and Assistant Surgeons were Scots and graduates of Edinburgh University Medical School.[9] Some, using the knowledge and experience gained in the Army, graduated MD after leaving the Service.

Surgeons and Assistant Surgeons after only a few years gained much practical expertise and many were knowledgeable researchers into tropical diseases, hygiene, venereal diseases and cholera.[10] They inspected the men regularly, advised the Commanding Officer on disease prevention and treated the sick and wounded, frequently at great personal risk. Best known amongst their number are probably Surgeon Munro of the 91st and 93rd[11] and Surgeon Goldie Scot of the 79th.

From amongst the establishment of officers various men would be chosen for appointments within the battalion on a long or short-term basis, such as Adjutant, Instructor of Musketry, Signals Officer, Machine Gun Officer, and Mess, Band and Pipe Presidents. With the development of the range and complexity of the weapons available to the infantry soldier and the training and tactics required in their deployment, specialist officers in Musketry and Signals for example became increasingly important.

Officers were not recruited in the sense that the men were recruited, nor did they form a separate class in the Prussian sense. In 1820, officers obtained a commission in the infantry of the line by nomination from the Commander-in-Chief supported by a certificate that they were both a gentleman and a Christian. Thereafter their name was placed on a list at Horse Guards to await a vacancy. Patronage played an important part in this process and particularly in ensuring that their name came forward for any regimental vacancy that occurred.

When for example John Walter Wedderburn, eldest son of John Wedderburn of Auchterhouse, obtained his commission in the 42nd in 1841 his opportunity came as a direct result of the influence of his uncle Walter, 5th Earl of Airlie. Even then he had had to wait for some time. He wrote in his diary on 26th October 1841:

> Having always had a great liking for a red coat, and my name having been down for nearly two years on Lord Hill's private list for a Commission in the Line I was agreeably surprised this forenoon by getting a letter . . . saying I was appointed to an Ensigncy in the 42nd Royal Highlanders . . . I did feel very proud today, and although only 17 years old, already looked upon myself as a big man and an officer.[12]

Most commissions, like Wedderburn's, were obtained by purchase until it was abolished by Royal Warrant of 20th July 1871. The regulation prices were laid down in the Warrant of 1821, and an Ensign paid £450 for a line commission. There was no medical examination and as a result serious anomalies could arise, such as Ensign James Webster of the 79th. Commissioned in 1847, he was 5′ 7″ in height, 19 stone 4lbs. in weight and measured 48 inches around the waist. His Commanding Officer rather naturally complained: 'My good God what am I to do with such a recruit!'[13]

A limited number of non-purchase commissions were awarded by the Commander-in-Chief to men of line regiments, but by far the majority purchased their first commission in Highland regiments before 1871. Between 1820 and 1858 the Royal Military College, Sandhurst operated to all intents and purposes as a military public school providing the minimum of military education to boys between 13 and 18. In 1820 ten free places were available, but the free system was abolished shortly afterwards and students paid between £40 and £125.[14] The entrance examination for Sandhurst comprised

> . . . the first four rules of arithmetic, simple and compound, with Cornelius, Nepos or Caesar in prose and Virgil or Ovid in verse . . . or . . . arithmetic only, as high as the rule of Three with Vulgar and Decimal fractions.[15]

All this was not considered as a 'severe test' by the thirteen and a half year old John Alexander Ewart, later of the 93rd.

In 1832 the Whig government abolished the financial vote to the College which was forced to become self-supporting, and numbers fell below 200, with a high rate of failure. Conditions were spartan in the extreme, and in order to obtain a Commission without purchase from the College candidates had to pass six subjects out of a formidable list which included Euclid, military surveying, higher mathematics, conic sections, the attack and defence of fortresses, general history, Latin, French and German. Between 1838 and 1848, 650 cadets entered the College, 350 obtained commissions without purchase, 200 failed and 150 obtained commissions with purchase.[16] In the 1830s the College had no library, no books, no canteen, and no recreation rooms, and while Ewart obtained his commission without purchase, as a result of his ability and diligent study, his success was in no way assisted by the extensive bullying which pervaded the College.[17]

There were thus two methods of entry into the infantry as an officer, by purchase or without purchase through Sandhurst, or by purchase or without purchase from Horse Guards.[18] In 1849 applicants for first commissions were required to pass a qualifying examination,[19] and following the enquiry into the system of purchase and sale of commissions in the army of 1857,[20] Sandhurst was reformed,[21] but only gradually, and it took a mutiny at the College in 1862 and the appointment of the Committee on Military Education in 1868 to bring any sort of sound military curriculum into being. These measures took place under the eye of an officer of the 42nd, Sir Duncan Alexander Cameron, who was Governor of the Royal Military College between 1868 and 1875.

As a result of the abolition of purchase in 1871, the question at once arose of the future of Sandhurst. The intention was that a commission would be awarded as soon as the qualifying examination had been passed by an officer candidate, but when a large number passed the examination at the first attempt it was found that there were more officers than vacancies in the regiments. To encourage officers to attend Sandhurst, those who had passed 1st Class were given two years' ante-date, those of the 2nd Class one year's ante-date, and others were given the opportunity to study specific subjects abroad. Amongst these was the man later to become General Sir Ian Hamilton of the Gordon Highlanders, who elected to study in Germany. Even then there were still no vacancies in the Gordons and he was first gazetted into the 12th (East Suffolk) Regiment.[22] By 1873 all candidates were obliged to attend Sandhurst, except the top six from the qualifying list, and this rule was itself finally abolished in 1878.[23]

A feature of this background of obtaining a commission before 1871 had been a series of 'cramming schools' and institutions which had sprung up largely as a result of the 1849 regulations. Some schools had already prepared their scholars for a military life in some way, such as Charterhouse which in the 1870s had a specific class known as the 'Woolwich farm' or Army Class, and Wellington College, founded in 1859 in memory of the Duke of Wellington, which had the specific object of educating the sons of officers with a view to a military career. Most candidates however used 'crammers' of which there were several in the London area.

The Scottish Naval and Military Academy in Edinburgh existed primarily as a training centre for the East Indian Service, but it was also used to cram for military entrance examinations. An Academy was instituted in Edinburgh in November 1787 under the superintendence of Major D'Asti, with premises in the Waterloo Place area.[24] It was virtually defunct by 1825, and Lt. Scott the

Superintendent was dead when, in that year, Major General Stewart of Garth asked Major Charles Downes if he would be interested in setting up a Military Academy in Scotland. Entitled the Scottish Naval and Military Academy, it opened sometime after 1825 in the Elder Street Hall, St. James' Square, which according to Downes was

> . . . a room . . . which was built over two small shops each about 5 yards square. One of these was appropriated to teach military exercise in; but it was damp and only just fit for a dog kennel . . . There was a front kitchen at some distance in St. James' Square to teach the mathematics in.[25]

By 1827 classes included Fortification, Military Drawing, Surveying, Levelling, Mathematics, Navigation, Persian, Hindostanee, Arabic, Fencing and Gymnastics.[26]

Shortly afterwards the Academy moved to George Street where the lack of order among the students led to 'idleness and riot'. Downes complained:

> As soon as I had left them [the students] to attend to my own classes upstairs, they took cinders from the fire, strewed them upon the table and danced upon it . . . . Whilst others sat with their hats on at the upper windows and their legs outside, throwing cinders into the street at the passengers.[27]

When the Academy moved to London Road, sometime before 1831, there were 140 students, but Downes had a serious argument with the Board of Management regarding discipline and the Academy went into decline. However, amongst those known to have received their basic military education here was Bertie Gordon, the charismatic and important Lieutenant Colonel of the 91st.[28]

After 1878 all officer candidates attended the course at Sandhurst with the exception of those commissioned from the ranks. The course was of one year's duration, and while it had improved immeasurably, it was still essentially a general education with an emphasis on field sketching and manly sporting pursuits. Count Gleichen remembers in the 1880s that

> . . . there was a good deal of drunkenness . . . and among a certain set it used to be the correct thing to return from their Saturday and Sunday leave in a somewhat advanced state of intoxication.[29]

Nevertheless there was a comprehensive course of learning, with standards and examinations to be passed, although the regiments were still expected to furnish the more practical side of a young officer's training. The officers who passed out of Sandhurst from the 1870s onwards were destined to play an important historical role. The students of the 1870s and early 1880s were to furnish the leading commanders of the First World War; those of the 1880s and '90s the field commanders, while those of the late 1890s and 1900s who commenced the war as Captains, if they survived, were Lt. Colonels in 1918. Those who graduated after 1900 were mainly still subalterns in 1914 and the majority were killed early in the war, or survived to fight as senior commanders in the Second World War, as for example Wavell, who was Commissioned into the Black Watch in 1901, and Victor Fortune, also of the Black Watch, gazetted in 1903.[30]

While at Sandhurst the students were styled Gentlemen Cadets, and before passing out they were entitled to choose three regiments, in order of preference, to which they wished to be gazetted:

> There was great excitement before the Gazette . . . the Scottish and Irish Regiments seemed to give the most anxiety [and] . . . there were instances of Cadets with Irish names being very angry about being gazetted to the Highland Light Infantry.[31]

Those with family connections, or fathers and relatives in regiments, tended to get the regiment they wanted, and because of long historical associations and close family links between the noble and landed families of Scotland, by far the majority of officers in Highland regiments had pre-regimental associations of some kind or another, resulting in a considerable continuity, which continues to this day, as Highland battalions still virtually insist on some form of pre-association with the regiment prior to acceptance.

Between 1820 and 1872[32] the statistics of the nationality of officers of the kilted Highland battalions show a general trend of, firstly, small numbers of Irish officers with the exception of the 78th, who in 1850 and 1872 had ten in each of these years; secondly the growing numbers of English officers throughout the period; but thirdly, the dominance of Scots officers, particularly in the 42nd and 79th, whose English and Irish officers never outnumbered the Scots.

The 92nd and 93rd also maintained a fair consistency in this respect, but the numbers of Englishmen increased in these regiments during the 1860s and '70s.

Of the remaining regiments, the 91st had the highest proportion of Scots officers. The 72nd and 74th are notable for the numbers of Englishmen, while the 73rd and 75th are dominated by English and Irish.

As will be seen later, the nationality of the officers is important because they could, by their allegiances and interests, shape the character of the regiment to which they belonged. The statistics however may well be deceptive. The son of a serving Scots officer born in Ireland, while his father was serving there, might for example well declare this in the returns, but it is unlikely that he would consider himself Irish. Taken at face value, however, the figures would appear to be roughly correct.

The overall percentage on the figures available during the period 1820 to 1872 brings out a slightly different balance and shows in particular how badly the 93rd fared for Scots officers, although their 54.5% is still above any of the trews or line regiments.

% Nationality of Officers 1820-1872

Kilted regiments		
42nd	English	19%
	Scots	73%
	Irish	8%
78th	English	28%
	Scots	55%
	Irish	17%
79th	English	20%
	Scots	68%
	Irish	12%
92nd	English	32%
	Scots	59%
	Irish	8%
	Foreigners	1%
93rd	English	28%
	Scots	54.5%
	Irish	17%
	Not Known	0.5%
Highland Trews and Line Regiments		
72nd	English	48.5%
	Scots	34%
	Irish	17%
	Foreigners	0.5%
73rd	English	55%
	Scots	15%
	Irish	29%
	Foreigners	1%
74th	English	40%
	Scots	38%
	Irish	22%
75th	English	60%
	Scots	16%
	Irish	24%
91st	English	34%
	Scots	47%
	Irish	18%
	Not Known	1%

It has long been assumed that between 1820 and 1920 officers were drawn primarily from the aristocracy and the landed gentry, and statistics appear to support this conclusion:

Status Group of Officers in the British Home Army[33]

	Aristocracy	Landed Gentry	Middle Class
	%	%	%
1780	24	16	60
1830	21	32	47
1875	18	32	50
1912	9	32	59
1930	5	6	89
1952	3	2	95

These statistics are however often used as a form of social comment and criticism, which is not always entirely justified. The Highland regiments had, as has already been illustrated, an unusual and virtually unique background, and Highland social structure did not conveniently fit into three limited status groups.

What, then, is meant by 'landed gentry' in relation to Highland officers? It is clear that the term must be carefully used, for although there were in the Highlands landlords of considerable standing, many of the estates had capital value but little revenue income. It had also long been the custom to distinguish the more common surnames by associating them with their farms, home area or estates, however large or small they might be, for example Archibald Campbell of Glendaruel. Sometimes a family was entitled 'of' a particular place after direct association with that place had ceased, and the 'of' was merely used to establish a branch or division of a particular family. In Scotland this practice was extremely common and was accepted and formalised by the Lyon Court. Many of the estate proprietors were not rich as the term 'landed gentry' implies, and with the growth of fishing, shooting and stalking as popular Highland-based sports, a new form of landed gentry emerged in the Highlands, usually with money and sometimes with middle-class origins.

A study of the Army list of 1839, with particular reference to the officers of the 42nd, gives a good idea of the structure of a Highland regiment before the Crimean War, and the subsequent reforms, and shows the kind of officers being attracted to the service. Research on the individuals has brought out some of their origins and social position, together with their length of service and the nature of their promotion.[34]

The Colonel of the 42nd in 1839 was Sir George Murray. A distinguished General and statesman, he was the second son of Sir William Murray Bart. and Lady Augusta Mackenzie, seventh and youngest daughter of George, 3rd Earl of Cromartie. Sir George was born at the family seat of Ochtertyre, Perthshire on 6th February 1772. He was educated at Edinburgh High School and Edinburgh University and was first commissioned into the 71st Regiment on 12th March 1789. He later served in the 34th and the 3rd Foot Guards in Flanders, Holland, Germany, the West Indies, Gibraltar, Egypt, the Baltic, Portugal, Spain, France, Ireland, Canada and again in France after Waterloo.

In 1813 he was Colonel of the 7th Battalion the 60th Regiment and in 1817 transferred to be Colonel of the 72nd, before becoming Colonel of the 42nd in

The 42nd (or Royal Highland) Regiment of Foot, 1839[35]

Colonel

Years' Service 51 — **P** Rt. Hon. Sir George Murray, G.C.B. & G.C.H. **Ens.** 12 March, 1789; **Capt.** 16 Jan. 94; **Lieut.- Col.** 5 Aug. 99; **Col.** 9 March, 1809; **Major-Gen.** 1 Jan. 12; **Lieut-Gen.** 27 May, 25; **Col.** 42nd Highlanders 6 Sept. 23.

Full Pay	Half Pay	

Lieut. Colonel

15	$5^7/_{12}$	George Johnstone, Cornet, p 5 Aug. 19; **Lieut.** p 9 Nov. 21; **Capt.** p 17 Nov. 25; **Major,** p 3 Oct. 26; **Lieut.-Col.** p 23 Aug. 39.

Majors

25	$2^5/_{12}$	**P** James Macdougall, **Second Lieut.** 11 June, 12; **Lieut.** 8 Sept. 13; **Capt.** p 10 Sept. 25; **Major** 23 Oct. 35.
15	0	Duncan Alex. Cameron, **Ens.** 8 April, 25; **Lieut.** p 15 Aug. 26; **Capt.** p 21 June, 33; **Major,** p 23 Aug. 39.

		Captains	**Ensign**	**Lieut.**	**Captain**	**Brev, Maj.**
26	$2^1/_{12}$	Daniel Frazer	31 Oct. 11	13 June 16	p 5 Nov. 25	28 June 38
15	0	Charles Dunsmure	9 Apr. 25	p 7 Nov. 26	p 30 Jan. 35	
14	0	William Guthrie	p 22 Apr. 26	p 20 Mar. 27	p 24 Feb. 37	
14	0	Archibald Campbell	p 26 Nov. 25	p 25 Dec.28	p10 Mar. 38	
15	0	Geo. Burrell Cumberland	11 Apr. 25	31 Dec. 28	p 30 Mar. 38	
25	$1^8/_{12}$	Wm. Beales	24 June 13	13 Dec. 21	12 Aug. 36	
14	0	Thomas Tulloch	p 25 June 26	23 Oct. 28	p12 July 33	
16	0	Lord Cecil Gordon	p 8 july 24	p 17 June 26	p 22 July 36	
18	$7^4/_{12}$	George Montagu	8 Dec. 14	p 31 Oct. 22	p 22 Oct. 25	28 June 38
		Lieutenants				
14	0	Colin Campbell	p 8 Apr, 26	3 Dec. 29		
10	0	J. Cameron Macpherson	p 10 Sept. 30	p 21 June. 33		
8	0	Alexander Canmeron	24 Feb. 32	p 30 Jan. 35		
8	0	Hon. Robert Rollo	p 10 Aug. 32	p 25 Sept. 35		
8	0	Thomas Kinlock (sic)	p 14 Sept. 32	p 24 Feb. 37		
9	0	Lord Chas. Lennox Kerr	p 5 Apr. 31	p 2 May 34		
7	0	H. Maurice Drummond	p 4 Dec. 32	p 15 Dec. 37		
7	0	Geo. Duncan Robertson	p 14 June 33	p 10 Mar. 38		
7	0	Atholl W. Macdonald	p 9 Aug. 33	p 24 Apr. 38		
5	0	G.W. Macqarie	p 25 Sept. 35	p 31 May 39		
4	0	Duncan Cameron	23 Oct. 35	1 June 39		
3	0	Arch. Colin Campbell	p 24 Feb. 37	p 23 Aug. 39		
		Ensigns				
2	0	James Hunter	p 17 Nov. 37			
2	0	W.J.H. Johnstone	p 16 Mar. 38			
2	0	James Grant	p 30 Mar. 28			
2	0	Sir F.W. Dunbar, Bt.	p 24 Apr. 38			
1	0	Farquhard Campbell	p 30 Nov. 38			
1	0	Henry Sholto Douglas	p 31 May 39			
1	0	Thos. Rob. Drum. Hay	p 2 Aug. 39			
1	0	Thos. Francis Wade	2 Nov. 38			

8	0	**Paymast.** - J. Wheatley, 12 Oct. 38; **Ens. & Adjt.** 20 July, 32; **Lieut.** 3 Apr. 35
4	0	**Adjutant.**- Duncan Cameron (Ens.), 30 Oct. 38
21	0	**Quarter-Master.**- **P W** Finley King, 31 Dec. 18.
30	0	**Surgeon/** - **P** James Paterson, M.D., 25 May 26; **Asssist.- Surg.** 22 Aug. 11; **Hosp. - Assist.** 7 June 10.
14	0	**Assistant-Surgeon.** - James M'Gregor, 12 April, 26; **Hosp.-Assist.** 5 Jan. 26.

p indicates Commission by purchase.
P served in the Peninsula or the South of France.
W present in the actions of the 16th, 17th or 18th June 1815.

1823. While therefore he had never served in the 42nd, he had served with them. He had family connections in Perthshire and Cromarty and was a man of great ability, influence and patronage.

In 1818 he was made Governor of Edinburgh Castle and in 1819 Governor of the Royal Military College, Sandhurst (to 1824). In 1823, the same year as he took the Colonelcy of the 42nd, he was elected Tory MP for Perthshire (to 1834). He was a Fellow of the Royal Society and a Lieutenant General of the Ordnance. He held the office of Master General of the Ordnance until 1846, transferred to the Colonelcy of the 1st Royals in 1843 and died in London in 1846.

He was thus a man of wealth and no little power. A man of his political, military and social position could bring it to bear in relation to appointments to the Regiment for first commissions, changes in station (by ensuring that the Regiment was kept away from unhealthy climates), and the standard and quality of the dress of the Regiment. He finally widened the opportunities of patronage available to men and officers seeking appointments or promotion.

Through his interest in 1825 the 42nd were armed with the 'Long Land Tower' musket, the only regiment of foot to which it was issued, and in 1840 they were the first regiment to receive the percussion musket.[36]

The Lieutenant Colonel Commanding was George Johnstone, believed to be related to the family of Westerhall, Langholm, Dumfriesshire. Johnstone had purchased his commission in the Grenadier Guards in 1819 and, after having been on half-pay, had purchased his Majority in 1826 and his Lt. Colonelcy in 1839. He therefore came into the Army after Macdougall, Frazer, Beales and Montagu and had purchased his Majority and Lt. Colonelcy over Macdougall. While a Captain of the Guards was deemed to be equivalent to a Lt. Colonel of a line regiment, Johnstone must nevertheless have had funds to finance his steps and obtain command, which alone would have cost him £5,800, if not more.

He did not command for long relative to the tenure of command for the period, and after going on half-pay in 1843, he eventually died in London on 16th April 1874. Apart from the possible connection with Westerhall his background remains unidentified. His name does not appear in *Burke's Landed Gentry*, and he may well be an illustration of how an outsider with no connections in a Highland Regiment could purchase command without having any interest, or family, or geographical link with a national corps.

Of the two Majors, James Macdougall was by far the senior. He obtained his commission and promotion to Lieutenant without purchase, which was not at all unusual in time of war. He was not initially commissioned into the 42nd, but after having spent some time on half-pay he purchased his full-pay Captaincy in 1825. He was a seasoned campaigner, having been present at Nivelle, Nive, Orthes and Toulouse (1813-1814). His background is unknown, but he was certainly not a man of means, for although he purchased his Captaincy in 1825, he did not purchase his Majority and obtained his Lt. Colonelcy of the Reserve Battalion in 1846 through seniority, aged possibly 51 after thirty years' full-pay service. He retired in 1850 and died in 1876. The absence of any information on Macdougall, together with his name, might imply that he was one of the few surviving Officers from the old Highland tacksman class, but this must remain conjecture.

The second Major, Duncan Alexander Cameron, was commissioned without purchase in 1825. He was born in 1808, the son of Sir John Cameron of Culchenna, and purchased all his remaining steps until, in 1854, he commanded the 42nd at the Alma and later the Highland Brigade at Balaclava. During the Maori Wars (1863-1865) he commanded the British forces, but received official censure when he refused to exact retribution against the Maoris by the burning of Pa House. Between 1868 and 1875, at a critical period of its development, Cameron was Governor of the Royal Military College, Sandhurst. He married Flora Maclean, daughter of Dr. Andrew Maclean, in 1873, aged 65, and died with the rank of General at Blackheath on the 8th June 1888. He appears to have been an intelligent and capable commander, whose career certainly suffered as a result of the New Zealand incident. Despite his Highland name, Wedderburn criticises him as 'another infernal Englishman'.[37]

Daniel Frazer was the longest-serving of the ten Captains and, along with George Montagu, had been granted Brevet rank the year before in 1838. They had both been Captains of Companies since 1825 and had been purchased over by Johnstone and by Cameron. Frazer was first commissioned, without purchase, into the 8th (or the King's) Regiment of Foot. His background is unknown and he does not seem to be related to any of the major lines of the Frazer or Fraser families in Scotland. He was married and his son, Captain Rowland Aynsworth Frazer of the 42nd, was killed at Sebastopol in 1855. For all their length of service, Frazer, Beales and Montagu had not been present in the Peninsula or at Waterloo, and Frazer and Beales would have stood out in the Battalion as older Captains, men from a previous war that had ended over twenty years before, but who remained by design or necessity Captains of Companies.

Charles Dunsmure was certainly a man of means. In 1843 he purchased his Majority and in 1849 he is reputed to have purchased the Lt. Colonelcy of the 42nd for £7,000.[38] He was actually gazetted Lt. Colonel on 15th February 1850 and went on half-pay on the 1st of April in the same year, as a result of the reduction of the Reserve Battalion.

William Guthrie was the second son of John Guthrie of Guthrie, Convenor and Depute Lieutenant of the County of Forfar. The Guthrie family was of some antiquity in Scotland and the castle was founded in 1468 by Sir David Guthrie of Guthrie and enlarged and extended in 1848. The main wealth of the family in the nineteenth century came from the possession of rubber estates in Malaya, and the Guthrie plantations were still in existence after the Second World War. William's elder brother John had served in the Regiment between 1829 and 1832, when he had gone to half-pay, retiring in 1836. William had purchased all his steps, went to half-pay as a Captain, and died in 1880. His family were influential in Forfarshire circles and owned rich farmlands. Although only the two brothers served in the Regular Battalions, the name Guthrie came to be associated with the Regiment as a 'Black Watch' name, largely through the service of members of the family in the Territorial and Volunteer Battalions.

Archibald Campbell was nephew of Elizabeth Campbell, 5th of Glendaruel, Argyll, and on her death inherited the estates in 1824 to become Archibald Campbell 6th of Glendaruel. He had at least two ancestors in the 42nd, Colonel John Campbell who died in 1795, and Captain Archibald Campbell who died in 1768. He married Elizabeth Hume and later Christina MacLaren by whom he had a son, William MacLaren Campbell who became a Brigadier General and served in the Black Watch. Archibald's eldest surviving son, Robert, 7th of Glendaruel, sold the family lands sometime before 1921. Archibald Campbell had funds at his disposal, for he purchased all his steps to Captain. He retired as a Captain in 1840, became Depute Lieutenant of Argyll, the first Colonel of the Argyllshire Volunteers, and died in Ayr in 1875. Archibald is one of the few officers of the 42nd of the period with direct Highland connections as opposed to Perthshire or Forfarshire links.

It is believed that George Burrell Cumberland was an Englishman. Wedderburn hated him. 'I wish to heaven', he wrote, 'all these infernal Englishmen were out of the Regiment and at the devil.'[39] This comment was aimed particularly at Cumberland who, in the absence of the Lieutenant Colonel, commanded the 42nd during part of their tour in Halifax, Canada, in 1852. By all accounts he was disliked by the men also. Donaldson, a retired soldier, commented to Wedderburn, 'Oh Sir, I would like to see the Major's head in that puddle'.[40] Cumberland objected to the pipes, piobaireachd and reels in the Mess and complained that Wedderburn and his companions did not pay enough attention to their soldiering.[41] Cumberland retired in 1855 without accompanying the Regiment to the Crimea and died at Wolvers Dean, Andover, ten years later. While Wedderburn is lavish in his criticism of this man, it cannot be said that being an Englishman made him a bad officer. His position however illustrates aspects of some of the complex nuances associated with kilted Highland regiments.

The 42nd, being the oldest surviving Highland regiment, were, and still are, extremely proud of their history and origins. Having been founded well before the other kilted battalions, they had assimilated much of the character of the eighteenth-century Hanoverian army and had had time to develop fully their own regimental character and codes of internal behaviour. Before 1820 a high proportion of their officers had been Highland gentlemen who, in the strict sense of the word, would not necessarily fall into the category of landed gentry; but they were no less gentlemen for all that, such was their pride and individualism. Codes of conduct were set by these men, and outsiders such as English and Irish, being few in number, had to conform or suffer censure. The pressure on both sides could be extremely subtle and could well lead to an entrenchment of views when a Highlander could be at his most infuriating and an Englishman at his most stubborn.

The 42nd were noted by Wheately, with some pride, as a regiment that was left to itself, where the officers did not bother or interfere with the men unless required.[42] Cumberland's attention to detail in respect of inspections, drills, guards and barrack regulations was thus deeply resented and taken personally by officers and men, who were perhaps only too keen to lay the principal blame on his nationality. The conduct of some of the junior officers and senior NCOs does not seem to have helped, for there were, and still are, subtle pressures which can be applied in these cases. Cumberland hated pipes and reels, so undoubtedly the Pipe Major played that little bit longer at Mess and playing was encouraged at every opportunity, with fiddle, flutina and Gaelic songs thrown in.[43] The lack of understanding was bitter and resentful:

> So much for having a d—d thick headed Englishman Commanding a Highland Regiment, and as every Gazette seems to bring more Englishmen into the Regt. the sooner it drops the title *Royal Highland* the better.[44]

Nothing is known of the background of William Beales. He was probably not a man of funds, for he had served twenty-five years on full pay and never purchased a step. In 1844 he went on half-pay as a Staff Officer of Pensioners and died as Lt. Colonel in St. Helier, Jersey in 1868. Such employment would imply that he did not have a private income of any kind and that patronage obtained him the employment, in the light of his lengthy and loyal service to the Army.

Thomas Tulloch may well have been related to the Tullochs of Dingwall, but this is not confirmed. He came to the 42nd from the 94th, purchasing his Captaincy in 1833. He became Lt. Colonel in March 1855, but went to half-pay in October 1855 and retired as Colonel in 1859. He died in London in 1866.

The first member of the 'aristocracy' in the list is Lord Cecil James Gordon. Born in 1803, he was the fifth son of the 9th Marquis of Huntly. In 1850, when he married Emily Moore, he assumed the name Gordon Moore and he died in 1878. He joined the 42nd from the 17th of Foot in 1838, and while he had a title and his family had money, he inherited none of the family estates. Gordon is an excellent example of the dilemma faced by the junior sons of large families of the nobility. Only one could inherit, and as the fifth son he had virtually no chance whatever of assuming the title and he therefore had to find employment in an occupation suitable to his social status and background.

George Montagu is unidentified, but his name would suggest a relationship to the Duke of Buccleuch. Whoever he was, his heart was certainly not in soldiering or the 42nd. Of his eighteen years' service he had spent seven years four months on half-pay, having joined the 42nd from half-pay of the 52nd as a Captain and Brevet Major in 1839. He retired to half-pay again in 1842 and did not return to the Regiment. While it may be entirely unwarranted, it would appear that Montagu represents the worst of the complaints about mid-nineteenth century officers, obtaining promotion by purchase, spending much of his time on half-pay instead of with his Regiment, and transferring to a national corps with which he had no direct association, remaining for only a short period.

The junior Captain, Robert Williamson Ramsay, has the family name of Dalhousie, but no connection can be traced. He came as a Lieutenant without purchase from the 62nd in 1832 and left the 42nd in 1841.

Of the thirteen Lieutenants, the senior is Colin Campbell of South Hall. He was the second son of John Campbell, 3rd of South Hall, a mansion with estates extending to 19,736 acres at Inverchaolain, Argyllshire. Colin was born in 1801 and died unmarried in 1859. One of his relations, Edward Parker Campbell, 6th of South Hall, served with the Black Watch in Egypt in 1882, and it was he who eventually sold the estates during the period 1914 to 1917. Colin retired a Lieutenant in 1839 and died in the Isle of Man.

John Cameron Macpherson also came from a Highland family. He was the third son of Duncan Macpherson of Cluny and Catherine Cameron, youngest daughter of Sir Ewen Cameron of Fassifern, Bart. Macpherson purchased all his steps to Major by 1855 and obtained a Brevet Lt. Colonelcy. He died in Stirling in 1873.

Alexander Cameron was the son of Captain Ewen Cameron of the 79th Cameron Highlanders and belonged to the family of Cameron of Glennevis. He commanded the 42nd from 1855 and, after surviving the Crimean War and the major actions of the Indian Mutiny, died of fever at Bareilly, India, on 9th August 1858.

The Hon. Robert Rollo was the third son of John, 8th Baron Rollo of Duncrub, Perthshire. The 8th Baron was a man of considerable wealth and in 1836-37 had employed the architect William Burn to renovate and extend Duncrub Park, a house which was demolished in 1950.[45] Rollo rose to the rank of General in 1880 and became Colonel of the Black Watch in 1888. He therefore soldiered through the period of major changes which took place between the time he purchased his Ensigncy in 1832, until he died, still Colonel of the regiment aged 92, in 1907.

Thomas Kinloch was probably related to the family of Kinloch of Kinloch, Perthshire. He certainly had funds enough to purchase all his steps to Majority and retired in 1844, probably due to ill health, as he died in 1848 at Logie in Perthshire.

The third titled Officer was Lord Charles Lennox Kerr. A Lowlander, he was born in 1814, the first son of the second marriage of the 6th Marquis of Lothian. He exchanged to the 42nd from the 6th of Foot in 1834 and went on half-pay as a Captain in 1844, retiring in 1848. He was Lt. Colonel of the 3rd Militia Battalion Black Watch and died in 1898.

Henry Maurice Drummond was born in 1814 the sixth son of Adam Drummond RN, 7th of Megginch Castle, Perthshire. In 1859 he married Charlotte Elizabeth Hay of Seggieden, Perthshire and assumed the name Drummond-Hay. He was to become Lt. Colonel Commandant of the Royal Perthshire Rifles and was a JP and Depute Lieutenant of Perthshire. He retired from the 42nd as a Captain in 1852 and Wedderburn attributes this to Drummond's disgust with Cumberland.[46] He was related by his marriage to Ensign Thomas Robert Drummond Hay of Seggieden and it was probably while serving with the 42nd that Henry met Thomas's sister Charlotte, although the families would almost certainly have known each other in Perthshire.

George Duncan Robertson is the second officer of direct descent from a Highland chief. Robertson was the eldest son of Major General George Duncan Robertson of Struan, and he himself became the 21st of Struan, Perthshire, 18th Chief of the Clan Donnachaidh. He was born in 1816 and in 1839 married Mary-Stuart, daughter of Major Menzies, formerly of the 42nd, who lived at Avondale, Stirling. After purchasing both his steps, Robertson left the Regiment a year after his marriage and he died in the Isle of Wight in 1864 aged 58.

Charles Murray was probably the sixth son of John Murray of Murraythwaite, Dumfries, but this is not confirmed. After purchasing all his steps to Major he went on half-pay in 1856 and retired in 1860. He died in 1874 at Kendal.

Atholl Wentworth Macdonald may well have been related to the Macdonalds of Sleat, who historically had Wentworth in the family name. He purchased all his steps to Captain and retired in 1844, probably through ill health, for he died in February 1845 at Florina, Malta, where the regiment was stationed.

George W. MacQuarie was the second son of Colonel Charles MacQuarie of the 42nd, who had lands in Mull, and George died there in 1894. He was also related to the Maclaines of Lochbuie, and the account for his uniform is amongst the Lochbuie collection at the Scottish Record Office.[47] After purchasing his Captaincy in the 42nd in 1844 he exchanged to the 63rd in 1853 and later became Paymaster of the Military Train, going on half-pay in 1862.

Duncan Cameron, born in 1819, belonged to the family of Cameron of Inverailort, Moidart, Inverness-shire, his father being Major General Sir Alexander Cameron. Cameron was Commissioned in 1835 and became Adjutant in 1838, a post which he held until 1840, when he retired and Atholl Wentworth Macdonald took over. Cameron died in 1874. He purchased neither of his steps and was probably without funds, but not from the ranks. The duties of Adjutant required experience and ability and the post was often filled in Highland regiments at this time by men commissioned from the ranks of the Senior Sergeants. Cameron's predecessor in the office of Adjutant had been John Wheately, known to have been commissioned from the ranks and the Paymaster in 1839. Cameron married the first daughter of George Mackay of Bighouse and he had a brother, Arthur Wellington Cameron, who was born in 1827 and who commanded the 92nd Highlanders.

The junior Lieutenant was Archibald Colin Campbell of Renton. He purchased his way to Captaincy and between 1843 and 1845 he acted as Adjutant, retiring as a Captain and Brevet Major in 1855. He died at Mordington House, Berwickshire in 1866.

None of the eight Ensigns had more than two years' service. James Hunter was the eldest son of Charles Hunter JP DL, of Seaside and Glencarse, Perthshire. Hunter was born in 1816 and he would thus be 20 when he purchased his Ensigncy. In 1845 he exchanged to the 13th of Foot and died as a Captain and Staff Officer of Pensioners in Chester in 1860.

There is no indication that Ensign William James Hope Johnstone was related to Major Johnstone, for William James, born in 1819, was the eldest son of John James Johnstone Hope MP JP DL (who achieved fame in the Annandale Peerage Case). William James was known as 'Younger of Annandale', Dumfriesshire. In 1841 he married the Hon. Octavia Sophia-Bosville Macdonald, youngest daughter of Lord Macdonald. William had two brothers who served in the 92nd, one in the diplomatic service, one in the Hon. East India Company, and one in the Royal Navy. He retired as a Lieutenant in 1840 and died at Annandale in 1850 aged only 31.

The Hon James Ogilvie Grant was the fourth son of Francis William Ogilvie Grant, 6th Earl of Seafield, Cullen House, Banffshire. As a result of his elder brothers dying unmarried or in childhood and of his nephew also dying unmarried, James himself became 9th Earl of Seafield in 1884.

He was born in 1817 and served in the 42nd between 1838 and 1841, when he sold out as a Lieutenant. He was MP for Elgin and Nairn from 1868 to 1874 and was also a Depute Lieutenant and Lt. Colonel of the Elgin Volunteers. He died in 1888. He married three times, in 1841, 1853 and 1875, and by his second marriage to Constance Helena, fourth daughter of Sir Robert Abercromby of Birkenbog, he had a son Robert, who served in the Gordon Highlanders. One of James's younger brothers, the Hon. George Henry Essex Grant of Easter Elchies, Craig Ellachie, served in the 42nd between 1841 and 1865, and James the 11th Earl served in the 3rd and 5th Battalions of the Queen's Own Cameron Highlanders in the Great War and died of wounds in 1915.

Another titled Officer was Sir Frederick William Dunbar Bart., of Boath, Nairn, the eldest son of Sir James Dunbar of Boath RN and Helen Coull of Ashgrove, Elgin. In 1840 he retired as Ensign and he married in 1842 Caroline-Maria, daughter of William Garden, and died in 1851.

Farquhard Campbell of Aros, Mull, purchased his Captaincy in 1846 and sold out in 1849. He died in 1881.

Henry Sholto Douglas purchased his Ensigncy in 1839 and retired by sale as a Captain in 1848. He lived for a time at Bonjedward and Timpindean, Roxburghshire.

Thomas Robert Drummond Hay of Seggieden was to be related by marriage to Henry Maurice Drummond of Megginch. Seggieden, in Perthshire, was a fine but modest mansion built around 1775 amid rich farmlands. The house was eventually demolished in 1970.[48] Drummond Hay purchased his steps to Captain by 1848. In 1851 he exchanged to the 78th probably as a result of the tension in the Battalion which Wedderburn directly attributes to Major Cumberland. Hay was a great friend of Wedderburn and they would sit up in the evenings together in the West Indies singing and playing the flutina and guitar.[49]

The junior Ensign, Thomas Francis Wade, was son of Colonel T.F. Wade who had served in the 42nd between 1809 and 1826. Wade junior exchanged as a Lieutenant to the 98th in 1841 and retired in 1847.

Two senior men occupied the positions of Paymaster and Quarter Master with non-combatant commissions. Paymaster John Wheately joined the 42nd as a private soldier aged 17 in 1817. Ten years later he was acting Sergeant Major and he was commissioned Ensign and Adjutant without purchase in 1832. He became Paymaster in 1838. He moved to the Depot Battalion in 1855, was appointed Major (without purchase) in 1860 and retired as Lt. Colonel in 1866. He died in 1882.

The Quarter Master, Finley King, enlisted as a private soldier in 1803. He served in the Peninsula between July 1809 and August 1812, including the Battles of Busaco and Fuentes d'Onor, and was present at Quatre Bras and Waterloo. By 1818 he was Sergeant Major of the 42nd and in that year was appointed Quarter Master. He went on half-pay in 1840 and died in Guernsey in 1842. His son Robert Henry King was assistant Surgeon of the 42nd between 1848 and 1852.

Finley King, like Quarter Masters Alexander Cruikshanks of the 79th and William MacKintosh of the 93rd, must have been a very remarkable man. They had all seen considerable action and in the Army of 1839 were regarded as 'military curiosities',[50] men who were carefully looked after by their regiments, where they represented a link with arduous battles and campaigns, which had already been taken to the heart of regimental history.[51]

It is difficult to decide how Wheately and King were treated in the Battalion in the light of their social origins. While they may not have been treated as equals amongst the officers, there is no suggestion that they were not treated with the utmost respect.

Surgeon James Paterson MD also served in the Peninsula. He had commenced service as a Hospital Mate in 1810 and had served with the 45th, the 13th and the 46th before he joined the 42nd in 1835. He received his MD from Glasgow University in 1818, retired on half-pay in 1841 and died in Edinburgh in 1866.[52]

The Assistant Surgeon, James M'Gregor, had joined the 42nd as a Hospital Assistant in 1826. Between 1820 and 1822 he had attended St. Andrews University and he further attended Marishcal College, Aberdeen between 1834 and

1835. He was appointed Surgeon of the 42nd in 1841 and moved to the Staff in 1842, retiring on half-pay in 1858 with the honorary rank of Depute Inspector General of Hospitals. He died at Fonab, Perthshire in 1874.[53]

These details bring out several important points. Firstly, in 1839 the 42nd may be seen as a prestigious and desirable regiment to which to belong, and this is reflected in the social status and background of the identifiable officers. The 42nd were, after all, the senior Highland regiment, who had acquitted themselves well at Quatre Bras and Waterloo, and this was the era of growing general interest in things Highland and Highland associations. Six Officers had titles and fall into the category of 'Aristocracy', three others had links with Highland clan chiefs.

Secondly, in the light of the ultimate recruiting areas assigned to the 42nd by the Brigade Depot System of 1872 and the Territorial System of 1881, it is most interesting to see the numbers of officers with links in Perthshire and Forfarshire, nine known and identifiable in all. Four officers are linked with Argyllshire families, two with Inverness-shire and one each with Aberdeenshire, Banff and Nairn. It might be expected that the 42nd's officers would have been drawn from a wider Highland area, particularly in the light of the regimental origins, and the answer may lie in the fact that the 42nd were expensive to belong to and many truly Highland families could not at this time afford the costs. It may emphasise, too, the growing prosperity of the Perthshire landholding community.

The trends shown in the 93rd Descriptive Roll Book appear to be continued and extended in the 42nd at this time, and the 42nd's Roll of Enlistments for 1840 shows that recruits for the ranks were coming from all over Scotland, with growing numbers from Lanarkshire, Renfrew, Aberdeen, Edinburgh and Perth.[54] It would appear therefore that officers were no longer commanding men they knew personally prior to enlistment, as had been the case when the Watch were raised, and yet they were still being led by Scots from north of the Forth/Clyde line.

Thirdly, seven officers are known to have been the eldest sons of their families; however, these men tended to leave the Battalion early, presumably because of family commitments. Ten men are second or lesser sons. Families tended to be large by modern standards, and it is interesting to note the alternatives which other brothers took up by way of occupation, particularly in other Highland regiments and the East India Company. No officer is identifiable as a son of the clergy. Because of the size of the rest of their families and the lack of opportunity of direct inheritance, twenty-two officers may be classified as coming from the families of the landed gentry, but few would be classified as landed gentry in their own right, although some purchased country estates and houses after they left the army.

Fourthly, it is clear that many of these men would have known each other prior to service in the Regiment. There are interrelationships too through marriage, an illustration of the closeness of society in general and of the relationships within the Regiment. Much of this closeness and interrelationship, in the difficult circumstances of service in Ireland and the subsequent service of the Battalion in small garrisons in the Ionian Islands and Malta, may account for some of the internal conflicts which Wedderburn encountered.

Fifthly, the desirability of one particular regiment may well have been based not only on its history and national associations, but also upon its location. In 1841 the 42nd moved to the Ionian Islands and in 1842 to Malta. While these locations might now be considered highly desirable, in 1841 they carried with them a serious risk of disease. Probably even more unpopular would have been the move to Bermuda in 1847. Thus, within ten years, by 1849, twenty of these Officers had left the Regiment and one, Macdonald, had died at Malta in 1845. While it might be expected that the senior officers would have died or been promoted, particularly noticeable is the loss of the Ensigns who served for an average of 6¼ years with the Regiment. Service may therefore have been looked upon as an extension of a young man's education as opposed to a long-term career, much like a Short Service Commission nowadays. Apart from Lt. Colonel Cameron who died at Bareilly in 1858, none of these officers is known to haved died in action or at war, or from disease contracted in war. Some of these men were, it also seems, simply not prepared to go to war. Miss Murray wrote to her brother, Captain J. Murray of Polmaise, on 10th January 1855:

> A detachment of 70 men of the 42nd leave this (sic) today under the command of our friend Cluny—all the officers have, except him, Major Murray and the young Ensigns, sent in their papers! They have really shown themselves a set of *spoons*. Cumberland has sold out and Major McPherson who is on his way here has sent in his papers, in short they are no longer like the old 42nd which was such a distinguished Corps. I daresay *Col.* Cameron thinks he is well quit of them.[55]

Sixthly, whatever might have been the earlier motives of Highland officers, it is clear that the system of purchase and sale operated to its full extent in a Highland regiment as in any other. It might have been expected therefore that there would have been far more clearly identifiable English and Irish officers, and yet it seems that the Highland regiments were still able to retain their nationality in their officer corps in open competition, perhaps as a result of their retention of Highland dress, or the selective patronage of the powerful Colonel of the Regiment.

Finally, it is of interest to note that several of these officers, apart from undertaking duties as Justices of the Peace and Depute Lieutenants, which would have followed largely as a result of their landed interests, also became officers in the Volunteer movement, which was closely linked to the Lieutenancies but not founded until twenty years after the list.

In general the kind of officers found in the 42nd at this time are a reflection of the officers of the other kilted battalions, and the nationality figures show that when the proportions are projected to 1872, a slight shift has taken place away from Scottish officers towards Englishmen. This is partly the result of the large influx of officers during the Crimean War and Indian Mutiny, but may also be accounted for by the contemporary popularity of particular Regiments, the 78th being known as 'the saviours of India', and the 93rd as 'the Thin Red Line'.

The list also illustrates the practical workings of purchase, promotion, exchange and half-pay. The system of purchase was established in the British Army by 1720 and the Warrant of 1821 set down the rates charged for each rank. However, the practice grew up of 'over regulation payments', and the real price for an officer was much higher than the regulation rates:

Line Regiments' Regulation Prices

Rank	Regulation	Difference in Value between Commissions
Ensign	£450	—
Lieutenant	£700	£250
Captain	£1800	£1100
Major	£3200	£1400
Lt. Colonel	£4500	£1300

An officer had to serve two years as a Subaltern, i.e. Ensign and Lieutenant, before he could be promoted to Captain and six years as a Commissioned Officer before he could become a Field Officer, i.e. Major. Promotion also required the sanction of a Senior Officer and certification of an officer's fitness for higher rank in the Quarterly Returns. There were in addition regular confidential reports on officers.[57]

In 1850 examinations for promotion from Ensign to Lieutenant and Captain were introduced,[58] but seniority and not merit was the guiding principle behind promotion. An officer could not be promoted by purchase over the heads of more senior officers of the same rank if the latter had also indicated their intention to buy, and no officer however good could be promoted without purchase over the heads of men of the same rank, but with longer service. Thus, Frazer was a Lieutenant before Beales or Montagu, but Montagu would have had to ensure that Frazer did not intend to purchase for the Captain's vacancy on 22nd October 1825, and Ramsay was in the same position with regard to Campbell, who was two years his senior.

No purchase price was payable in the case of a vacancy caused by death, hence the toast, 'To a bloody war or a sickly season', or in the case of an increase in establishment, retirement of an officer on full pay after thirty years' service, or in certain circumstances where an officer retired on half-pay after twenty-five years' service. Ranks above Lt. Colonel could not be purchased or sold.

An officer could exchange with another man in another regiment providing both were in agreement, but payment was prohibited except where there was a difference in value in the commissions, as between the Guards and the Line. The system of exchange was used to hasten the opportunities of promotion, to avoid serving in certain stations or to enable an officer to serve with a particular regiment. For example, Lieutenant John Alexander Ewart served initially in the 35th Regiment. He had not had to purchase his Lieutenancy but in 1848 had the chance to purchase to Captain. He paid the regulation of £1800 together with £700 over regulation, the latter being made up of £425 which his father gave him and £275 which was subscribed by the other Subalterns of the 35th. Ewart then made contact with exchange agents in London (intermediate brokers who put officers wishing to exchange in contact with one another), and organised his exchange with Captain N.S. Buchanan of the 93rd.[59] It was common for money to pass in order to arrange a deal of this nature.

Purchasing and exchanging into a regiment was very unpopular with the officers *in situ*, who remained in exactly the same position on the promotion ladder, with a stranger in their midst and less chance of their own promotion. Lieutenant Parke of the 72nd complained in 1854 that while the Regiment had got rid of an unpopular Commanding Officer in Lt. Colonel Freeman Murray, an outsider had purchased his way in:

> We are all sorely disappointed in getting another Lieutenant Colonel from a strange Corps, this is the eleventh in succession appointed to command us never giving promotion in the Corps.[60]

Because of the strict limitations of establishments, manipulation of the system and enhanced over-regulation payments were common and the abuse was overlooked, provided it was not blatant. Complex negotiations and deals were the result. In order to get the Lt. Colonelcy of the 79th in 1841, Lauderdale Maule had to get rid of Andrew Brown, a fellow Major but Maule's senior. Brown wanted to be a Lt. Colonel but did not want to command the 79th; Maule wanted both. Thus Maule had to find a Lt. Colonel who would firstly exchange with Brown once he was promoted, and then would agree to sell out to Maule. He found Lt. Colonel John Carter of the 1st Royals who wanted to exchange and sell out to half-pay. In theory this was not permitted and so Carter had to join the 79th, wait a few months and then sell out. Maule wrote to his brother:

> You see Carter cannot sell for some months to come even after he has exchanged because the HG [Horse Guards] won't sanction a proceeding which would look like a direct job. Carter is nominally in Command, he signs, I however am Prime Minister and . . . everything.[61]

So Brown was promoted Lt. Colonel on 8th June 1841. It would appear that Maule paid at least part of his regulation price for this, and other officers who would have benefited in their turn may have contributed also. Brown then exchanged with Lt. Colonel Carter of the 1st Royals on 29th October 1841. Carter joined the 79th and applied to sell and go to half-pay, which he did on 14th June 1842, on which date Maule duly achieved his object and became Lt. Colonel of the 79th.

By leaving his Majority, Maule made a vacancy which he had agreed to sell to John Stewart Smyth. Maule delayed as long as he could, but Smyth could not raise the money and, being £500 short, had to step aside for another.[62]

In the 1850s the War Office tried to curtail the practice of exchange by ruling that an officer was not permitted to exchange unless through ill health or after twenty-one years' service.

The departure of one officer could be encouraged by his fellows subscribing to an unofficial payment to him in addition to the regulation and over-regulation price, or an officer whose vacancy was sought might demand a lump sum or allowance before he would consent to leave or go to half-pay, or he might ask for additional money to help to buy his own promotion.[63]

An officer could leave the service and sell his commission, recouping his outlay, but he had no automatic right to a pension and many officers chose to go on half-pay. The half-pay list was a parallel system of vacancies and an officer on the half-pay list was paid a sum virtually amounting to a retaining fee. A half-pay officer could obtain promotion on the half-pay list, but was only paid at the rate of the rank he had last held on the active list. No officer was allowed to purchase two steps on half-pay without having served in the intermediate time two years on full pay.[64] Half-pay was used by men who wanted a prolonged period of absence from the army because of health or personal affairs, those awaiting promotion opportunities on the active list, or those in the transition stage of retiring or selling out. Many officers were on half-pay with no intention whatever of returning to the army. The government consistently tried to reduce the half-pay list,[65] but by allowing the system to continue relieved themselves of their obligation to pay officers pensions and on reduction of the service were simply able to place men on half-pay at short notice.

Unattached pay was restricted in 1818 to a list of 120 unattached Generals on a standard pay of £456 p.a. These men were on the rolls of their regiment but in name only.

Until 1833 an officer who had not purchased his Commission was not allowed to sell it until he had served twenty years, but after 1833 a non-purchase Ensign could sell after twelve years, a Lieutenant after fifteen years and higher ranks after twenty years.

By way of contrast to the list of 1839, it is interesting to see the effect of the two-battalion system and to look at the structure of the Black Watch in 1891. Ten years after the system had been introduced, it might be expected that the 42nd and the 73rd would have become inextricably intermixed, but this is not the case. Purchase ended twenty years before this list, yet several of the senior officers are listed as having purchased to Lieutenancy.

In spite of being the old second battalion of the 42nd and 'The Perthshire Regiment', the 73rd obviously had few Scottish officers, and in the main those who came from the 73rd in 1881 stayed with the 2nd Battalion, while, presumably to keep the peace, a 73rd man commanded the 1st Battalion and a 42nd man commanded the 2nd Battalion. It would be wrong to assume that either the 42nd or the 73rd was a second-rate battalion or inferior to the other, but it is difficult to see how rivalry and jealousy could not have existed amongst the officers at this time, particularly on the part of the 73rd, whose personality as a regiment was effectively swallowed up by the 42nd, whose dress and general character they adopted. It is indicative of this process that the Black Watch Museum is only able to display one small room of 73rd items, a situation which arises out of necessity rather than design. The 73rd were an old and gallant regiment, but very little is known about them apart from their general history.

The Black Watch (Royal Highlanders) 1891

Years' Ser. Full Pay	Half Pay	
		Colonel. Hon. Robert Rollo,[1] **CB. Ens.** p10 Aug. 32; p25 Sept. 35; **Capt.** p5 Nov. 41; **Bt. Major,** 20 June 54; **Bt. Lt. Colonel,** 12 Dec. 54; **Major** p5 Jan. 55; **Lt. Colonel,** 10 Aug 55; **Colonel,** 23 Feb. 58; **Major General,** 6 March 68; **Lieut. General,** 1 Oct 77; **General,** 19 Dec. 80; **Colonel** 93rd Highlanders, 5 Apr. 80; **Colonel,** Black Watch, 9 June 88.
32	6/12	Lieutenant Colonels, - 2 Alexander Ferrier Kidston, **Commanding the Battalion,** 29 Jan. 87; **Ensign,** p9 Nov. 58; **Lt.** p2 Dec. 62; **Capt.,** 12 Feb. 73; **Major,** 1 July 80; **Bt. Lt. Colonel,** 21 May 84; **Lt. Colonel,** 1 July 85; **Colonel,** 21 May 88.
30	...	1 William Gordon, **Commanding the Battalion,** 29 Sept. 88; **Ensign,** 15 Oct. 61; **Lieut.** p2 Oct. 63; **Capt.** p22 Jan 67; **Bt. Major,** 1 May 80; **Major,** 1 July 81; **Lt. Colonel,** 11 July 86; **Colonel,** 11 July 90.

		Majors	**Ensign or 2nd Lieut.**	**Lieut.**	**Captain**	**Brev. Maj.**	**Major**
29	...	2 Howel Gunter	8 July 62	p23 June 65	7 July 74	...	10 July 81
26	...	1 p.s.c. Richd. Hugh Lambert Brickenden	18 July 65	11 Jan. 67	29 Sept 77	...	25 July 83
26	...	1 Andrew Gilbert Wauchope CB CMG (Bt. Lt. Colonel, 21 May 84; Colonel, 21 May 88)	p21 Nov 65	23 June 67	14 Sept 78	...	14 Mar. 84
22	...	1 Andrew Scott Stevenson (Bt. Lt. Col. 2 July 85; Colonel 2 July 89)	p17 Mar 69	28 Oct. 71	19 June 79	...	1 July 85
22	...	1 Edward George Grogan	p24 July 69	28 Oct. 71	19 June 79	...	4 Dec. 85
25	...	2 George Francis De Bude Davidson	p2 Mar. 66	p19 Feb. 67	11 Nov. 76	...	11 July 86
19	...	2 Charles Albert Bushman	...	14 Aug. 72	11 Dec. 78	...	20 Aug. 90
16	...	2 John Henry Collier Coode	...	10 Sept 75	17 Apr. 82	...	27 Aug. 90

		Captains				
16	...	Archibald Morden Carthew-Yorstoun, Adjutant 6 (Fifeshire) Vol. Bn. Royal Highlanders	...	20 Nov. 75	25 Oct. 82	
18	...	1 Herman Frederick Elliot	...	9 Aug. 73	25 July 83	
15	...	2 Albert Wiley	...	28 Oct. 76	28 Nov. 83	
18	...	Lord Alexander Kennedy, Adj. 5 (Perthshire Highland) Volunteer Battalion Royal Highlanders	...	12 Nov. 73	29 Dec. 84	25 June 85

The Black Watch (Royal Highlanders) 1891 (contd.)

Years' Ser, Full Pay	Half Pay	Captains (contd.)	Ensign or 2nd Lieut.	Lieut.	Captain	Brev. Maj.	Major
14	...	Ernest Maxwell Wilshire, Adjutant 3 Battalion Shropshire Light Infantry	13 Oct. 77	25 May 78	15 May 85		
13	...	Henry Edward Maxwell, Adjutant 8 Battalion King's Royal Rifles	...	11 Sept 78	15 May 85		
12	...	2 Douglas Campbell Mercer	22 Jan, 79	29 Sept 80	20 Oct. 85		
12	...	Charles Graham Moulton-Barrett 4 Vol. Bn. Royal Highlanders	13 Aug. 79	26 Feb. 81	20 Oct. 85		
19	...	Edward Parker Campbell, Adj. 5 Vol. Bn. Argyll & Sutherland Highldrs.	...	17 Jan. 72	4 Dec. 85		
16	...	Alexander Gordon Duff, Aide de Camp to Major General H. Wilkie	...	28 Apr. 75	4 Dec. 85		
18	...	Charles Grant Adj. 5 (Glasgow Highland) Vol. Bn. Highland Lt. Inf.	...	9 Aug. 73	14 Jan. 84		
16	...	1 Thomas Francis Archibald Kennedy	...	27 Jan, 75	20 Jan. 86		
12	...	St. George Edward William Burton, Adj. 3 (Dundee Highland) Vol. Bn. Royal Highlanders	13 Aug 79	1 July 81	15 Nov. 86		
12	...	Thomas Mowbray Martin Berkeley, Adj. 1 (Dundee) Vol. Bn. R. Highldrs.	13 Aug 79	1 July 81	29 Jan. 87		
12	...	Percy John Caton Livingston, Adj. 3 Battalion (Perth Militia)	22 Jan. 79	1 July 81	21 Apr. 87		
12	...	John Grenfell Maxwell, DSO (Bt. Major, 17 Aug. 89), serving with Egyptian Army	22 Mar. 79	1 July 81	28 Nov. 87		
9	...	Kenneth Murchison Massie-Cox-Murchison, Adj. 2 Vol. Bn. R. Highldrs.	...	10 May 82	12 Mar. 88		
9	...	1 Alfred Campbell Bald	...	10 May 82	21 Nov. 88		
9	...	1 Norman William Cuthbertson	...	9 Sept 82	7 Dec. 88		
9	...	2 Henry Clare Filmore	...	9 Sept 82	22 Jan. 89		
9	...	1 Duncan Alexander M'Leod	...	9 Sept 82	27 Nov. 89		
8	...	2 Thomas Souter	...	24 Jan. 83	17 May 90		
8	...	2 James Deane	...	10 Mar. 83	5 June 90		
8	...	1 Walter Gordon Wolrige-Gordon, Adjutant 14 July 88	...	12 May 83	5 June 90		
7	...	2 George Herbert Lyle Galbraith	...	6 Feb. 84	27 Aug. 90		
7	...	1 Hugh Rose	...	6 Feb. 84	22 Oct. 90		
		Lieutenants					
7	...	1 David Lorraine Wilson	...	6 Feb. 84			
7	...	2 John Stuart	...	14 May 84			

The Black Watch (Royal Highlanders) 1891 (contd.)

Years' Ser. Full Pay	Half Pay	Lieutenants (contd.)	Ensign or 2nd Lieut.	Lieut.	Captain	Brev. Maj.	Major
7	...	1 Harrie Jennings-Bramly	...	23 Aug. 84			
6	...	1 William MacLaren Campbell	...	7 Feb. 85			
6	...	1 Hon. James F. Thurlow Cumming-Bruce	...	29 Aug. 85			
6	...	1 Alexander Campbell	...	25 Nov. 85			
5	...	2 John George Rennie	...	30 Jan. 86			
5	...	Alexander Kenneth Gillespie, A.S. Corps	...	30 Jan. 86			
5	...	2 Hon. Alan David Murray, Adj. 29 May 89	...	30 Jan. 86			
5	...	1 David Baird	...	8 Dec, 86			
4	...	2 Francis Andrews Ferguson-Davie	26 Feb. 87	29 May 89			
4	...	1 Edward Sidney Herbert	4 May 87	27 Nov. 89			
4	...	1 Colin M'Lean	4 May 87	27 Dec. 89			
4	...	1 Henry Scott Turner	21 Dec. 87	17 May 90			
3	...	2 William MacFarlan	11 Feb. 88	31 May 90			
3	...	1 Thomas Owen Lloyd	9 May 88	5 June 90			
3	...	2 Erle Godfrey Elton	22 Aug. 88	13 Aug. 90			
3	...	2 Charles Herbert Philip Carter	14 Nov 88	20 Aug. 90			
2.	...	1 Robert Henry Pitcairn	9 Jan 89	27 Aug. 90			
2	...	1 Adrian Grant-Duff	23 Mar 89	22 Oct. 90			

		Second Lieutenants	2nd Lieut.
2	...	2 Charles Edward Stewart	10 Apr 89
2	...	2 Cecil Eykyn	6 July 89
2	...	2 Ronald Adrian Mackenzie Ewart	9 Nov 89
1	...	2 Archibald Rice Cameron	1 Mar 90
1	...	2 Arthur Ernest Heald	3 May 90
1	...	1 Colin William MacRae	28 June 90
1	...	2 John George Harry Hamilton	8 Oct 90
1	...	1 Edwin Sandys Dawes	29 Oct 90
1	...	1 Alexander Johnstone Nicol	29 Nov 90
1	...	1 Henry Andrew	29 Nov 90

Paymasters. - 1
-2

8 ... Quarter Masters. - 1 Charles Sinclair, 28 Nov. 83; Hon. Lieut.
1 William Webb, 14 May 87; Hon. Lieut.

Figures 1 or 2 before a name indicates serving with the 1st or 2nd Battalion.
p.s.c. Passed Staff College.

Of the men themselves on this list, the Colonel, the Hon. Robert Rollo, is the only survivor from the 1839 list. The ratio of Captains and Majors has altered and it is noticeable how many Captains are detached for service with the Volunteers and Militia and not necessarily to units directly associated with the Regiment.[67] Some well-known names are here: Andrew Gilbert Wauchope who was to be killed at Magersfontein in command of the Highland Brigade; Hugh Rose of Kilravock, whom Corporal MacFarlane remembers as the gentlemanly Commanding Officer of 1913-1914;[68] John Grenfell Maxwell, who commanded the 2nd Egyptian Brigade at Omdurman; the Hon. Alan David Murray, later to be Earl of Mansfield, and Adrian Grant Duff, a skilled and able soldier who, after passing Staff College, became Assistant Secretary of the Committee of Imperial Defence and commanded the 1st Battalion Black Watch in 1914. He is remembered with great respect by Mr. MacFarlane as a man who was a knowledgeable and professional soldier and who was a serious loss to the Battalion and the Division when he was killed in action on the Aisne in September 1914.[69]

A large number of these men had seen active service including the Ashanti War, Egypt and the Sudan. The 73rd, who had remained in India until 1878, had only seen home service since, and it would be the 42nd officers who had the medals, a factor which cannot have been lost on them at the time.

It is noticeable that many of the young officers, Second Lieutenants and Lieutenants, have Scottish associations, and this probably reflected an effort on behalf of the Regiment to recruit Scotsmen not only into the rank and file, but also into the officer corps.

The points brought out here also apply to the linking of the 92nd and the 75th, but are not so marked in relation to the 93rd and 91st, or the 78th and 72nd. The officers of the 79th were of course unaffected, as they remained a single unlinked battalion, but they were alarmed at the possibility of disbandment or amalgamation with the Guards, as this amalgamation would have been particularly expensive, apart from the inevitable friction that would have ensued.[70]

The 1891 list also illustrates the increasing professionalism of officers. All the serving officers had passed an entrance and promotion examination and all who had been commissioned after 1878 had attended Sandhurst. Among the officers of the Regiment who had attended the School of Musketry at Hythe, was Wauchope. One officer, Richard Brickenden, had passed Staff College; Cameron, Grant-Duff and Cuthbertson were to follow, and all would have taken part in manoeuvres and exercises involving units larger than their own battalion, either in Aldershot, Egypt or Malta.

The pattern is indicative of the broadening of an officer's education and the changes in attitude that followed the introduction of new weapons, tactics and drills, together with lessons learned from the Franco-Prussian War. There was still however an underlying prejudice amongst officers against the professionalism of theoretical training and the Staff College, reflecting the paramount importance in many officers' minds of 'the Regiment' over and above personal ambition.[71]

The Senior Department of Sandhurst moved to a house in Sandhurst in 1820 and catered for fifteen officers per year.[72] There was an entrance examination and the subjects of study included higher mathematics, surveying and military drawing, astronomy, fortification, French and German. Candidates had to be over 21 with not less than four years' service at home (three abroad).[73] The Department was neither popular nor prestigious, and in 1854 only six officers were attending.[74] Ewart of the 93rd remembers in 1844 that the students lived in rooms in 'Tea Caddy Row' and 'were cooked for by an old woman called Shaw'.[75] The course lasted between two years and eighteen months and gave no guarantee of advancement when completed. 'Going back to school' was not popular with officers and the course was seldom used to its best advantage and was regarded by many as two years' rest.

In 1858 competitive examinations were introduced for entrance, and in 1862 the Staff College was built at Camberley. One officer per regiment was allowed to attend at any one time, a condition which meant that an officer with good results might fail the entrance examination because an officer of the same regiment had scored higher marks; but only one could attend, and the man failing had to sit the examination again.[76] A new syllabus of training was introduced with examinations and lectures,[77] but in general officers' attitudes did not change:

> In those days [the 1890s] the general opinion of the Army was still that Staff College Officers were a set of shirkers who left their Regiments with a view to an idle two years at the College, to be followed by loafing and well paid jobs in the plums of the profession.[78]

Spencer Ewart of the 79th who attended Staff College in 1890 recorded:

> A great drawback in my opinion to the Staff College at the time of my residence there was the sacrifice of every other consideration to the horse, unless one talked all day long of this animal, rode with the 'drag', subscribed to the coach, (which nobody knew how to drive) and dressed like a bookmaker, one ran a considerable risk of being unfavourably reported on by the authorities or being shunned by one's associates as a pariate![79]

Count Gleichen however concluded that his tour of Staff College had been '. . . two intensely interesting and valuable years', which were rounded off by attachments to the Cavalry and the Artillery.

The Highland regiments had a good record of attendance at the Senior Department and Staff College, but in the Gordon Highlanders

> . . . there was a great tradition that the Regiment was everything and any departure from the sealed pattern was frowned upon. No Officer had ever volunteered for Staff College, for active service or for anything. They lived and fought as a Regiment, without personal considerations . . .[80]

In the Cameron Highlanders a similar attitude prevailed under Colonel Leith, as recorded by Spencer Ewart when he dined for the first time with the Regiment on joining at Gibraltar in 1882:

> At Mess I sat that evening between Colonel Leith and Captain Murray. Old Leith was very affable and told me the 79th had got two things to thank God for, one that they had never had a man with the Victoria Cross, the other that they had never had a Staff College man. He was certainly one of the old school.[81]

In the minds of many officers there was therefore a conflict of loyalties as far as ambitions outwith the Regiment were concerned, and in the Highland regiments, where tartan, clan, home area and regimental loyalty were deeply cherished, it might be expected that this conflict would be most marked. However, with the exception of the Gordons and the Camerons a broader view was taken in the Highland regiments, and while only a minority of officers were Staff College trained, personal ambition was not subordinated to regimental cohesion and most regimental officers from the 1870s onwards found themselves posted away from their regiments to staff posts at some point after passing out of the College. Brickenden for example became Garrison Instructor at Malta in 1876.[82] Lt. Colonel Knollys of the 93rd was the first p.s.c. (Passed Staff College) officer to command a Highland regiment, and in 1877 the 93rd alone had four officers p.s.c.[83]

The 1891 list shows that the abolition of purchase had not materially altered the social structure of the battalion, and there are no long lists of men commissioned from the ranks, except Charles Sinclair and William Webb the Quarter Masters and Captain Thomas Souter, who was commissioned from the ranks of the Queen's Own Cameron Highlanders and who returned to that battalion as a Major in 1899.[84]

The list also brings out the extensive use of Brevet rank in the later Victorian Army. The Brevet, in theory elevation of rank without pay, had been introduced by William III purely as reward, but had come to be governed by some form of rule of seniority, although staff appointments and meritorious service also came into play. Thus Wauchope, for example, in 1891 held two ranks, Major in his Regiment and Colonel in the Army. When with his Regiment he was under command of his Colonel, but in the Army he was of equal rank to him. The system caused major difficulties and was one of the principal reasons for the command breakdown that led to the surrender of the 1st Battalion Gordon Highlanders on 27th August 1914. In this case Lt. Colonel Neish commanded the Battalion and his second-in-command was Colonel W.E. Gordon VC who held Brevet rank and was therefore senior in the Army but junior in the Battalion. In the confusion and darkness of the early hours of 27th August, the Battalion collected several soldiers of other regiments, and Gordon was entitled to take command of a composite force, which he did, much to Neish's displeasure. Thinking themselves surrounded, Gordon advocated fighting their way out, while Neish proposed surrender. The officers and men, without leadership or clear orders, and unable to decide whom to obey, reluctantly and bitterly laid down their arms.[85]

The nationality and social status of officers of the Highland battalions remained remarkably consistent between 1820 and 1914.[86] Then, because of sheer necessity caused by high officer casualties, the criteria for officer selection changed. Men were promoted in large numbers from the ranks, fifty for example in the 1st and 2nd Battalions of the Black Watch, of whom nineteen were killed in action.[87] Money had nothing to do with fulfilling the fighting role and a basic standard of education, fitness and primarily experience became of importance. The influx however of these officers and men from civilian life led to major dissatisfaction regarding army pay, and it was because of them that pay was eventually raised in 1919.[88] This emphasised that officer selection was largely based on economic considerations prior to 1914, when governments were ready to criticise the limited class base of officer recruitment, but were not prepared to pay for the solution.

Highland regiments, therefore, had the standard structure of command of the Infantry of the Line, but the kilted battalions in particular recruited officers with national associations and origins in the 'landed gentry'. The training, selection and education of officers improved throughout the century, but the purchase system and emphasis on 'the Regiment' militated against serious academic pursuits. The linked battalion system and the changes in officer structure within the battalion could well have resulted in a falling away of Highland spirit but it did not, and while regimental numbers were cherished and are still used today, the linked battalions assumed Highland characteristics. Men commissioned from the ranks were highly regarded, but were few in number until 1914, when the system of officer selection and financial obligations and requirements broke down due to heavy losses, especially amongst junior officers, and the very nature of the War. So many of these pre-1914 officers were killed that a continuity in nationality, family, service and regimental association was effectively broken. It will therefore be interesting to look more deeply into the nature and character of these men and to examine their financial circumstances.

NOTES

1. Following the defeat of the Army Regulation Bill the purchase of Officers' Commissions was abolished by Royal Warrant of 20th July 1871.
2. See for example the letters of Lt. Col. Hon. Lauderdale Maule GD/45/14/634(3) 1-84. Gibraltar 26.6.1846. 'The moves have been fixed and the 79th goes on this Autumn to the West Indies. I was in hope that some little interest might have been made to get the Regt. to Jamaica. I wrote long ago to the Colonel and to one or two others to try and get this done . . .'
3. WO/43/871 and Warrant of 6.6.1852, 'Clothing of the Army is no longer to be provided by the Colonels of Regiments out of 'off reckonings''.
   Warrant Regulating the Provision of Clothing, Necessaries, Great Coats, Accoutrements and Appointments for Corps of Infantry 21.6.1828. GD/225/Box 42/B1.xi. (Includes the abolition of Warrant Men).
4. In 1858 Grenadier and Light Companies were abolished and the Companies simply numbered 1-10. In 1865 the ten Companies were designated by letters instead of numbers and in 1873 two Companies were made Depot Companies.
5. 'Comparative View of the Pay of Officers in the French and British Service'. 1835. Edinburgh University Library Special Collection P/384, pp. 17-18.
6. An Officer, *Fifteen Years of Army Reform* (Edinburgh: 1884), pp. 29-30: ' . . . [after abolition of purchase] . . . the dissatisfaction became so rife and so generally displayed, that in September 1873 the Commander in Chief found it necessary to issue a General Order, forbidding the Officers of the Army to continue further discussion on the disadvantages which they considered to have resulted to their position and interests'.
7. See Chapter 3.
8. PP 1822 XIX c.570 and GD/139/450; Letter from Robert McBeath 78th Highlanders to George Sinclair of Brabster, 13.9.1828.
9. John D. Gomrie, *History of Scottish Medicine* (London: 1932), pp.740-757.
10. See, for example, Daniel Blair MD, *Some Account of the last Yellow Fever Epidemic of British Guiana*, ed. John Davy MD. FRS. (London and Edinburgh: 1850). The research in this book covered the outbreak of yellow fever amongst the 72nd at Barbados in 1847 and the 92nd at Barbados between 1841 and 1842.
11. Surgeon W. Munro, *Records of Service and Campaigning in Many Lands* (London: 1887), 2 vols. and Surgeon W. Munro, *Reminiscences of Military Service with the 93rd Highlanders* (London: 1883).
12. Diary of Col. J.W. Wedderburn, BWRM, 28/714/1.
13. Letters of Lt. Col. Hon. Lauderdale Maule GD/45/14/634(4) 1-98 12.6.1847.
14. PP 1854-55 XII c 317 pp. iii-vii.
15. Lt. Gen. John Alexander Ewart, *The Story of a Soldier's Life* (London: 1881), Vol. 1, p. 19.
16. Brigadier Sir John Smyth VC, *Sandhurst* (London: 1961), pp. 86 and 97.
17. Lt. Gen. John Alexander Ewart, *The Story of a Soldier's Life, op.cit.*, p. 35.

18. PP 1849 XXXII c 120, Return of Non Commissioned Officers, Royal Military College Cadets and Private Gentlemen who have obtained Commissions without purchase.

Date	NCO	RMC Cadet	Private Gentlemen
1830	11	19	43
1831	12	19	40
1832	5	29	21
1833	8	22	16
1834	18	16	36
1835	16	24	22
1836	16	25	38
1837	34	42	24
1838	36	27	34
1839	26	33	83
1840	25	25	40
1841	46	28	108
1842	27	26	206
1843	17	28	75
1844	33	27	119
1845	17	28	75
1846	58	34	203
1847	41	21	83

19. PP 1849 XXXII c 532.
20. PP 1857-58 XXXVII c 498.
21. PP 1857-58 XXXVII c 127, and PP XVIII c 2262.
22. Ian B.M. Hamilton, *The Happy Warrior* (London: 1966), p. 12.
23. Brig. Sir John Smyth VC, *Sandhurst, op. cit.*, and Anthony Bruce, *The Purchase System in the British Army 1660-1871* (London: 1980).
24. *Rules of the Military Academy Edinburgh,* SUSM.
25. Second letter by Major Charles Downes to the subscribers of the Scottish Naval and Military Academy, CL., YU 548/B29246.
26. *The Edinburgh Almanac 1827, op. cit.*, pp. 273-274, and CL., YU 548/B21809.
27. Major Charles Downes, Letter to the Subscribers of the Scottish Naval and Military Academy 1832, CL., YU 548/B29327.
28. G.L. Goff, *Historical Records of the 91st Argyllshire Highlanders, op. cit.*, p. 247.
29. Major General Lord Edward Gleichen, *A Guardsman's Memoirs* (London: 1932), p. 14.
30. Brig. Sir John Smyth VC, *Sandhurst, op. cit.*, p. 133 and *Officers of the Black Watch, op. cit.*
31. Quoted *Ibid.*, p. 163. An amusing example of the anxiety generated among gentlemen cadets as to their choice of Regiments is cited by David Niven who stated his order of preference of Regiments as:
   '1. The Argyll and Sutherland Highlanders
   2. The Black Watch
   3. Anything but the Highland Light Infantry'.
   In 1928 he was commissioned into the Highland Light Infantry. David Niven, *The Moon's a Balloon* (London: 1973), p. 63.
32. The series of Monthly Returns to the War Office (WO/17) ended in 1864. The 1872 figures are taken from PP 1872 XXXVII c 315 and c 171.
33. P.E. Razzell, *Social Origins of Officers in the Indian and British Home Army 1758-1962, British Journal of Sociology*, Vol. XIV, Sept. 1963, pp. 248-260. These figures are in fact very deceptive and illustrate the importance of the study of individual regiments, as even today it would be difficult to find a Guards Battalion with 95% of its officers being drawn from the 'middle class'.

34. *Army Lists* 1820-1920. *The Scots Peerage*, ed. Sir James Balfour Paul (Edinburgh: 1914), Vols. I-LX. *Officers of the Black Watch, op. cit. Dictionary of the Landed Gentry*, Sir Bernard Burke (London: 1858). John Stewart of Ardvorlich, *The Camerons* (Stirling: 1974). *Debrett's Illustrated Peerage, Baronetage, Knightage and House of Commons* (London: 1866). *Dictionary of the Peerage and Baronetage*, Burke (London: 1876). *History of the Landed Gentry*, Burke (London: 1879). *Burke's Landed Gentry* (London: 1937), 15th Edition.
35. *Army List*, 1839.
36. Archibald Forbes, *The Black Watch* (London: 1896), p. 275.
37. Diary of Col. J.W. Wedderburn, BWRM, 28/714/1, 17.10.1853.
38. E. and A. Linklater, *The Black Watch* (London: 1977), p. 94.
39. Diary of Col. J.W. Wedderburn, BWRM 28/714/1, 15.4.1852.
40. Ibid., 21.4.1852.
41. Ibid., 15.4.1852 and 16.5.1852.
42. Diary of Lt. Colonel John Wheately 42nd, BWRM, also reprinted in the *Red Hackle*, Regimental Magazine of the Black Watch, July 1922, p. 8.
43. Diary of Col. J.W. Wedderburn, BWRM 28/714/1, 31.12.1851.
44. Ibid., 5.12.1851.
45. Binney, Harris and Winnington, *Lost Houses of Scotland* (London: 1980).
46. Diary of Col. J.W. Wedderburn BWRM 28/714/1, 6.5.1852.
47. GD/174/1708/11.
48. Binney, Harris and Winnington, *Lost Houses of Scotland, op. cit.*
49. Diary of Col. J.W. Wedderburn, BWRM 28/714/1, 16.5.1848.
50. Letters of Lt. Col. Hon. Lauderdale Maule, GD/45/14/634(4)99-184, of 22.11.1848.
51. When Alexander Cruikshanks of the 79th was leaving the Battalion in 1848, Lauderdale Maule wrote to Fox Maule trying to obtain him a position. 'Quebec, 5.9.1848. My old Quartermaster is leaving me—Cruikshanks— after 44 years hard service in the 79th—you must remember him. Get him made a poor Knight of Windsor, it is barely a favour to ask, he has the strongest claim and poor fellow he will not last very long—you will make a note of this? . . . I am quite sure that none can have a stronger claim than the man who began with Copenhagen and ended with Waterloo.' Letters of Lt. Col. Hon. Lauderdale Maule, ibid.
52. Drew, *Commissioned Officers in the Medical Services of the British Army 1660-1960* (London: 1968), Vol. I p.212.
53. *Ibid.* p.277.
54. Roll of Enlistments of the 42nd 1795-1893, BWRM, 2285.
55. GD/189/2/867, Murray of Polmaise Papers.
56. Extract from the 1821 Warrant.
57. Gwyn Harries-Jenkins, *The Army in Victorian Society* (London: 1977), pp. 82-84. While these reports did tend to be of a negative nature, it is clear that if an officer was not efficient he was removed or advised to leave. When Major General Sir Guy Campbell inspected the Depot of the 79th at Castlebar in June 1847 he reported, 'Major Ferguson has made a special report to me of the complete inefficiency of Ensign Place, which is herewith transmitted. This officer I consider unfit for the Service as stated in Major Ferguson's letter—but there is nothing whatever against this young Gentleman's character—simply the want of capacity to learn what is required'. Ensign Place retired within the month. WO/27/364/67147.
58. WO Circular 14.5.1850. PP 1857 IX c.101.
59. Lt. Gen. John Alexander Ewart, *The Story of a Soldier's Life, op.cit.*, p. 122.
60. Diary of Lt. William Parke, QOHRM, 13.4.1854.
61. Letters of Lt. Col. Hon. Lauderdale Maule GD/45/14/634(2) 1-93 31.8.1841 and 11.11.1841.
62. Ibid., 1.7.1841 and 14.6.1842.
63. Ibid., 1.14.1838 and 16.7.1838.

64. Regulations for sale of Retired Full and Half Pay Commissions, 25th April 1825.
65. PP 1849 XXXII c 360.
66. Army List 1891.
67. This was the result of the 1881 reforms and the compulsory removal of Captains after twenty years and of Majors after twenty-seven years to clear the blockage of promotion. Many of these Adjutants' posts had been occupied by long-serving Captains and Majors, especially men promoted from the ranks, such as Henry Mackay, former Sergeant Major and Adjutant of the 79th, who became Adjutant of the Forfar and Kincardine Militia Artillery between 1855 and 1865. In 1881 ' . . . several score of Adjutants of the Auxiliary forces—upon an arbitrary limit of age suddenly fixed—were with only about a month's notice literally kicked out of their appointments and placed on a retired allowance of only a very few shillings a day . . .' An officer, *Fifteen Years of Army Reform, op. cit.*, p. 32.
68. Cpl. Frank MacFarlane, oral history archive, op. cit.
69. Ibid.
70. In 1892 the Wantage Committee proposed either to disband the Queen's Own Cameron Highlanders or to amalgamate them with the Guards. In a spirit of optimism but not necessarily of understanding they wrote, 'The above measure [amalgamation] would probably not be unacceptable to the Cameron Highlanders as it would give them increased pay and prolonged periods of home service. There would doubtless be difficulties of a personal character to overcome . . .' PP 1892 XIX c 6582 pp. 36-37.
71. Brian Bond, *The Victorian Army and the Staff College, 1854-1914* (London: 1972), p. 97, and p. 19.
72. PP 1854-55 XII c 317 pp. iii-26.
73. Major A.F. Mockler Ferryman, *The Annals of Sandhurst* (London: 1900), p. 89.
74. One of the major limiting factors on the numbers of officers attending the Senior Department was the regulation that when a regiment was on foreign service the officers of that regiment were not allowed to attend the Senior Department. This was a serious obstacle for the Highland regiments who spent such a long time abroad. PP 1854-55 XII c 317 p. 22 para. 473.
75. Lt. Gen. John Alexander Ewart, *The Story of a Soldier's Life, op.cit.*, p. 80.
76. In 1877 Lieutenant W. Prevost passed the Qualifying examination but could not attend because another 91st Officer had gained higher marks. *Army List 1877.* Evelyn Wood, of the 17th Lancers, had to exchange to the 73rd to get around this rule. Evelyn Wood, *From Midshipman to Field Marshal* (London: 1906), Vol. 1, p. 205.
77. GO Horse Guards 23.5.1860 No. 752.
78. Major General Lord Edward Gleichen, *A Guardsmans Memoirs, op. cit.*, p. 110.
79. Diary of General Sir Spencer Ewart, RH/4/84/1.
80. Ian B.M. Hamilton, *The Happy Warrior*, op. cit., p. 19. This is not in fact correct as in 1830 Captain John Browne of the 92nd was a student at the Royal Military College. WO/17/437.
81. Diary of General Sir Spencer Ewart, RH/4/84/1. 3.1.1882.
82. Army List 1876.
83. Army List 1877; 'p.s.c.' was introduced in the Army List of 1876.
84. *Historical Records of the Cameron Highlanders*, Vol. 2, p. 181, *op. cit*; Captain Souter was promoted for gallantry at Tel-el-Kebir.
85. Memoir of Captain Alex. D.L. Stewart MC of Achnacone, GHRM.
86. Under the Army reforms of 1881 it became possible to transfer as an Officer from a Militia to a Regular Commission. This, together with the clearly defined territorial districts, produced a substantial number of local landed Officers for the Regular Battalions. In due course, as the Volunteer Battalions were incorporated in the territorial local Regiments and adopted the same uniforms and designations, there developed the same sort of interchange between them and the line battalions. By

1914 the Highland Battalions probably had more local Officers and men than at any stage since their formation. The author has to thank Lt. Colonel A.A. Fairrie for this information.

87. *Officers of the Black Watch 1725-1952, op cit.* Many Highland officers were mixed up in other battalions, particularly those promoted from the ranks, but it was the sheer numbers of men killed that brought about a break in the chain of continuity that had been so prominent in Highland regiments. Of the officers of the 1st Battalion Black Watch who left Aldershot for France, for example, Major and Quarter Master Fowler MC was the only one who remained with the Battalion in 1918, and at the end of the war no officer of the 1st Battalion Queen's Own Cameron Highlanders was still with the Battalion from 1914.

88. General Sir Ian Hamilton, *The Soul and Body of an Army* (London: 1921), p. 78.

CHAPTER 5

The Character and Nature of Highland Officers

What, then, was the character of these officers of the Highland battalions, for studies of nationality and family background say little about what they were actually like. Many were intensely Scottish and proud of it, even though those who had spent their childhood in Scotland were often sent to England to 'unlearn their Scottish lingo'. While those who were Scots had accents, those accents would certainly not have been as pronounced or as regional as those of the men, and those Scots officers who went straight to their battalions prior to 1878 may well have had stronger Scottish accents than might even now be 'acceptable', although these would have been softened by lengthy periods abroad and the social pressures resulting from a number of English and Irish officers in the battalion.

With the development of the major English public schools and the growth of Victorian opinion as to how exactly a gentleman should speak and behave these accents began to disappear. In his letters Lieutenant Colonel Maule of the 79th often inserts a comment in the vernacular, which implies that he did not actually speak that way. These comments do not necessarily take the form of jibes and are often used in an endearing, almost complimentary, way which does not appear patronising.[1] This distinction in accents which seems to have developed in the last quarter of the nineteenth century into almost intolerance in some regiments (but not necessarily Highland regiments) could have set apart those commissioned from the ranks with a regional brogue, but it is difficult to say that as a result their careers were affected, because frequently several other factors were involved, such as financial resources, the nature of their commissions, their age and educational abilities.

An example is William McBean of the 93rd who was born in Inverness. He enlisted in the 93rd, was commissioned, commanded the Regiment and retired with the rank of honorary Major General. When he was dying in his lodgings in London in 1878, Surgeon Munro went to see him. Munro wrote of his visit:

> I found him in bed in a little room not 10 feet square at the very top of the house . . . . 'What ails you man?' (McBean replied), 'Ther's something gone wrang wi ma futt an' I've had a Doctor in to see it'.[2]

From this account it seems therefore that McBean spoke with an accent until his death and his promotional opportunities were not affected. Thus, as far as accents are concerned it would be wrong to draw too rigid conclusions, with social and class implications. Anglicised many of these officers may have been, but the figures show that in the Highland kilted battalions the majority were

Scots. An anglicised accent does not make an Englishman, and much depended upon contemporary fashion and social behaviour.[3]

Gaelic speakers were entirely another matter. Firstly, these would almost certainly have been restricted to the Scots officers, as learning Gaelic was extremely unlikely in the period 1820 to 1920: most people were unlearning the language at this time. Secondly, of the Scots officers, unless they came from the Highland area they would not have been native Gaelic speakers. For example, none of the Forfarshire/Perthshire-based officers of the 42nd of 1839 are likely to have spoken the language, and the same applies to the Lowlanders and the English. However, it could well be the case that men like Archibald Campbell of Glendaruel, Colin Campbell of South Hall, J. Cameron Macpherson of Cluny and George Duncan Robertson of Struan were amongst the native speakers. There is little evidence however that any officers in the Highland battalions used Gaelic in ordinary conversation or communication. Letters, diaries, order books, platoon notebooks are all in English, although Burgoyne records that Adjutant William McDonald of the 93rd drilled the Glengarry Militia in Gaelic in Canada in 1838,[4] and Goff asserts that in the 91st 'up to 1839 a squad was always drilled in Gaelic'.[5] While Gaelic-speaking officers were used in recruiting, the language was most prominent in song and verse.[6] As for other languages, Latin, French, Spanish and German also appear in many letters, memoirs and diaries and may well have been interjected in conversation. For those who served in India or Ceylon, Hindustani, Urdu or Tamil were sometimes officially learned, but more likely were used simply in everyday language to communicate with servants and tradesmen.[7]

Officers were accepted with speech defects, and a stammer was not uncommon, for example Lieutenant Scott of the 92nd about whom the Inspecting Officer remarked in 1847:

> Lt. Scott has at times a considerable impediment in his speech but he is in all other respects perfectly fit for the Service.[8]

Such an impediment must have been a serious drawback in the issuing of orders and at drill.

It is often imagined that Highland officers looked like the ideals portrayed in *The Gentleman's Monthly Magazine of Fashion and Costumes de Paris*,[9] with carefully groomed features, broad shoulders, narrow waists, a well-turned knee and almost feminine hands and feet. Photography was to prove a rude awakening and prints, sketches and oils produced in the period 1820 to around 1850 can only ever be considered as a guideline. Certainly Highland officers were, throughout the one hundred years under consideration, seriously dictated to by fashion as well as by the regulations in force.

Hair from the 1820s onwards always tended to be short, but not necessarily closely trimmed. In the 1830s and 1840s beards and moustaches were not worn, but bushy whiskers extending sometimes to the jawline were in fashion, together with a curl of hair brought forward across the temple in front of the ear. In 1854 permission was given for infantry officers to grow moustaches.

During the Crimean War, officers, like the men, dispensed with the razor and frequently wore full beards with the hair relatively long around the collar. With the popular development of photography at the time these men can be seen as they actually were, and the image is very different from the prints of a few years before. These photographs show men with much more rounded features, probably as a result of the contemporary diet and the quantities of alcohol taken, a feature particularly noticeable in photographs of other ranks. The uniforms are colourful and decorative but not very well fitting or immaculately pressed and clean. In any group of officers setts of tartans vary at this period, and it is obvious that these men did not concern themselves with some of the minutiae of dress regulations.

The beards, moustaches and more relaxed approach persisted amongst the officers of the Highland regiments through their service in the Mutiny and India after 1858. The 42nd did not return to Portsmouth until 1868, the 79th in 1871 and the 93rd in 1870. The 78th returned in 1859 and the 92nd in 1863.[10] Absence from contemporary European fashion and the prevailing climate would certainly have affected their appearance at this time.

Gradually through the 1870s and 1880 moustaches only were worn with the hair much thinned and shortened, frequently with a centre parting to accentuate a broad forehead, considered at the time a physical attribute. By Queen's Regulations, paragraph 60 of 1896, moustaches were made obligatory for all officers.

The wearing of the kilt by officers is a difficult question. It is often assumed that the kilt was worn to the exclusion of trousers in the kilted battalions, but this is certainly not the case. In the early part of the nineteenth century the kilt had, it seems, come to be considered as the poor man's dress, an interesting curiosity but not the dress of a gentleman or a man of means. Officers were happy to have their portraits painted and their photographs taken in the kilt, but were not required to wear it to the exclusion of trousers. This does not necessarily imply an anglicisation or lowlandisation of the Highland officer corps and may simply be a reflection of contemporary attitudes in fashion. Certainly tartan trews and, for mounted officers, tartan breeches, became an integral part of a Highland officer's dress, accompanied by complex regulations as to the various orders of dress for set occasions.[11] About 1820, an observer of Highland officers commented:

> I cannot help noticing an unaccountable practice in some Highland Regiments where the officers seldom appear in the Feile Beg except on field days and on particular occasions! . . . Having sometime since lived four or five years where the 78th were stationed I must exonerate that Corps from the above reflections, Officers and men always being dressed in proper regimentals.[12]

Colonel Cuming of the 79th wrote of his regiment in Ireland in 1846:

> The Officers seldom wore the kilt in those days and unless something exceptional took place it was only worn at half yearly inspections. The men wore it constantly, but it was some years after this time that it became at all general with the Officers. In

'marching order' the Officers wore the undress blue frock coat, trews, and forage cap, shoes and white gaiters.[13]

In the winter season in Canada, and sometimes in the heat of India or the West Indies, the kilt was abandoned by all ranks for practical purposes.[14] The popularity of the kilt in later years may be attributable to the effect on fashion of the Queen and Prince Albert who were openly enthusiastic about wearing the 'National Dress'. It became common for officers to possess 'mufti' (civilian) kilts, and at Chobham Camp in 1853, the first major exercise in the United Kingdom since the Napoleonic Wars, kilts were a prerequisite of entry to the Highland Gathering held there. Wedderburn noted in 1853, however:

> The Colonel spoke to me about wearing the mufti kilt, as he does not like it, so I shall now never appear out of uniform and if all goes well I hope to be soon out of this (would be) Highland Regt. which is ashamed seemingly of its dress, (at least the Officers are) . . . . I have been more disgusted today than I have been for an age . . .[15]

For duty and active service the kilt was retained, except for mounted officers, during the Afghan War, the Egyptian Campaign, the Sudan, the Tirah Campaign and the South African War. During the First World War, apart from field officers and transport men, the kilt was worn by all ranks, adapted to field conditions by the addition of a khaki apron.[16]

Height and physical proportions varied amongst officers and as has been seen in the case of Ensign Webster, it was possible to find an officer of a size and shape totally unsuitable for the physical demands of soldiering or alternatively the wearing of uniform, particularly the kilt. Colonel Cuming describes Webster's first parade:

> Webster was an excellent fellow, but so stout that he was quite a sight in his way; he was only nineteen years of age, but nearly twenty stone in weight. He was very handsome, not tall, about five feet nine. In walking he waddled along slowly, and he seldom mustered up a run. When he joined no one would believe he was a real Ensign gazetted, the whole appearance of the man was so utterly absurd. His first appearance in uniform was very trying and the shouts of laughter that greeted him as he waddled across the square in a tight jacket and trews to 'fall in' with a lot of thin and hungry-looking recruits must have been very galling, but he was possessed of a great good humour and was full of fun.[17]

Such physical proportions do not appear to have deterred officers from seeking commissions or from being accepted by the War Office. A notable example is Lieutenant General Frederick William Traill Burroughs of the 93rd, who inherited the island estate of Rousay, and who was probably under five feet in height.[18] In some interesting handwritten notes in a copy of Burgoyne's *Historical Records of the 93rd Sutherland Highlanders*, E.S. Wood, a fellow officer, wrote in the margin, 'Burrough—Little b He was a finicky little beggar having been educated abroad.[19] To the men Burroughs was known as 'wee Frenchie', and it seems he was extremely sensitive regarding his height, taking care to be seated when photographed in a group.[20]

A dark complexion in the latter part of the nineteenth century could also be a source of difficulties for a Highland officer. Wood writes of an officer he calls 'Baboo Middleton':

> This Baboo Middleton was a dark man, so dark and baba like that the Bank of Bengal would not employ him. Middleton was no doubt bullied by some of the 93rd and some of the Officers who so bullied him very nearly lost their Commissions. It was a foolish thing of his Mother and the Authorities to put him in a Highland Regiment when of course he looked absurd in the kilt.[21]

As regards general appearance, Maule was particularly scathing about some of his fellow officers in the 79th in 1836. He selects an officer who he calls 'Tom', probably Thomas Dundas, for special descriptive attention:

> Tom is my Sub [Subaltern] in the first Company. I can make nothing of this fellow. He looks like the ghost of a strolling player in deep meditation on the means of procuring a meal. He blushes like a boarding school Miss and after a dinner night might easily be mistaken for a runaway lamp post. . . . I must get rid of him before the summer for in the kilt I could compare him to nothing but a two legged tobacco pipe surmounted by a soap bubble.[22]

Artificial aids to a good appearance were not discounted and it is believed that Colonel Mackenzie of the 78th, who commanded the Regiment during its tour in Canada 1868-1871, wore a toupee and dyed his hair. Officers also studiously avoided having their photographs taken wearing spectacles, and even a monocle is unusual in Highland regiments. In the nature of things, some of these men must have had sight defects.

Dental health and appearance is very difficult to assess. Because the photographic process demanded a timed exposure of the wet plate, instant photographs were impossible. Hence there are few smiles and, most important of all, no open mouths. Indeed, an open mouth was considered a 'yokel' characteristic. Several officers complain however of toothache, Wedderburn for example on the 3rd April 1851: 'Had beastly toothache all day'. Eventually on the 2nd June he could stand it no longer:

> I had such toothache this mg (morning) that I turned dentist and lugged the villain out excepting a little bit which will follow one of these days.[23]

When Captain, later Colonel, A.S. Leith Hay of the 93rd suffered from toothache in Montreal in September 1844 he did not have Wedderburn's courage to turn dentist and an Indian made him fill his mouth three times with coarse salt, and he then 'put an nail in the ground to take the pain away'. Leith Hay was extremely surprised when the remedy seemed to work.[24]

Several officers lost arms or eyes during their service, a handicap that did not incapacitate them or prevent them from continuing to serve. John Alexander Ewart, for example, had his left arm shattered by round shot during the Indian Mutiny and the arm had to be amputated. He was invalided home, exchanged to the 78th and took command of that Regiment in 1858. In 1877 he commanded the Allahabad Division and was afterwards appointed Colonel of the 92nd and the 93rd.[25] General Sir Ian Hamilton of the 92nd had his left wrist broken at Majuba by a Boer bullet:

> . . . the hand always remained a pathetic but neatly manicured wreck. Between the withered fingers he could hold a letter or a cigarette, but for all practical purposes it remained useless.[26]

Extensive periods of foreign service in the heat of India or the West Indies, or in the intense cold of Canada, coupled with a badly balanced diet and an excess of alcohol, could leave officers with prematurely grey hair and heavily marked complexions, the sun and smallpox all playing their part. Few of these characteristics are evident before the advent of photography.[27]

How often or how much these men washed is unknown. In barracks their facilities were no better than those of the men during the period 1820 to c.1860, in that there was seldom any form of running water except for a pump which might not be situated inside the barrack wall. Officers usually purchased a wash stand with their equipment, but washing the whole body in warm fresh water with soap was probably rare. In foreign stations, particularly the West Indies, South Africa, Malta and India bathing was popular in the sea or in water 'tanks'. Washing hair or having a bath is very seldom mentioned, and as a result hair looks dull unkempt and these men must have had a personal smell that would be totally unacceptable in modern society, conditioned to deodorants and high-quality soaps.

In field conditions and, it is suspected, in the rigours of the Canadian winter, officers simply did not take their clothes off. In the Crimea during the winter of 1853-1854 John Cheetham McLeod of the 42nd took off his shoes each night, but did not actually remove his clothes for eight months between September 1853 and April 1854.[28] There is no reason to suppose that he was unique, and in such circumstances lice must have been common. J.A. Ewart of the 93rd records in the Crimea in January 1855:

> It was difficult to wash, on account of the frost, both sponge and towel being like pieces of wood; the water in my tent being generally hard frozen. What caused me more annoyance, and certainly more loss of blood than the Russian guns, were the fleas, which literally swarmed in the trenches.[29]

As standards of personal hygiene, barrack conditions and cosmetic preparations improved, so too did the physical appearance of officers. There are many officers from the 1870s onwards who are outstandingly handsome and most are immaculately groomed. The photographs, particularly in the 1890s and 1900s, show tall, fit, clean, good-looking, well turned out men with a personal assurance about them that has none of the rough edges of the earlier period, and whose appearance is undoubtedly enhanced by the beautifully tailored and high-quality uniforms and a well worn kilt (i.e. a kilt put on correctly). This appearance is partially the result of the groupings of the photographs themselves and also the quality and cleanliness of the uniforms.

During active service in India, Egypt, South Africa and in the First World War, uniforms and cleanliness were quickly adapted to local conditions and the availability of washing facilities, water and clothing replacements. Even khaki, once impregnated with mud, was almost impossible to keep clean and kilts were ruined by constant saturation in water and slime. Officers, after the first few months in 1914, took to wearing Other Ranks' tunics to prevent themselves being the target of snipers, and baths although available were still considered a luxury.[30]

The accent and appearance of officers varied widely in Highland regiments and in many cases did not conform to the projected ideal. A more intangible consideration was that of being a 'gentleman'. As the meaning of the word seems to have changed to include a man's background and financial situation as well as his moral conduct and bearing, it is difficult indeed to pin down the term 'gentleman'. It is seldom mentioned or defined by Highland officers of the period 1820 to 1920, and it appears to have derived from a combination of birth and a code of unwritten conduct that was acceptable at any one time amongst the officers of a regiment. Thus in 1839 Lieutenant Andrew Agnew of Lochnaw of the 93rd wrote:

> . . . this [the 93rd] . . . is in point of society, among ourselves, a very second rate Corps . . . of course I except two or three, Aylmer, Buchanan and one or two others who are as nice gentlemanlike fellows as ever breathed (I am writing in strict confidence pray, let no one but my Mother see this) but Spark (Lt. Col. Spark the Commanding Officer) was not *born* a gentleman and there is a certain breeding necessary, particularly to a Commanding Officer — neither was Arthur and you cannot fancy how disagreeable it is doing duty under either. Though composed of rather odd material, MacGregor's (Lt. Col. Duncan MacGregor's) high principles and thorough gentlemanlike bearing kept us together pretty well, but now we have a sad reverse.[31]

Agnew was in fact at this time short of money, fed up with Canada and anxious to get his Company, all of which factors may have affected his attitude to Lt. Colonel Spark, but in this letter he does bring out the important point that although a man was not born 'a gentleman', he could by bearing and manners acquire the necessary attributes and that land, title or money were not essential prerequisites.

Thus the acceptance of men from the ranks was possible: men like Cruikshanks of the 79th, Wheately of the 42nd, William McBean who commanded the 93rd and Gilbert Gunn and Alexander Yeadon of the Camerons. These men were greatly respected and their humble origins did not prevent them from being completely accepted as gentlemen. Frank Richards, the only private soldier known to have published a study of life in the ranks in India before the First World War, notes that in his Battalion, the Royal Welch Fusiliers, the Quartermaster commissioned from the ranks ' . . . did not on that account regularly dine at the Officers Mess. He was merely invited once a week on guest night'.[32]

There is no indication that this practice took place in Highland regiments. Colonel Cuming remembers in 1847:

> Quartermaster Alexander Crookshanks (sic), or 'Auld Crooky' as he was called was the last of these grand soldiers who, in the 79th, had fought in the Peninsula and Waterloo. All the rest had passed away by death, discharge or to pension. He had been forty years in the Regiment, and had served in most of the actions in Spain and finally at Waterloo. He was a fine old man and very interesting to talk to. He delighted in dining at Mess and always sat amongst the youngsters. He used to tell us any amount of stories of his younger days . . . What stirring tales he told us of incidents at Fuentes d'Onor, Salamanca, Toulouse, Waterloo and the occupation of Paris. He was a hard featured old fellow, but had always a kindly pleasant smile on his face.[33]

While many of these men commissioned from the ranks may have stayed away from Mess because they either had quarters assigned to them consequent upon their jobs or because they were married, any suggestion that they were only invited on formal occasions is flatly denied by both Frank MacFarlane of the 1st Battalion the Black Watch[34] and Major Dan Bonar of the 2nd Battalion the Highland Light Infantry (the 74th).[35] Major Bonar is particularly adamant on this point and emphasises that the officers of the 74th were too well mannered to even think of such discrimination.

An aspect of the term 'gentleman' which is relevant to the officers of the Highland battalions is the Highland character itself. In a hostile and isolated environment and in a country with a relatively small population where people know one another, innate good manners, hospitality and pride were held in greater store than any wealth or title. In this sense the term 'gentleman' in Highland society had no social bounds and had no implications of class.

The qualities of loyalty and bravery were not defined or expanded upon by Highland officers. They were expected, almost taken for granted. Loyalty was often of a more general character than merely to the Regiment. It implied loyalty particularly to the Monarch and especially to Queen Victoria, who quite openly regarded the Army as 'Hers' and took an extraordinary personal interest in individual regiments and Officers.[36] The feeling was certainly reciprocated, and whatever might have been their personal differences or political opinions, officers were in no doubt as to where their personal allegiances lay. On Queen Victoria's Jubilee the *79th News* summed up the opinion of all ranks when it was stated, 'We can thank our God that we have a Queen to whom it is so easy to be loyal'.[37]

Many officers also became deeply attached to their men and to their regiments and were not afraid of showing their affections in this respect. Lieutenant Agnew relates of the departure of Lieutenant Colonel Duncan MacGregor from the 93rd:

> Never did a Commanding Officer leave a Corps more justly beloved and admired . . . . We had a grand dinner the day before he left us . . . when we sat down there were several white handkerchiefs in requisition . . .[38]

Amongst them was MacGregor's handkerchief, and according to Agnew, MacGregor wept quite openly at leaving his beloved Regiment.

Indicative of these scenes of parting and of regimental Highland loyalty is the farewell speech of Sir Colin Campbell to the Highland Brigade in the

Crimea. It is not only a fine piece of prose, but it also brings out the affection, loyalty and emotion which the Highland battalions generated:

> Soldiers of the 42nd, 79th and 93rd! old Highland Brigade; with whom I passed the early and perilous part of this war, I have now to take leave of you: in a few hours I shall be on board ship, never to see you again as a body — a long farewell! I am now old and shall not be called to serve any more, and nothing will remain to me but the memory of my campaigns and of the enduring, hardy, generous soldiers with whom I have been associated, whose name and glory will long be kept alive in the hearts of our countrymen. When you go home, as you gradually fulfill your term of service, each to his family and his cottage, and you tell the story of your immortal advance in that victorious echelon up the heights of Alma and of the old Brigadier who led you, and loved you so well, your children and your children's children will repeat the tale to other generations, when only a few lines of history will remain to record the discipline and enthusiasm which have borne you so stoutly to the end of this war. Our native land will never forget the name of the Highland Brigade, and in some future war the nation will call for another one to equal this, which it can never surpass. Though I shall be gone, the thought of you will go with me wherever I shall be, and cheer my old age with a glorious recollection of dangers confronted and hardships endured: a pipe will never sound near me without carrying me back to these bright days when I was at your head, and wore the bonnet you gained for me, and the honourable decorations on my breast, many of which I owe to your conduct. Brave soldiers! Kind comrades! Farewell![39]

Surgeon Munro recalls leaving the 91st at Dover in 1850:

> That I was no longer an Officer of the 91st was a positive grief to me. Next day I dined at Mess as a guest. After dinner my late brother Officers drank my health, wished me God speed and each presented me with some little token of remembrance. As I took leave the Officers accompanied me to the barrack gate, dear old Dalrymple walking on one side of me and Patterson on the other, while the Band followed playing 'Auld Lang Syne'.[40]

These men too were certainly brave. In modern terms their leadership training was negligible, even in 1920, but they knew exactly what was expected of them, and at battalion level, in battle and under appalling conditions, they displayed a courage that is unteachable. Often an officer who was not held in great regard by his men would appear at his best in these circumstances. Robert Sinclair, a soldier of the 93rd, wrote of Lt. Colonel Ainslie at the Battle of the Alma in 1854:

> He rode in our front during the whole action and when he saw some of the men wavering under the tremendous fire he strove to animate them with courage and in his whole conduct displayed a noble example of fortitude, coolness and presence of mind . . . his actions bespoke him to be the true soldier as well as the gentleman. I never had any particular regard for him until that day . . . I had formed the idea that he was a very proud and distant gentleman but . . . no soldier who had had the opportunity of seeing him could ever think of him with any other feeling but that of pride to say that he belonged to the same Army as himself.[41]

At the Battle of Langemark, on 22nd October 1914, Captain John Orr of the 1st Battalion the Queen's Own Cameron Highlanders found himself outnumbered and isolated with no hope of reinforcements or support and so, with three men of his Company, he charged into the advancing Germans and was never seen again.[42] Their act was not rash, or ill conceived on Orr's part, merely brave, and it epitomises the self-sacrifice and cool courage of these men, without show, publicity or ostentation, following what they believed to be the responsibilities of a Highland officer.

Such expectations and responsibilities in respect of their conduct under fire were taken extremely seriously by officers, for failure in such circumstances reflected upon themselves and their regiments. The resulting pressure could be intense and could bring about bitter and unnecessary recriminations when officers, overcome sometimes by circumstances far beyond their control, failed to come up to expectation in battle. As there was little general or even medical understanding of stress-related behaviour, the stigma of breakdown or evacuation with what came to be known as 'shell shock' was deeply felt, and few regimental historians will name officers so affected or state exactly what happened to them and how they broke down. The general impression is that death is easier to record than a display of fear, or failure by an officer to take the kind of action which in hindsight seems all too obvious. Such omission has led to considerable suspicion falling on numerous regimental histories as to their veracity. The idea that all Highland officers must be handsome *and* brave was in point of fact an unrealistic burden to place on these men who, after all, were, in the final analysis, only human.

Thus a good deal of time and effort was taken up in exonerating officers at Majuba, where three Companies of the 92nd were present:

> . . . after the disaster there was a great deal of heart burning, one regiment blamed the other, a fierce controversy as to 'who ran first? Did anyone see anyone run?' etc.[43]

After Tamai on the 13th March 1884 the 1st Battalion Black Watch were taunted with the cry of 'Broken Squares'.[44] The surrender of the 1st Battalion Gordon Highlanders in 1914 led ultimately to an action in the Court of Session for slander and damages.[45]

While a great deal is made of these kind of events to 'prick the bubble' and break the myth of the Highland regiments and their officers, it must be kept in mind that, as Lord Saltoun wrote in 1978 of the Gordons' surrender, ' . . . it's very easy to be critical in an armchair',[46] and when placed in perspective these events are simply unable to overshadow hundreds of chronicled incidents of dogged perserverance and personal self-sacrifice.

It would be wrong to assume, however, that Highland officers lived in their battalions in harmony all the time, for they certainly did not. Particularly in the first half of the nineteenth century, many officers were forceful and forthright martinets who were not averse to freely expressing their opinions on others, especially their fellow officers. This is partly attributable to the pressures induced by the purchase system and financial considerations, partly contemporary behaviour and partly the result of the heavy drinking which also pervaded society at large.

It is evident that prior to the Crimean War officers of intelligence and ability were seriously under-employed. They were young, active and in search of adventure and challenge, and although they were often fully employed in running their companies and the operation of the battalion day-to-day, there was very little opportunity for them to expand upon their military knowledge or training. Before the exercise at Chobham in 1853, in which the 42nd, 79th and 93rd took part, there had been no major military exercise in the United Kingdom since the Napoleonic Wars. Although the 93rd saw 'action' in Canada during the Rebellion in 1839, none of the kilted Highland battalions saw a major battle between 1815 and 1854. What they did perform were strenuous and difficult duties in aid of the civil power in Ireland, in Scotland and in the Midland industrial towns, together with extensive periods in Canada, Gibraltar, South Africa and the West Indies. Only the 78th were in India between 1820 and 1856 where they lost heavily from cholera.

It is often argued that officers must indeed have had an idle, boring life, but the boredom was in the quality not the quantity of work in many cases. Life was largely governed by the extent of daylight hours and the climate. In the absence of telephones, electric light, air conditioning and motorised transport everything took a great deal longer to do. Ledgers, roll books and accounts all had to be painstakingly written out by hand and checked without the aid of calculators. In every station there were guard duties, convict guards, inspections, drills, ball practice, courts martial and boards of inquiry. J.W. Wedderburn noted on 6th May 1848:

> I was in orders for a Commissariat Board at 11 o'clock. I had therefore to wait in no very good humour 'till that hour to inspect candles (a most gentlemanlike employment truly . . .) . . . .[47]

Moving from station to station meant marching there with hired horses and carts, when the regiment, its women, children, officers, men, horses and belongings would all take to the road. There were in addition work parties to supervise and pay, for much military labour was used in building fortifications, roads and wharfs.

While a great deal of work was left in the hands of the senior NCOs, particularly the Sergeant Major, an officer's life was by no means the round of idleness that is often portrayed. For intelligent men, however, the duties must have been very monotonous, and as many remained unmarried until they were at least senior Captains, their society came largely from within their own number. Between fifteen and thirty officers living closely together under such circumstances could, and did, generate friction.

There were sometimes, but not often, open and abusive arguments such as that which took place in 1824 in the public gallery of Stone Barracks, St. Ann's Garrison, Barbados, outside the Officers' Billiard Room of the 93rd. Two officers of the 35th were primarily involved, shouting abuse at each other, but it is evident from the court martial report that officers of the 93rd were also present and may have taken part.[48] In Jamaica, in the same year, there was a serious altercation between Captain Warren and Ensign Wilton, both of the 92nd. When the dispute was investigated, sworn statements were taken from officers and it was subsequently found that some of these did not entirely comply with the truth. As a result Paymaster James Hope Johnston was severely reprimanded. Warren was dismissed the Service, and it seems that Quartermaster Daniel Callagy was dismissed also.[49]

It is difficult to untangle some of the apparent trivia in such cases and establish the grounds for accusations and stories. For example, in December 1824 and January 1825 two officers of the 91st were court martialed at Up Park Camp, Jamaica on the charge of conduct unbecoming the character of an officer and a gentleman. The two officers, Captain T. O'Doherty and Lieutenant T.G. McIntyre, had made public statements to the effect that an Ensign had thrown a glass of wine in the Commanding Officer's face and that the latter had taken no action except to reprimand the Ensign on parade next morning. O'Doherty was found guilty and dismissed and McIntyre was severely reprimanded.[50] The incident may now appear confusing and trivial; at the time it was obviously of great moment, especially to O'Doherty who lost his commission, but it does show an underlying uneasiness and lack of harmony, all of which may have been induced by a combination of stress, heat, alcohol, isolation and fear of disease.

When a senior officer was unpopular, it was not merely a case of 'soldiering on' until he moved to another posting in two years' time. As we have seen, strangers could buy their way into a Highland regiment and stay for as long as they wished. For the *in situ* officer, fond of his regiment and not wishing to exchange, there was considerable temptation to make the superior officer feel unwanted and to openly express that opinion by argument or action. The open and extremely hostile disputes between Bertie Gordon and Lieutenant Colonel M.G.T. Lindsay of the 91st are legendary.

Lieutenant Colonel Martin George Thomas Lindsay commanded the 91st from 1842 to 1848. He was neither popular nor efficient. He had purchased into the 91st from the 78th and commanded at a time when the 91st were undertaking difficult and trying duties in Cape Colony. The Regiment was broken up into detachments at isolated frontier posts together with a number of men on St. Helena. In 1842 a Reserve Battalion was formed and both Battalions took part in the Kaffir War of 1846-47 which involved a series of abrupt and bloody skirmishes, long and dangerous marches either on foot or in ponderous ox-drawn wagons and months in outlying forts and frontier stations, seldom more than broken-down cabins or huts, frequently roofless, without even the most basic of facilities.

Bertie Edward Murray Gordon was astute, eloquent, efficient, totally dedicated to the 91st and extremely abrasive. The conflict between these two men started right from the beginning of their relationship when they sailed together from Kingston, near Dublin, on 2nd June 1842 on board the transport ship the *Abercrombie Robinson*. During the voyage to the Cape several men died of typhus and one man was lost overboard. The ship arrived off Table Bay on 25th August; on the 27th Lieutenant Colonel Lindsay disembarked and most of the other Officers were allowed ashore, leaving Gordon in command of the soldiers, women and children on board. During the night of the 27th a gale blew up and in the early hours of the 28th the starboard and port cables snapped and the ship was driven towards the shore by the wind and the huge rollers. Amidst a terrible storm of thunder and lightning the *Abercrombie Robinson* grounded and at daybreak one of the ship's cutters managed to get through the surf to the beach with a cable. Surf boats were brought to the shore and Gordon issued orders for evacuation as the ship gradually broke up.

The surf boats took off the women and children, the invalids and some of the men who had drawn lots for their places, but at 10.30 a.m. on the morning of the 28th these boats were called away to assist the convict ship *Waterloo*, also grounded and breaking up in the storm. Gordon maintained calm with the able assistance of Acting Sergeant Major Murphy, Colour Sergeant Phillips and Sergeant Murray amongst others and eventually effected evacuation of 450 men using one cutter. The men took their arms and accoutrements; the knapsacks, regimental possessions and regimental stores were all lost. Fifteen men of the 99th Regiment, fourteen sailors, four women, fourteen children and 143 convicts died aboard the *Waterloo*, but not one single life was lost from the *Abercrombie Robinson*.[51]

If there had been any dispute between Lindsay and Gordon on the voyage out, it is not recorded. However a bitter argument started shortly afterwards. Gordon discovered that Lindsay had sent no adequate account of the wreck to Horse Guards and was not prepared to give Gordon or his subordinates any credit for their conduct in saving the lives of all on board. Instead Gordon was sent to an isolated post at Fort Cradock, beyond the Fish River, which comprised a roofless building with no barrack furniture, no fires, no medical arrangements and no cooking equipment, apart from what the men carried with them. Gordon requisitioned for stores:

> 'I am by no means satisfied', he wrote, 'that the dry flooring upon which ⅓ of the detachment will have to spread their palliasses, in rooms without fireplaces, may not be productive of sickness in the approaching cold of this season.'

He went on to order:

8 Tables for soldiers rooms
4 Tables for Sergeants rooms
9 Forms for soldiers rooms
9 Hair Brooms
6 Mops
6 Scrubbing Brushes
4 Stools for Sergeants Rooms
1 Table for Guard Room
1 Form for Guard Room

1 Table for Defaulters Room
1 Form for Do.
4 Large Black iron (sic) for kitchens[52]

In early May the roof of the building was still unfinished and men were falling sick.[53] Gordon asked for clothing for the men and cooking utensils:[54]

> The camp kettles brought here by the Detachment under my Command and which have been in use for three months are beginning to wear out and will soon be unfit for cooking in.[55]

Eventually the furniture arrived in mid-May. Ordered to march the fifty miles to Fort Beaufort later in the same month, he was unable to do so because the Commissary Clerk could not produce the cattle and waggons due to cattle disease.[56] After marching for four days Gordon reached the Fort, only to receive a critical letter from Lindsay regarding his requisition for his unsheltered detachment.[57] Acrimonious letters persisted from Lindsay regarding requisitions, in reply to which, and several other niggling enquiries, Gordon remained remarkably restrained.

Gordon however became extremely annoyed when his Cradock detachment was charged £15 Barrack Damages, and he wrote to Lindsay:

> The sum of £15 charged against the Cradock detachment for what was falsely described as dammages by the proprietor of the half finished and unwholesome tenement in which they were lodged for six weeks, but which was in reality only fair wear and tear . . . from the senior sergeant down to the youngest soldier is felt to be a heavy and most unjust grievance . . . [58]

Gordon's apparent siding with his men in this instance cannot have helped at all, but Gordon could not contain his anger when Lindsay wrote to him in late October 1843:

> Lt. Col. Lindsay requests to be informed what steps have been or are intended to be taken to settle the accounts of the Transport Mess [i.e. the Mess aboard the Abercrombie Robinson] by the Committee appointed in [the] Cape for that purpose?[59]

Having lost nearly all his possessions and almost his life in the wreck of the *Abercrombie Robinson*, Bertie Gordon was indeed angry:[60]

> . . . Lt. Col. Lindsay charges me with having failed to prefer a claim against the estate of the late Major Ducat and also with having failed to collect certain sums due . . . At a meeting of certain Officers of the Regiment . . . which was summoned yesterday by Lt. Col. Lindsay I was expressly and publicly told by Lt. Col. Lindsay that it was my duty to collect the money referred to—that the responsibility for the deficiency of £248.19.9. which has been owing to certain tradesmen in Dublin for stock supplied to the transport Mess nearly 18 months ago was on my shoulders . . .
>
> Feeling deeply aggrieved by charges of this nature I beg to request that . . . all the circumstances connected with the non payment be laid before his honour the Col.

> Commanding . . . to ascertain whether I am justly chargable with the failure of duty which Lt. Colonel Lindsay has affixed to me.[61]

Lindsay refused and Gordon thereupon refused to co-operate with the Committee. Eventually, in February 1844, the matter reached the Commander-in-Chief who closed ranks with Lindsay against the outraged Captain:

> The C in C considers the whole thing an internal matter . . . [he recommended that the matter be brought to] . . . a satisfactory settlement and thus free the Corps from the unfavourable impression left by the whole character of the correspondence . . . . His Excellency is nevertheless strong in his determination to bring any Officer to a Court Martial whom Colonel Lindsay shall report to him as refusing to obey his orders, or whose conduct towards him shall evince a spirit to resist his authority, or to refuse him that support to which he is entitled.[62]

By the 17th March Bertie Gordon was applying for sick leave and by April he was on board the transport *Sir Charles Napier* on his way home. In 1845 Lindsay closed down the Officers' Mess of the 91st.

Once at home Gordon had a distinct advantage. On 5th August 1844 he submitted direct to the Duke of Wellington his full report on the wreck of the *Abercrombie Robinson*, the details of which seem to have been unknown, presumably because Lindsay had been careful not to praise or bring attention to his rebellious Captain. Wellington wrote on the report:

> I have never read anything so satisfactory as this report. It is highly creditable not only to Captain Bertie Gordon and the Officers and troops concerned, but to the service in which such an instance has occurred of discretion and firmness in an Officer in command, and of confidence, good order, discipline and obedience in all under his command even to the women and children. I wish that I had received this statement after this misfortune had occurred.[63]

Nevertheless, Lindsay retained command of the 91st and Bertie Gordon was employed as Brigade Major at Chester. Finally, in 1848, Gordon achieved satisfaction. The Annual Inspection Report of the 91st for that year is remarkable in its outspoken criticism. Major General Lord Fitzclarence noted dirty barracks, dirty arms and the fact that ' . . . due attention has not been paid to the cleanliness and comfort of the men's messing'. The Regimental Books were badly kept and Colonel Lindsay commanded without 'zeal or ability'. The musicians could 'hardly play at all' and Fitzclarence summed up:

> I certainly never saw any Regt. in HM Service appear so slovenly under arms and what astounded me mostly was the apparent want of knowledge of Lt. Col. Lindsay to rectify all these errors.[64]

Originally attached to his report was a confidential report on Lindsay which is now missing. Later in 1848 Lindsay retired and Gordon returned to the Regiment, ultimately to command.

The whole episode demonstrates the depth and intensity of the personal differences which could occur between officers and how these differences could spill over into public arguments. It also illustrates the extraordinary difficulties under which officers worked in outlying posts and how ultimately inefficiency was not tolerated, even at this early date, when it is often assumed that the Army in general was at its lowest ebb.[65]

Lesser internal arguments were also common, and it is obvious that factions amongst the officers of Highland regiments were frequent. Agnew of the 93rd for example refers to:

> . . . internal arguement having cemented more firmly a little band of brothers; Haliday, Buchanan, Trevelyan and myself and one or two others . . .[66]

Wedderburn's differences with Cumberland brought him closer to men like McLeod, Hay, Chisholm and Archie Campbell. In general these arguments were transitory and all would sit down at Mess and enjoy a convivial evening, or dance reels or race or hunt together, when minor differences seem to have been forgotten.

In the Crimea there occurred a special relationship between officers that can only come from hard work and dangers shared. The feeling continued through the Mutiny when Officers united to face the common enemies of the mutineers, the heat and disease; few personal disputes are recorded at this time. After the Battle of the Alma, Surgeon Munro records:

> We all knew that we had fought and won a great battle . . . the thought in everybody's mind and the words on every lip were, 'What will they say at home? and will they think that we have done our duty? . . . Friends shook each other by the hand as if they had first met after long years of separation.[67]

However, after the storming of the Sikandarbagh at Lucknow in 1857, a great argument took place amongst the officers of the 93rd as to who was 'first through the breach', and who therefore considered themselves entitled to the Victoria Cross. The honour was claimed by F.W. Traill Burroughs amongst others, and he cherished a lifelong grievance that his claim was not recognised. It is interesting that when Sir Colin Campbell decided that three Victoria Crosses were to be awarded to the Regiment, to be determined by the votes of the officers, the NCOs and the private men in their turn, the officers voted for Captain Stewart in preference to Burroughs and Ewart, Stewart being 'a popular figure in the regiment'.[68]

The kind of division which Hamilton experienced in the 92nd with regard to ambition and personal advancement was probably not unusual in the 1870s, although it is clear that by this time there was a much greater and more complex mental and physical challenge to officers. Many of the differences between officers were also submerged in the extensive growth of Victorian Highland regimental pride, which resulted in arguments being 'kept in the family' and carefully omitted from regimental records. Nevertheless pressures were still there. Second Lieutenant the Hon. S. Fraser, a Militia Officer of the 3rd Battalion Gordon Highlanders, remembers joining the 1st Gordons at the outbreak of war in 1914, when two officers of each Regular Battalion were exchanged with two Militia Officers to try to ensure continuity of standards and procedures:

> Neither Hay nor I were precisely popular because it was explained to us that everyone resented the loss of the two comrades who had been left for the 3rd Battalion. However we tried by modesty and zeal to dissipate; and were careful, as instructed not to venture to acknowledge the private soldier's salute unless indisputably alone.[69]

Getting rid of an officer was not always exclusively a command decision, and prior to the abolition of purchase it could not always be achieved easily. If an officer was unsuitable, unacceptable or unpopular, it was not merely a case of posting him elsewhere as might be the case nowadays. An officer before 1871 purchased his commission in a specific regiment, for a specific rank, and he could therefore be sent to the depot or on a detachment of the regiment, but he could not be moved out without his consent, unless for disciplinary reasons. As a result internal pressures were brought to bear upon such an officer, which seem in many cases to have been none too subtle. Men like Maule of the 79th were blunt to the point of rudeness, and every officer that he mentions in his letters that he intends to get rid of, soon goes. If 'Tom', referred to by Maule as the 'two legged tobacco pipe surmounted by a soap bubble', is in fact Thomas Dundas, then he exchanged to the 22nd Regiment in 1841. Maule quite openly writes, 'I have got rid of Isham and now want to exchange one or two more . . .' But Maule admits:

> Skene is a vulgar devil wh(o) has deep roots and will be troublesome to eradicate. There are one or two more I would like to pull up and out.[70]

Exchange was in reality a highly unsatisfactory solution, for it meant that the useless officer merely became a burden on another regiment. The Commanding Officer of the 78th wrote to General Sir John Wilson from Trincomalee, Ceylon on 18th April 1833:

> We have a last got rid of Mr. Wingate, but had I entertained the least idea that he would have remained in the Service after giving in his resignation I would have made a much stronger case against him. The Queen's have him now, but it is lamentable . . . [that] . . . a worthless fellow should be retained . . . when truth and even common honesty in his dealings are strangers.[71]

Maule would dearly have loved to get rid of Buchanan whose dissipation resulted in his contracting syphilis and gonorrhoea as well as having considerable debt in the Regiment, but while he had sufficient evidence to court martial him, this was avoided to prevent disgrace falling on the Regiment and Buchanan's family.[72] There were therefore official and social boundaries within which the system of removal had to operate.

Excessive internal chaffing and pressure on an officer could lead to severe repercussions as recorded by E.S. Wood in the case of 'Baboo Middleton', who was 'bullied' by his fellow officers of the 93rd on account of his colour. While Wood does not enlarge upon the trouble these officers got into, there may well have been a specific incident and an internal inquiry.[73]

It is known that 'Subalterns' Courts' took place in the Victorian and Edwardian Army, where an Officer would be 'tried' by a mock 'court' of his fellow officers for an alleged 'offence' which might have comprised breaking the acceptable code of conduct. Sometimes the proceedings were conducted in pantomime fashion, with slapstick, costumes, gales of laughter or just plain fun as Spencer Ewart of the 79th records of the 'trial' of Captain Roderick W. Macleod of Cadboll and Invergordon in Egypt in 1883. Macleod had legitimately gone on leave after Tel el Kebir but his fellow officers were very jealous of his ability to pay the £30 passage money, and on his return to the Regiment he was seized and tried,

> . . . on a charge of absenting himself from the Regiment without due cause for seven months thereby causing his brother Officers to do his duty. He was sentenced to stand champagne to the Captains and Subalterns of the Regiment at Mess for two nights.[74]

Sometimes however the proceedings were more serious and had unpleasant results. In 1911 four Subalterns joined the 2nd Battalion Gordon Highlanders in India, Findlay, Dobie, Graham and Cochrane. For some reason these four had great difficulty fitting into the life of the Regiment. Described by A.D. Greenhill Gardyne, the Senior Subaltern, as 'four rather extra awful people', who needed 'very strong instructions in the simplest facts of good manners', it was Findlay and Graham who were eventually tried by their fellow Subalterns late in the evening after a guest night in Mess. Whatever the original intention had been of this 'trial', it went seriously wrong when Findlay's mother wrote a letter of complaint to the War Office. Undoubtedly in an unhappy situation and probably under some pressure, Findlay then absented himself from the Regiment and had to be brought back to the Battalion at Lucknow for the Enquiry. This Enquiry finally concluded in May 1912 that there had been a 'misunderstanding of intention' on Findlay's part. Greenhill Gardyne as Senior Subaltern received a reprimand over the incident, but shortly after it was discovered that Findlay's evidence had not been entirely balanced and he was re-arrested with the possibility of a court martial. This was however set aside and Findlay was given a further six months' extra trial with the Regiment before he finally sent in his papers in August 1912. Undoubtedly smarting from his reprimand, in the tense atmosphere generated by this whole unpleasant incident Greenhill Gardyne parted from Findlay with bitter words.[76] It must indeed have been an unhappy time in the Battalion.

How many such 'courts' of this nature there were and when they took place is unknown, but this particular case does illustrate the problem. If a group of people are living together in an organised and disciplined society and one of their number does not conform to the group mores, but at the same time does not actually commit a breach of discipline, it is only human nature that the remainder of the group should exert pressure on the dissenting individual to conform. Exerting such pressure does not necessarily put the majority in the wrong, for the dissenter might be entirely unheeding of tactful or more gentle indications of how he should behave and unable to appreciate that for the benefit of the majority he should either conform or leave.

In spite of these differences between officers, many of which were the result of contemporary manners, Highland officers express deep respect and affection for many of their comrades. Their communal life under difficult circumstances bred a particular affinity that lasted even after they left the service, an affinity that is often understood with difficulty by those who have not actually served in a Highland regiment. Some of that feeling is reflected in Colonel Cuming's description of his fellow officers. Here he is not only recording the facts, but he projects part of the character of the men, accepting their good and bad points and emphasising their individuality, for although there were good officers and bad officers in Highland regiments, as in any other, Highland officers were certainly not characterless, their foibles and attributes all contributing to the folklore of the regiments.

Among the officers of the 79th described by Colonel Cuming in Quebec in 1848 were:

> Captain . . . Sir Richard Taylor, who was a most popular man in the Regiment, a jovial Irishman, fond of society, and great in a social point of view; his beaming face at a big dinner party was an institution in itself; he was the life and soul of the Mess, the more the wine went round and the longer we sat, the more his cheeks shone with good humour and enjoyment, but never on the 'wettest' of nights did I see him overtaken. This speaks volumes for his head, as I don't think he ever shirked his liquor.
>
> Captain Reeve was open, hearty and generous. He was not clever, and was therefore a 'butt' for the humorist. He was slow to take in a joke; when others laughed, Jock Reeve was pondering, but sometime after he would burst out into hearty roars for no apparent reason, but his intimates knew that he had at last mastered the point of the joke whatever it might be. He was my Captain for a couple of years, and a kinder or better fellow I never knew. He was a fine handsome fellow, over six feet, and looked grand in the kilt. He was very popular and deservedly so, being a thorough gentleman.
>
> Captain Andrew Hunt— 'Andy' as he was familiarly called. I shall have much to say of him hereafter, as I served many years in his Company. He drank hard at times, and during the intervals was as sober as a judge; then he was much shocked at seeing others in the condition. He was terribly wild in his habits, an excellent dancer, very handsome and exceedingly popular with the other sex.
>
> Captain McCall was a kindly good creature. His name was William, but he was always called Charles; why I don't know. He was of a very practical turn of mind. He was a great dandy, always dressed in the extreme of fashion. His Company was always known as the 'Lancers', for some reason connected with its Captain. He never was 'exactly sure' of anything. His talents lay in riding; he was a neat horseman and was the Regimental race rider.
>
> Keith Ramsay Maitland was perhaps the best and most sensible man in the Corps, over six feet, good looking, very gentlemanly and taking in his manner and

address. There was no man in the Regiment I respected more. He was the pleasantest companion I ever met. He was a great reader, very shrewd, and, to use an expression of his own, he knew 'the length of every man's foot in the Regiment'. He was very popular, respected and esteemed by all the officers, and beloved by the men.[76]

The internal differences, arguments and criticisms have an interesting side-light. The arguments between officers are essentially between Officers of one regiment, within that regiment, where they appear to have felt entirely justified in criticising and conflicting with one of their own. Adverse comment from outside however had, and still has, the effect of producing internal unity. Mr. William Boag of the Scottish United Services Museum and a former member of the Highland Light Infantry (71st/74th) once said to the author, '*I* can say the 74th was a useless Regiment, but *you* can't'. The argument is totally illogical, but it goes a long way to explaining how major differences of opinion and internal struggles could have taken place and yet at the same time regimental pride and *esprit de corps* amongst the officers of Highland regiments could have been maintained at such a high level. It is all part and parcel of the élitist aspect of these regiments, part of their unique history and part of the key to their strength and survival.

Officers of Highland regiments between 1820 and 1920 therefore seldom conform to the models so often portrayed. They are intensely individual and sometimes impatient and taciturn. In accents and manners they were influenced by contemporary fashion and their physical appearance varied widely. While they frequently disagreed amongst themselves, sometimes seriously, they were nevertheless regimentally proud and were prepared to undertake arduous, dangerous, repetitive and unpleasant duties for what will be seen to be little personal financial reward.

NOTES

1. Letters of Lt. Colonel the Hon. Lauderdale Maule, GD/45/14/634 (1) 8.5.1839: ' . . . you as an old soger know what billets are...' and GD/45/14/634 (3) 1-84: '. . he [an unknown officer] is Exchangd., not one of the auld 79th'.
2. Surgeon William Munro, *Records of Campaigning in Many Lands*, *op. cit.*, Vol. 11, p. 419. A further example is Hector Macdonald of the Gordon Highlanders: see Trevor Royle, *Death before Dishonour* (Edinburgh: 1982).
3. The author remembers her own godfather, Colonel George David Bruce DSO, 1st and 61st Madras Pioneers, who in spite of a lifetime of service in India spoke with an educated but nevertheless Scottish accent which he never commented on as being a drawback to him.
4. R.H. Burgoyne, *Historical Records of the 93rd Sutherland Highlanders* (London: 1883), pp. 84-85.
5. G.L. Goff, *Historical Records of the 91st Argyllshire Highlanders*, *op.cit.*, p. 122.
6. Diary of Col. J.W. Wedderburn, *op.cit*; Wedderburn mentions several times 'Archy Campbell' singing Gaelic songs. In the 79th several officers are known to have been native Gaelic speakers, notably Colonel Gilbert Gunn (1866-1948) who was well known in the Regiment for his Gaelic singing. *79th News*, Vol. X, no. 108, March 1910, p.32.

7. A few isolated words still survive and are used in the Army today although very few people know whence they originated, such as 'dhobi' (washerman or washing), 'char wallah' (tea man), 'Tiffin' (snack), 'Toddy' (an alcoholic drink tapped from a palm tree), 'cushy' (easy), 'jildi' (hurry).
8. WO/27/367.
9. *The Gentleman's Monthly Magazine of Fashion and Costumes de Paris* (London). While illustrations from the magazine are often used to show Highland dress and the 'Piccadilly Highlanders' in a manner which almost amounts to ridicule, it must be remembered that these were plates and designs, often accompanied by tissue patterns, that were intended for tailors and are in reality no more representative of the human shape than modern fashion design drawings.
10. Horse Guards order of 1.5.1857 regulated against the wearing of 'long hair and whiskers', but it is clear that in regiments abroad this order was not always obeyed.
11. Orders of Dress the 2nd Battalion Seaforth Highlanders 1884, QOHRM., and Orders of Dress the Black Watch c.1902, BWRM.
12. *79th News*, Vol. VIII, No. 90, p. 1.
13. Diary of Colonel Cuming, *79th News*, January 1935, p. 79. Sadly only two extracts of this manuscript were published in January and April 1935 before the document was stolen from a car in London and never seen again. *79th News*, July 1935, p. 245.
14. Diary of Col. J.W. Wedderburn, BWRM 28/714/1. 6.5.1852 Halifax, Canada: 'Parade and a short drill — the first of this year wearing kilts for the summer', and 22.5.1848 Bermuda: 'Shell jackets and white trousers taken into wear this morning'.
15. Diary of Col. J.W. Wedderburn, BWRM 28/714/1.
16. The khaki apron was first introduced during the South African War. The kilt was a source of considerable pride to the Highland regiments, but was also difficult to wear in active operations in extremes of climate and was consistently under attack after the introduction of khaki. Writing on the health of the troops in the Tochi Field Force of 1897 in which the 2nd Battalion Argyll and Sutherland Highlanders took part, the Principal Medical Officer noted the better health of the Highlanders and their 'superior physique' in comparison with the 3rd Battalion Rifle Brigade, but he did not consider the dress of the Highlanders suitable for active service especially in hot weather. *Operations of the Tochi Field Force 1897-98* (Quetta Pakistan: 1978), pp. 58-59. In 1902 attempts were made to abolish the kilt but were unsuccessful. *79th News*, Vol. 5, No. 61, 1.5.1902, p. 1. At the outbreak of the First World War the War Office tried to introduce a 'universal khaki kilt' but General Sir Spencer Ewart and other influential Highland officers seem to have been instrumental in preventing this. Letter, General Sir Spencer Ewart to Murray of Polmaise, 20.12.1914. GD/189/2/1081 (4).
17. Diary of Colonel Cuming, *79th News*, January 1935, p. 79.
18. William P. Thomson, *The Little General and the Rousay Crofters op. cit.*, p. 62.
19. R.H. Burgoyne, *Historical Records of the 93rd Sutherland Highlanders, op.cit.* (ASHRM copy).
20. William P. Thomson, *The Little General and the Rousay Crofters, op. cit.*, p. 62 and photograph 2a.
21. E.S. Wood MS notes on R.H. Burgoyne, *Historical Records of the 93rd Sutherland Highlanders, op cit.*, Stirling Castle.
22. Letters of Lt. Col. the Hon. Lauderdale Maule GD/45/14/634 (1) Quebec 10.3.1836.
23. Diary of Col. J.W. Wedderburn, BWRM 28/714/1, 3.4.1851 and 2.6.1851.
24. Diary of Captain A.S. Leith Hay 93rd 1844-1846. GD/225/39/8 Leith Hay Papers, p. 19. Toothbrushes were however used, as is evidenced by the Betting Book of the 78th: 'Perth. 2.4.1831. Mr. Fisher bets Mr. Montgomery one bottle of wine that the girl in Cameron's shop that served us out the toothbrushes has got red hair. — Lost by Montgomery'. *Betting Book of the Officers Mess 78th Highlanders 1822-1907* (London: 1909) QOHRM.

25. Lt. Colonel W. Gordon Alexander, *Recollections of a Highland Subaltern* (London: 1898), pp. 165-166.
26. Ian B.M. Hamilton, *The Happy Warrior, op. cit.*, p. 46.
27. See for example Fenton's photographic portraits of General Sir Colin Campbell or General Sir George de Lacy Evans in Lawrence James, *1854-1856 Crimea — The War with Russia from Contemporary Photographs* (Thame, Oxfordshire: 1981), pp. 49 and 45.
28. 'A Scotsman in the Crimean War — Unpublished letters of John Cheetham McLeod', *The Red Hackle*, No. 211, December 1984, p. 13.
29. J.A. Ewart, *The Story of a Soldier's Life, op. cit.*, pp. 320 and 378.
30. Diary of Lt. Robert Lindsay Mackay, the 11th and 1/8th Battalion Argyll and Sutherland Highlanders, ASHRM. 11.1.1917: 'Had a bath in Albert an event always worth chronicling'.
31. Letters of Andrew Agnew of Lochnaw, 93rd. GD/154/745.
32. Frank Richards, *Old Soldier Sahib* (London: 1983), p. 156.
33. Diary of Colonel Cuming, *79th News*, January 1935, p. 84.
34. Corporal Frank MacFarlane. Oral History Archive, *op. cit.*
35. Major Dan Bonar, 2nd Battalion Highland Light Infantry (74th), in conversation with the author. Major Bonar enlisted as a Boy Piper aged 15 in the 2nd HLI (the 74th) in 1914 when the Battalion was stationed at Aldershot. The Battalion, although officially the 2nd HLI, clung to the old regimental number 74th and in spite of being Light Infantry and based at Hamilton, still considered themselves Highland and entirely separate from the 1st Battalion the 71st. The use of the old number and the distinction between the two Battalions persisted until the amalgamation of the 1st and 2nd Battalions in 1947 and did not die out even then amongst the older soldiers. Major Bonar still prefers to be known as an old 74th man.
36. David Duff, ed., *Queen Victoria's Highland Journals* (Exeter: 1980), pp. 25, 28 and 161.
37. *79th News*, No. 32, 1.7.1897.
38. Letters of Andrew Agnew of Lochnaw 93rd, Halifax, NS. 20.7.1838. GD/154/745.
39. Farewell speech of Sir Colin Campbell to the 42nd, the 79th and 93rd near Kamara, Crimea 9.5.1856. Quoted *Historical Records of the Cameron Highlanders*, Vol. 1, pp. 182-183. The 92nd arrived in the Crimea and joined the Highland Brigade at Kamara. On 9th May 1856 they had marched out with the other three Regiments of the Brigade, but Sir Colin dismissed them before making his speech, much to their annoyance. Hence the emphasis *old* Highland Brigade.
40. Surgeon William Munro, *Records of Service and Campaigning in many lands, op. cit.*, Vol. 1, p. 239.
41. Notebook of Robert Sinclair. RH/4/141.
42. *Historical Records of the Cameron Highlanders, op. cit.*, Vol. 3, p. 69. Captain John Orr was a particularly good-looking man, the ideal Edwardian officer of a Highland regiment; according to his nephew General Sir Peter Hunt, Orr was known as 'Beauty Orr', a nickname which he hated. Another example of a good-looking and equally brave officer was Captain Charles Findlay of the 1st Camerons who was killed commanding his Company in the attack on the Dervish position on the Atbara river in 1898. Six foot six inches tall, he was the 'beau ideal' of the British officer, and his loss was so keenly felt by the nation that Queen Victoria insisted on being godmother to his son who was born after his death, the baby being christened Victor. The author has to thank Lt. Colonel A.A. Fairrie for this information.
43. Quoted, John Crouch, 'Majuba', *Soldiers of the Queen — Journal of the Victorian Military Society*, No. 26, September 1981, p. 30. The defeat of a composite force of three Companies of the 92nd, two Companies of the 3rd Battalion 60th, two Companies of the 58th and elements of the Naval Brigade, of which a total of only 352 men were actually engaged on the hill (Ian Hamilton says 365), took place at Majuba, near Lang's Nek, Natal on 27th February 1881.

44. The action at Tamai in the Sudan took place on 13th March 1884 against Osman Digna. The 1st Battalion Black Watch formed the front face of the Second Brigade square. When ordered to charge, they left a gap between themselves and the remainder of the square. Through this gap hundreds of the enemy got into the square, and in the smoke and confusion the rear rank of the Black Watch were forced to turn about to defend themselves. For many years afterwards it was a common taunt in public houses and canteens for soldiers of other regiments to order, within the hearing of Black Watch soldiers, 'Two pints of broken squares!'
45. Brevet Colonel William Eagleson Gordon VC v John Leng and Co. Ltd. (the Proprietors of the *People's Journal*), 1919 Session Cases, p. 415. Gordon won his action and obtained £500 damages.
46. Letter of Lord Saltoun to Ian Stewart of Achnacone, 1978. GHRM.
47. Diary of Lt. Col. J.W. Wedderburn 42nd, BWRM 28/714/1.
48. WO/91/13, p. 290.
49. WO/91/13, pp. 281-282.
50. WO/91/13, p. 314.
51. Scrap Book History of the 91st Highlanders presented to the Officers' Mess 1st Battalion Argyll and Sutherland Highlanders by Lt. Colonel H.G. Robley 17.7.1883. ASHRM, R/50.
52. Letter Book of Captain Bertie Gordon 91st, South Africa 1843-1846. 24.4.1843. ASHRM.
53. Ibid., 9.5.1843.
54. Ibid., 1.5.1843.
55. Ibid., 22.5.1843.
56. Ibid., 25.5.1843.
57. Ibid., 30.6.1843.
58. Ibid., 12.9.1843.
59. Ibid., 8.11.1843.
60. Ibid., 10.11.1843.
61. Ibid., 12.11.1843.
62. Copy letter Commander in Chief to Lt. Colonel Lindsay. Ibid. 16.2.1844.
63. G.L. Goff, *Historical Records of the 91st Argyllshire Highlanders*, *op. cit.*, p. 110 and Scrap Book History of the 91st Highlanders, *op.cit.*, ASHRM.
64. WO/27/380 Annual Inspection Report of the 91st 1848. Fitzclarence was a strict disciplinarian. Colonel Cuming remembers him inspecting a draft of the 79th in 1847: 'Lord Fitzclarence was Commanding the Portsmouth Garrison at this time and announced his intention of inspecting the detachment before embarkation. We were drawn up in the Barrack Square, where this fat and pompous specimine of a martinet entered the gate. He stood a hundred yards off, scowling at us a minute or two, then bawled out that the men were not sized properly and ordered the Officers to fall out and do it properly. He then condescended to look at us; fortunately he knew nothing about the Highland Dress so we got off lightly'. Diary of Colonel Cuming, *79th News*, January 1935, p. 80.
65. The wreck of the *Abercrombie Robinson*, five other ships, the *Waterloo* and a cutter on the 27th and 28th August 1842 was completely overshadowed by the wreck of the *Birkenhead* on 26th February 1852, when detachments of the 91st and the 74th were present.
66. Letters of Andrew Agnew of Lochnaw. GD/154/754. 25.11.1839.
67. Surgeon William Munro, *Reminiscences of Military Service with the 93rd Highlanders*, *op. cit.*, p. 19.
68. William P.L. Thomson, *The Little General and the Rousay Crofters*, *op. cit.*, p. 78, and Diary of F.W. Traill Burroughs, NLS, MS 2234.
69. MS Account of the 1st Battalion Gordon Highlanders in the area of Le Cateau August 1914 by 2/lt. Hon. S. Fraser, later Lord Saltoun. GHRM.

70. Letters of Lt. Col. the Hon. Lauderdale Maule, GD/45/14/634/3 (1-84) 28.4.1844.
71. Letter Book of Colonel Martin Lindsay 78th, Ceylon 1831-1836. Lindsay of Dowhill Papers GD/254/697/1.
72. Letters of Lt. Col. the Hon. Lauderdale Maule, GD/45/14/634 (1) 6.3.1839, (2) 1-93 11.11.1841, (3) 1-84, 8.3.1843.
73. E.S. Wood, MS Notes on R.H. Burgoyne, *Historical Records of the 93rd Sutherland Highlanders, op.cit.*, Stirling Castle.
74. Diary of J. Spencer Ewart, RH/4/84/1. 28.3.1883.
75. Diary of A.D. Greenhill Gardyne, RH/4/59/8.
76. Diary of Colonel Cuming, *79th News*, January 1935, pp. 83-84.

CHAPTER 6

Officers' Finances

'. . . "heads" the Treasury wins, and "tails" the Officer loses . . .'[1]

An important consideration in an officer's life was money. Even in Highland regiments, which were not considered expensive by Guards or Cavalry standards, it was difficult to keep pace with financial demands without some form of private income. The rates of pay were established in 1806 and remained virtually unchanged for over a hundred years. The Royal Commission on the Purchase and Sale of Commissions of 1857-58 noted the rates of pay:

Pay of Officers	**per day**	**per annum**
Lt. Colonel	17/-	£310.5.0d
Major	16/-	£292
Bt. Major	13/7d	£247.17.11d
Captain	11/7d	£211.7.11d
Lieutenant (over 7 years)	7/6d	£136.17.6d
Lieutenant	6/6d	£118.12.6d
Ensign	5/3d	£95.16.3d[2]

The rates of officers' pay remained virtually unaltered until 1st January 1914, and by 1919 Officers were paid as follows:

Pay	**per day**	**Rations**	**Married pa**	**Unmarried pa**
Lt. Col.	47/6d	2/1d	£1242	£1184
Command Pay	10/-			
Major	31/6d	2/1d	£768	£684
+5 years	37/-		£868	£784
Captain	23/6d	2/1d	£622	£517
+7 years	26/-		£667	£562
Lt.	16/-	2/1d	£448	£375
+7 years	19/-		£503	£429
2/Lt.	13/-	2/1d	£394	£320
+2 years	16/-		£448	£375

NB: The Married pa figure includes lodging, fuel and light and furniture allowance.[3]

The rise in 1919 was closely linked with contemporary discontent and the necessity of retaining the services of officers and soldiers while at the same time offering them some sort of parity with civilian rates. The increases were long overdue.

In addition to his pay in the nineteenth century an officer could expect certain allowances. A 'non-effective allowance' was given to the senior Lieutenant Colonel and Major of the Regiment of about £20 per annum, and a 'contingent allowance' was granted to Captains of Companies, which could vary from £18 to £102 per annum according to the number of men under the Captain's command. This latter allowance was intended

> . . . to indemnify the Officer for his liability to pay for the repair of arms, for the burial of soldiers and to pay their debts when their effects were insufficient.[4]

While the officer was supposed to make a small profit, it was by no means guaranteed. In addition the officer actually present and in command of a regiment received an allowance of 3 shillings per day, called 'Command Money', Brevet Majors received 2 shillings per day extra and Lieutenants after seven years service received 1 shilling per day 'Additional Pay'. When living out, an officer could receive a 'Fuel and Light and Lodging Allowance'. For his soldier servant an officer was given 1/6d per day, and in the tropics where soldier servants were not permitted to be employed, he received a 'Black Servants Allowance'. An allowance of 'Rations of Provisions' was also given in the Colonies together with a special 'Colonial Allowance' in some Colonies, 'in consideration of the great expense of the necessaries of life'. A 'Mess Allowance' was first granted in 1811. It was given to regiments in the United Kingdom and later extended to regiments stationed in the West Indies, St. Helena and the west coast of Africa. In Queen's Regulations and Orders for the Army of 1844 its object is stated as being:

> . . . to enable Regimental Officers of every rank, but more especially of the junior . . . s, to enjoy the comfort and advantages, which it is calculated to afford, by placing it in the power of every individual to drink a moderate quantity of wine daily at or after dinner, on reasonable terms, and such as his rate of pay may fairly justify.[5]

Certain officers also received rewards for their distinguished services of various amounts, such as Major General R.C.H. Taylor of the 79th who was rewarded by £100 per annum[6] for his long and distinguished service between 1835 and 1882, and officers could also receive additional pay when qualifying as interpreters and of course during campaigns, Prize Money.[7]

Set against this were all sorts of expenses, obligatory and otherwise, which did not necessarily involve extravagance. Prior to the abolition of purchase an officer had already paid £450 for his commission; he was then required to equip himself with his uniform, camp equipment and furniture, and items of uniform were expensive, as can be seen from Meyer and Mortimer's account of 1835 for an officer of the Black Watch:

Edinburgh
G.W.Macquarie Esq.
42nd Royal Highlanders
1835 Octr. 19 To Meyer and Mortimer, Army Clothiers

A fine blue cloth regulation Forage cap with band regtl. ornament & oilskin cover	£2.2.
A blue cocked highland Bonnet mounted with cockade & gilt sphinx	£0.15.
A full dress Regimental Highland Bonnet mounted with black ostrich feathers & sphinx	£9.19.6d
Oil silk cover for Do.	£0.10.6d
A Scarlet Vulture feather	£0.16.
A Japaned case and padlock	£1.2.
A Saxony Scarlet cloth dress Jacket with blue cloth collar and cuffs ditto and flaps laced with rich gold lace regimental buttons	£10.10.
A pair of gold embroidered skirt ornaments	£0.13.
A pair of rich gold bullion Epaulettes with silver thistles	£5.5.
Japaned case for Do.	£0.6.6d
2 Saxony blue cloth Frock coats with silk skirt linings & regimental buttons	£5.5.-£10.10.
2 pair of Shoulder Scales with silver thistles	£3.10.
2 pair of fine worsted tartan Trowsers 25/-	£2.10.
1 Do. soft Do. Do.	£1.5.
1 fine Do. Do. Do.	£1.1.
2 pair red & white tartan hose 7/6	£0.15.
A rich crimson silk Highland Sash	£5.5.
A buffalo leather slinged Shoulder belt	£1.9.
A Regimental Breast Plate	£2.10.
A Steel mounted Highland Sword	£4.14.6d
An engraved silver shoulder Broach	£1.5.
A gilt mounted highland Dirk with knife and fork ebony handles & Cairngorm stones	£6.16.6d
A patent leather slinged Waistbelt with Regimental Plate	£2.2.
A white goatskin Regtl. Highland Purse mounted with gold lace on top gilt shield & 6 gold bullion tassles	£5.15.6d
A buffalo leather belt for Do.	£0.2.6d
Box for Do.	£1.1.
3 black silk Stocks 5/-	£0.15.
3 pair White buck gloves 6/-	£0.18.
3 Do. doe Do. 3/-	£0.9.
6 Do. cotton Do. 1/6	£0.9.
2 Patent leather Stocks 4/-	£0.8.
A fine blue cloth circle cloak with cape lined with scarlet shalloon gilt Lion's Head clasp & etc	£5.15.6d
3 pair White Patent flannel pantaloon drawers 16/-	£2.2.
3 pair Do. cotton ditto 6/-	£0.18.
1 Do. Do. gloves	£0.1.6d
1 pair dress shoes	£0.17.
A portable Iron Tent Bedstead with curtains hair matress, Bolster feather pillow, 3 Blankets 2 pair sheets and counterpane. Box & Valese	£17.17.
A Wainscot canteen complete with Brass Plate with name for Do.	£0.5.6d
A portable Mahogany chest of Drawers with oak backs and bottoms Writing Desk patent locks & bound with brass	£16.10.
2 Cases for Do.	
Box for Sword	£0.3.6d
painting name on boxes & etc.	£0.7.6d
	£136.17.6d

Additonal items were also required and a Meyer and Mortimer estimate of 1906 for the dress items alone, excluding civilian clothes or sports kit, totalled £63.17.0. for the Gordon Highlanders.[9] More fortunate were some of the retired, militia or territorial officers who rejoined their battalions in 1914. The

Hon. S. Frazer, later Lord Saltoun, recalled as an officer of the 3rd Militia Battalion ordered to the 1st Battalion Gordon Highlanders that:

> In general no one would cash a cheque owing to the moratorium—but at least the Secretary of the Carlton Club consented to cash me two cheques of £2 each. I was short of a coat and telephoned Mr. Alfred Moss of Moss Bros. and told him of my financial difficulties and asked if he would take a cheque. He told me to come and help myself to anything I needed, that he would take a cheque if I wished, but he did not care if he were never paid.[10]

Officers not only had to pay for clothing and accoutrements, they also required furniture and utensils which they had to carry with them wherever they were posted, for only a bare room was provided for them when trooping or in station at home or abroad. Messrs Hill and Millard for example advertised a 'complete outfit' of barrack and camp furniture comprising a bed, two chairs, stool, chest of drawers, wash stand basin, table and trunk for £28.10/- in 1866.[11]

When John C. Stewart joined the 72nd in 1850 and arrived at Hadfield Barracks, Bristol to join the Regiment, he had no bed linen or furniture and had to rely on the generosity of his fellow officers:

> 'I am going down this evening,' he wrote 'to get some sheets and linen in Bristol. I have got the loan of a bed till my own comes . . . .'[12]

Having arrived in his regiment, an officer was faced with further expenditure. He was required to pay subscriptions to the Mess; in 1903 this amounted to thirty days' pay, i.e. £7.17.6d, together with subscriptions to the Band, Pipe and any sports funds which the regiment might have, and monthly bills for his servant, washing and other extras. Lt. John C. Stewart related his problems to his mother:

> Hadfield Barracks 1.11.1850
>
> My Dear Mother,
> My tailor's bill in London came very high . . . a dress coat . . . is £4 odds and the whole came to £116 odds. The only thing I want now is my boots, that bootmaker is very lazy, however I think I have given him a rattler today that will make him exert himself.
>
> This is the first of the month and I have all my bills to pay we don't pay them ourselves we pay orders on Mr Lawrie the Army Agent they are monthly bills the washing is £1 a month and the servant is the same, his regular pay is 10/- but extras are always £1—1 have a good deal to pay this month but I hope to get through. I am trembling for the £80 as I am afraid it is too little however I will try.[13]

Agents' fees were also charged, as can be seen from the account of Ensign Arthur Pitcairn of the 42nd:

Agents account before joining *Ensign Arthur Pitcairn* 42nd Royal Highlanders. Ensign Arthur Pitcairn with Sir Edwd. R. Borough Bart, Armit and Co.

1840	To fees of Commission	£4.11.10d
	Subn. to Mess Fund on Appt	£7.17. 6d
	Do. to Band on Do.	£5. 5.
	Do. to Do. to 30th June	8. 3d
	Do. to Mess and Newspapers to Do.	7. 0d
	Paid postage	1.
		£18.9.8d
	By pay at 5/3d / day fm. 15th May to 30th June 1840	£12. 6. 9d
	Balance charged to the paymaster	£6. 2. 11d

Dublin 16th July 1840
Borough Armit and Co.[14]

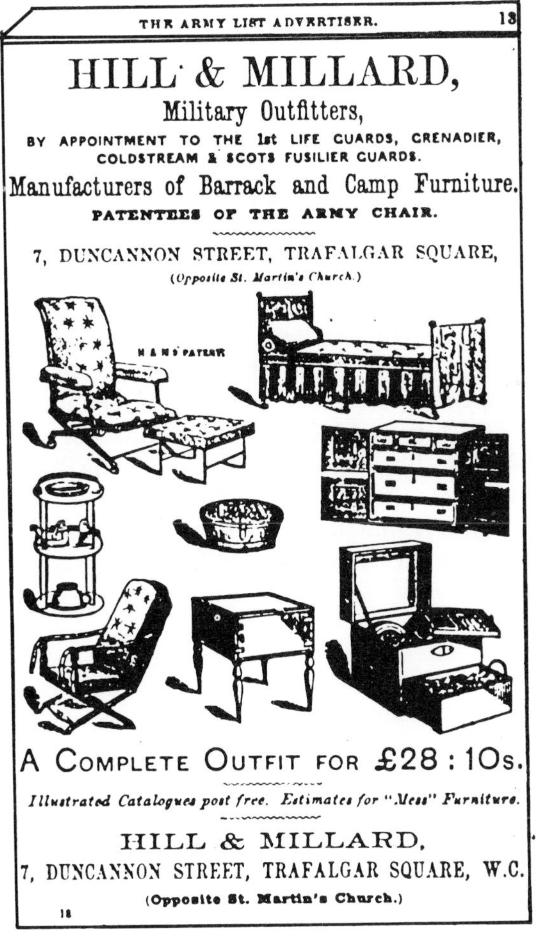

These Army Agents mentioned by Stewart and in Pitcairn's account formed a vital link in the financial management of a Regiment and Officers' affairs. Originally acting as Clerks to the Colonels of the Regiments, Agents dated from the middle of the seventeenth century. In return for their services they received 2d in the £ from the pay of the Regiment, but part of their complex pay responsibilities were removed when Army Paymasters were appointed in 1797.

Until 1801 the Irish Establishment was entirely separate from the British Establishment, hence regiments required Agents and Irish Agents, a legacy which persisted for many years afterwards. The position of Agent was sought after, and these commercial firms would pay for the privilege and the profit of acting for a regiment, their appointment being sanctioned by the Secretary at War. In 1827 there was a total of thirteen Agents, but by 1878 only eight remained. Most Highland regiments favoured Cox & Co., although in 1839 the 91st were using Messrs. Barron & Smith, Westminster and the 79th were using Mr Lawrie.[15] In 1847 the Colonel of the 79th, Lt. General Sir James MacDonnell, 'sold' the 79th to Cox & Co., presumably receiving a profit for himself on the deal. Lt. Colonel Lauderdale Maule writes to his brother:

> Our Colonel is quite unworthy of the 79th—I wish to God he would give it up—He has sold the Regt. to Cox & Co. receiving so much p.a. and leaving all to them. They of course keep us in everything close to the wind. Alas, would that old Sir R. Fergusson had us still.[16]

Agents were further affected by the clothing warrant of 1854 when Colonels of Regiments ceased to have a pecuniary interest in regimental dress,[17] and in 1881, when Colonels of Regiments became Honorary, Agents were selected by the War Office, both Battalions under the two-battalion system being obliged to have the same Agent. By 1891 only three Agents remained, Cox & Co., Holt & Co. and Sir C.R. McGrigor, McGrigor going bankrupt in 1922. In 1905 Cox & Co. opened a Bombay Branch, followed by a Calcutta Branch in 1911, but in 1923 the Company was taken over by Lloyds Bank Ltd. It was not however until 31st December 1971 that the Ministry of Defence finally ceased paying Army Officers through Army Agents and Paymasters and computers took over.[18]

Throughout their existence, however, Agents had become much more than mere administrators of regimental pay, officers' pay and general finances. They acted as brokers upon whom officers could draw bills of exchange, forwarding agents for the dispatch of articles while the regiment was abroad and agents for promotion, allowances and widows' pensions. It seems too that they were intermediaries for official correspondence when the regiment was overseas. In 1847 Lt. Colonel Maule wrote from Gibraltar:

> Cox & Co. write out that we go in November to Nova Scotia.[19]

The wide range of Agents' duties, together with the invaluable services which they rendered to officers and their worldwide reputation and respectability, is reflected in the note written by an Officer in 1923 when Cox & Co. were taken over by Lloyds:

> Bombay 15th April 1923.
> This is my last cheque on the 'old firm', I dedicate to the immortal memory of Messrs Cox & Co of 16 Charing X London & Hamby Road Bombay, who fed and clothed me over the space of a quarter of a century and whose cheques I cashed in the Continents of Africa, India & Canada—& from Bunya's shop in the Himilayas to a shack in the Canadian Backwoods.
> F.O. Bower, Major
> late of the 18th Foot 'the Royal Irish'.[20]

Having joined the regiment and incurred the basic expenses, young officers were immediately put on the drill square with the recruits and taught their drill. On graduating there is evidence to suggest that it was common practice for the sergeant to expect payment. In 1850 Ensign Dowbiggin of the 71st wrote to his uncle Lt. Colonel Lauderdale Maule of the 79th:

> My Dear Uncle Lauderdale,
> I have some bills that I owe to the Regt. such as wine for formal guests or ante-room subs . . . that have accumulated since I got my Commission and which I knew nothing of . . . There are also the fees that the Drill Sergeants and Sergeant Major expect on my being dismissed drill which I have no money for as Mule M . .?. . gave me 25£ when I left England and that is my allowance till Xmas
> £25 for Mess
> £7 for Fees on Drill.[21]

Money was also paid by a young officer to his first guard who, presumably if the money had not been paid, could have put all sorts of difficulties in his way. Colonel Wedderburn's first guard in the 42nd was at Drummond Castle on 11th September 1842 guarding Queen Victoria. He remembers:

> I was on guard at night and visited my sentries every half hour, had to pay my footing this being my first Guard, £1 to the Sergeant and 2£ to the men.[22]

It is by no means certain when this practice died out, but it was certainly not used in the 42nd/73rd and the 79th in 1913 and 1914.[23] In addition in the late 1850s it was the custom in the 42nd for an officer when married to buy all the men in his company drinks in the canteen. Archibald McIntosh, a private soldier of the 42nd, records:

> Another Officer named Scott [Captain Francis Cunningham Scott, younger of Malleny] rejoined the Regiment from leave of absence, while he was away he had married a Minister's Daughter at Calcutta, when he joined we carried him round the barracks according to custom and he payed for our allowance of drink at the Canteen.[24]

These informal expenses were indicative of the internal social pressures that could exist within a battalion and induce an officer to spend far more than he would have wished or was able to afford and about which Regulations could do little. When Ian Hamilton joined the Gordon Highlanders in India in 1876 he wrote to his brother:

> The thought of all that is spent on one's stomach is simply disgraceful, but in a Regiment like ours one cannot help it. Champagne is always flowing. No one is allowed to pass through the station without being a Regimental guest—all that sort of thing.[25]

The Committee of 1903 to inquire into an officer's expenses recognised these informal expenses and attributed them to the 'style of living habitually adopted by the majority of his brother officers'.[26] Attempts were made to prevent extravagant messing charges and commanding officers were urged to resist extra expenditure, but a 'style' once adopted was difficult to cut down. A well-equipped band with all the latest instruments, pipe banners, special accoutrements for the Pipe Major and Pipes are examples of the calls that would be made on an officer's pocket. In 1860 the 91st, at Kamptee, India, purchased Pipes and Lt. Colonel Bertie Gordon wrote in Orders:

> Two Captains of the Regiment have incurred considerable expense in procuring from Scotland and presenting to their Companies three handsome sets of Bagpipes.[27]

In addition the purchase and engraving of silver became almost obligatory in some regiments when an officer was promoted, married or left the battalion. While the 79th seems to have had little silver in the officers' mess, the 72nd had a particularly fine collection dating from 1801. In 1820 officers of the 72nd 'donated' one day's pay per month for a year to the Plate Fund and by 1823 the Regimental Plate and Cash was valued at £1799.7.1½d[28] Some of this silver was donated by bets:

> Lost by Colonel Monkton to Major Carter—2 large silver decanter stands—On Major Carter walking on stilts from the Society House to the Governor's Guard.

and:

> Lost by Lt. A. Maclean to W. McKenzie—2 Pint Silver Decanter Stands—On sporting his hand 'Ginger or no Ginger.'[29]

Living together within the geographical and social confines of a battalion and its Officers' mess, it would have been difficult not to conform in relation to this kind of expenditure, and those who could not afford the social life would certainly have been conspicuous. As messes became more permanent, formalised mess rules imposed payments upon officers. 'Rules of the Mess' were already in existence in the 79th before 1849 and were probably introduced by Lt. Colonel Lauderdale Maule about 1844. Until 1860 it was the custom of the 79th for an officer to give 'Promotion Wine' and not plate, but it was agreed in that year that a scaled donation would be given to the Plate Fund on promotion:

Ensign to Lieutenant	£4
Ensign to Captain	£6
Ensign to Major	£10
Ensign to Lt. Colonel	£15.[30]

Such donations were 'optional' but would have been difficult to avoid. 'Billiard Tables' (1860), 'the Hunt Fund' (1850), 'The Boat Fund' (1868), 'the Pipe Banner Fund' (1881), a fund for the purchase of Mess Furniture (1883), 'Tennis Fund' (1887), 'Newspapers and Magazines' (1888), watches to the members of the Regimental Football Team (1894), the '79th News' Regimental Magazine (1895), Band Instruments and Officers' Stable (1895), Photograph Albums (1896) and Mess Servants' livery are all mentioned in the Minute Book of the Officers' Mess of the 79th,[31] and while they were an extremely distinguished regiment, they were not generally considered expensive.

Before 1871 officers coupled these lesser costs with the major expenditure of purchase and purchase of promotion at actual cost together with the financial manipulations and deals that were required to make a place for themselves. Even in 1903 the Committee of Enquiry established initial expenses at £200 and current expenses at £155.16.3d and concluded that a private income was required by an officer to meet 'necessary' expenses:

Initial Expenses. Infantry.	
Uniform and Cases	£97. 2.6
Mess Contribution (para 948) King's Regs. 30 days pay	7.17.6
Furniture	35.
Plain clothes, kit and servant's outfit, say	60.
	£200.

Current Expenses.	
Mess subs. 8 days pay @ 5/3d	£2.2.
Incidental Mess Expenses 10/- / month	6.0.
Share of Mess Guests	3.0.
Messing 365 days (less 60 days leave) @ 4/- / day	61.0.
Moves and Manoeuvres	5.0.
Repairs and upkeep of uniform	10.0.
Washing and mending linen @ 20/- / month	12.0.
Soldier servant @ 10/- / month	6.0.
Clothing for soldier servant yearly	5.0.
Subscriptions to Regimental Cricket Club	3.0.
Drink and Tobacco	15.5.
All other expenses, plain clothes, travel etc.	27.9.3
Total Necessary Expenses	£155.16.3
Deduct 365 days pay @ 5/3d	95.16.3
Balance to be met by private income	£60.0.0[32]

In the light of the above, this figure of £60 must be considered as very conservative when applied to the Highland regiments, also taking into account the ordinary expenditure of moderate eating, drinking, keeping a horse and having something left over for leaves. Only the heavy losses and the prolonged and destructive nature of the First World War changed the style of living amongst officers which, while practised in India in the 1920s and '30s, was never again really reinstated in the Highland battalions on such an extensive scale. The 1903 Committee could only recommend cutting down on regimental entertainments, substituting a 'two horse brake' for the 'Regimental Coach', moderation in regimental packs of hounds, doing without polo tournaments in the UK, and minimum changes of uniform.[33]

It is certain that many Highland officers were not wealthy and that much of their finance for general necessary expenditure was obtained not from a large family or personal income, but from loans, bills, delaying the payment of tradesmen or obtaining the money from parents or relatives. Lt. Colonel Lauderdale Maule is a fine example; he was the second son of Lord Panmure, one of the largest landowners in Forfarshire, his brother was Fox Maule, Secretary of State at and for War, Member of Parliament and influential reformer. Yet as a result of a family dispute neither son had any money at all apart from what they earned through public office or the Army. Lord Panmure gave an irregular small allowance to Lauderdale and reluctantly paid the regulation price for his promotional steps, but until their father died in 1852, both brothers were obliged to borrow heavily and lived in decidedly straitened circumstances. Finances were their constant concern and in 1850 the two brothers jointly owed the Union Bank in promissory alone £6285, with no possibility of meeting this debt until their father's death.[34]

There was very little opportunity for the Highland officer to get money by alternative means in the period 1820 to 1920. While looting did take place in the Crimea and during the Ashanti War and prize money was awarded, it was only in the Indian Mutiny that there was any real opportunity for valuable items to be acquired. E.S. Wood of the 93rd in his manuscript notes writes of some of his fellow officers:

> Captain Roderick Glenlyon Hamilton Burgoyne—'Poor Roderick', was always hard up as I believe his father (also a soldier) had been before him.
>
> Major William Gustavus Alexander Middleton—'Tony'. He was no friend of mine and when I got into the Grenadiers (i.e. the Grenadier Company) after the Crimea he became the Captain of it and I had hard work to keep out of trouble. He himself was a poor man yet he liked the society of rich ones. As he was dying a letter came saying he had come into a considerable sum of money—thus he was no longer on his pay—but it was too late and I believe he knew nothing about it.
>
> Major Walter Scott Mackenzie—'The Nobbler'. He I believe married a rich woman.[35]

The men were aware when an officer was poor, and Private McIntosh of the 42nd noted in his diary:

> One of our Officers named McLeod got married here to one of Barclay's Daughters, which set him on his feet as he was very poor. Barclay is an Indigo Planter and was at one time a soldier in the East India Company Service, and bought his discharge.[36]

Marriage was therefore an option but debt was more likely. As regards the truly Highland officer it must be remembered that many Highland estates and farms were, between the period 1820 and 1920, undergoing serious physical and financial transition which left them in the situation of having capital assets but little revenue, and it was not always easy for them to have cash in hand without bonds being granted. Some officers fell so seriously into debt that commanding officers were forced to intervene to prevent a scandal that might reflect upon the regiment. Lieutenant Alexander Buchanan of Powis of the 79th, who joined the Regiment in 1838, was already in debt by 1841 and his father had to pay up on his behalf. Some of the trouble he seems to have brought upon himself, and his Commanding Officer, Lt. Colonel Maule, on hearing of the debts, sent for him, warned him, transferred him to another company, gave him a month to pay his mess bill and kept watch; a month later the situation was no better:

> That confounded ass Buchanan owes about £370 I cannot tell you how disgusted I am with the fellow's folly . . . I have taken his Mess Debts upon myself to save him from being put under arrest . . . he has been seen gambling, not in his own Regiment, for we do not play, (thank God!) but with Officers in other Corps. Meanwhile I advise India or a retirement from the service. This is the second time he has forfited his word in the 79th and he will do so again; depend upon it.[37]

Lt. Colonel Maule, who from his own personal circumstances can have had little sympathy with Buchanan, personally took him back to the depot of the 79th in 1842. After further transgressions Buchanan was deprived of the depot adjutancy and was 'recommended to leave the Regiment', which he did in 1843, leaving debt behind him in the 79th.[38]

Very few officers of Highland regiments were court martialed after 1860, and because anonymity was preserved in relation to linking names with cases, it is difficult to tell whether all the cases are related to debt. For example between 12th and 19th August 1853, Lieutenant W.D. Stewart of the 93rd was tried by court martial at Chobham Camp. Wedderburn mentions this court martial, but does not expand on the charge.[39] The Judge Advocate General's record of the period is missing in War Office records, but in 1853 it is known that there were eighteen courts martial of officers, the charges including embezzlement, debt, drunkenness and foul language.[40] No individual identifications are possible, but Stewart certainly left the service.

It is seldom that officers express dissatisfaction with their income from army pay, however, and most appear to have come to terms with their financial circumstances. The rates of purchase, promotion and pay were laid down and well understood, and when an officer joined he knew exactly what his pay was to be and very few complained about it. What rich and poor felt alike, however, were the hidden costs arising out of duty for which the Treasury refused to take any responsibility and which were offloaded on to the officer to become yet another burden on his pocket. A source of severe criticism was the expense of evacuation of sick and wounded officers particularly during the Indian Mutiny, a cost which had to be met by the officers themselves. Lt. Colonel Gordon Alexander cited the case of John Alexander Ewart of the 93rd who lost his arm at Cawnpore and had to set out 628 miles across India to Calcutta under his own arrangements to find a ship for home.[41]

A 'passage allowance' was available, but was not given automatically; it had to be claimed and that claim it seems was often disputed. Bertie Gordon of the 91st wrote to his Agents in 1844 objecting to his being charged 3/6d per day 'Messing' on board ship when he returned from South Africa, stating that he was an 'invalid' and was therefore entitled to the allowance. It appears however that he paid his own fare home, agreeing the figure of £40 with the ship's captain.[42]

Officers also had to pay for their own medicines if they were not available from the medical chest, and again Bertie Gordon when ill with rheumatic fever in 1843 had had to buy medicine from the apothecary's shop as the hospital chest could not supply him with what he required. It would seem that his claim for this account was not met.[43] As for the Medical Officers themselves, on campaigns they had to meet much of the cost of their equipment to be effective on active service. Munro of the 93rd supplied his own case of surgical instruments and also additional medical comforts for his patients. He also had to purchase two horses, one for himself and one for his equipment panniers, at a cost which far exceeded the allowances.[44]

A poor officer who could not afford the difference between the allowances and the actual cost of a horse, the possession of which was a virtual necessity for practical purposes alone, sometimes had to leave. Lieutenant Agnew of the 93rd noted:

> . . . poor Pole has had to leave the Regiment in consequence as he cannot afford to keep a horse . . .[45]

When officers were ordered from station to station and were forced to sell their horses and possessions, there was no guarantee that they would recoup their outlay.[46]

Personal items lost by officers, particularly in the field, had to be replaced by the officers themselves or more likely through the generosity of their friends and relations. The letters of officers serving in the First World War are notable for their consistent requests for items. An example is Second Lieutenant Alistair Jameson of the 1st Camerons who wrote hurriedly to his Mother in February 1917: ' . . . I must ask you to send me a shirt and collar . . .' A week later he wrote again:

> I have lost all my washing and shaving things again. I require 2 small towels, 2 razors and strop, lather brush, glass (to see my pretty face in), brush, comb, tooth brush and basin. I was coming from the line after relief & got stuck with a lot of men in a trench over the waist in mud. It took us 12 instead of 2 hours to reach our destination, which I did in boots and socks, shirt tails, jacket and tin hat only. I thought my number was up that night.[47]

During the long retreat of 1914 many officers lost all their possessions except for those they stood up in. Lieutenant A. Stirling of the 2nd Argylls wrote on 25th August 1914:

> At last we were told where the billets were. It was still raining. Some of the men could hardly get one foot in front of the other. After seeing the gun horses fed I had a wash, the first since Valenciennes, at the place of watering engines and turned in. I was very comfortable for I had all my kit on the machine gun waggon and so got into my pyjamas and my flea bag and had a real good sleep. I was the only one who could do this for all the kit was with the transport and we heard that the waggon on which was some officer's kit, had to be abandoned and burnt the day before.[48]

By 29th August 1914, wounded and a prisoner, Stirling was in a less fortunate position:

> At this time my worldly possessions were reduced to 1 coat, 1 shirt, 1 boot, 1 sock, 1 pair of breeches (cut), 1 broken watch and chain, 1 pipe and my snakeskin belt with my knife.[49]

Compensation to officers or issue in lieu for personal items and uniform lost on duty was rare, and Bertie Gordon does not appear to have received anything for the loss of his possessions in the wreck of the *Abercrombie Robinson*; Lauderdale Maule, in spite of his financial difficulties, seems to have borne much of the loss of the baggage and regimental possessions aboard the *Lady Cremorne* wrecked en route to Quebec in 1848.[50] Lieutenant A. Stirling also records on several occasions using his own money to buy food for his men when the transport failed to appear or the Quarter Master refused to issue rations:

> I managed to buy an enormous round loaf of bread which I gave to the section to stave off the pangs of hunger. [The following day] . . . the men had been issued with about quarter rations and had managed to light fires and boil tea in their canteens, so they did not start on empty stomachs. That is all except the poor machine gun section, who belonged to no Company and got nothing from the rapacious hands of the Quarter Master Sergeant. I could get nothing for them there so . . . I went to several shops but could get no bread at all or any kind of substantial food, so I bought as much chocolate as my pockets could hold.[51]

One of the most annoying and illogical charges which an officer encountered was the tariff duties payable on imports to Canada in the nineteenth century. The tariffs covered all items, even uniforms, and most important for the officers who drank, alcohol, as in Canada the 'Prince Regent's Allowance' to assist in the purchase of wine in the mess was not given. Lauderdale Maule of the 79th complained in 1849:

> Yesterday we paid duty alone on the supply of Champagne amounting to upwards of 40 per cent! . . . our clothes, uniform everything that we get are subject to duty 12 or 10 p cent on the value![52]

Thus, while a complex system of allowances was open to the serving officer, these frequently did not meet necessary expenditure, nor were they easy to obtain, and officers of Highland regiments were placed at a distinct disadvantage as a result of the lengthy periods which their battalions spent abroad. If an allowance had to be obtained from London, a letter from India, Canada or the West Indies could take months to arrive and the reply correspondence, directed through Agents, would take the same time to return.

Some officers were extravagant, spendthrift and incautious, particularly in their leisure activities, but it would appear that overspending and illegitimate debt were not acceptable in the Highland regiments. Income from pay in no way compensated officers for their outlay, but many young men got into financial trouble simply because they were neither equipped nor prepared for the 'hidden' costs. Succinct as usual, Lt. Colonel Maule of the 79th sums up the problems:

> I have had enough of young gentlemen joining from their Mother's apron strings with a £5, a Bible and the parental blessing—running slap into every extravagance, parents refusing to pay, the onus thrown upon the system in the Army, claims becoming pressing and then insolvent, young gentleman's promotion stopped to pay his debts and said young gentleman becoming disgusted, then indifferent, next wreckless—taking refuge in low company and strong drink and finally if not cashiered sent home to his friends ruined in his morals and constitution mind and body a swindler and a drunkard . . . from all such plagues may God deliver me and the 79th![53]

Finally, there were the financial implications of patronage, which in Highland regiments appears to have extended far beyond the bounds of providing men's drinks in the canteen on marriage or paying 'footing' on a first guard. While the wider aspects of patronage will be discussed later, there is no doubt that the majority of Highland officers cared deeply about their regiments and their soldiers, and were prepared to financially assist those with whom they had served. Against the background of Highland poverty and emigration this has important implications in understanding the officer/soldier relationship, certain aspects of individual emigration and the strength and depth of nineteenth- and early twentieth-century Highland regimental feeling.

This idea of the 'Regimental Family' is the subject of considerable criticism and derision in the 1980s,[54] and the financial aspects of patronage are often misunderstood by those who fail to appreciate the complex interplay of regimental feeling, Highland pride, nineteenth- and early twentieth-century attitudes to poor relief, military discipline, Scottish religious attitudes and the intensity of Highland regimental comradeship, and look only on financial patronage as being 'patronising' and degrading.

In 1854, a former soldier of the 42nd, John Currie, walked from Glasgow to

Rosebank, Roslin looking for John Wedderburn. Wedderburn wrote in his diary:

> To my astonishment my late servant boy John Currie came here tonight wishing me to help him out to Nova Scotia.[55]

Wedderburn gave him the money and the return fare to Glasgow and Currie returned eleven days later to say goodbye to him:

> . . . met John Currie near Straiton and he returned with me to Edinburgh as he was on his way to Rosebank to bid me adieu. I again paid his way to Glasgow as he is to sail on Monday to Nova Scotia.[56]

Wedderburn's diary was kept for his own amusement and was not intended for publication in any form. He records the incident in a matter of fact way and as a retired officer could gain no prestige from the event, nor apparently did John Currie lose face in Wedderburn's, or his own, eyes by his request, and he also felt sufficiently confident and comfortable in their relationship to return to Rosebank and thank Wedderburn personally. The passing of money demeaned neither the giver nor the receiver.

How many soldiers were assisted to emigrate in this way is unknown. Few officers left such detailed documentary evidence as Wedderburn, but given the situation in the Highlands to which many discharged long-serving soldiers returned, it is possible that their number could be quite considerable. Although there is no written proof, it is possible that either Lauderdale Maule or his brother Fox, who had also served in the 79th, assisted the emigration of the former Sergeant Major of the 79th, John Mackay, who went to New Zealand in 1854,[57] and Lauderdale had certainly intended to pay for Quarter Master Robert Jameson's son to be sent to Sandhurst.[58]

F.W. Traill Burroughs of the 93rd, apparently contrary to all the characteristics he exhibited in the management of Rousay, paid a pension to the mother of Donald Maclean, a soldier of the 93rd killed at Lucknow.[59] John Wedderburn gave money prizes to his men in a competition for turning out in 1853,[60] and when Major Cumberland banned dogs aboard the troopship *Resistance* returning from Canada in 1852, Wedderburn sent his own dog Grouse and paid for the Pipe Major's dog Fanny to travel home aboard the Mail Ship, so that they would not have to be left behind or sold.[61]

Officers subscribed to numerous charities and funds associated with their service, from the fund formed to assist the Creole Mrs. Seacole who had operated the 'British Hotel' in the Crimea,[62] to the funds raised to assist women and families left at home on embarkation of the regiment,[63] and the various regimental associations, one of which, the 91st, was formed according to Goff as early as 1864.[64] Officers also subscribed to the endowment of beds at Queen Victoria School, Dunblane, opened in 1908 for the education of the sons and orphans of servicemen.[65]

There were therefore pressures of all kinds, coming from many sources, on the funds of a Highland officer in the period 1820 to 1920. Failure to balance these pressures with the income available left an officer with four basic choices: acknowledge poverty and the inadequacy of his income and accept his fellow officers' censure, if any, go into debt in the hope of better times, exchange to a cheaper regiment, or sell out.

It is difficult to tell in fact which were 'expensive' regiments amongst the Highland Corps as the position often depended upon the commanding officer of the moment. It would appear that the 92nd were relatively reasonable until the late 1860s when by Ian Hamilton's account it was certainly costly, and it seems to have remained so until the commencement of the First World War. The 42nd were desirable as a prestigious regiment but Wedderburn makes no complaints about costs. The 79th were very expensive during the tenure of command of Lauderdale Maule largely because of the number of uniform changes he introduced, but the 78th and the 93rd appear to have been entirely reasonable with the 93rd probably marginally cheaper as several of their commanding officers were not rich men. Of the Highland regiments wearing trews, the 72nd lived in the greatest style, their investment in plate alone causing considerable expense to the officers. The 74th was a prestigious regiment but not necessarily expensive, and the 91st, 73rd and 75th all seem to have been entirely reasonable.

On the whole costs tended to rise as the century progressed and as mess establishments, military bands, pipe bands and leisure pursuits became more sophisticated according to the contemporary fashion. The cost or style of living of the officers in a regiment did not however have any relationship to its efficiency or battle potential although it might affect morale in general, when officers and men felt that they belonged to a regiment that could afford a high standard of entertainment and an expensive and generous lifestyle.

Finally, in the light of the imbalance between income from pay and legitimate expenditure, even if kept at a minimum, it is small wonder that a commission was viewed by an officer in an entirely different light, that attitudes in many cases were not governed by a professional approach to soldiering and that officers clung to their extended leave periods, hunting, shooting and polo. They after all had in many instances made a major capital investment and also paid handsomely for serving their country, a price which the government was conspicuous in its refusal to meet.

NOTES

1. Lt. Colonel W. Gordon-Alexander, *Recollections of a Highland Subaltern, op. cit.*, p. 153.
2. PP 1857-58 XXXVII c498, p. 10.
3. PP 1920 XXVIII c119, Appendix 1, p.112.
4. PP 1857-58 XXXVII, c498, pp. 84-85.
5. *Queen's Regulations and Orders for the Army*, July 1844, p.130. In Queen's Regulations of 1858 this paragraph was amended to read: 'The principal object of this allowance is to enable the Officers of a Regiment, of every rank, but more especially of the junior ranks, to enjoy the comfort and advantages of a mess, without incurring expenses which their pay is not calculated to meet'.
6. PP 1872 XXXVII, c 575, p.81.
7. General Sir Ian Hamilton, *Listening for the Drums* (London: 1944), p.61; 75th Regiment Delhi and Lucknow Prize Roll. GHRM.
8. GD/174/1708/11. See also GD/244 Box 24, Estimate of clothing and accoutrements for an Officer of the 79th c.1845. It is noticeable that Macquarie's account does not include a kilt, the tartan for which would have been purchased in the Regiment and made up by the Regimental Tailors.
9. Lt. Colonel A.D.Greenhill Gardyne, *The Life of a Regiment, op. cit.*, Vol. III, p. 479.
10. MS account of the 1st Battalion Gordon Highlanders in the Le Cateau area August 1914. GHRM.
11. *Army List 1866*, p,13. Suppliers of Highland officers' clothing and equipment included Messrs Meyer and Mortimer, who had premises at 105 George Street, Edinburgh; Messrs. Moss Brothers, of Covent Garden, London; Messrs Jardine and Coy., Forth Street, Edinburgh; and Messrs William Anderson and Sons Ltd., Military Tailors, of Edinburgh.
12. Letters of John C. Stewart QOHRM.
13. Ibid.
14. BWRM. 395 File H5 P-Q.
15. J.D. Turner, 'Army Agency', *Journal of the Society of Army Historical Research*, Vol. XII 1934, pp. 27-46.
16. Letters of Lt. Col. the Hon. Lauderdale Maule, GD/45/14/634/4 1-98, Gibraltar 28.1.1847.
17. Royal Warrant 6.6.1854.
18. George and Anne Forty, *They Also Served* (Speldhurst, Kent: 1979), p. 145.
19. Letters of Lt. Col. the Hon. Lauderdale Maule GD/45/14/634/4 1-98 Gibraltar 5.7.1847.
20. Quoted R.M. Jones, 'Cox and Co.—Army Agents', *Journal of the Society for Army Historical Research*, No. 164, December 1962, pp. 178-186, and XVIV, No. 180, December 1966, pp. 195-204. Unfortunately none of the accounts of the Highland regiments have survived at Lloyds Bank which is a great loss as the accounts of Cox and Co. could have answered so many questions on the financial and internal management of the regiments.
21. GD/45/14/634/5 57-121. This is in fact a letter from the man to become famous in the 'Look after Dowb' telegram of 1855 from Lord Panmure to General Simpson. Georgina Maule, sister of Fox (Lord Panmure) and Lauderdale, married W.H. Dowbiggin in 1833 and Ensign Dowbiggin was their son; the intensity of the Maule family dispute goes a long way to explain why Panmure should have added a postscript to an official telegram which originally read, 'I recommend Dowbiggin to your notice, should you have a vacancy and if he is fit'. Cecil Woodham-Smith, *Florence Nightingale* (London: 1950), p. 267.
22. Diary of Col. J.W. Wedderburn 11.9.1842 28/714/1. BWRM.

23. Cpl. F. MacFarlane 1st Battalion Black Watch and Pte. R. Lobban 1st Battalion Cameron Highlanders. Oral history archive, *op.cit.* Drill money was authorised in the 79th by Standing Orders of 1819 which stated: ' . . . he [the officer] pays the guinea for his instruction to the Drill Sergeant'. Standing Orders of the 79th, 1819. QOHRM. In 1843 an attempt was made in the 79th to stop the practice of Guard Money when the Commanding Officer disapproved of 'the old practice of a guard asking for money from a new subaltern on his first guard'. Regimental Standing Order Book, 79th Highlanders, QOHRM 144/79. 21.7.1843. The practice however was still in existence in the Queen's Own Cameron Highlanders in 1882 when J. Spencer Ewart records, 'I was subaltern of the day "on my own". I had to give a sovereign to the Quarter guard; this being the customary fee for the first time an officer turns out a guard'. In the same year Ewart writes, 'I carried the Regimental Colour and had to pay the usual fee of £1 to the escort due on the first occasion of carrying a colour'. Diary of J. Spencer Ewart RH/4/84/1 8.1.1882 and 19.4.1882. Lt. Colonel Angus Fairrie informs the author that it is still the practice in the Queen's Own Highlanders for the subaltern to stand drams for the escort.
24. Diary of Pte. A.W. McIntosh. BWRM 421 (3591(1)).
25. General Sir Ian Hamilton, *Listening for the Drums*, *op. cit.*, p. 114.
26. PP 1903 c1421, p. 5.
27. Commanding Officer's Rough Order Book 91st Highlanders, 29.11.1860. ASHRM r/16.
28. Record of Donations of Plate 72nd Regiment. QOHRM.
29. Ibid.
30. Minute Book of the Officers' Mess 79th Highlanders 1844-1899 MS/1161 and Mess Rules adopted by the Officers of the 79th Highlanders, Quebec, 1st May 1849 MS/149/79, QOHRM.
31. Ibid.
32. PP 1903 X c1421, p. 7.
33. *Ibid.*, p. 14.
34. Letters of Lt. Col. the Hon. Lauderdale Maule GD/45/14/634/6 45-107.
35. E.S. Wood MS notes on R.H. Burgoyne, *Historical Records of the 93rd Sutherland Highlanders*, *op. cit.*, ASHRM.
36. Diary of Pte. A.W. McIntosh 42nd, Vol. 1, pp. 156-157. BWRM 421 (3591(1)).
37. Letters of Lt. Col. the Hon. Lauderdale Maule GD/45/14/634/2 1-93 25.11.1841.
38. Letters of Lt. Col. the Hon Lauderdale Maule GD/45/14/634/3 1-84 8.3.1843. Amongst those to whom Buchanan owed money was Alexander Cruickshanks, the veteran Quarter Master of the 79th.
39. WO/93/18, and Diary of Col. J.W. Wedderburn 42nd. BWRM. 12.9.1853.
40. PP 1857-58 XXXVII c499. An example of an officer court martialed and cashiered for drunkenness is Captain Colin Maxwell of the 93rd (of Dargarval House, Bishopton) who was court martialed at Sebastopol on 22nd October 1855. E.S. Wood notes on R.H. Burgoyne's 'Historical Records', 'Burgoyne is kindly silent why he left. He was cashiered for being drunk Poor Beggar!' MS Notes of E.S. Wood on R.H. Burgoyne, *Historical Records of the 93rd Sutherland Highlanders*, *op. cit.*, ASHRM, and WO/93/1B.
41. Lt. Col. W. Gordon Alexander, *Recollections of a Highland Subaltern*, *op.cit.*, p. 166.
42. Letter Book of Captain Bertie Gordon 91st, 13.8.1844. ASHRM.
43. Ibid., 25.7.1843.
44. Surgeon W. Munro, *Records of Service and Campaigning in Many Lands*, *op. cit.*, Vol. 1, p. 46.
45. Letters of Lt. Andrew Agnew of Lochnaw, 7.4.1840 GD/154/745.
46. Just before he retired in December 1860, Lt. Colonel Alexander Leith Hay of the 93rd who was stationed at Sabathu, India, began the process of selling up before returning home. While treasured personal possessions were undoubtedly retained,

books, furniture, linen, glass and saddlery were all auctioned off in lots, emphasising the peripatetic lifestyle that military families had right up to the end of the Empire in the 1950s and 1960s. Leith Hay's sale was conducted over several months and most lots were sold within the Regiment. His collections of pigeons and birds was obtained by Colour Sergeant Charles Allan of the 93rd and items were bought by private soldiers and sergeants in ones and twos, Private John Webster of No. 3 Company for example buying the Mynah Bird for 9 Rs. Certain personal items were sold to Officers of the Regiment, Dr. Munro buying the portable armchair. Most of the books were purchased by private soldiers, but native Indians, presumably servants or contractors, also bought items. GD/225 Box 42.

47. Letters of Sydney B. Jameson, HQ 1st Army and his son Alistair Jameson, 7th and 2nd Seaforth Highlanders and 1st Cameron Highlanders. NLS, MS/10305 and *Historical Records of the Cameron Highlanders*, *op.cit.*, Vol. III, p. 224.
48. Diary of Colonel A. Stirling, 2nd Battalion Argyll and Sutherland Highlanders, property of Colonel J. Stirling (Retd.), kindly lent to the author.
49. Ibid.
50. Letters of Lt. Col. the Hon. Lauderdale Maule, Quebec 7.7.1849 GD/45/14/634/4 99-184.
51. Diary of Colonel A. Stirling, 2nd Battalion Argyll and Sutherland Highlanders, *op. cit.*
52. Letters of Lt. Col. the Hon. Lauderdale Maule, Quebec 7.7.1849 GD/45/14/634/5 57-121.
53. Ibid., Quebec 15.3.1849. GD/45/14/634/5 1-56.
54. Myna Trustram, *Women of the Regiment* (Cambridge: 1984).
55. Diary of Colonel J.W. Wedderburn 7.2.1854. BWRM. 28/714/1.
56. Ibid., 18.2.1854.
57. Letters, papers and information on the Mackay family kindly lent to the author.
58. *79th News*, No. 98, July 1908, p. 204.
59. William Forbes-Mitchell, *Reminiscences of the Great Mutiny* (London: 1910), p. 239.
60. Diary of Colonel J.W. Wedderburn 6.6.1853. BWRM. 28/714/1.
61. Ibid., 27.5.1852.
62. Ziggi Alexander and Audrey Dewjee (eds.), *Wonderful Adventures of Mrs Seacole* (Bristol: 1984), p. 237.
63. For example the 79th Cameron Highlanders Wives' and Children's Fund 1892, *79th News*, 1903, No. 70, p. 1, and James McKay, *Reminiscences of the Last Kafir War* (Grahamstown: 1871), p. 125.
64. G.L. Goff, *Historical Records of the 91st Argyllshire Highlanders*, *op. cit.*, p. 241.
65. Archives of Queen Victoria School, Dunblane.

CHAPTER 7

Locations, Barracks and Living Conditions

A considerable amount of energy in research and reforming zeal has been expended upon the barrack and living conditions particularly of the Victorian Army, but much of this work was, and still is, directed entirely towards the Army at home.[1] It is important therefore when looking at the Highland regiments to see exactly where they were between 1820 and 1920 and to look more closely at individual cases to see whether the general conclusions on army living conditions applied to these regiments. Locations at home and abroad, together with experience on active service, affected the character of the regiments as much as their unique dress or the forceful individuality of their commanding officers, and the tables of outline locations in Appendix II bring out some important points.

Firstly, the location details must be broken down for kilted regiments (42nd, 78th, 79th, 92nd and 93rd) and for Highland Line and Trews Regiments of Foot (72nd, 73rd, 74th, 75th and 91st) and secondly, by the natural division which occurs in 1881, with the dual battalion system, when it was proposed to have one battalion at home and the sister battalion overseas on an equal time basis. Therefore taking the kilted Highland battalions between 1820 and 1881 by whole years and dividing the service between home service, foreign service and active service, a pattern begins to emerge.

All the kilted battalions saw home, foreign and active service and, proportionally, during the sixty-two years under consideration, very little time was spent in Scotland. Much of the time spent in Ireland was in aid of the civil power, and England was not a regular station for the Highland kilted battalions, although the 78th, the 79th and the 93rd were all used to assist in the industrial and political unrest in the 1830s and early 1840s. The 42nd, 79th and 93rd took part in the pre-Crimean Camp of Exercise at Chobham in 1853 and all the kilted battalions ultimately passed through Aldershot, the first home hutted and tented camp, purpose-built with training areas attached, purchased by the Army in 1853.[2]

The table brings out clearly that by far the greater proportion of the time of the kilted regiments was spent in foreign and active service occupying particularly stations in India, Gibraltar, Canada and the West Indies. The 78th spent a remarkable twenty-four years on foreign service in India, a figure which excludes their active service in the Indian Mutiny, and they and the 79th managed to avoid the West Indies, the latter probably because of the influence of Lauderdale Maule. Between Waterloo and the Mutiny the 92nd as a Regiment saw no active service at all, having been reduced to a Staff and Band at Gibraltar to supply men to other regiments, and they arrived, much to their

SERVICE LOCATIONS OF KILTED HIGHLAND REGIMENTS (in whole years) 1820-1881

Location		Regiment 42nd	78th	79th	92nd	93rd
Home Service	Ireland	8	13	5	13	8
	Scotland	5	6	8	5	7
	England	8	5	9	1	10
	Home Service totals	21	24	22	19	25
Foreign Service	Gibraltar	8	2	10	6	2
	Malta/Ionian Islands	14			6	
	West Indies	4			11	11
	Canada	1	4	14		9
	Indian/Ceylon	9	24	12	14	10
	Aden		4			
	Crimea (not active service)				1	
	Foreign Service totals	36	34	36	38	32
Active Service	Canada, Crimea, Aden, India, Persia, Ashanti, Afghanistan, South Africa	5	4	4	5	5
% Time on Home Service		34%	39%	36%	31%	40%
% Time on Foreign and Active Service		66%	61%	64%	69%	60%

disgust, too late in the Crimea to see action. It is especially noticeable that the kilted Highland regiments were seldom used in Africa, with the exception of the 42nd who took part in the Ashanti War in 1873,[3] and the 92nd who were at Majuba in 1881. The kilted regiments are associated with India, but apart from the 78th, this is a modern misconception until the period of the Mutiny and after, when they began to be included in the regular rota of Indian Service in the British garrison. The 78th and the 92nd also served in Afghanistan, the latter taking part in Roberts's historic march from Kabul to Kandahar.

The percentage totals of foreign and active service show that these kilted Highland battalions were primarily active, working, fighting service units who spent very little time in their homeland and as much as 69% of their time between 1820 and 1881 overseas. When at home their primary duties were in Ireland where they seldom kept together as a battalion but were broken down into detachments, scattered over a wide area and lodged in several barracks or billeted on the local population.

By contrast the Line and Trews Regiments of Foot who were Highland or were linked to Highland regiments in 1881 show a slightly different pattern.

These Highland Line and Trews Regiments of Foot spent very little time in Scotland, the 75th none at all and a greater proportion of their time in England. Again however their foreign and active service totals outweigh their home service and the 73rd and 74th spent 73% of their time overseas. The 73rd and the

SERVICE LOCALITIES OF HIGHLAND LINE AND TREWS REGIMENTS OF FOOT 1820-1881

Location		Regiment				
		72nd	73rd	74th	75th	91st
	Ireland	4	5	9	13	13
Home Service	Scotland	4	1	3		4
	England	11	11	5	12	11
	Home Service totals	19	17	17	25	28
	Gibraltar	4	1	4	6	
	Malta/Ionian Islands		8	5	2	3
	West Indies	3		13		9
Foreign Service	Canada	3	4	8		
	India/Ceylon	15	15	9	11	8
	Cape of Good Hope/ St. Helena	11	5		10	11
	Hong Kong/Japan		3	1		
	Singapore/Penang			2		
	Foreign Service totals	36	36	42	29	31
Active Service	Cape of Good Hope, Kaffir Wars, Crimea, Montevideo, Afghanistan	7	9	3	8	5
% Time on Home Service		31%	27%	27%	40%	45%
% Time on Foreign and Active Service		69%	73%	73%	60%	55%

75th did not go to the West Indies and the 75th and the 91st did not serve in Canada; all however served in South Africa, the 74th and the 91st having three years' active service there during the Kaffir War of 1851-1853. The 73rd and the 74th were also sent to the Far East for a short time. Only the 72nd were in the Crimea, but all these Regiments were involved in the Indian Mutiny or its aftermath and the 72nd were also in Afghanistan.

Overall it is again clear that these Highland Line and Trews Regiments were primarily hard-working, foreign service units who did not spend lengthy periods in home barracks, and when they were at home their stay in any one place was remarkably short. Alternatively, overseas postings in an area could be as long as thirteen years (the 72nd and the 75th in the Cape of Good Hope), either together as a battalion, or broken down into detachments. Thus while home barracks played their part, they are by no means the whole story.

There is no clear indication as to why the Kilted and Line and Trews Regiments were used in this way. Some of the locations may be accounted for in patronage and influence, but it is difficult to say exactly why none of the kilted regiments served on the African continent between 1820 and 1873. The changes in recruiting patterns and the number of English and Irish in some of the Line and Trews Regiments may account for their short service in Scotland, but it does not account for the small amount of time spent in their home country by the Kilted Regiments. It could be that part of the explanation lies in a total lack of sympathetic feeling and understanding of the Kilted Regiments on behalf of the War Office, fear of an increase in desertion rates while at home in Scotland, or concern over the Highland economic situation and an underlying fear of potential unreliability given Highland poverty and emigration; but there is no direct evidence of this.

The object of the two-battalion and territorial system of 1881 was not only to provide a firm home base for recruiting, but also to try to ensure an equality in the number of regiments at home and abroad. It is clear from the following table that in relation to the kilted Highland battalions this did not happen, and consistently their percentage figure of foreign and active service exceeds 50% in both the first and the second battalions.

SERVICE LOCALITIES OF HIGHLAND KILTED REGIMENTS (in whole years) 1881-1920 INCLUSIVE

		1/BW 42nd	2/BW 73rd	1 Sea-forth 72nd	2 Sea-forth 78th	1 Gor-dons 75th	2 Gor-dons 92nd	1 Cam-erons 79th	2 Cam-erons (1897)	1 ASH 91st	2 ASH 93rd
	Ireland	5	8	6	1	4	8	3	1	1	5
Home Service	Scotland	7	4	5	8	3	4	7	2	5	7
	England	2	7	5	5	7	6	7	1	8	4
Home Service	Totals	14	19	16	14	14	18	17	4	14	16
	Gibraltar	4						3	2		
	Malta	3		1		4		3	2	3	
Foreign	Egypt	1		4		1	2	5			
Service	South Africa	3							4	4	3
	India/Ceylon	6	12	11	15	8	11	2	4	6	15
	Constantinople					1					
	Hong Kong/ China								2	4	
Foreign Service Totals		17	12	16	15	14	13	13	14	17	18
Active Service (Egypt, Soudan, S. Africa, France, Flanders, Mesopotamia, Palestine, Hazara, Chitral, Italy, Bulgaria, Georgia, Tochi)		9	9	8	11	12	9	10	5	9	6
% Home Service		35%	48%	40%	35%	35%	45%	42%	17%	35%	40%
% Foreign and Active Service		65%	52%	60%	65%	65%	55%	58%	83%	65%	60%

In the years between 1881 and 1920 moves became more regular and frequent although the time spent in India as a whole could still be up to sixteen years on one tour, as in the case of the 2nd Battalion Seaforth Highlanders. There was an attempt to bring all the kilted battalions home to Scotland, but their stay was short and service in Ireland continues although it is less than during the 1820-1881 period. Ireland was after 1881 not only a garrison station, but was also used for extensive field training especially at the Curragh, a camp built on similar lines to Aldershot. In Scotland there was a serious shortage of training facilities and ranges, and while the kilted battalions returned for morale, recruiting and public relations purposes, it was not the most practical of locations from the military point of view.[4]

The 78th left Canada in 1871 and no Kilted Highland Battalion returned there for garrison duties in the period 1881 to 1920 in line with British reluctance to expend further resources on Canadian defence, gradually improving relations with the United States of America after the 'Trent' affair in 1861; and the federal union of the Provinces of Canada, New Brunswick and Nova Scotia in 1867.

Much of the foreign service of the Highland Kilted Battalions between 1881 and 1920 is linked with active service in Egypt, the Sudan and the North-West Frontier, and while every Kilted Battalion saw action on one front or another during the First World War, six battalions also served in the South African War of 1899-1901. The active service percentages are therefore high and the Kilted Battalions built up a considerable fighting reputation during the period 1881 to 1920, gaining coveted and well-deserved battle honours in arduous and hard-fought campaigns.

The construction of the barracks and quarters occupied by these Highland soldiers varied widely at home and abroad. All barracks however, whatever their construction or location, comprised certain basic ingredients, not all of which were to be found in every barrack at any one time. These ingredients were:

Officers' Quarters and Mess
Sergeants' Quarters and Mess
Soldiers' Quarters
Married Soldiers' rooms
Kitchens
Wet and dry Canteen
Hospital
Barrack Square
Stables
Privies for men and women
Urinals
Ablution Rooms
Wash house
Ash Pits
Rainwater collecting tank and/or well
Dead House

Guard Room
Cells
Black Hole
Coal Yard
Forage Store
Forge
Barrack Master's Store
Magazine
Cleaning Shed
Drill Shed
Butcher's Shop
Tailor's Shop
Quarter Master's Store
Pioneer's shop and armourer's workshop
School Room
Recreation Room
Reading Room
Library
Fives Court
Drying ground

The barracks may be classified by their nature and their history: firstly, ancient forts and garrisons, secondly, purpose-built barracks of the eighteenth and early nineteenth centuries and thirdly, barracks and camps built after 1850.

Dealing firstly with home barracks, that is barracks in England, Scotland and Ireland, much of the psychology behind their location and construction was based on official concern regarding the concentration of soldiers in any one place, fear of invasion, internal unrest and civilian opposition to large numbers of soldiers in their midst. At home therefore there were the ancient forts and garrisons some of which were of considerable antiquity, Stirling Castle, the Tower of London, Dover Castle and Edinburgh Castle being fine examples. Now regarded as major tourist attractions, they were, between 1820 and 1920, still working barracks and were garrisoned as defensive positions, arsenals and military stores and were occupied and guarded as such. The living accommodation of the men together with their wives, families and associated horses and equipment was fitted into these ancient and frequently picturesque fortresses which in the nineteenth century were adapted without any reverence for their history; but in fact their twentieth century survival, relatively intact, depended very much upon their eighteenth, nineteenth and twentieth century occupation by military units, a factor often overlooked by modern historians. Their modern military occupation is in fact part of their history, and while military necessity required structural alterations which damaged some of the ancient fabric, military occupation saved many of these buildings from total ruin.[5]

An example of an old home fort barracks is Stirling Castle. Here the ancient and beautiful buildings were occupied and adapted for the practical requirement of the garrison. Once a royal residence, the Castle's history as a fortress ended after the 1745 rebellion. It remained however a fort and garrison containing a large supply of ordnance, and several buildings, including the Great Hall built by James V in 1529, were adapted to accommodate soldiers' barracks. In 1801 this Hall, with its magnificent oak hammer-beam roof, was partitioned and divided into barrack rooms and it was here that Private Archibald McIntosh of the 42nd served in 1858 prior to embarkation for India:

> Tuesday 3rd June 1858.
> I did not like soldiering in Stirling, there is no sport here. I seldom went out, but when I did it was mostly to the Bridge of Allan which is a nice clean place.
> —'I spent most of my time in barracks at the 'Ladies Look Out' where I could get a very good view of the surrounding country, I dare say it is the reason it got that name.
> —The barracks here are very small, and each room has two flats, the upper one being reached by a ladder which goes through a trap door cut in the floor [The Great Hall].
> —The building the Canteen is in [the Palace built by James V] is very beautifully carved out in front with all sorts of faces and a life size figure of the 'Modest Maid' in the centre, the barrack in that building is called the 'Lions Den'.[6]

The physical and structural limitations resulting from the position and nature of these ancient fortresses is evident in the Interim Report on the Barracks and Hospitals in the North British District of 1859, which described the barracks in Stirling Castle as '. . . the worst barracks we have seen anywhere'.[7]

There was little in fact that could be done with the external dimensions of the massive, soundly constructed stone buildings and thus internal divisions had no reference to existing windows or ventilation:

> The old Parliament House [the Great Hall] has been cut up by staircases, floors and partitions, so as to make three flats of tolerably good rooms ranging from 11 feet 9 inches to 14 feet high in the upper rooms which are carried into the roof. There is a considerable amount of window space on opposite sides, apparently on account of the large size of the old windows. All the rooms except two have stoves instead of fireplaces.
> There are Sergeants' rooms partitioned off from the landings on the two upper floors ... The Sergeants' Mess is on the ground floor. It has no Mess kitchen.
> The barrack accommodation in the Palace is of a very inferior character. The old halls of the building have been crowded with men not only on the floors but on the galleries carried round the walls, exhibiting one of the worst barrack arrangements in the three kingdoms.[8]

At Stirling Castle there was a school room under the armoury and two ablution rooms, one under the Great Hall and one under the Quarter Master's store. A 'very dark room' was used as the women's wash house and next door to it was the cleaning shed. There were two cook houses, one of which was underground, and two ash pits in large cellars. There was no drill shed and the passages of the main buildings were used for drill in wet weather. In 1859 water was supplied by the Stirling Water Company and a rainwater collecting tank with 136,000 gallon capacity. There were drinking fountains and privies but the latter had no doors and drained down the rock face to a large pit below. The

Forts, Garrisons and Barracks in Scotland 1820-1920

1:2500000

Black Hole was situated under the palace. Most of the floors in the barrack rooms were of wood but some in the Palace were flagged. The Hospital was outside the Castle in the Argyll Lodging. The rooms and barracks in the Castle were lit by gas in 1859 and the general conclusion of the report of that year was that:

> Stirling Castle offers an example of the inconvenience arising from an attempt to put buildings to a purpose for which they were never intended.[9]

While certain internal improvements were made and additional modern facilities introduced into Stirling Castle, the basic barrack accommodation remained virtually unaltered right up to the time that the Depot of the Argyll and Sutherland Highlanders left the Castle in 1963.

The general situation was also evident at Edinburgh Castle where ancient buildings were adapted for barrack purposes. Parliament Hall was used as a hospital, in the Palace were barracks, and the Canteen with barracks was on the other two sides of Crown Square.[10]. The 'New Barracks', Mills Mount and Argyll Battery Barracks were below Foogs Gate. Mills Mount Barracks were described by George Miller of the 71st (HLI):

> In 1865 they were double breasted, that is rooms on each side, said rooms were short and narrow, a crush to get past the tables and the bed irons. Nothing between the slates and the eye, while here and there if you had a smack for astrology you could spend sleepless hours looking at the stars and planets through holes in the roof.[11]

After the First World War the barrack block on the north side of Crown Square was demolished to make way for the National Shrine, and plans for the Hospital Block were begun in 1893 on the site of the old ordnance store, the design and construction of the Hospital Block being an extremely vexed question as it altered the profile of the Castle from the north and west sides.[12]

Picturesque though these old fortresses may be today, in 1820 they were still considered to have a practical purpose as barracks, defensive positions and arsenals for, seventy-five years previously and within living memory, the Jacobites had attempted and failed to take Edinburgh and Stirling Castles and their structures were still looked upon and maintained as working garrisons. It was only with the increase in interest in things Scottish and Highland, the romance of Scotland resulting from the writings of MacPherson and Scott, the growth of tourism and the long peace at home that the great Scottish castle garrisons came to be viewed in a different light. As demands for increased public access grew and historical maintenance was required, particularly on the Parliament Hall and Palace at Edinburgh Castle, the responsibility for this structure was gradually assumed by the Ministry of Works.[13] The cost of repairs to Queen Mary's Rooms, unused by the military since 1836, was assumed by the Commission of Works in 1876.[14] Later, in 1895, it was proposed to hand over St. Margaret's Chapel, Parliament Hall and the Argyll Tower,[15] and by 1915 the Office of Works had taken over the whole Castle. Thus when the question arose regarding the charges for entry for the relations of soldiers and visiting friends in 1915, HM Office of Works was able to write to the War Office:

> The G.O.C. in Chief does not seem to realise that Edinburgh Castle has been transferred to this Department subject to Military occupation.[16]

Secondly, in home barracks there were the purpose-built barracks and forts of the eighteenth and early nineteenth centuries. These fall roughly into three groups, Irish barracks, Highland Forts, and barracks from the period of the French and Napoleonic Wars. Irish barracks form a group of their own

Barracks and Stations: Ireland 1820-1920

1:2,500000

100 miles

because of the historical background which caused their building and their continued maintenance and occupation by the British Army up to 1921. The largest single complex of barrack accommodations listed by the 1859 Commission report is Royal Barracks, Dublin.[17] It was built in 1704 and extended in 1793 for 1917 men in the form of three large squares several stories high, named Royal Barracks, Palatine Barracks and Cavalry Barracks. Standing adjacent to the River Liffy, whose smell was none too pleasant on a warm summer's day, outwardly it looks a bare, barren, unwelcoming place, destitute of any of the romance associated with the great castle forts of Scotland. Leaving Royal Barracks for the healthier environment of Tidworth in 1907, the *79th News* noted:

> . . . we must remember that distance lends enchantment to the view. We are now inclined to forget the searching odours of the Liffy [and] the squalor and filth of the slums which surrounded us . . . .[18]

All the Highland regiments were stationed here or passed through these barracks between 1820 and 1920, and apart from the addition of certain facilities and the improvement of the area of space per man, the barracks in 1920 were in much the same condition as they were in 1820. The rooms were generally long and narrow and were originally intended to house men in berths of two in two tiers. Thus, when single beds were introduced the rooms were cluttered with furniture and the report of 1859 noted that:

> . . . before the beds are folded down the tables have to be removed, and when down, the beds cover the floors so closely that only a narrow passage . . . is left.[19]

By 1904, when the 1st Cameron Highlanders were stationed at Royal Barracks, some of the rooms had been subdivided by partitions: 'Cubicles are all the go here and the Company seem very taken up with them'.[20] It was here also that the Battalion was introduced to dining rooms which were not altogether popular at first, and when the Battalion returned to Aldershot in 1909, eating in the barrack rooms was reintroduced:

> On arrival at Aldershot we resumed the old barrack-room system of Messing as opposed to the Dining Hall system. The two methods, like the question of 'Bread and Biscuits' produce divided opinions.[21]

Water at Royal Barracks was obtained from a pond in Phoenix Park and from St. James's Harbour, and drainage was direct to the Liffy. While the barrack may have been entirely adequate in its dimensions and layout when it was built, it proved to have severe limitations when attempts were made to adapt it to later nineteenth and twentieth century standards.

The majority of other Irish barracks were constructed upon what came to be known as 'the standard Irish pattern' and were built approximately between 1786 (Eniskillen) and 1813 (Kilkenny). They were of stone, built in blocks either two or three stories high, with ablutions, cook houses and sundry buildings separate and they were usually encompassed by a wall. Kilkenny, built in 1813, was described as:

> . . . arranged on the common plan to many other Irish barracks. They are in houses each of which has a central passage and staircase with a barrack room opening out of the landings on each side, and a non-commissioned officers room between each two soldiers rooms.[22]

There were stone staircases and wooden landings, the windows being on one side of the rooms, four to each barrack room, with two fireplaces to each room. The rooms were 33 feet long, 18 feet wide and 10 or 11 feet high and housed between 17 and 19 men. When John Wheately of the 42nd served here in 1820 the barrack was relatively new; he comments that Nenagh barracks, built on a similar pattern, was 'a nice comfortable little barrack'.[23]

What is surprising about these Irish barracks is the numbers they were intended to accommodate: 1169 men at Birr, for example,[24] 1755 at Cork, stone-built in 1800, and 946 at Buttevant, built in 1810. The rooms held approximately ten to twenty-five men and the size of the accommodation can be roughly gauged from this. In 1859 a consistent complaint regarding these Irish barracks was the lack of ancillary buildings such as drying rooms, laundries, adequate cook houses, cleaning sheds, drill sheds, ablutions, drained latrines and privies and married quarters, and therefore much of the cooking, all of the eating and the drying of clothes took place in the barrack rooms, a situation that was entirely acceptable when the barracks were built, but which became unacceptable as the moral, military and sanitary reforms of the second half of the nineteenth century grew in popularity and effect.

Of the purpose-built barracks and forts of the eighteenth and early nineteenth centuries there are the three main Highland forts, Fort William, Fort Augustus and Fort George, together with the barracks at Berwick upon Tweed, the last of which was designed in 1700 and occupied in 1721, and was the first purpose-built barrack on the British mainland. As the Irish barracks had been built to garrison Ireland, so the Highland forts had been built to overawe the Highlands after the 1715 and 1745 rebellions. In 1833, when a barrack survey was carried out, apparently by the Board of Ordnance, the viability of Fort William and Fort Augustus was already in question.[25] It was believed that these forts had to be kept up under the Act of Union, but nobody seemed to be quite sure, and certainly no maintenance had been carried out since they were built.[26] Fort Augustus in 1859 had no latrines, bath houses or wash houses, and the urinals and privies were open holes in the wall draining directly to the loch below.[27] The Reserve Companies of the 72nd were stationed here and at Corgarff Castle in 1830.

The massive Vaubanesque Fort George was unique of its kind in Scotland. It was begun in 1748, completed in 1770 and was intended as a strategic military base to overawe the Highlands, being designed to hold over 2000 men. As a military base it has been continuously occupied since and in 1986 was entirely renovated and restored.[28] The large stone buildings and barracks were well and soundly constructed, but the 1859 Commission had hardly a complimentary word to say about the facilities within its walls and the hygienic conditions under which the men lived.[29]

Finally, of the home purpose-built barracks of the eighteenth and early nineteenth centuries there are the 'Napoleonic' barracks on the mainland of Britain. These were built in the alarm and panic generated by the French Wars on very similar lines to the Irish barracks. Their hasty construction meant that even in 1820 they were probably ill repaired and out of date in their facilities. They generally comprised stone or brick blocks of several stories, with three or four sets of large barrack rooms on each floor. The complex at Canterbury, where the 93rd were stationed in 1834, is a good example; there were altogether four barracks at Canterbury, Cavalry Barracks built in 1795, Artillery Barracks built in 1802, North Gate Barracks built in 1803, and Infantry Barracks built in 1806, housing altogether 2000 men, women and children. Infantry Barracks were of brick, in two blocks, two stories high, each with three sets of rooms. The privies, ashpits and ablution rooms were separate buildings behind each block. In 1858 the whole was lit by candles, there were no baths and the kitchen had no ovens. Fluid refuse and effluent was run off in open drains.[30] Similar blocks were built on Western Heights, Dover (1800), Dundee (originally built in 1760 and extended 1796/97), and at Perth (1792/93) which had been intended as a Cavalry Barrack.

Unusual amongst this category of home barracks was Shorncliffe, which comprised 192 huts holding 25 men each and was highly favoured as a barrack by the Commission of 1858,[31] and Weedon in Northamptonshire built in 1806. The barracks and large ordnance store at Weedon were built of brick around the Grand Union Canal in a position in England at the maximum distance from the sea in any direction and was secretly intended to be the final retreat of Royalty in the event of invasion. The barrack blocks were of considerable size, two stories high, with stores, prison, chapel and stables on the ground floor. The rooms held between 11 and 20 men each, there were sergeants' rooms on each flat, some rooms had two open fireplaces in them and in 1859 the whole was lit by gas. There was adequate accommodation for tailors' shops, school room and sergeants' mess, but the ablution rooms and privies, which were not connected to the drains, were at some distance from the barrack blocks.

Large quantities of ordnance were brought here in the 1830s during the revolutionary scares, and the Report on Barracks of 1833 noted:

> The storehouses and armouries are the most magnificent buildings . . . 100,000 muskets have been sent away . . . 100,000 remain . . . There are also very good barracks . . . in short all is on a magnificent scale at Weedon and the keeping up for so long a time of such an establishment is quite beyond my comprehension.[32]

The 93rd were at Weedon in 1834 and 1852, the 73rd in 1821 and the 91st in 1831.

There is a small category of barracks which were built between the Napoleonic and the modern periods and these reflect an interesting change of attitude towards internal security in mainland Britain and the seriousness with which contemporary industrial unrest was viewed. Such was the nature and location of industrial unrest after Peterloo that a number of barracks were built in the midland manufacturing districts to accommodate troops employed in aid of the civil power. Billeting was unpopular and entirely unsatisfactory as troops could not be kept together, housing conditions were bad, and there was a danger of subversion. Lt. Colonel Maule of the 79th wrote to his brother from Newcastle under Lyne in June 1839:

> I propose for the sake of the men to concentrate the two Companies at Newcastle [under Lyne] . . . now that the men are to remain in the district, it seems highly advisable to have them together, not only for the purpose of drill, but because Lane End is a very loose quarter and I am afraid of the soldiers becoming too intemate with the people.[33]

Thus, Salford Infantry Barracks were built between 1820 and 1821, Bury in 1845, and Fulwood (Preston) in 1848, and there were also barracks at Burnley and Stockport. They were all, it appears, stone-or brick-built, candlelit, ill-drained buildings with the minimum of facilities and were probably never intended to be permanently occupied.[34]

The final category of home barracks occupied by the Highland battalions were those which were purpose-built from the time of the Crimean War onwards. The War had emphasised the need for a greater proportion of a soldier's time to be spent on practical field training, and the Reports of the Barrack and Hospital Improvement Commission showed that in general living conditions were inadequate to keep a soldier fit and healthy for his job. First amongst these stations is Aldershot. In fact, the planning of Aldershot had begun before the War when in 1852 the first reconnaissance of the area was made. Building began in 1854 and it was intended originally to have 1200 wooden huts with tented areas in two Camps, North and South.[35] The huts were lit by oil lamps and gas estimates were obtained in 1855, while heating was from stoves although some brick fireplaces were installed, again in 1855.[36] The structures were guaranteed in the same year by the contractor for thirteen years, but the huts deteriorated when unoccupied in the winter, and by 1889 they were neither wind nor waterproof. Some of the North Camp was rebuilt in brick by the early 1890s, but South Camp was still in the form of wooden huts.[37] Even in 1866 the 74th found that the buildings had been so heavily painted that they constituted a serious fire risk and iron fire surrounds were introduced, but the unlined huts were very cold and held frost on the inside of the walls. The large iron stoves in the middle of the rooms had a pipe to the roof and a good fire soon made these red hot, burning kit and hands if they came too near.[38]

Largely on account of its physical deterioration Aldershot was not a popular camp, but this lack of popularity may also have had something to do with the work done there. The camp had a great levelling and standardising influence on the British Army primarily because large-scale exercises could be carried out with formations greater than a battalion. Every Highland battalion passed through here before 1914 and it is clear that whereas a Highland regiment could be run on a personal and individual basis, particularly in India, at Aldershot, within easy reach of London and the War Office, standards, procedures and regulations were fully enforced and the individuality of commanding officers was suppressed.

The camp at the Curragh, in Ireland, was built on very similar lines to Aldershot and there were several other camps on a smaller scale. However, the primary building of new barracks took place after the Localisation and the linked battalion system was introduced in 1872. As a result of the considerable advances in medical knowledge regarding hygiene, health, living space and drainage these barracks were built to a high standard and most survive to be occupied today. An excellent example as far as the Highland regiments are concerned is the Brigade Depot at Inverness (Cameron Barracks). By 1872 the only surviving viable barrack in the area was Fort George, but for the purposes of the linked battalion and depot system it was deemed that the fort was unsuitable as depot accommodation and accordingly the building of the Inverness Depot commenced in 1877. Re-named Cameron Barracks, it was built to a high standard of construction and design with gas lighting throughout, purpose-built married quarters, wash basins, foot baths, night urinals, cleaning and drying rooms, coffee bar, canteen, library, reading room, stores and drill shed.[39]

Other barracks built in Scotland in this later period were Redford Cavalry and Infantry Barracks, Edinburgh. By the turn of the century it was clear that Edinburgh Castle was simply unable to accommodate an infantry battalion to the hygiene and living standards required, especially as there was continual pressure by the Ministry of Works to claim buildings and open them to the public. The Army, therefore, after years of guarding and residing in this ancient fortress, found themselves in the position of an unwelcome occupier in the twentieth century, but Redford was not completed until 1914 and was not occupied by the Regular Highland Battalions before the First World War, and when the 1st Battalion Cameron Highlanders left Edinburgh in August 1914, they left from Edinburgh Castle, the last full peacetime battalion to occupy the fortress.[40]

The overseas barracks occupied by the Highland battalions fall roughly into the same categories, that is, firstly, ancient fortresses, the majority of which were in India, the forts at Delhi, Lahore, Attock, Jamrud and Agra being fine examples. Some of these forts were not only old defensive positions but were in addition beautifully decorated with formal carvings, mosaics, audience rooms, gardens and fountains. In the case of the Fort at Delhi, barracks were built in the nineteenth century by the British within its walls and these are still used by the Indian Army today.

Secondly, there were the purpose-built forts, constructed primarily to defend the growing Empire, and as islands and areas were captured, extended or colonised in the eighteenth and nineteenth centuries, fortresses were built or

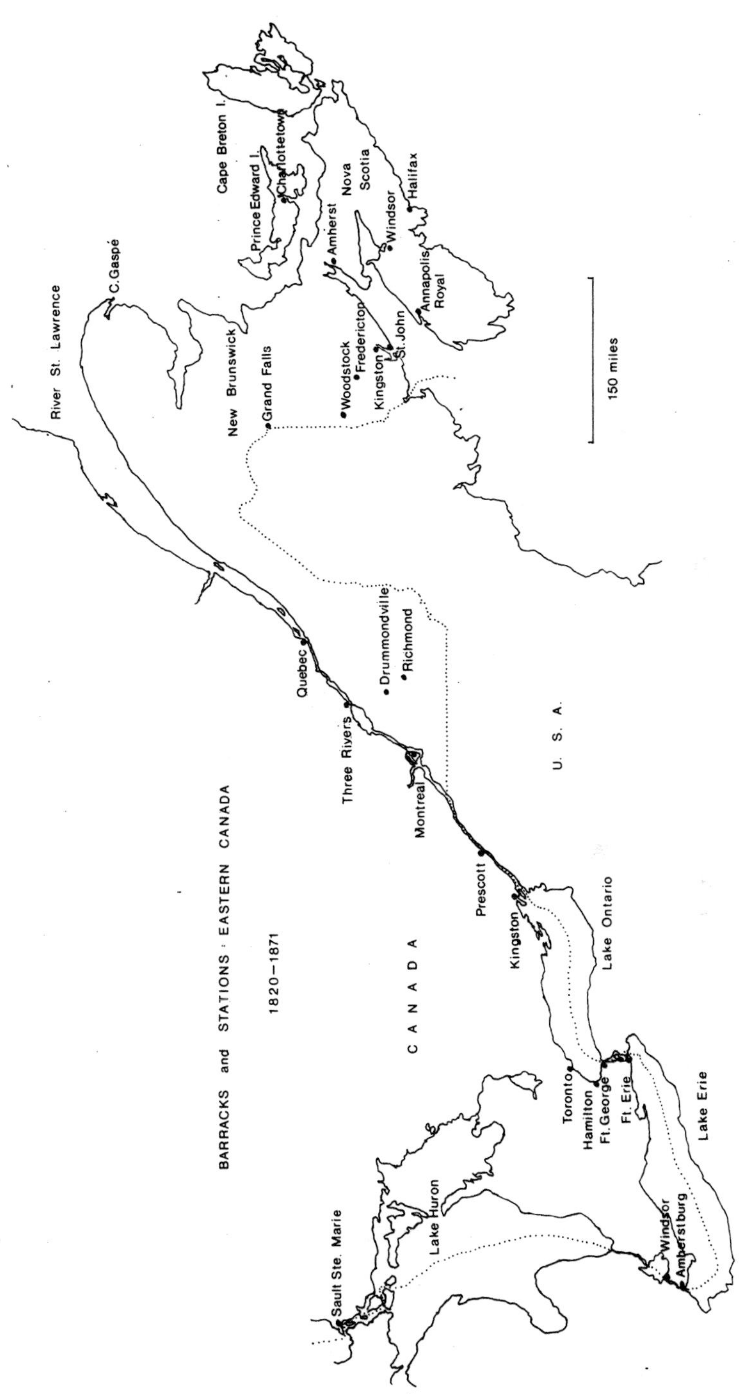
BARRACKS and STATIONS · EASTERN CANADA
1820–1871
River St. Lawrence
C.Gaspé
Cape Breton I.
Prince Edward I.
Charlottetown
New Brunswick
Grand Falls
Woodstock
Fredericton
Kingston
St. John
Amherst
Nova Scotia
Windsor
Halifax
Annapolis Royal
150 miles
Quebec
Drummondville
Richmond
Three Rivers
Montreal
U. S. A.
CANADA
Prescott
Kingston
Lake Ontario
Toronto
Hamilton
Ft. George
Ft. Erie
Lake Erie
Sault Ste. Marie
Lake Huron
Windsor
Amherstburg

adapted all over the world. Some of the largest and most impressive defensive positions which still survive today are in Canada. Following the wars between Britain and America in 1812 and 1815, tension between the two countries remained, and in 1825 Sir James Carmichael Smyth, Royal Engineers, was commissioned to study Canadian defensive positions, with a chain of supporting forts along the sensitive border with the United States.

In Nova Scotia the rebuilding of the defences at Halifax started in 1828 and was officially not completed until 1856. By 1861, £233,882 had been spent by the British Government on the fortress and several barracks, with the star-shaped citadel overlooking Halifax harbour comprising casemates, a ditch, magazines, stores and bastions, housing 764 NCOs and men and 18 Officers.[41]. Gas lighting was installed here in 1844.[42]

In Lower Canada work on the Citadel at Quebec began in 1820 and was finished in 1831. The barracks in the Citadel must have been basic and unsophisticated and would have had few amenities. They were heated by wood fires and lit by candles and oil lamps.[43] The 79th were stationed here from 1825 to 1828, from 1834 to 1836 and again from 1848 to 1851, and the 93rd were also in Quebec from 1843 to 1848 and the 74th in 1841.

Reinforcing the defences at Isle aux Noix, Montreal commenced in 1818, and here officers' quarters, guard house barracks and stores were built.[44] There were in addition several small forts of earth, stone and timber construction, built and garrisoned as outstations.

In Upper Canada there were few permanent fort defences, except at Kingston, but there was always a problem of access here until the completion of the Rideau Canal in 1832, one bank of the St. Lawrence being American-held. Fort Henry was built between 1832 and 1836, Toronto Fort was in ruins and a new stone barrack was built at Fort York, known as Stanley Barrack, in 1840. There was a star-shaped earth redoubt named Fort Mississauga which guarded the Niagara River, and Fort Malden at Amherstburg which was garrisoned until 1859.[45] When the 79th were at Kingston and its out stations in 1829 and 1830, this was the edge of a virtually untouched frontier. In winter, when the cold forced the abandonment of the kilt for grey trousers in the 79th, the individual outstations were totally isolated by snow and the unmade roads.[46] These bitter weather conditions in Canada meant that for up to five months of the year the men were virtually confined to their barracks and very little exercise, drill, work or training of any kind took place except guard duties.[47] Colour Sergeant Joseph Wylie Stevens of the 72nd, then serving with the 22nd, remembered that in Canada,

> Winter generally commenced in September . . . the snow lies all the winter through [and] the frost is severe. The city of Fredricton was at that time [1866] built only of wood and during the quiet hours of night what would appear to be pistol shots was heard cracking in all directions but it was in reality simply the nails of the wood giving way.[48]

Across the Atlantic was the important fortress of Gibraltar, captured by the

British in 1704 and successfully defended between 1779 and 1783. On this inhospitable rock isthmus was built a series of siege defences, gun emplacements, barracks and stores.[49] The principal barracks which the Highland Regiments seem to have occupied were Windmill Hill Barracks, Europa Point Barracks and South Barracks, all of which were stone-built on conventional lines on the shelves of flat land at the south end of the Rock. Detachments also occupied the smaller and more isolated barracks on the east side at Catalan Bay. When the 72nd and 79th were at Gibraltar in 1841, there seems to have been adequate accommodation and some of the married men had huts which were separated from the main barrack blocks,[50] while all the buildings were lit by oil lamps and candles.[51] Because the defences and barracks have been continuously in use for such a long time and because they were radically altered and extended before and during the Second World War, it is difficult to say exactly what the barracks looked like internally in the nineteenth century. The two principal difficulties in Gibraltar were drainage and water. In 1832, the shortage of fresh water was so acute and the smell of the barrack and town drains so strong that proposals were made to flush the drains with seawater,[52] and until the construction of rainwater holding tanks on the rock, the supply of fresh water was often uncertain and unhealthy, causing epidemics of fever as in 1828-29, when the 42nd lost 54 men and the 73rd 32 men.[53]

Over a thousand miles to the east of Gibraltar lay the island garrison of Malta, given by the Emperor Charles V to the Grand Master of the Order of St. John of Jerusalem in 1530. The island was taken by Napoleon in 1798 and, after blockade, was captured by the British in 1800, whose possession was confirmed in the Treaty of Vienna in 1815. There were two main barrack areas here, enclosed in the fortress walls of St. Elmo and Florina, with two subsidiary forts of Manoel and Tigne, all overlooking the beautiful harbour of Valetta. The barracks, some of them old palace buildings, were of stone, with verandahs, and were at least two storeys high, built around open squares, but in the first half of the nineteenth century they were probably without any sort of sophisticated sanitary facilities.[54] When the 42nd were here in 1844, they were in the barracks at Fort St. Elmo and later moved the short distance to Florina. Sergeant John Grant, of Aberdeen, who was the Pay Master's Clerk in the 42nd, wrote to his girlfriend Margaret Wilson from St. Elmo in 1844:

> We have a fine airy situation in St. Elmo and a delightful view comprising the City of Valetta, the Grand Harbour, [and] Cattoneia and scarcely a day passes without a sail in sight, wafted along by the gentle breezes of the Mediterranean.[55]

Additional accommodation was built west of Valetta at St. George's Barracks and St. Andrew's Barracks and at Pembroke Camp, a hutted musketry training camp built sometime before 1892. In general it appears that Malta was a more popular station than Gibraltar, a situation that may not have been related to

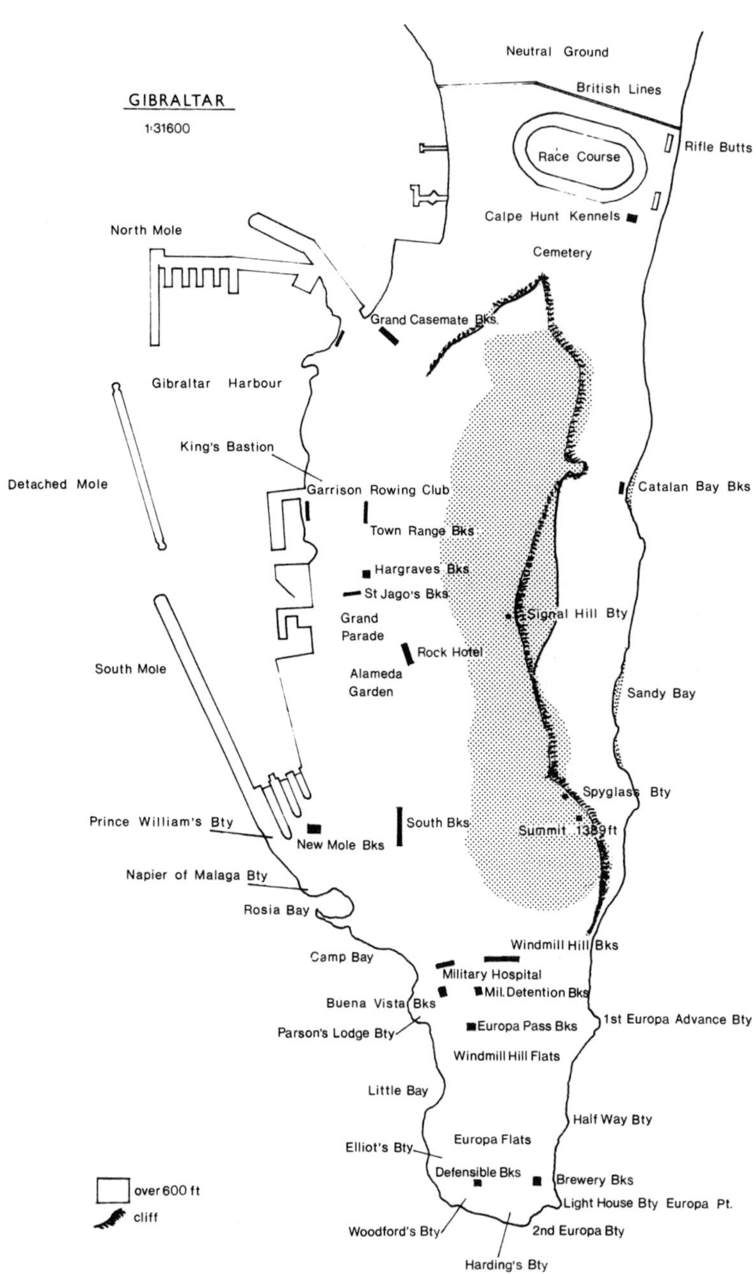
GIBRALTAR
1:31600
Neutral Ground
British Lines
Race Course
Rifle Butts
Calpe Hunt Kennels
Cemetery
North Mole
Grand Casemate Bks.
Gibraltar Harbour
King's Bastion
Detached Mole
Garrison Rowing Club
Catalan Bay Bks
Town Range Bks
Hargraves Bks
St Jago's Bks
Signal Hill Bty
Grand
Parade
Rock Hotel
South Mole
Alameda
Garden
Sandy Bay
Spyglass Bty
Prince William's Bty
South Bks
Summit 1389ft
New Mole Bks
Napier of Malaga Bty
Rosia Bay
Windmill Hill Bks
Camp Bay
Military Hospital
Mil. Detention Bks
Buena Vista Bks
1st Europa Advance Bty
Parson's Lodge Bty
Europa Pass Bks
Windmill Hill Flats
Little Bay
Half Way Bty
Europa Flats
Elliot's Bty
Defensible Bks
Brewery Bks
over 600 ft
Light House Bty Europa Pt.
cliff
Woodford's Bty
2nd Europa Bty
Harding's Bty

barrack conditions, but to the climate of Malta, its size and its diverse population and character.

On the continent of Africa there was a wide variety of stations that were occupied by the Highland battalions. The 42nd, the 79th and the 92nd had taken part in the great battles in Egypt in 1801 under General Sir Ralph Abercrombie, including the remarkable assault landing at Abukir Bay and the Battle of Alexandria, but it was not until 1845 that British presence returned to the area with the establishment of an overland route for mail and passengers, organised by Lieutenant Waghorn of the Honourable East India Company (H.E.I.C.) Navy. Then, in 1869, with the opening of the Suez Canal, Egypt, and the Canal area in particular, came to be of vital strategic importance as the shortest route to India. The main presence was French, however, and not British, and the French were largely responsible for training and organisation of the Egyptian Army of the Khedive and for building many of the barracks in Cairo, such as Kasr-el Nil. In 1875 Disraeli, with Rothschild money, acquired the controlling interest in the Suez Canal Company and in 1878 the dual control system, British and French, was established over the tottering Egyptian finances.[56] Militarily, the prime influence was still French, however, and when the schoolboy J.S. Ewart, later of the 79th, came here in 1879 to meet his father, J.A. Ewart of the 93rd, who was coming home from India, he remarked upon the French officers and the French training of the Egyptian Army.[57]

When however in 1882 Arabi Pasha led a revolt and a force was sent to bombard and occupy the Canal area, it was British and not French, the latter being concerned about the more immediate problem of their German neighbours. The 42nd, the 72nd, the 74th, the 75th and the 79th all served here at this time, occupying the old Citadel at Cairo, Kasr-el Nil Barracks and Abdin Palace. Kasr-el Nil barracks were intended for native troops and were very fine buildings, three stories high, with high airy rooms protected by verandahs and surrounded by open parades, while the Citadel was a fortress of considerable antiquity.[58] When the 79th arrived at the Citadel in September 1882, after the Battle of Tel-el-Kebir, the barrack rooms had formerly been occupied by native troops, who had used the rooms as latrines. The place was filthy and work parties from the Highland regiments spent several days cleaning up so that it could be occupied.[59] At Kasr-el-Nil the whole barrack was infested by lice living in the plaster and behind the woodwork, and many men preferred to sleep on the verandahs or in the open.[60] On 7th November 1882, when stationed at the Citadel, Sergeant Hunter of the Camerons fell through a hole in the floor of a barrack room and discovered, along with Lieutenant J.S. Ewart, an extensive system of underground passages, dungeons and magazines, which housed hundreds of swords and spears, suits of chain mail and brass cannon.[61]

But the African continent in 1820 was largely unexplored. Cape of Good Hope, extending to about 112,000 square miles, was taken from the Dutch in 1795, but returned to them in 1802, then re-taken in 1806, an action in which the 93rd took part. At Cape Town there were two forts, the Castle and Amsterdam

Fort, and barracks for some 2000 men, all built by the Dutch. In later photographs these barracks appear to be bleak, stone-built, small-windowed buildings of two or three stories, constructed around an open parade square, and they are unlikely to have had any more than the most basic of facilities.

The hinterland to the north and east was unexplored frontier territory on the edge of known civilisation, and as formal rule was gradually extended a series of forts were built, Fort England at Grahamstown and Fort Brown, and beyond the Great Fish River, Fort Retief, Fort Beaufort, Fort Hare, Fort Cox, Fort Wiltshire and Fort Peddie. As has been seen from the accounts of Colonel Bertie Gordon of the 91st before and during the First Kaffir War, these forts and outstations were isolated and sometimes without furniture. The 72nd, the 73rd, the 74th, the 75th and the 91st all served here and Sergeant James McKay of the 74th records that although the forts may have had only basic facilities, these were none the less welcome after months of living and fighting on the Veldt:

> What with hot days, dusty roads, hard beds on the scorched, burnt or green grass, spare diet and unwashed clothes, we needed a little renovating; and when I stretched myself on an iron bedstead in the Fort Beaufort barracks, and had the pleasure of sitting at a table in the Sergeants' mess-room, I thought myself the happiest thing alive and wondered why I had not appreciated life in a barrack room before.[62]

All around the African coast there were a series of British forts and garrisons protecting British trading interests, but on the western offshore island of St. Helena, 1200 miles from the mainland, there was one of the most isolated and unusual garrisons. The island belonged originally to the H.E.I.C., but was transferred to the Crown and was garrisoned by the British during the imprisonment of Napoleon, and afterwards as an important water point and supply base for ships. The 91st were stationed there between 1836 and 1842 and in 1840 were responsible for the removal and disinterment of Napoleon's body:

> James Town, the only town the place can boast of, is situated at the bottom of a wedge like ravine, enclosed on each side by barren and overhanging precipices. It consists of a long straggling street running up a valley, with steep hills on each side . . . Lime being scarce, the stone of which the houses are chiefly built is cemented with mud. There was a church, botanical gardens, a hospital, a tavern and barracks. The latter where the 91st were quartered, are at the top of the street, about half a mile from the landing place, and are built on an artificial terrace overlooking a little stream which flows through the town. The terrace is nearly in the shape of an oblong, lying lengthways to the valley, and divided into two parts by a range of two-storied buildings, built of stone, and designed to hold six companies of infantry as well as Officers' Quarters. The military Hospital lies still further up the valley, and is placed in a pleasant and salubrious position.[63]

High above the town was Ladder Hill Battery with further accommodation for two companies, and connecting the two was a 700-foot flight of 699 steps. Companies stationed at the top were relieved every six months, but had to attend all daily parades at the main barracks in the town, and while the island

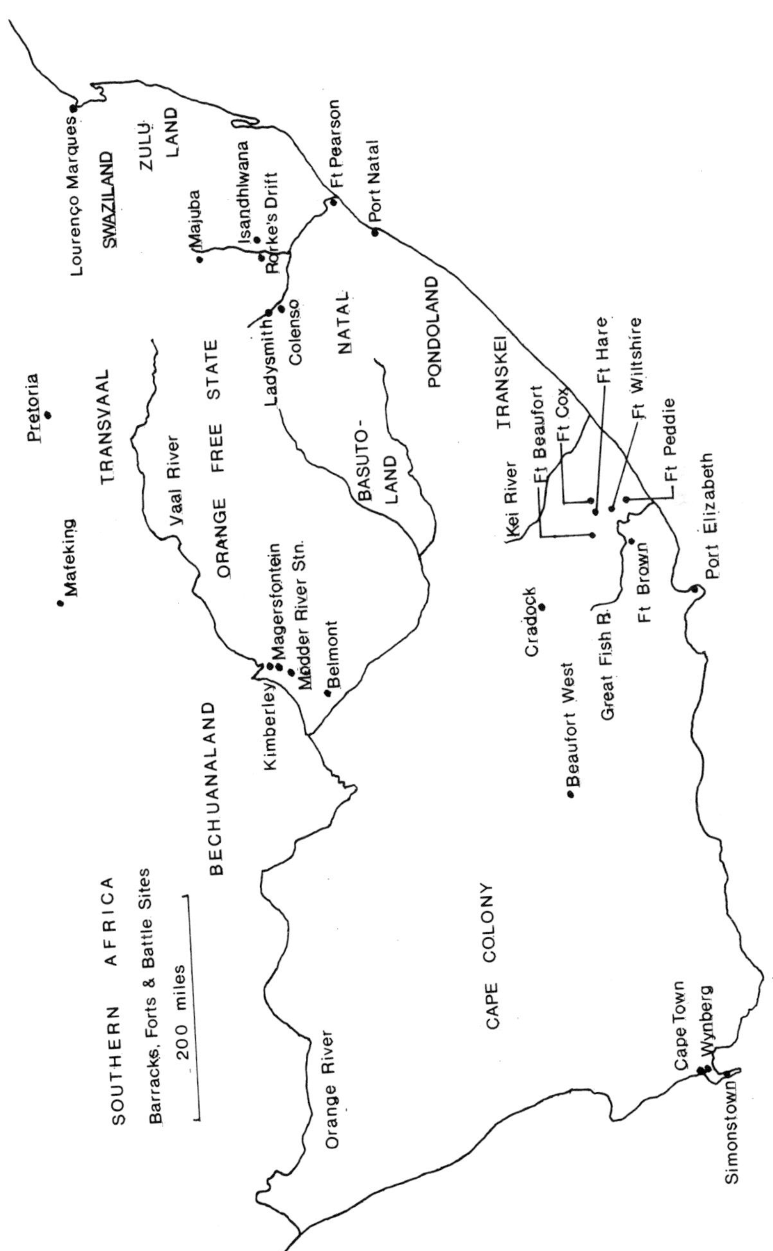
SOUTHERN AFRICA
Barracks, Forts & Battle Sites
200 miles
Orange River
CAPE COLONY
Cape Town
Wynberg
Simonstown
BECHUANALAND
Kimberley
Magersfontein
Modder River Stn.
Belmont
Mafeking
Pretoria
TRANSVAAL
Yaal River
ORANGE FREE STATE
Beaufort West
Great Fish R.
Cradock
Ft Brown
Port Elizabeth
Kei River
Ft Beaufort
Ft Cox
Ft Hare
Ft Wiltshire
Ft Peddie
TRANSKEI
BASUTO-LAND
PONDOLAND
NATAL
Ladysmith
Colenso
Majuba
Rorke's Drift
Isandhlwana
Port Natal
Ft Pearson
ZULU LAND
SWAZILAND
Lourenço Marques

was verdant and beautiful, it was an isolated and lonely place to be stationed and drunkenness was always rife.[64]

Barracks in India occupied by the Highland Regiments between 1820 and 1920 varied greatly in appearance, design and construction, from ancient mud and stone fortresses, such as Jamrud, west of Peshawar,to the Vaubanesque Fort William at Calcutta, or the hill station barracks at Murree. With the exception of some of the forts, military stations were built on the cantonment principle of a military town separate from the native town and bazaar. The stations were sometimes fortified, or fortifiable, and possessed all the basic requirements of their inhabitants, with a cantonment bazaar, shops, brothels, barracks, mess houses, married quarters, stables and parade ground all in one area. Construction was largely governed by the climate, barracks being built to allow air to circulate, but at the same time to stop the sun shining inside, and there were thus high ceilings, verandahs, doors at either end of the building, large windows covered with 'tatties' and a louvred upper section. Many cantonments were constructed on the bungalow principle of timber or brick, whitewashed internally and elevated to deter ants, rats or snakes. To prevent snakes and insects dropping from the ceiling, the roof space was sometimes sectioned off with canvas. In 1893 Ian Hamilton of the 92nd arrived at Mooltan and described his first impressions of a station bungalow:

> . . . the bungalow itself [was] whitewashed with a deep verandah [and] was rather nice inside; two rooms with bathroom and a central room for a living room set out with photographs and a few sporting prints. The ceiling consisted of a sheet of white canvas stretched out straight across, called a 'chat' . . . every now and then something would scamper across the canvas ceiling and sometimes it squeaked—seeing my startled expression Shaw Kennedy [of the 41st] told me it was only a rat being pursued by a snake, unless it was a courtship between a couple of bats.[65]

Water was obtained from wells, rivers or rainwater tanks and, being often contaminated by inadequate drainage, was the source of fevers, cholera and bowel complaints. Attached to the barracks were the guard rooms, school, reading rooms, latrines and ablutions, and while native Indians could usually only enter the cantonment with the sanction of the Quarter Master, who issued a tin or metal pass for the purpose, it was often difficult to keep control of the sanitary arrangements and to retain what Europeans considered to be cleanliness. Colonel Bertie Gordon complained in the 91st Orders at Kamptee in 1860:

> The result of the Quarter Master General's last inspection of the Officer bungalow portion of the 91st lines has proved the existence of dirt and disorder to a considerable extent, affecting the sanitary condition of the cantonment. The causes of complaint are that the native servants use the back portion of the Godowns as necessary places . . . .[66]

Latrines either drained through a bed of charcoal, which was often used to

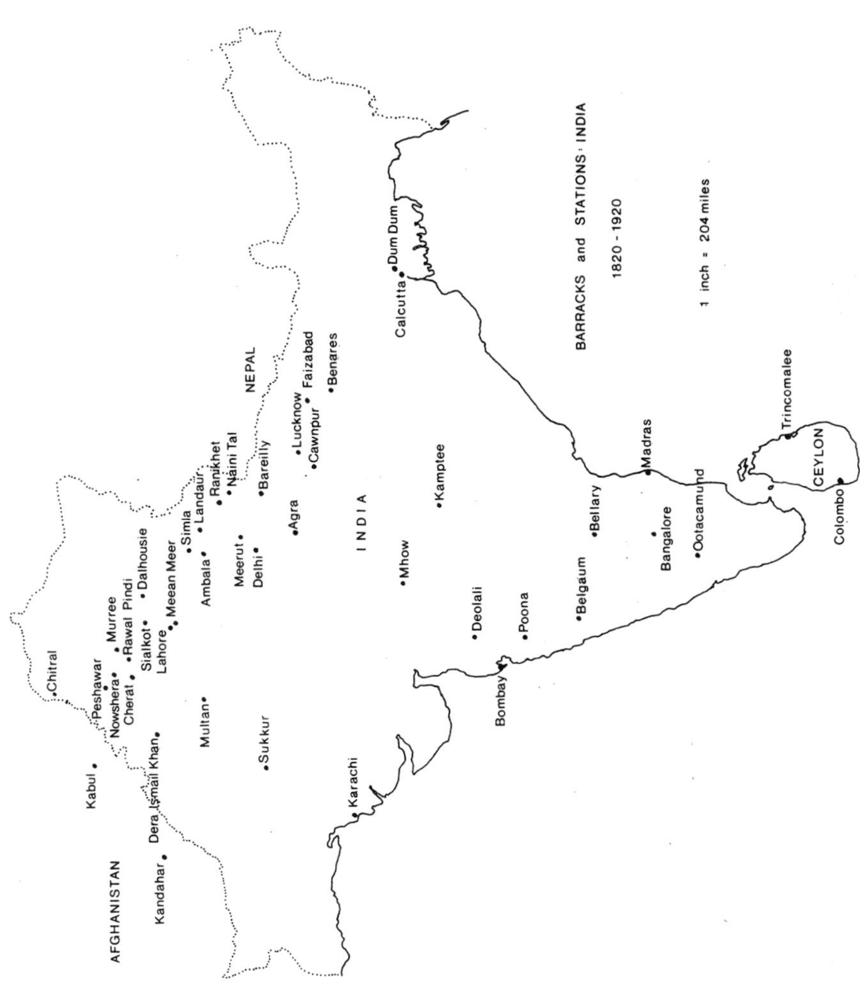
BARRACKS and STATIONS: INDIA
1820 - 1920
1 inch = 204 miles
AFGHANISTAN
Kandahar
Kabul
Dera Ismail Khan
Chitral
Peshawar
Nowshera
Cherat
Murree
Rawal Pindi
Sialkot
Lahore
Dalhousie
Meean Meer
Multan
Sukkur
Karachi
Simla
Ambala
Landaur
Ranikhet
Naini Tal
Meerut
Delhi
Bareilly
Agra
NEPAL
Lucknow
Cawnpur
Faizabad
Benares
INDIA
Mhow
Kamptee
Calcutta
Dum Dum
Deolali
Poona
Bombay
Belgaum
Bellary
Bangalore
Madras
Ootacamund
Trincomalee
CEYLON
Colombo

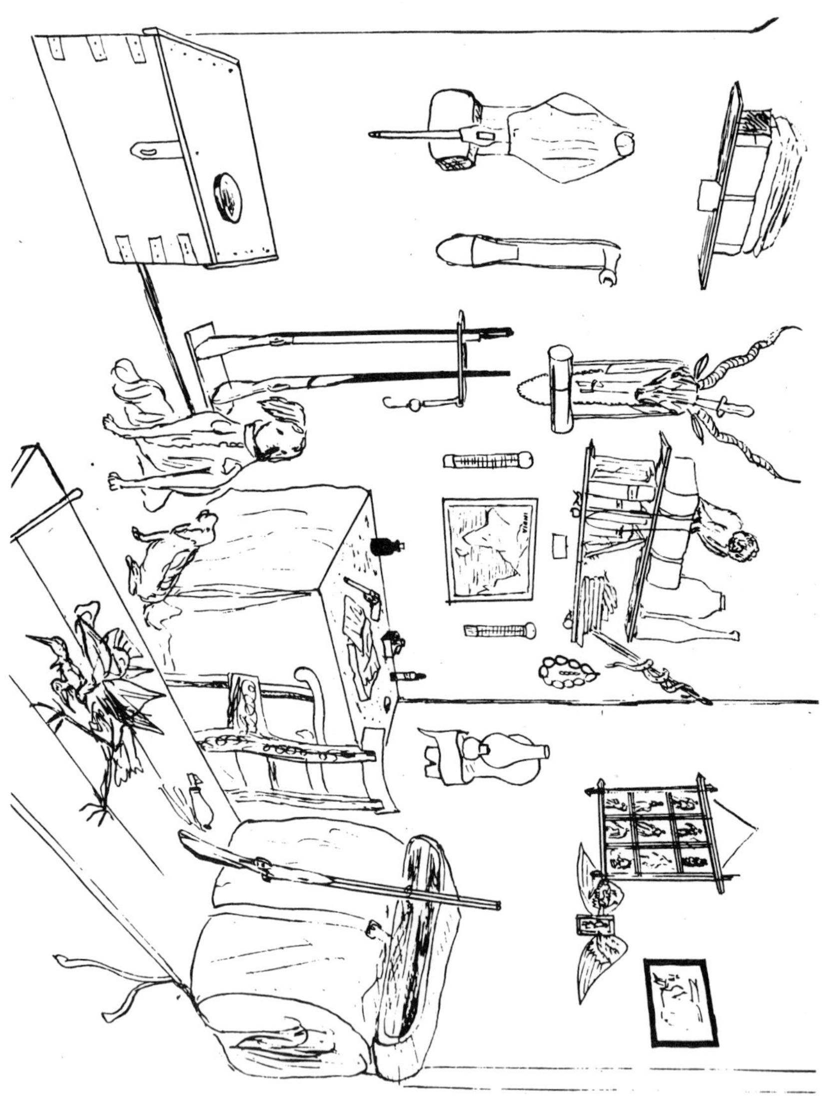

'My Corner', a pen sketch by Sergeant Major George Whitfield Anderson of the 72nd Highlanders, Sailcot, India 1877. Anderson was born in Rhynie, served 25 years with the 72nd and died as a Colonel in the Egyptian Army on 31.8.1915 aged 59. He was editor, compiler and instigator of the Regimental Magazine *The Albany Monthly Record*. SUSM.

deface the walls,[67] or they were supplied with dry earth and sand, the latrine and urinal walls being 'leepoyed' each week with a four-inch-thick layer of mud clay and dung.[68] In the bungalows, which were usually assigned to the married officers and senior NCOs, or shared by several unmarried officers, washing and toilet facilities were situated in the bungalow itself:

> Every bedroom in the house had its own bathroom, furnished with a tin bath, a washstand and a thunder box. This was an extremely comfortable commode, with arms and a bucket. When the session was over, the user of the thunderbox opened the bathroom door that led outside and yelled. The bucket was taken away immediately, emptied and returned with creosol solution in the bottom. Another distinctive feature of the bathroom was the Bromo. It is doubtful if in the length and breadth of India, any other lavatory paper could have been found. It came, in a certain number of sheets at a time in a black and yellow container, on the front of which was printed a great deal of information about its apparently almost miraculous properties and the warning that those who did not take advantage of these would certainly suffer from what was described as the painful 'and almost universal complaint called piles'. The bath stood on a slightly raised platform, with built up sides and a draining hole. Hot water was poured in from copper vessels . . . and the bather added the cold from a huge Ali Baba jar with a tin dipper. The dirty water was tipped on to the platform by the sweeper and ran outside through a hole in the wall. To lie in water heated over charcoal, or better still, as in the hills, wood, is an experience that bathers in tap water can never know, to their deprivation.[69]

Dust, rain, insect life and, above all, heat were the main problems in Indian barracks, and thus ceilings were high and ventilated and were fitted with a system of punkahs operated by the wallah squatting on the verandah outside pulling a rope. In the 91st at Kamptee in 1860, fifteen punkah wallahs were employed by day in the hot season and eighteen by night.[70] Native Indians were also employed to splash water on the 'tatties', heavy mats of woven roots hung over the doors and windows, through which the air passed and cooled. Water was also spread over the barrack area to lay the dust. Much of the conduct of cantonment life was governed by the number of native Indians who had to be employed. Because of the strict caste regulations one man could not do another man's job if that job was associated with another caste. In addition there was the working principle that everyone should have at least a small slice of the employment cake and that all those employed required a boy to assist them. Thus it was impossible to get anything done without employing tailors, barbers, sweepers, gardeners, watchmen, water carriers, cooks, bearers, washermen and so on, all of whom were vital and most of whom were underemployed.

While summer heat was a tremendous problem in the Punjab and Central India, in stations like Bangalore life was, and still is, much more pleasant, even pre-monsoon. The 2nd Battalion the Cameron Highlanders were at Bangalore in 1910. This beautiful city was in the old Madras Presidency, and although some of the headquarters, messes and barracks are now no longer occupied by the Indian Army, in 1910 the cantonment was impressive:

On walking through the barracks one cannot but be struck with the general appearance of the bungalows and the grounds. A staff of trained men daily exercise supervision over the native sweepers, whose duty is to remove all undesirable elements from the vicinity of the barracks, and keep them clean and healthy. The bungalows are large stone buildings, very airy and wonderfully cool in the hot weather. The water the men drink is kept in locked tanks and their food is served up by specially trained soldier cooks. No native is allowed to cook for men of this Battalion. The men have their own library and billiard room as at home.[71]

In this cantonment there was, in addition, a gymnasium, two covered swimming pools, a bungalow for the Army Temperance Association, a regimental theatre, and a cycle shop.

On the plains, the heat in the summer months was intense, and was accompanied by a hot wind, cloudless skies and burning sun. Everything assumed a gritty texture as dust invaded everywhere. Military life adapted accordingly and the men rose early for parades, were restricted to barracks during the day and completed the remainder of their work in the cool of the evenings. In fact the only comfortable time of day was the few hours around dawn, but pre-monsoon the temperature in Central India and the Punjab seldom falls below 80°F, day or night. In 1895 the 93rd were at Mian Mir a few miles south of Lahore:

As may be expected the cantonment has a very dry and parched appearance, and there is a large accumulation of dust upon the road, which when the wind rises, does not add very much either to the beauty of the country or the pleasure of travelling. As a matter of fact, however, few can be seen out of their bungalows during the day, except those whose duty it is to draw the mid-day lotion from the canteen (this is done in cans supplied for the purpose in which it is taken to the bungalows and issued to the thirsty individuals who possess the necessary), or the much abused punkah coolie, who can be dimly seen under his straw shelter, giving the punkah lever the minimum of 'kinching' compatible with moving it at all. The sentries of the quarter guard are about the only other animate objects that can be seen, and they pass their two hours 'sentry go' as best they can under the meagre shelter afforded by the verandah, scorched with the hot air that with almost furnace heat comes over the maidan in front of the guardroom and blinking at the glare outside and the hot vapour that dances in seemingly countless eddies before their eyes.[72]

With the increase in the numbers of British troops in India after the Mutiny, several hill stations were built or enlarged,[73] to which the invalids, women, children, band boys and at least some of the service companies in turn would retreat during the hot season. In Southern India, these stations were primarily situated in the Nilgiri Hills, in and around Ootacamund, the old summer headquarters of the government of the Madras Presidency. The 74th came to this area in 1855 and Sergeant John Tulloch wrote to his brother in Glasgow recording the scene:

. . . marched back to Madrass and a short time encamped there, then marched up the country to Trichinopoly this is the hottest place in the east, it is quite possible to lay a piece of beef, on a stone, any time from 8 o'Clock in the morning, till 4 PM, and it will be ready for eating directly, the men say their is only a sheet of foolscape paper between it and the other place . . . Marched to the Neilghery hills, stationed at Jackatalla, this place is 8000 . . . Feet above the level of the sea, it is the highest part of the Neilgheries, it is very cold up their but I liked it well, I used to keep some poultry, such as cocks and hens, the soldiers lived in mud built huts. They are building a fine barracks there, believe me that Aurther Seat in Edinburgh is nothing to the Neilgheries.[74]

Other hill stations in Southern India included Poona, Belgaum and Bellary and, in the North, Cherat, south of Peshawar, Simla, Solan, Dagshai and Sabathu and a complex of stations in the Murree Hills and at Dalhousie. Today these stations are primarily tourist resorts, but they were built initially with military labour and their resemblance, particularly that of Murree, to Perthshire, is remarkable.

Much of the information on foreign service barracks occupied by the Highland battalions between 1820 and 1920 is sketchy and must be gleaned from the drawings, photographs and memoirs of those who occupied them and, in the case of India and Pakistan, from the author's own observations, for while there was an important and informative study of home barracks in 1858-1859, no comprehensive barrack study was ever carried out on foreign stations, where in fact these Highland regiments were for the greater part of their service. A great deal of information is needed on what these barracks and their amenities actually looked like between 1820 and 1920, as regimental photograph albums tend to show people and not places, and all too often a diarist will record:

> Expect to be able to make Calcutta this evening. Cast anchor opposite Fort William . . . Disembarked at 4 o'clock p.m. and marched into barracks at Fort William . . .[75]

or:

> Attended the barrack church with the men. Went round rooms etc. at the men's dinner hour,[76]

without actually saying what the Ghats on the Hooghly looked like, how they got ashore, what Fort William looked like in 1857 or the nature of the barrack accommodation inside, and they frustratingly fail to give a description of the barrack church, the men's rooms, the men, or their food and how it was cooked. It is particularly interesting that there appear to be very few detailed soldiers' descriptions of Canada and the West Indies, that day-to-day events are seldom recorded and that barracks, trooping and landing, in what would now be considered an exotic or romantic country on a great adventure, is almost taken for granted.

It must be remembered, too, that the Commission of 1858-1859 was the Barrack and Hospital *Improvement* Commission. They looked primarily at sanitary arrangements and were obsessed with the introduction of fresh air and the miasmatic approach to disease, and took little account of the important necessity of educating soldiers to keep themselves clean by the simple process of washing themselves and their clothes in water and soap, of drinking less, of taking regular exercise and of taking some kind of care in their sexual relations. The Commission, too, operated in the heady era of sanitary and military reform following the Crimean War and was led by the zealous Sydney Herbert. Herbert's capacity for hard work was legendary and his contribution to the Royal Commission on the Sanitary Condition of the Army can never be underestimated, but it must be remembered that he was not a soldier and that his proposals were not always in keeping with the actual situations in which soldiers found themselves. When Fox Maule became Secretary of State at War in 1846, he took over from Sydney Herbert; Lauderdale Maule was of course delighted that his brother, an ex-79th officer, should hold such an important office, but Lauderdale's letters would appear to indicate that amongst soldiers, Victorian social reformers were not always appreciated:

> I Congratulate you sincerely on your improving prospects, what you communicate is with me safe—*Much* Much does the Army want a practical man in that position . . . utopian theory [is] all very well for the study of Lord Howick or Sydney Herbert but impossible in practice . . . .[77]

It should be kept in mind also that Herbert was Secretary of State at War in 1852 in the Aberdeen administration and that he was blamed for much of the failure of supply in the Crimean War, criticism which he felt deeply as much of it centred around his Russian parentage.[78]

Thus, while the value of the Commission in hospitals and barracks, Army medical statistics, the Medical School at Chatham and the code of regulations of the Army Medical Department cannot be underestimated, the work on barracks must be looked at in the light of the foregoing. The conclusions of the Commission on the barracks at home make dramatic reading: hardly a barrack, with the possible exception of Shorncliffe, escapes criticism, but giving each man 600 cubic feet and ventilation by louvred doors, vents in the roof and holes in the windows was an oversimplification of the solution. Basic maintenance, internal barrack cleanliness and personal hygiene were too often overlooked and could have contributed greatly towards improved conditions, for in cold northerly stations with a limited coal supply, much of it being sea coal, men simply stuffed up the vents with paper and rags, shut the doors and windows, did not take their clothes off and washed only their hands, faces and knees.

In addition it must be remembered that the housing conditions from which many of the nineteenth century Highland battalion recruits came were often worse than anything British Army barracks could produce. In Scotland:

> The tenements had many small houses, or flats, so that in 1871 32.5 per cent of Scottish houses had only one room; 37.6 per cent had only two rooms. By 1911 the

proportions were 12.8 per cent and 40.4 per cent. Moreover in 1911, 56 per cent of one-roomed houses had more than two persons in each room, so had 47 per cent of those with two rooms.[79]

> . . . the general standard of water supplies in Scotland in 1864 could only be described as precarious, unsatisfactory and in some cases grossly and permanently polluted.[80]

> . . . [and] it is still true that the outstanding feature of most towns and villages . . . [in Scotland about 1895] . . . was their filthy condition from the sanitary point of view, though it was thought that a great improvement had been brought about by the cessation of throwing household refuse into the streets, following the provision of ash pits . . .[81]

In the North-West and the Islands it was still common practice in the 1890s for a family and their animals to be housed under the same roof during the winter, and:

> . . . from the very early days of organised sanitary supervision, one of the major problems in Highland Counties turned on how to persuade the inhabitants away from the very general practice of accommodating animals in the same house as human beings.[82]

The Medical Officer of Health for Inverness was forced to bring test cases against four Harris crofters in 1894 to try to stop this practice, but he met with only limited success.

Unless therefore barrack conditions worldwide are looked at in perspective with existing civilian conditions, particularly civilian Scottish conditions, it is unrealistic to lay too great an emphasis on the

> . . . poor design and faulty construction coupled with overcrowding inadequate ventilation and sewage disposal, neglected sanitation and faulty lighting and heating [in barracks] . . . .[83]

This is not a military excuse but a question of realistic contemporary comparison, an appreciation of the considerable expenditure involved and an understanding of the practical and physical limitations of nineteenth and early twentieth-century scientific knowledge, and of the prejudices which delayed the application of that knowledge.

Barrack life was not however conducted in a series of bare rooms, and the fixtures and fittings form an important part of any study of living conditions in the Highland regiments from 1820 to 1920. Private Archibald Watt McIntosh of the 42nd gave his impressions of the interior of a barrack room at the Depot at Aberdeen on his arrival there on Tuesday 12th January 1858:

> The party of Recruites which had been made up, left Edinburgh this day. We were to sail from Granton at 6am but owing to the stormy state of the weather we could not sail before 12 o'clock. We sailed at that hour and after a very rough passage we landed at Aberdeen at 9½pm very tired and sick. When we got up to the barracks all

the men were in bed the Tattoo being at 8 o'clock. Some of them got up, stirred the fire and showed us our beds. I was very glad to get into mine as I was very tired and soon dropped off asleep. When I woke in the morning I found myself on the floor, the bed being too narrow I had fell out, I was stiff and shivering with cold, the snow was about a foot deep on the barrack square—I must now tell you how a soldiers room is regulated and cleaned—Every soldier has a bed to himself which he makes up every morning in the following order, viz, The Tick which is filled with straw is rolled up, tied with a belt and placed at the head of the Iron Stretcher, the blankets are folded in four, the sheets also in four and covered with a Rug are placed on top of the Tick, a Ticket having his Name, Regiment, Number, Company, Rank and Squad is placed at the head of his bed in his bed clothes.

Bed Ticket.
N° 8 COMPANY
255
p^{t} A. WATT. M^{c} INTOSH
N° 1 SQUAD

The kilt is hung on two pegs at the head of his bed, the Accoutrements on the right peg, the Purse and Gaiters on the left one, the Knapsack is on a shelf at the head of the bed, the Feather Bonnet on the right, Canteen on the left, the Rifle is placed in a stand also at the head of the bed, there is a place for everything and everything goes in its proper place—We do Orderly Man in turns whose duty is to clean up the room, wash the tables and forms, lay the dishes for Breakfast, after that is over he washes them, puts them past, and cleans the Room, at Dinner and Tea time he does the same.

A Bugle sounds at 10 minutes to 8, that is called the 'Quarter Bugle' when the breakfast is brought from the Cook House and laid on the Tables, another Bugle at 8 O'Clock is called the 'Sit Down' when the Orderly Officer comes round the Room to see if anyone has a complaint to make, the same thing is done at Dinner time, but not at tea time.[84]

Descriptions of this nature are not common, but it is important to note that McIntosh makes no reference to inadequate sanitary arrangements or dilapidated barracks and that he emphasises, 'each soldier has a bed to himself', illustrating at least one of the improvements that had taken place since 1820. Much of a soldier's life centred around his barrack room, around his own allocated bed space and his few possessions and equipment, and these domestic arrangements showed a remarkable continuity in time and location.

Barrack rooms were used for eating, sleeping, sometimes for cooking, writing and recreation and at night for urinating, and were fitted out accordingly. In 1820, a room 53 feet by 20 feet would be expected to hold 44 men, but the area of floor space was greater than could be expected because the men were accommodated in double bedsteads of two tiers. These bedsteads were built of wood and may well have been free-standing.[85] They comprised two levels of wooden 'trays', similar to old wooden bread trays, with a raised edge surround. As the bedding was double, it is unlikely that there was a central dividing plank, and one berth was designed to hold two men. These bedsteads were probably very similar to those used in Salvation Army shelters in the 1890s, although these had central dividing planks.[86] G.W. Anderson of the 72nd asserts that these 'berths', as they were known, were shared by three soldiers, and he illustrates a small sketch of a barrack room in 1820 showing double, two-tiered wooden bedsteads,[87] but where ceilings were low, particularly in attics, single tier double berths were used.[88] Standing Orders of the 79th in 1819 state:

> The name of every man and his comrade are to be posted at the foot of each berth and the same at his place in the arm rack. In all barracks, Sergeants are to have a whole berth to themselves.[89]

These berths, also known as cots, were supplied with double palliasses and double sheets and blankets.[90] In many cases the palliasses were filled with straw which was nicknamed 'soldiers' feathers' ' . . . every feather being fully a yard long [and] commonly called by the Scottish farmers "clean bed straw . . .".'[91] After the straw had been used in soldiers' beds it was sold,[92] but in Barbados corn husks stuffed the palliasses, in Dominica 'trash', in Demerara plantain leaves, and in Canada and some parts of the West Indies, hair.[93]

The allocation of men to these double berths was not random and was part of the larger military structure, as the Standing Orders of the 79th record:

> The Captain . . . having formed his Company thus equally, he will then arrange comrades. Every Corporal, Private and Drummer, will select a comrade of a rank differing from his own i.e. front rank and rear rank and is never to change him without the permission of his Captain. Comrades are always to have the same berth in quarters. The Corporal's comrade should either be the chosen man or some other steady man of the squad who can occasionally aid him in his duty; and the Drummers Comrades are the odd men of any two squads, when there are any.[94]

Writing in retrospect, Lt. Colonel Wheatley records life in the 42nd:

> . . . until 1825 [there were] . . . what was called the 'double berths', they were wooden erections made for two men to sleep together below and two men above . . . the upper were generally preferred because the lower had to put up with the dust etc. that came from above, moreover there was better accommodation of racks etc.[95]

In 1824 the new single iron bedstead was introduced, with bedding adapted accordingly. Initially 12,000 were ordered at a cost of £15,000, the new single bedding and the alteration of bedding in store from double to single costing £12,500.[96] It would appear from Ordnance estimates that these single bedsteads were used for home service only,[97] but in 1828 the Account of Extraordinary Expenses of the Army included 'iron bedsteads and bedding supplied for barracks at foreign stations . . .',[98] and iron bedsteads certainly arrived in Jamaica in 1830, where wharfage was paid on them of £59.3.3½d.[99] In 1830 these iron bedsteads were being made under contract to the Ordnance Department by Keasley Brothers,[100] but by 1835 they were being made by several contractors throughout Britain, and those for Ireland were made there under a separate contract.[101] Palliasses and bed sackings, the cords for tying them and some 'striped cotton', probably for sheets, were made at the Penitentiary at Millbank and there were separate contracts in 1828 for blankets, sheets, and cotton and woollen rugs.[102] Pillows or pillow cases are not mentioned.

One pattern of the iron bedstead folded in the centre and was 'put up' during the day, with the bedding on top. This entailed stripping off the bedding, placing it on the floor and folding or unfolding the frame. In 1838, Lieutenant Hall, Barrack Master of the Tower of London, submitted a bed design in which the bottom section of the bed simply slid into the head section. In 1839 ten of these new bedsteads were sent to Edinburgh for troop trials and the pattern was finally adopted in 1844, Lieutenant Hall receiving £200 for his efforts. The design stopped soldiers putting their bedding on the floor and lessened the damage to floors and ceilings, as it was obviously a popular sport to let the ends of the bedsteads drop with a crash on the floor when the beds were 'put down'.[103] Various adaptations of the single iron bedstead survived into the twentieth century.

The folding of the bedsteads was in fact a compromise between giving each man his own bed and not building extra barracks to cater for the reduced space per man. At night, however, when the beds were put down there was often little floor space left, particularly in long narrow barrack rooms. These iron bedsteads were free-standing, and knocking them against the whitewashed plaster walls caused damage and mess. Individual Barrack Masters frequently introduced rules insisting that the bed irons be one foot from the wall.[104] In Gibraltar, 79th Orders required the beds to be six inches from the walls, although this order may well have had the object of stopping men from stuffing items down the beds during inspections.[105]

It would appear that when the old double, two-tier berths were in use before 1824, the wall space between the heads of the berths was used for arm racks and that shelves for a soldier's possessions were not allocated to each individual, but centrally situated along one wall of the room. War Office records suggest that cast-iron barrack fittings for individual bed spaces were experimented with around 1827, with a musket rack, shelf and iron rail with hooks for each soldier.[106] While some of these centralised shelves were retained, it became the practice to give each soldier a shelf above his bed, together with a series of wooden pegs, or wooden half-moon bridle heads referred to by Private McIntosh of the 42nd, on which dress and accoutrements were hung.

There is evidence to show that personalisation of the bedspace was allowed in certain Highland regiments and that while equipment and clothing had to be kept in a certain place, neatly folded and laid out, photographs, drawings, 'pin ups', clocks and caged birds were allowed, together with the Victorian fashion of decorating the front of the shelves with paper cut into fancy designs. Some men, or their wives or girlfriends, made their own rugs for their beds from scraps of uniform or material, stitched into a patchwork. Each man was also provided with a wooden box to hold his possessions. These stood at the foot of each bed and were much the same as the boxes which were permitted to married men and their families when trooping.[107] In 1880 a General Order forbade the use of these barrack-room kit boxes at home,[108] but prior to this, in the 1870s it had become common practice, in the 79th at least, for the men to keep a few personal items in 'knick knack' boxes:

> During the time that the 1st Battalion was stationed at Edinburgh Castle the use of small boxes for holding knick knacks had steadily crept in, to such an extent that nearly every man possessed one. The consequence was that on each man's shelf there was displayed an advertisement of somebody's blacking or blacklead. An order was at last issued to Company Officers that if men really required to have such boxes, they were in future to be covered with tartan or some other material.[109]

The withdrawal of the men's boxes at home was not popular, and Colonel Leslie of the 1st Camerons commented to the Wantage Committee in 1891:

> I think the men should be provided with a box, with a secure lock and key wherein to keep his small belongings . . . at present they have absolutely nowhere to keep their little odds and ends.[110]

Women and children also lived in these barrack rooms, but there is evidence to suggest that from an early date, where possible, married families were allocated separate rooms from those of the single men, one barrack room being shared by several married families, separated by partitions, curtains or blankets. 79th Orders of 1838 at Dublin stated:

> If the Commanding Officer has any complaint again made to him that the Married Men's Beds are not made up, curtains opened and children properly dressed before the breakfast hour, he will without exception turn those offending out of barracks . . ..[111]

In Gibraltar three years later the married men had their own huts,[112] and at Inland Island, Bermuda in 1848, John Wedderburn of the 42nd noted:

> Got up at 6½ o'ck. Saw my [men's] kits at 12 o'ck and my married rooms afterwards.[113]

Single beds were provided for the married families and small children probably shared an iron bedstead or used hammocks. Otherwise the women and children were subject to the same provisions and regulations as the men and they formed an important part of regimental society.

Each barrack room was also supplied with a table, or tables, and forms. These were most probably entirely constructed of wood, the table possibly being trestles and a detachable board top.[114] About 1844, if not before, the ubiquitous design of wooden table top with cast-iron legs in a half-moon shape and a 'form with iron legs' came into use,[115] and this design survived even into the author's own memory. At these tables men ate before the advent of separate dining rooms, squads being divided into messes of 10 to 18 men. In 1819 squad messes of the 79th were supplied with two table cloths, knives, forks, spoons and dishes,[116] but it is not known whether the provision of table cloths was a general one, or was widely and regularly practised. Certainly there are several photographs of New Year dinners in barrack rooms with table cloths in use, and Ordnance Estimates of 1821 include 'Huckaback, table cloths 7 foot by 4 foot'.[117] In 1833 the 6d share of a table cloth was deemed to be 'an article which a soldier cannot do without'.[118]

Bowls and plates were probably stored during the day on a wall rack, or on a shelf which was often hung from the ceiling above the central table, while a knife, fork and spoon formed part of a soldier's 'necessaries', i.e. those items he was required to possess and pay for. These latter items were stamped, sometime after 1830, with the soldier's number to prevent theft and aid identification and were traditionally known as eating irons. Plates were of tin, enamel or earthenware, and cheaply made earthenware bowls, sometimes with a regimental pattern, were popular for porridge, milk and tea.

Coal was carried to the barrack room and stored there in coal boxes, which appear in early plans as a fitting and were probably made of wood; large metal coal scuttles were introduced later. The fireplace was fitted with a metal grate and fire irons. The old-pattern grates were considered by the Barrack and Hospital Improvement Commission to be highly inefficient and a new pattern was introduced. The front bars were detachable and it was common to use them, run through a broom handle, as a weight to dry rub the barrack floors.[119] The introduction of the new pattern grates together with the official separation of the functions of cooking and heating led, in 1862, to a revision of coal allocations. The year was carefully divided into three: winter (November-March), Summer (June-August), and Spring and Autumn (April, May, September and October) with the ration divided accordingly. Less fuel was given to the new barrack-room grates and there was a new and separate allowance for cooking.[120]

With only one fireplace or stove (or two in larger rooms), there was probably a pecking order amongst the men for the beds closest to the fire or away from a draughty door, similar to the order used in bothies in the east and north-east of Scotland.

The inadequacy of lighting in the corridors of barracks and the distance of the privies and urinals from the barrack rooms meant that each barrack room was supplied with a urine tub for communal use at night, and these probably also served as spittoons. The subject generates a considerable amount of horror amongst modern historians and the smell was undoubtedly offensive when they were not probably washed, tarred or limed, but it must be remembered that it was still common after the Second World War to have, and to use, chamber pots, in even the most respectable houses and hotels, and buckets are still supplied in H.M. Prisons.

Chamber pots were experimented with in barrack rooms before 1861, but as Sir Alexander Tulloch reported:

> They were found not to answer. The men in the first place would not use them—they objected to its being an unseemly sight under their beds; so much so that they said they would be ashamed to introduce any of their friends into their room; that while

> they were sitting at their meals it was not very pleasant to see them under their beds and at last I found that they put them upon the shelves with the other crockery . . . They objected that in sweeping under the beds they knocked the handles off and that in moving out their beds they broke them.[121]

Until barracks were built with complete internal plumbing, adequate corridor lighting and night urinals, such as at Cameron Barracks, Inverness, urine tubs continued in use. It was quite simply unrealistic to expect a man to get up in the middle of the night, go down probably two flights of stairs and outside, on a winter's night at Edinburgh Castle, across Crown Square and find his way to the privies to relieve himself. The subject illustrates a part of the character of the nineteenth- and early twentieth-century soldiers, in that however hard the reformers, philanthropists, officers or Sanitary Commissioners tried to initiate alterations in conditions, or tell a soldier what was good for him, many soldiers were deeply conservative and in certain areas resisted 'improvements' which they considered interference. The introduction of dining rooms and the withdrawal of pewter pots in canteens are also good examples. Men purposely put too much water on dining-room floors when washing them after meals, so that they would still be wet and unusable for the next meal, and a great many glasses were broken before the drinking 'schools' could be persuaded not to pass drinks hand to hand at closing time, as was the practice with the pewter pots.[122] The men's reaction to the introduction of single beds is not recorded, but it may very well have been unpopular as thin blankets, a limited coal supply and a cold damp climate meant that soldiers resorted to practical solutions to keep warm at night:

> In this climate the soldier should have an extra blanket; they all ask for it, and to keep themselves warm, they either sleep in a portion of their clothes or put two beds together to obtain the advantage of four blankets, or they stop the ventilation.[123]

The cleanliness of the barrack room was achieved by brushing floors, removing the fire ashes and blacking the grate. Urine tubs were removed, washed, limed or tarred and replaced, windows were opened and bedding was aired or taken outside and laid in the sun in the summer months.[124] Standing orders of the Highland regiments, from those of the 79th in 1819 onwards, consistently urge tidiness and cleanliness, but it is clear that the soldiers were constantly careless and inattentive to the process of trying to improve their own hygiene conditions. At Aldershot the Commanding Officer of the 78th noted in 1861:

> . . . some of the men are in the habit of making water against the walls of the privies instead of using the urinals and also emptying the urine tubs into the privies instead of the urinals and . . . many of them are not emptied until late in the morning after the barracks have been cleaned.[125]

Later in the same year 78th Orders noted:

> A report having been made to the Commanding Officer that some men are in the

> habit of making water in the ablution rooms, the regiment is warned that any soldier who is detected in the commission of so dirty a proceeding will be severely punished.[126]

And at Gibraltar in 1866:

> The Commanding Officer has received a letter from the Chaplain of the Church of England complaining of the filthy condition in which the Chapel is left on the men of the regiment quitting it at the termination of the Presbyterian service, the floors being covered with spittle in every direction. The non commissioned officers will check the practice of spitting on the floors . . .[127]

It is small wonder therefore that to achieve any sort of order, cleanliness, or even consciousness of the dangers of disease, there had to be regular and detailed inspection and parades, and until individual and collective awareness of hygiene was achieved, the only alternative to chaos was enforcement.

There is no doubt however that barrack rooms and the ancillary buildings were difficult to keep clean. Sums spent on basic maintenance consistently failed to keep pace with ordinary wear and tear, let alone neglect or misuse, and the commissariat and barrack labour department were inefficient and frequently 'on the make', and appeared to have a remarkable lack of interest in the welfare of the soldier. The frequent and often heavy charges for barrack damages were bitterly resented by occupants, largely because they could not see that their money was being put to the direct use of replacements or repairs. The sweeping of the stone or wooden floors generated a great deal of dust, and it was for example always necessary to brush down walls prior to whitewashing, otherwise the result was a series of grey smears of accumulated dirt.[128] The privies, ablution rooms, ash pits, urinals, and refuse tips were all in the barrack area and sometimes on a hot day were uncomfortably close to the living quarters. The 1858-59 Sanitary Commission advocated that ablution and bath rooms should not be in the same building where the men ate and slept, but this recommendation did very little to encourage the men to use the facilities:[129]

> The ablution accommodation should never be less than for 10% of the force; and in all future barracks the ablution rooms should, if possible be so distributed that the men can reach them, whenever possible under cover, though they should not be under the same roof as the sleeping rooms.[130]

Privies comprised a screened or walled-in area, not necessarily covered, with as many as ten holes and buckets, tubs or a drain to a cess pit beneath. They were communal and usually without cubicle divisions, except for officers' privies.[131] Newspaper was probably used for toilet paper, while supplies of paper were delivered by barrack masters after 1862.[132] Urinals were also communal and were either drained to pits or main drainage systems, but many had no water piped to them.[133]

A great deal of ash accumulated from the many coal and wood fires and this was thrown in a central area and removed periodically, usually by contractors; in Stirling Castle ash was thrown into a cellar which was dug out and cleaned when full. Ablution rooms initially probably only comprised a pump or water tubs. As barracks came to be connected to town water supplies, taps were introduced, in a long line from a single pipe, below which was a slate table with a beaded edge or basins. The 1858-59 Commission frequently recommended extending and ventilating these rooms, but there is no mention of heating the water, or the rooms, in winter. The floors were plain stone or were covered with wooden gratings and there were sometimes wall pegs for hanging up clothes and towels.[134] Baths were rare at the ratio of 4 per 100 men or less. In Edinburgh Castle in 1907 there was a total of six bathrooms and Colonel McIntosh of the 2nd Battalion Seaforth Highlanders wrote to HQ Scottish Command complaining:

> The present bathrooms are very inadequate in point of numbers (6) . . . [and] . . . they are scattered over the whole barracks.[135]

However, even when the Ministry of Works proposed to convert the disused military prison into a bath house, eight baths were considered quite adequate for 650 men, although there were proposals for the provision of hot water.[136] Corporal MacFarlane remembers the baths at Aldershot as being made of slabs of slate, 'like coffins', with the water supply and drain being controlled by an NCO outside the bathroom. Taking a bath was hardly considered worth the trouble, as the NCO often had to be paid to prevent him from cutting off the water in mid-bath.[137]

Refuse from the kitchens and dung from the stables were sold privately, the 'refuse fund' in many regiments providing an important source of income to benefit families, and to provide books, magazines and sports equipment, or as in the case of the 78th in Gibraltar in 1866, the profits were distributed as a small monthly sum to each man.[138]

Prior to the 1860s some cooking was still done on the barrack-room fires while the remainder was done in kitchens. The basic equipment in these kitchens was boilers of which there was usually two, one for meat and one for potatoes, and the main criticism of the Sanitary Commission was that kitchens had no roasting or baking facilities, so that the ration of beef and bread together with vegetables, usually potatoes, and flour and oatmeal, was generally served in the form of soup or stew, with porridge. Cooking utensils were few and the cooks were either the women assigned to the duty from each company, or the duty men, who before the advent of dining rooms cooked and carried the meal in kettles from the kitchens to the company and squad barrack rooms.[139]

Barrack lighting was provided by candles, oil lamps or gas. Candlesticks were provided with barrack utensils and the candles, either dip or mould, were issued on a scale by the pound,[140] but before 1862 this scale of issue was deemed to be inadequate and a witness to the 1861 Commission on Recruiting commented:

> The quantity of light given to a soldiers barracks by the supply of candles now authorised is not sufficient.[141]

Oil lamps provided a better light and were on issue together with oil, wicks and globes, but the latter had to be kept clean and no doubt frequently cracked and broke.

The installation of gas provided a different light altogether. The pipes were fitted into the barrack rooms, running across the ceiling, with a jet and tap suspended so that it could be reached at a convenient height, usually above the central table. From photographs it would seem that for a normal size of barrack room, holding ten to sixteen men, one jet was provided per room, that filaments and globes were not included in the fitting, and that the gas was low pressure. From the evidence it would appear that in some cases the supply of gas to the rooms was centrally controlled, either from outside the barrack room or from a central control tap, and in 1860 the War Office laid down that gas was to be turned off half an hour after tattoo roll call, and on again half an hour before sunrise.[142] At Edinburgh Castle gas was installed in the barrack rooms before 1860 and the 78th Order Book notes:

> Complaints having been made to the Commanding Officer of the great irregularities in the burning of the gas in barracks. Officers commanding companies are requested to see that no gas whatever is burnt during the daytime except in those rooms where it is absolutely necessary on account of their extreme darkness. Lights are to be put out at 10 o'clock except in the passages . . . the married people are in the habit of burning lights after hours contrary to the regulation.[143]

The restriction on lighting however caused all sorts of problems on a dark morning when the men were trying to turn out, wash and dress, and a writer in the *79th News*, poking fun, but equally making his point, wrote, under the title 'What the folks are Saying', at Malta in 1895:

> . . . That half an 'oor o' the gas in the morning wid be a great boon as shaving in the dark wi' a bint razor and cauld water is no what you wid ca' a luxury . . .[144]

While the installation of gas provided a safer and cheaper lighting system, the effect was generally dismal and Angus Cameron remembered joining the 79th at Cambridge Barracks, Portsmouth in 1853:

> When I entered the room that I was to sleep in it dampened my spirits a little. A large dismal room with 20 iron cots, a solitary jet of gas burning, three long tables endways in the centre of the room with forms to match and one solitary individual sitting at the table trimming a feather bonnet . . .[145]

Candles, lamps and gas however all contributed greatly towards the heat of the rooms, providing a particular warm, and not unpleasant, aroma, virtually unknown in modern society, brought up entirely on electricity.

It is clear therefore that Highland soldiers between 1820 and 1920 lived in barracks of many different types and origins, the primary service of the regiments being in fact abroad in much understudied foreign barracks, the majority of which have long since passed to the ownership of Commonwealth countries, and some of which are still occupied today. The barrack equipment and living conditions depended very much upon location and climate, but there is a strong thread of continuity running through British Army barrack life, which also was flexible enough to adapt to local conditions. There can be no doubt that between 1820 and 1920 the living environment of the Highland soldier in barracks improved considerably, an improvement which is attributable to the basic reforms before 1855, especially the introduction of single beds, the improvements and expenditure resulting from the Sanitary Commission, the education of the soldier himself, sometimes unwillingly, to accept order and cleanliness as part of his normal routine, the major scientific and medical advances of the century and the distinct change in contemporary attitudes to hygiene, sobriety and personal cleanliness.

It is evident from all the standing orders and regimental order books of the Highland regiments, that many of the commanding officers were in advance of the thinking of their time in trying to establish and maintain some sort of individual responsibility on the part of the soldiers, NCOs and officers in the orderly regulation of their daily lives, and that great emphasis was placed upon respectability and cleanliness. The difficulties faced by these officers were considerable as in many cases they worked against a background of ill-maintained buildings, an unhelpful if not hostile barrack department and the indifference or hostility of a number of soldiers who resented interference, would not wash unless ordered to march to bathing parade, stuffed up the ventilators with rags and paper and used every possible ploy to evade regulations.

In general it must be said however that the housing circumstances of the Highland soldier between 1820 and 1920 were better than those that he could have expected in civilian life, given Highland and Scottish industrial housing conditions of the period. Too often the Highland croft house or the bothy is portrayed as something romantic and desirable, while the barrack is portrayed as squalid, and while eyebrows are raised in horror at the sanitary facilities and habits of the soldier, it is entirely unrealistic to compare modern conditions and expectations with those of the nineteenth and early twentieth centuries.

Personal hygiene at the level which is now taken for granted in the second half of the twentieth century was not a prime consideration for these men, and it is important to set aside modern prejudices which often classify as worthless and undesirable those who drink, have venereal diseases and lice or do not wash too often. We should try to see these men as they saw themselves, for rough as they and their living conditions were, they were also proud, long-suffering, brave, tough men with constitutions of iron and endless humour and resilience.

NOTES

1. Alan Ramsay Skelly, *The Victorian Army at Home* (London 1977).
2. Lt. Colonel H.N. Cole OBE TD, *The Story of Aldershot* (Aldershot: 1951), p. xvii.
3. The 42nd were used with reluctance in this war as Wolseley was under strict instructions to conduct the campaign with the minimum loss of British lives and maximum efficiency, the War Office being concerned that Ashanti might become another Crimea. The 42nd were also under strength at this time and were made up by volunteers from the 79th. Wolseley wrote, '. . . when so splendid a Battalion as the 42nd is ready to my hand, when I see the martial spirit which animates both Officers and men, when I think of the vastly superior numbers of the enemy and I see myself entirely deprived of the large force of native auxiliaries upon which I have counted, when I remember how vitally important it is that the campaign should be short and decisive, I do not think that I should be acting wisely in keeping the 42nd Regiment at sea'. WO/33/26, Wolseley to Cardwell 18.12.1873.
4. Troops stationed at Edinburgh Castle used the ranges at Hunter's Bog, Arthur's Seat, and ranges were built adjacent to Fort George and at Longman Ranges, Inverness. Stobbs Camp at Hawick was bought by the Army in 1903; Barry Buddon Camp near Dundee was opened in 1892 and it was intended that this camp become the Aldershot of Scotland, while the building of Redford Cavalry and Infantry Barracks began in 1911. Ranges existed at Mugdock and Dechmont (Glasgow), Dreghorn (Edinburgh) and Blackdog (Aberdeen), and many towns had their own small rifle ranges used primarily by Volunteers.
5. The official guidebook to Stirling Castle makes no mention at all of the military occupation of Stirling Castle between 1745 and 1963. In fact it was an important arsenal, station and depot, through which thousands of men passed until 1963 when the Depot of the Argyll and Sutherland Highlanders finally moved out to be amalgamated with those of the other Highland Regiments at the Highland Brigade Depot, Bridge of Don, Aberdeen. J.S. Richardson and Margaret E. Root, *Official Guide, Stirling Castle* (HMSO, 1978).
6. Diary of Private A.W. McIntosh, 42nd, Vol. 1, p. 19. BWRM 421 (2591(1)-).
7. WO/33/8, 111, p. 26.
8. Ibid., pp. 27-28.
9. Ibid., p. 29.
10. The west block of Crown Square was used as the Sergeants' Mess in 1914.
11. *HLI Chronicle*, Vol. 111, No. 9, April 1903, p. 888.
12. Diary of General Sir J. Spencer Ewart 79th Cameron Highlanders RH/4/84/1 14.7.1893.
13. The restoration of Parliament Hall, Edinburgh Castle was in fact undertaken through the generosity of Thomas Nelson the Edinburgh publishers.
14. MW/1/183 (West Register House, Edinburgh).
15. Ibid.
16. MW/1/78. HM Office of Works to the War Office 16.4.1915.
17. WO/33/8 (66), and PP 1861 XVI c2839, p.15.
18. *79th News*, Vol. VIII, No. 95, January 1908, p. 4.
19. WO/33/8 (66).
20. *79th News*, No. 77, January 1905, p. 11.
21. *79th News*, No. 106, 1909, p. 218. The 2nd Battalion Cameron Highlanders first experienced Company Dining Rooms at Tientsin Barracks, China in 1908. *79th News*, No. 98, 1908, p. 184.
22. WO/33/7.
23. Diary of Lt. Colonel John Wheately, 42nd. BWRM.
24. The barracks at Birr were blown up by the IRA in 1921.
25. GD/225 Box 41. Leith Hall Muniments. Report on Barracks 1833.

26. Ibid.
27. WO/33/8 IX.
28. Lt. Colonel A.A. Fairrie, 'The Story of Fort George', *Queen's Own Highlander*, Vol. 24, No. 67, Winter 1984, p. 133.
29. WO/33/8 XIII.
30. WO/33/6A.
31. Ibid.
32. GD/225 Box 41. Leith Hall Muniments. Report on Barracks 1833 and Byron Rogers, 'Still Waiting for Napoleon', *Sunday Telegraph Magazine*, No. 375, December 18th, 1983, pp. 36-38. WO/33/7. Weedon is one of the most interesting and under-researched barracks in England. Of its kind it is unique. It housed large amounts of ordnance and ammunition in the nineteenth and twentieth centuries. In 1930 it became the central Ordnance Depot for small arms, machine guns and bicycles and between 1922 and 1938 also housed the Army Equitation School. In 1961 Central Ordnance Stores moved to Donnington and the buildings and ground were finally sold early in 1984.
33. Letters of Lt. Col. the Hon. Lauderdale Maule, 79th. GD/45/14/634/1 June 1839.
34. WO/33/6A. Bury was a defensible barrack. See PP 1861 XVI c2839, p.25.
35. Lt. Colonel H.N. Cole OBE TD, *The Story of Aldershot*, *op. cit*., p. 25.
36. *Ibid*., pp. 60-61.
37. Field Marshal Sir Evelyn Wood VC, *From Midshipman to Field Marshal*, *op. cit*., p. 193.
38. *HLI Chronicle*, Vol. V, No. 3, July 1905, p. 85, and Juliana Horatia Ewing, *The Story of a Short Life* (London: 1900) pp. 17-18.
39. Military Forces Localisation. Bill of Quantities for Erection of a Brigade Depot at Inverness, North Britain July 1877. QOHRM. In 1872 the 71st (HLI) and the 78th became linked Battalions. They were temporarily housed at Fort George but were allocated the new Inverness barracks. However the 1881 reforms joined the 78th to the 72nd as Seaforth Highlanders and the 71st to the 74th as Highland Light Infantry and the latter were taken out of the Highland District to Hamilton. The 79th Cameron Highlanders were left as the only single Battalion and were allocated the partially completed Inverness Depot, being temporarily housed at Fort George until Cameron Barracks was finished in 1886.
40. Diana M. Henderson (ed.), 'Private Reginald Lobban 1st Battalion Queen's Own Cameron Highlanders', *Queen's Own Highlander*, Vol. 24, No. 66, Summer 1984, pp. 29-32 and Vol. 24, No. 67, Winter 1984, pp. 137-140.
41. George F.G. Stanley, *Canada's Soldiers, 1604-1954*, *op. cit*., pp. 182-183.
42. WO/44/597. When the 72nd arrived in Halifax in 1851 Lieutenant William Parke recorded, 'Disembarked and marched to 'South Barracks' the very worst and dirtiest quarter I ever saw or was in. Officers were quartered in an old and large Hotel which was hired by the Government when Bks. were burnt down . . . all duties seem to be done in a most slovenly and casual manner, staff inefficient and idle, a contrast to the ever bustling officers of the W.I. I have a comfortable large room with (a) fine view of Harbour which is certainly beautiful'. Diary of Lt. William Parke 72nd, 24.7.1851 and 31.7.1851. QOHRM. See also Cameron W. Pulsifer, *British Regiments in Halifax* (Parks Canada, 1980) and Cameron W. Pulsifer, *The 78th Highlanders in Halifax 1869-71, The experiences of a Highland Regiment in a Garrison Town*, Vol. 1 (Parks Canada, 1983).
43. PP 1831 VI c 268.
44. E.L. Senoir, An Imperial Garrison in its Colonial Setting: British Regulars in Montreal 1832-1854. Ph.D. thesis, McGill University, Canada, 1976.
45. George F.G. Stanley, *Canada's Soldiers 1604-1954*, *op. cit*., pp. 185-190.
46. Regimental Standing Order Book 79th Highlanders, QOHRM. 144/79.
47. Lt. Colonel Maule of the 79th wrote from Canada in 1836: 'Of the Corps I can say nothing—we see but little of our men at this season—and besides it is impossible to

judge a soldier in their Canadian Winter Costume'. Letters of Lt. Colonel the Hon. Lauderdale Maule, 79th. GD/45/14/634/1 10th March 1836.

48. Reminiscences of Colour Sergeant Joseph Wylie Stevens, 22nd and 72nd. QOHRM M 79/6.

49. 'During the whole of its service in Gibraltar [1844-1846] the Regiment [the 72nd] was constantly employed in furnishing working parties and artificers to assist in the construction of the new line of fortification, extending from the Light House at Europa Point to Little Bay and from the New Mole to Chatham Centre Guard'. *Albany Monthly Record*, Regimental Journal of the 72nd Highlanders, Vol. 2, November 1877, p. 1. All the regiments who were stationed in Gibraltar at various times were required to supply soldiers for public works of maintenance and building, and as many as fifty-four 'daily labourers' were demanded from the 79th in 1848. WO/284/64 Garrison Orders Gibraltar 1.6.1848.

50. Regimental Standing Order Book of the 79th Highlanders, QOHRM, 144/79. 10.2.1841.

51. Ibid., 15.2.1841.

52. WO/44/139.

53. James Anton, *Retrospect of a Military Life* (Edinburgh: 1841), p. 345. Gibraltar has an unusual climate in that depressing clouds can hang over the summit for long periods of time. James Anton of the 42nd who served there in 1825 remembered 'The wind no sooner veers to the East, and settles in that point, than the evaporations borne along on the breeze, meet with an interruption from the lofty abrupt side of the rock collect in a cloud and continue to roll upwards like smoke from the mouth of a volcano. This is sometimes so dense that the sun is hid from the town by the thickly clouded vapours, until afternoon, while the isthmus north of the rock enjoys the rays without obstruction'. Ibid., p. 333.

54. General J.S. Ewart of the Cameron Highlanders was stationed in Malta in 1893 and lists the barracks at the time as: 'Verdale Palace, St. Elmo and St. Angelo, Inquisitor's Palace and Isola Gate, Florina, Pembroke Camp, Fort Manoel, Gozo and St. Francis Barracks'. Diary of General J.S. Ewart, RH/4/84/1 19.12.1893. NLS Map Division, Malta O.S. 1929 Sheet IV and V, War Office Geographical Section General Staff No. 3852.

55. Sergeant John Grant, 42nd, to Margaret Wilson 26.1.1844, BWRM. File H4 (42) Sec. G.

56. Michael Barthorp, *War on the Nile* (Poole: 1984), pp. 10-37.

57. Diary of General J.S. Ewart, RH/4/84/1.

58. NLS Map Division. Lower Egypt in 4 Sheets, Compiled at the Intelligence Branch, War Office, from the original French Survey in 1818-1882. Dept. No. 104-107. Map L 35.32.

59. Diary of General J.S. Ewart, RH/4/84/1, 16.9.1882.

60. Ibid., 30.10.1882.

61. Ibid., 7.11.1882. Two of the brass cannon were removed to become 79th Officers' Mess Coal Scuttles.

62. Sergeant James McKay 74th, *Reminiscences of the Last Kafir War, op.cit.*, p. 154.

63. G.L. Goff, *Historical Records of the 91st Argyllshire Highlanders, op.cit.*, pp. 82-84. WO/4/729-130.

64. *Ibid.* See also, 91st Highlanders. Register of Soldiers who have died while serving in the Regiment 1812-1881. ASHRM R/94.

65. General Sir Ian Hamilton, *Listening for the Drums, op. cit.*, p. 31.

66. 91st Commanding Officer's Rough Order Book, Kamptee 30.6.1860, ASHRM.

67. Ibid., 1860.

68. 91st (1st Battalion Argyll and Sutherland Highlanders) Permanent Order Book 1862-1884. ASHRM. 31.5.1865.

69. Veronica Bamfield, *On the Strength, The Story of the British Army Wife* (London: 1974), pp. 125-126.
70. 91st Commanding Officer's Rough Order Book, Kamptee 1860, ASHRM.
71. *79th News*, No. 109, May 1910, p. 78.
72. *The Thin Red Line*, Regimental Paper of the 2nd Battalion A and SH Vol. 2, No. 6, 1.6.1895, pp. 1-2.
73. Many of the hill stations and the roads to them were built by military labour; for example, the 79th and the Rifle Brigade built much of the road to Muree in 1865. Photograph Album C/45/951 1863-1873, QOHRM. The drill and football grounds at Muree were constructed by the 1st Battalion Gordon Highlanders in the season 1893-94.
74. Letters of Sergeant John Tulloch, 74th, to his brother 25.10.1855, kindly lent to the author by Mr. L. Tulloch, Ballyclare, Co. Antrim.
75. Lt. J. Wilson, 42nd, Diary of a Voyage to India from England 1857, BWRM.
76. Diary of Lt. Colonel J. W. Wedderburn, 42nd, Gibraltar 26.4.1846, BWRM.
77. Letters of Lt. Colonel the Hon. Lauderdale Maule, 79th, Gibraltar 16.2.1846, GD/45/634/3 1-84. In some foreign stations there were quite simply no barracks at all and the men lived in native-built huts.
78. Sydney Herbert's mother, Countess Catherine, was Russian-born. *Dictionary of National Biography* (Oxford: Oxford University Press), Vol. IX, p. 663, Sydney Herbert, First Baron Herbert of Lea, 1810-1861.
79. Report of the Royal Commission on the Housing of the Industrial Population in Scotland, 1918 para. 476, quoted R.H. Campbell and J.B.A. Dow, *Source Book of Scottish Economic and Social History*, *op. cit.*, p.223.
80. Thomas Ferguson, *Scottish Social Welfare 1864-1914* (Edinburgh: 1958), p. 182.
81. *Ibid.*, p. 173.
82. *Ibid.*, p. 120.
83. Alan Ramsay Skelly, *The Victorian Army at Home*, *op. cit.*, p. 28.
84. Diary of Private A. W. McIntosh, 42nd, BWRM 421 (3591(1)-).
85. WO/44/546.
86. See photograph of two-tier wooden berths in a Salvation Army shelter c.1890, *The Queen's Empire*, Part 6, The Homes of the Queen and of Her People (London: c.1897), p. 128.
87. Record Book of Plate, Books, Pictures Etc., presented to or acquired by the Sergeants' Mess 72nd Duke of Albany's Own Highlanders, now 1st Battalion Seaforth Highlanders, G.W. Anderson, QOHRM.
88. WO/44/546.
89. *Standing Orders for the 79th Regiment of Foot (or Cameron Highlanders)*, 1st May 1819. QOHRM. 142a/79.
90. PP 1824 XVI c15 p 37.
91. *HLI Chronicle*, Vol. 111, No. 9, April 1903, George Miller, 71st, p. 888.
92. PP 1861 XV c2762 para 5478.
93. PP 1824 XVI c60, p 26, PP 1828 XVII c28, p 24, PP 1829 XVI c17, p 35.
94. *Standing Orders of the 79th Regiment of Foot (or Cameron Highlanders)*, 1st May 1819. QOHRM 142a/79.
95. Diary of Lt. Colonel Wheately 42nd, BWRM.
96. PP 1824 XVI c15, p 37.
97. PP 1825 XVIII c35, p 36.
98. PP 1828 XVII c 56, p 9.
99. PP 1830 XVIII c 130, p 33.
100. PP 1830 XVIII c 210, p 4.
101. PP 1833 VII c 650, p 119 question 1290 and p 120 question 1305.
102. PP 1830 XVIII c 210, p 2.

103. WO/44/560.
104. PP 1861 XV c 2762, p 275, Evidence of Major Buckley.
105. 79th Regimental Standing Orders Book, 11.8.1836 and 15.2.1841, QOHRM. 144/79.
106. WO/44/551. John Fabb and W.Y. Carman, *The Victorian and Edwardian Army from Old Photographs* (London: n.d.), Illustration 43.
107. In the 79th in 1835 at Quebec the boxes for married men were 'three feet long, 18 inches wide and 18 inches deep, painted dark blue, with the soldier's name, number, company and regiment marked in the centre of the front side'. 79th Regimental Standing Order Book Quebec, 7.4.1835.QOHRM 144/79.
108. G.O. of 1.7.1880 No. 93.
109. *79th News*, Vol. 3, No. 37, 1.5.1898, p. 14.
110. PP 1892 XIX c 6582, para. 12379.
111. 79th Regimental Standing Order Book, QOHRM. 144/79.
112. Ibid., Gibraltar 10.2.1841.
113. Diary of Colonel J.W. Wedderburn 42nd, Bermuda 5.10.1848, BWRM. 28/714/1.
114. The table top was reversible and one side was kept for general use and the other side for inspections.
115. WO/44/560.
116. *Standing Orders for the 79th Regiment of Foot (or Cameron Highlanders)*, 1st May 1819, QOHRM. 142a/79.
117. PP 1822 XIX c 565, p 17.
118. PP 1833 VII c 650, p 178.
119. Cpl. Frank MacFarlane 1st Battalion Black Watch, Oral History archive, *op. cit.*
120. WO Circular 767 of 26.6.1862.
121. PP 1861 XV c 2762, p. 277 paras 5486-5488.
122. Lt. Colonel A.D. Greenhill Gardyne, *The Life of a Regiment*, *op.cit.*, Vol. 111, p. 345.
123. PP 1861 XV c 2762 para 5550, p 280.
124. Standing Orders of the 79th, 1835 Quebec, QOHRM. 143/79.
125. Regimental Order Book 78th Highlanders 1857-1866, SUSM. A242 72/78. Aldershot 20.5.1861.
126. Ibid., 23.11.1861.
127. Ibid., 15.2.1866. Spitting on the floors of the barrack rooms seems to have been a common habit. At Florina, Malta, in 1877 Orders of the 42nd record: 'The washing of floors is only allowed in barracks once a week, and should take place early in the morning so that the rooms and floors may have the whole day to dry. It would be well to omit the washing altogether on damp days. Dry rubbing should be freely used and the objectionable habit of spitting on the floors discouraged'. Permanent Order Book of the 42nd 1864-1886, BWRM 30/2271.
128. *Sutherland News*, No. 3, 1892, p. 4. General Regulations and Orders of the Army of 1822 discontinued the practice of washing barrack floors and substituted dry rubbing. In 1869 home barracks were whitewashed every two years, while lime was used on the urinals, drains and privies. WO Circular of 1.1.1869. Foreign barracks were whitewashed every two years by the Engineer Department and at intervals between by the occupying soldiers who were paid 4d per day for the work. WO Circular 606 of 11.7.1860.
129. WO/33/8 p. 6.
130. WO/33/7 Weedon.
131. WO/44/549.
132. WO Circular 788 of 28.10.1862.
133. In Aldershot in 1914 there were no flush toilets and privies still used the bucket system. Evidence of Cpl. Frank MacFarlane Black Watch, oral history archive, *op. cit.*
134. WO/33/8, p. 6.

135. MW/1/155 24.5.1907. SRO. During the summer months when they were most needed, baths were often closed, as for example at Shorncliffe in 1862. Regimental Order Book 78th Highlanders, SUSM A 242 72/78. 16.5.1862.
136. Ibid.
137. Cpl. Frank MacFarlane 1st Battalion Black Watch, oral history archive, *op.cit.*
138. Regimental Order Book of the 78th Highlanders, April 1866 Gibraltar, SUSM. A 242 72/78.
139. In 1863 a scale of cooking utensils was issued (WO Circular 828 of 13.7.1863) and in the same year one Sergeant Cook was allowed to be borne on the establishment, with training in his craft provided at Aldershot. HG Gen. Order 828 of 13.7.1863.
140. WO Circular 767 of 26.6.1862.
141. PP 1861 XV c 2762, p. 213.
142. WO Circular 573 of 27.3.1860. Gas fittings were standardised by the War Office and globes were available in 1877 for corridors, ante-rooms and officers' messes. Bill of Quantities for Erection of a Brigade Depot at Inverness, North Britain July 1877. QOHRM.
143. Regimental Order Book of the 78th Highlanders, 9.5.1860 and 14.9.1860, Edinburgh Castle. SUSM. A242 72/78.
144. *79th News*, Vol. 2, No. 17 1.1.1895 Malta, p. 18.
145. *79th News*, Vol. 2, No. 28 1.11.1896, p. 4.

CHAPTER 8

The Military Year: Duty, Marching and Trooping

In the varying physical and climatic surroundings of barracks and garrisons worldwide, Highland regimental life was conducted with remarkable continuity, revolving not only around discipline, rank and War Office Instructions, but also around national feeling, regimental music and individual and regimental pride. Many aspects of regimental life were the same as in other British regiments of foot, but Highland battalions retained a considerable individuality which reflected the interrelationships between officers and men and indeed between all the members and followers of the battalion, in the context of the regimental family.

The military year was divided, on purely common-sense grounds, according to season and location and it is clear that the inflexibility so often portrayed in British regimental life, in respect of dress and work in extremes of heat and cold, did not, in the main, occur in Highland regiments where it could be avoided. At home, the year was divided in two, winter and summer, commencing on 1st October and 1st April respectively. During the winter, moves, trooping and drills were kept to a minimum and training in the form of spring drills, musketry, route marching and transfers of station were generally reserved for the Spring, Summer and Autumn. In the Canadian winter both dress and routine were adapted to the bitter cold and Colour Sergeant Joseph W. Stevens of the 22nd and 72nd records about 1866:

> On landing in North America every soldier is granted the sum of £2 to procure a winter outfit which consists of a bearskin cap with flaps for covering mouth and ears, sealskin gloves, two under flannel shirts, two pairs of flannel drawers and a pair of long boots reaching over the knees. The greatcoats are also lined with thick flannel . . . In winter Drill is practically at an end. During the winter months we were often practised with snow shoes . . . [1]

During the hot seasons in the West Indies and India, dress and work were again adapted. Work in India during the hot season virtually ceased while men were confined to barracks, and physical labour in the West Indies was actually forbidden to European troops during the day in the hot weather. Thus when in the 1840s attempts were made to encourage soldiers in the West Indies to cultivate gardens for recreation and to improve their diet, the Commanding Officer of the 92nd

> . . . objected to the men . . . being employed during the day in this climate, [such work] being directly opposed to the General Orders for the troops in the West India Command.[2]

Dress was also adapted according to the time of the hot weather, the kilt giving way to shell jackets and white trousers for the 42nd during late May in Bermuda in 1848. By the beginning of November the Regiment reverted to tartan trews, and a week later preparations for drills began.[3]

While the red coat was retained in its various forms in many hot climates, it was nevertheless altered by being made up of a lighter material with the lining and padding removed.

The seasonal pattern was an accepted and expected feature of regimental life, and breaking the peacetime routine was bitterly resented. Private George Greig of the 93rd, who was born in Turriff and who enlisted in the Regiment aged 18 in 1852, served through the Crimea and the Indian Mutiny. In February 1859 when the regiment settled at Rawalpindi, they were already behind in learning the new drill book, and as the half-yearly inspection and the hot season approached, Colonel H.W. Stisted exchanged from the 78th to take command of the 93rd and immediately set about the belated drill instruction:

> Our Commander, having determined to brush up, had us out at early morning and let (sic) in the evening at drill, but it was getting now into the hot season and as at the rate of from 5 to 6 hours drill was crammed into the Regiment's head daily, the men began to grow extremely disaffected and instead of learning as they might have done under a better system, they on the contrary grew careless . . .[4]

The Regiment failed the inspection and extra drill was prescribed. In the light of the regiment's fighting history this was not popular:

> For the last four years we had been marching and counter marching from nearly one end of this vast Empire to the other, having no chance whatever of making ourselves acquainted with the new drill book.
>
> Long ere sunrise each day saw us away most drearily towards the drill ground . . . [and] after drill hours clusters of men could be seen at every point in evident consultation as to how their general condition could be bettered as it was becoming intolerable. One morning a whol (sic) company was found in a general state of—.[5]

The Highland regimental life cycle was also conducted in a manner and at a pace which was ordered but leisurely, particularly in the period 1820 to the 1870s. Thus Lieutenant Colonel Wheately wrote of the 42nd in Royal Barracks, Dublin in 1819:

> We were an easy Corps and it gave our non-commissioned officers no concern to have us on parade if the weather was at all unfavourable, whilst the — Regt. in barracks with us were paraded in the rooms, or clearing the ground of snow for parade purpose, we would be for days without dressing and when the pipes played off 'Ba—Ma Linah. ba ba ba—' even the roll was not called, at one time this winter 1819-1820 we were fully three weeks without turning out for parade.[6]

In these early days there was no concept of training or a state of readiness engendered by consistent fever-pitch activity, and it appears the Highland soldier expected and valued the time to himself and the modified pace, much of which was in tune with his national and local lifestyle. Sergeant George F. Miller of the 71st (HLI) wrote of military life in the 1850s:

> Let it be understood that *Duty* was duty in the old Corps. Rush and dash was not in it. Our Commanding Officer and Sergeant Major possessed great common sense. Hence breathing time was always considered . . .[7]

Even in 1913 and 1914 it is clear from the evidence of Private Reginald Lobban and Corporal Frank MacFarlane of the Camerons and the Black Watch that while emphasis was placed on training, individual skills, smartness and efficiency, there was still an important area of time and space left which allowed for relaxation and avoided unnecessary badgering and hounding. The primary impression given by these men is of two outstanding battalions, whose men were fit, well trained and had an intense regimental pride and who had been given time to develop and train without the necessity of 'beasting', oppression, or the subversion of individualism.[8]

The high points of the military year were without doubt the half-yearly inspections. As Private George Greig of the 93rd recorded, battalions and depots worldwide prepared for these events some months before with drill practice and rehearsals and the inspections could last for several days, covering all aspects of regimental life, from displays of kit and necessaries to subalterns' sword drill and the regimental books. To a young officer the whole idea presented a terrifying prospect, as General Sir Ian Hamilton records of the inspection of the 92nd at Mooltan in 1874:

> . . . [then] came the Annual Inspection . . . This ordeal had lain for weeks like a bottled nightmare under my pillow. In those days the Generals were not urbane, smiling personages saying please and thankyou . . . Not much! After you had been doing your level best you would be lucky to get off with a reprimand to smoke in your pipe. The dread morning broke. After Books—Cooks—Kitchen—Barrack Room and Kits came three quarters of an hour for breakfast; then Parade. Next day there would be a Field Day.[9]

It is interesting to note that the proforma used for the Report and Confidential Report of the Half Yearly Inspection of a Regiment of Foot, for example that of the 79th at Gibraltar in 1847,[10] contained a total of 112 questions upon which the Inspecting Officer required to be satisfied, covering all aspects of regimental life, welfare and efficiency. Physical checks were carried out of books and records, and subalterns were chosen at random to conduct drill. The whole procedure was probably just as searching as the modern equivalent ARU (Annual Review of the Unit).

Drill, being closely related to field manoeuvre and battle procedure, was an important aspect of these inspections, and battalion drill well conducted on the Dundas or Torrens system must have presented an imposing and remarkable sight. It was not until the 1870s and 1880s that drill became separated into parade drill and battle drill, the last remnant of the Dundas System, the

Eighteenth Manoeuvre, 'Advancing in Line', still being in use today.

These often misunderstood old manoeuvres were entirely logical and coherent and enabled large bodies of men to be moved in column or line, while maintaining the important positions of the Grenadiers, the Light Company, the Colours and the front-rank men, so that in the smoky confusion of battle every man knew exactly who should be next to him and where he was in relation to the rest of the Battalion.[11]

It would be convenient to be able to consider a Highland regiment as a static entity with each officer and soldier performing regular and standardised daily tasks, in a set pattern and dress, following textbook regulations with clockwork precision, but a projected ideal such as this ignores the individual and human factors in regimental life.

A Highland regiment was never static. Men fell sick, died, went on furlough, committed crimes, deserted or were away from the regiment recruiting. Some officers were more popular or more efficient, some drank and gambled, some left the regiment while others stayed for many years, surviving considerable dangers during their service. Thus while it is easy to deal in the generalities of day-to-day life, the regiment, its personnel, location, morale, numbers, state of health and overall efficiency were constantly changing at varying rates, while at the same time the concept of 'Regiment' remained virtually unchanged.

Indicative of this theme of change amidst constancy and the dangers of considering regiments without looking behind the facade at the individuals involved, is a study of the parade state of the 74th Highlanders at Fermoy on 26th July 1850.

On 27th July 1850 the 74th had a paper strength of 852 officers and men, but as can be clearly seen, dealing in overall figures can be very deceptive. Only 67% of the Regiment (573 officers and men) were on parade, while 33% (279) were for one reason or another not in the ranks; 20% being at other duties and 13% (112) not being with the Headquarters of the Regiment at all.

The burden of duty, particularly of guards and escorts, thus fell heavily on the 67% of the men who were present, not sick, prisoners or regularly employed and this situation could be made much worse by men being removed for garrison duties and for garrison labour and fatigue parties. Thus in Gibraltar, where the 79th supplied men for garrison duties, fortress and defence works, Lauderdale Maule complained:

> The soldier has three nights in bed and the 4th on guard [and] he is harassed by constant fatigue duties when not on guard . . .[13]

Where a regiment was in the United Kingdom, joined with its depot establishment and of similar strength to the 74th in 1850, the situation was somewhat easier, but maintaining and manning a separate depot, carrying out effective garrison duties abroad and running the regiment day to day undoubtedly placed considerable strain on regimental manpower resources.

In the 74th, the reasons for absence from parade although present with the Regiment are interesting. The guard of the day appears to have comprised two

74th Highlanders Parade State 26.7.1850 Fermoy, Ireland

	Colonel	Lt. Colonel	Major	Captain	Lieutenant	Ensign	Staff	Sgts.	Corporals	Drummers	Privates	
Total on Parade	1	1	1	8	9	5	5	34	28	13	468	573
On guard								2	2		24	
Cooks											10	
Batmen											5	
On fatigue								1			1	
Clerks								1			3	
Orderly to Colonel								1				
Prisoners in the Guard Room											2	
Attending Sick								2			6	
Attending Mess									1		4	
Attending Drill									1	1	2	
Recruits											36	
Sick In Hospital									3	1	41	
Sick In Quarters					1	1			1		6	
Sick Convalescent								1	1		6	
Total at Headquarters:	1	1	1	8	10	6	5	42	37*	15*	614	740
Recruiting								2			4	
On leave and furlough			1	1	1	2				1	9	
Absent without leave											8	
In prison by sentence of Court Martial											7	
In custody of civil power											2	
Invalids at Dublin										1	13	
Sick at Clonmell											1	
Detached at Mitchelstown				1	1			3	2		52	
Total Effectives	1	1	2	10	12	8	5	47	39	17	710	852

* In the return these figures read 'Corporals 38 Drummers 14', which could be a clerical error.

sergeants, two corporals and twenty-four men and it is unusual that at least one drummer is not included in this figure. The guard took duty for twenty-four hours and an officer would also be designated for duty that day. Depending upon the state of the country, elections, famine etc., guards could be much heavier in Ireland, particularly in Dublin, and twenty-six would probably be a relatively low figure. The cooks, one per company, would be designated for the day or the week. The batmen, clerks, orderly and sick and mess attendants were probably permanently employed old or favoured soldiers, placed in sheltered positions of trust and responsibility, while those at drill were probably defaulters. The thirty-six recruits would have their own parades and would not be permitted to parade with the battalion until they had passed their drill training and learned their duty, a situation which also applied to the young officers on first joining the regiment.

Spencer Ewart commenced his drill for example under Colour Sergeant Newall of the 79th in January 1882. Two days later he was Subaltern of the Day, 'on my own', and by the middle of the month he was competent enough to attend Adjutant's Parade as a marker, but he would still have been wearing an other rank's uniform for the purpose. His first guard was on the North Front of Gibraltar in March 1882, but the first big parade he was permitted to attend was not until April, when he proudly records: 'I went on my first Company Officers Parade and was put in command of one of the Companies'.[14]

This gradual process of introduction and preparation also applied to the men in the ranks, and passing out as a 'Dutyman' was a moment of pride for many. Private John Tulloch of the 74th wrote to his brother from Mitchelstown on 21st April 1852:

> . . . i am got my cloths and liring my drill i have turned against drinking altogether i intend to save up and come down to see you all after i get my dril leaned . . . i drel 4 times a day i am quit a green horn yet but well dam soon lern . . .[15]

Private A.W. McIntosh also writes in his diary:

> Thursday 14th January 1858. I began my drill today. I took very ill at first but I soon got used to it as it was very cold I used to put my hands in my pockets when we got "Stand at Ease" but they stopped me from doing that by serving me out with the undress of the Regiment which is trews having no pockets and a white shell jacket . . .
> Friday 16th April. I was dismissed drill today. I am now a Dutyman, no longer a raw recruit, but a drilled soldier fit for anything.
> Monday 19th April. I mounted my first guard today and walked about on duty very strict.[16]

Thus, the thirty-six recruits in the 74th parade state of 1850 were in the preparatory learning stage, unable as yet to take their place in the ranks. Also not present with the ranks were the sick who in total amounted to some 8% of the men at headquarters. It is interesting that some of the men are permitted to remain in quarters when sick, thus avoiding the 10d per day hospital stoppages and that others are convalescent and are probably on light duties.

Of the 13% of the Regiment who were not present at headquarters, a small party was recruiting, and these men may well have been operating in Glasgow and Lanarkshire. Only five years before the 74th had regained their 'Highland' title[17] and the Lieutenant Colonel Commanding at the time, in 1850, was the renowned John 'Jock' Fordyce who personally contributed towards the re-nationalisation of the 74th Regiment.[18] Sergeant James McKay of the 74th remembers:

> When Colonel Fordyce joined the 74th as Major, the Regiment had recently been created a Highland Corps, and when he obtained his Lieutenant Colonelcy and the command of the Regiment, to make it a truely Scottish Corps, he gave a portion out of his own pocket to all Scotch recruits joining . . . so that the regiment might become a truely national one, such as the 42nd, 79th, 93rd and other Highland Corps. Some of the recruits he got were not of the most sterling stuff, the recruiting parties kidnapping anything Scotch they could get their hands upon about the Tontine, Glasgow or Peter Crears Glasgow.[19]

Seven officers and ten men were on leave or furlough and eight men, a noticeably small number, were absent. Seven men were in prison by sentence of court martial and one man was in the custody of the civil power. The fourteen invalids at Dublin and the man sick at Clonmell illustrate an interesting aspect of regimental life in an age of limited communications. These men were already at some distance from headquarters, and when the Regiment moved to the Cape in March 1851 they were even more isolated as the 74th Depot then moved to Aberdeen. If they remained unfit and were not discharged, the question must be asked, what happened to these men and how did they return to their Regiment?

Finally, away from the Regimental Headquarters there was a detachment at Mitchelstown some ten miles from Fermoy, a quite usual situation for service in Ireland, where regiments often found it difficult to maintain cohesion when many detachments were required. The numbers at Regimental Headquarters, almost 100 men in excess of the modern infantry battalion, also illustrate the size of barracks which was needed to house the 74th in 1850.

It is important to remember too that 573 'on parade' is a deceptive figure in respect of bayonet strength. Some twenty men would be in the band, five to ten of the total number would have been boys or acting drummers, and it is known that the 74th had pipers at this time, as the annual inspection of the 74th in 1848 prompted a letter from the Adjutant General at Horse Guards dated 20th March 1849:

> With regard to the innovation introduced into the 74th Regiment of dressing the Pipers in the Kilt. The Commander in Chief orders its immediate discontinuance, and that the Pipers may wear the dress of the Regiment.[20]

Lt. Colonel Fordyce, who appears to have had a forceful character not unlike that of Lt. Colonel Maule of the 79th, replied:

> This mode of dressing the Pipers is no innovation but that ever since the Regiment was raised they have been thus equipt . . . there were always at least two or three Pipers equipped in the old kilted dress of the Regiment who played at its head, . . . I may mention that one of the Pipers now in the Regiment has worn the kilt for upwards of seventeen years and another for upwards of twelve years . . . The professional pride of the Pipers themselves (who are not easily procured) would be wounded by the change.[21]

There would in addition have been the men who were the regular tradesmen of the Regiment, tailors and shoemakers and men who filled particular posts such as the Canteen Sergeant and the Schoolmaster, and excluded are the women and children and any civilians employed by the Regiment, such as the Messman and the Bandmaster, who was at this time Bandmaster Hartong, a German civilian employed and paid for by the officers.

This man accompanied the Regiment to the Cape and was killed while on patrol near Fort Beaufort by the Kafirs after, it is believed, having been tortured for three days.[22]

Thus a regiment was never static. Men came and went constantly, going or returning from furlough, prison, sickness or detachment; joining as recruits, passing into the ranks or being specially employed. Parade states, too, are not the whole answer to a regiment's true strength, and the concept of 'Regiment' and regimental life must be considered in the light of the foregoing.

Whatever their strength or internal arrangement, the primary function of the Highland battalions was duty which took many forms, from fighting the enemies of the nation and guarding isolated frontier outposts, to the guard at Holyrood Palace and attending the Law Lords at Court. The latter was not popular and is described by Private McIntosh, then at Stirling Castle in 1858:

> Monday 17th May 1858. The Lords came here today for the Trials and we had to furnish a Guard of Honour for them, guard the Court House during the trial, escort them back to their Hotel at night and remain there all night—I was on several times but did not like the job very well, it was great humbug, and we were very glad when they went away.[23]

Most detested however of the non-active service duties was undoubtedly employment in aid of the civil power, which could place the Highland soldier in considerable danger and under a certain emotional and psychological strain.

In the absence of effective police forces and with no clear guidelines,[24] such as are now laid down in the Green Card system, Highland soldiers were frequently employed to control civil disturbances and unrest on the British mainland in the nineteenth and early twentieth centuries. In 1837, for example, the 79th were in Glasgow and Paisley. Lauderdale Maule, complaining bitterly, noted:

> Glasgow is the most wretched place I was ever quartered in . . . I have not seen the sun since I arrived here. I am quite sick of pipeclay—This marching about day after day is disgusting. There is a depression in trade, a consequent want of employment and food and we are here to prevent the weavers helping themselves.[25]

Although there seems to have been no large-scale disturbance in which the 79th were involved at this time, an interesting incident did occur which resulted in the death of 31-year-old Private James Smith of the 79th. In early March 1837 Private Smith and his friend, Private Donald Pollock, were returning to the

Gallowgate Barracks along Dalmarnock Road when they were stopped by James Wilson who made himself out to be a deserter from the 71st Regiment. Wilson agreed to go with Smith and Pollock but soon became 'obstreperous', made to punch Smith and then ran off. The soldiers did not pursue him, but carried on their way only to be met by Wilson and some twenty colliers who were lying in wait for them. They set upon the two soldiers shouting. 'Here they are, let's at them!' and amid taunts of 'shame' from the women at the windows above, Pollock managed to take shelter in a house, while Smith was chased, cornered and kicked and his bayonet taken and used against him. Some two hours afterwards Smith managed to get back to barracks where he died eighteen days later as a result of his injuries. From the reading of the trial papers it would appear that the soldiers were deliberately provoked and set upon by the colliers, and Maule for one was very angry when Wilson pleaded not guilty, a verdict of not proven was returned in respect of culpable homicide and he was transported for seven years in respect of the assault:[26]

> There is a rascal too condemned *only* to seven years transportation for murdering one of the 79th—a blackguard coal miner from Glasgow. Such fellows ought to work out their whole sentences in irons in the dockyards.[27]

After a short tour in Ireland the 79th were again used in aid of the civil power, this time at Salford, Manchester, Liverpool and Newcastle under Lyne. Maule wrote:

> We are in readiness for Manchester . . . I hope to God we shall not be part of the anti-Chartist array I cannot well imagine a more disagreeable service.[28]

Arriving in Manchester, he noted:

> The people . . . appear to have an ill feeling towards us . . . some fellows taunted us as we came in [to Manchester] with the prospect of having a pike or two in our 'shody guts'.[29]

While Maule complained bitterly of the provocation and the indiscipline of the Yeomanry and the Police,[30] the use of Highland soldiers in full dress kilt and regimentals was not without its more humorous and relaxed side:

> The Chartists are giving us much trouble. Liverpool is well enough as a quarter if we had a barrack to go to [but] . . . the people flock to see us and the women require regular demonstration that the men don't wear drawers![31]

It is well to remember that many of the Highland soldiers employed in duties of civil disturbance were young and not yet fully trained, as frequently in Ireland depot men were used to assist the civil power.

In 1847 Donald Cameron was serving with the Depot of the 79th at Castlebar:

> One day a call for all off duty to turn out with arms to the town for there was a row I got some other men and on with them and down to the square fell in with the rest got orders to fix bayonets and got someone to fix mine and got the gun on my shoulder and out we went through the town until we came to a public house and formed up in front of it facing outwards and a great noise inside soldiers, police and civilians fighting and a crowd gathering outside and throughing missiles at us until we stood at the carry. Looking at them a missile struck my firelock about my shoulder and the firelock striking my head I came to the charge the Commander at once put his sword under my firelock and told me to shoulder then a man came on horseback and spoke to the crowd ordering them to disperse which they were not willing to do and smashing going on instead he told them he would be forced to read the riot act if they would not go with that they began to move away and we got our own men out we returned to barracks.[32]

One of the difficulties about the use of troops in Ireland was the religion of the numbers of Irishmen serving in the regiments employed. In the main this did not present a major problem to the kilted Highland regiments before 1881 when the numbers of Catholic soldiers were small, but in the 73rd, 75th and 91st the high proportions of Irishmen and Catholics must have caused difficulties and may, in part, account for the deployment of these regiments.[33]

The intervention of the clergy in relations between the soldiers and the local population also caused some unusual problems, as did the question of Roman Catholic preaching. In a note in the standing orders of the 93rd of 1835 it is written that when Roman Catholic soldiers wished to attend Chapel they were to be marched there by an officer who was to remain present during the service:

> . . . whenever it is found that the clergy of the Roman Catholic Church are in the habit of using seditious and inflamatory language to their congregation, Officers Commanding detachments will take their men to the service of Mass only, marching them off when that is concluded.[34]

An additional feature of working in aid of the civil power was subversion, particularly in the 1860s, by members of the Fenian movement. One of the movement's primary aims under Devoy was the infiltration of British regiments, and it appears that he was particularly successful in the 75th and 73rd Regiments, the latter being claimed to be one of the 'crack Fenian Regiments' about 1866,[35] and it is believed that one of the main reasons why the Regiment was sent to Hong Kong and Japan in 1867 was the question of its unreliability.

An interesting sidelight of this infiltration by subversion is that so little is known about the 73rd and the 75th. When these Regiments were linked with the 42nd and the 92nd in 1881, there appears to have been a deliberate attempt to take them over, rather than take them on as equal partners. Instead of retaining much of their identity, as the 91st and the 74th appear to have done, the 73rd and the 75th were quickly converted, not only in dress, to be essentially '42nd' and '92nd', and while the 73rd had been the old second battalion of the 42nd, by 1881 the link was tenuous and the question has to be raised as to whether their Fenian leanings resulted directly in their being linked to and consumed by entirely loyal and primarily Protestant Scottish regiments.[36]

It may well have been the case also that there was amongst the kilted Highland regiments a deliberate recruiting policy aimed against Roman Catholics, and it is obvious that Lt. Colonel Maule of the 79th, for one, discouraged Catholic recruiting to his Regiment. Anxious to preserve the national identity of the 79th, he wrote in 1847, 'God defend us from Irish recruits and above all from Catholics!'[37]

Whatever the religious implications, the unpopularity of duties in aid of the civil power continued, and reading between the lines of the *79th News* of 1907, it is clear what the feelings of the 1st Battalion Queen's Own Cameron Highlanders were when they were called to Belfast in that year:

> . . . we arrived back in Dublin again on the 29th July, expecting a well earned rest. But it was not to be, for at 10pm that same night the order went forth to get ready for Belfast the following morning. The scene that followed must have closely resembled the night before Quatre Bras . . . we entrained for Belfast the next morning . . . our services were called for on the nights of the 11th and 12th August, when the natives of the "Falls" district entered into a nut-cracking competition with the Police, and several of the military had the opportunity of experiencing what it is like to be struck with a "Belfast kidney" (a paving stone) and also of listening to the elocutionary powers of the "Falls" damsels . . . [38]

With the growth of the organised labour movement and the use of strikes to remedy grievances, the Army continued to be involved in internal security matters, and during the Railway strike of 1911 the 1st Battalion Gordon Highlanders were for example ordered to the 'disturbed areas' of Sheffield to guard the railway stations. Although supplied with live ammunition, the Battalion had strict, clear and definite instructions in respect of the use of force, and there seems to have been more curiosity than animosity regarding their deployment.

While these duties were not popular, their unpopularity, particularly in Ireland, was not necessarily related to a lack of sympathy on the part of the soldiers. It is difficult to believe that Highlanders serving in Ireland in the 1820s, '30s and '40s were unaware of Highland emigration, poverty and hunger, and there is evidence to suggest that they contributed what they could from their own rations and gave to the local population.[39]

The desperate people were however a serious problem and at Elphin, near Castlebar, in 1847, the young Edward Cuming records:

> There was a small barrack here sufficient to accommodate the detachment, but I had to rent a small cottage for myself. There was still terrible distress in the country; the beggars were legion, and my garden was constantly full of them, all squatting round the window, begging for something every time I made my appearance; it would have been impossible to relieve such numbers. They became so troublesome that I at length determined on a plan to keep them out. I selected two of the strongest and sturdiest old women to sit at my gate all day, and I paid them a couple of shillings a week, supplying them also with tobacco, in return for which they guaranteed that no one else should enter the garden and that I should enjoy

uninterrupted peace. The money was well invested and they fulfilled their contract conscientiously.[40]

Most interesting of all however is the use of Highland troops in aid of the civil power in Scotland but outwith the Lowland manufacturing towns. The noticeable shortage of information about this suggests that Highland regiments were carefully kept out of their home area, but this is not entirely the case. During the disturbances of 1792, popularly known as Bliadhna nan Caorach (the Year of the Sheep), three companies of the 42nd marched through Inverness and Dingwall to Boath, but there was no confrontation.[41] In 1827 a party of the 74th Depot was dispatched to Corgarff to assist Excise officers in the suppression of smuggling.[42] In 1839 a detachment of the 78th, then in Glasgow, went to Harris to the estate of Lord Dunmore to deal with disturbances amongst the distressed and desperate crofters, and it does not require a great deal of imagination to appreciate the psychological and emotional difficulties of Highland soldiers and officers so employed. Unfortunately there appears to be very little evidence as to what actually happened during these incidents, how the soldiers reacted and how they were greeted by the local population, some of whom may have been regimental pensioners or had relations amongst the 78th.[43]

Frequently English and Irish regiments were used, as for example in 1843 when the 87th Regiment (The Royal Irish Fusiliers) were employed to assist at religious disturbances at Loge and Resolis,[44] and the same Regiment were used in the potato riots at Inverness in 1846.[45] Two companies of the 27th (Inniskilling) Regiment were employed during the food riots at Wick and Invergordon in 1847[46] and the employment of these troops may well have been part of a deliberate policy to avoid conflicts of loyalty amongst Highland soldiers. For while the Depot of the 71st (HLI) drilled in Huntly square as a show of strength in 1842 to place a Minister at Glass[47] and a detachment from the 56th Brigade Depot (92nd and 93rd) went to Fraserburgh in 1874 in aid of the civil power,[48] large bodies of armed Highland troops were kept away from Highland disturbances.

At the Battle of the Braes in 1882 in Skye, Marines, gunboats and Glasgow Police were used and they were again employed in the collection of rates in Skye and Tiree in 1886.[49] An interesting corollary to these latter events was the residual strength of Highland opinion at the time. In 1886 two sergeants and thirty-two men of 'H' Company 1st Inverness (Inverness Highland) Rifle Volunteers, Queen's Own Cameron Highlanders, based at Portree, sent a letter as follows:

Portree, 1st Nov. 1886

To Major Macdonald, Portree,
Sir,—Taking into account the present military proceedings in Skye, we the undersigned members of 'H' Company, beg to tender our resignations as members of the corps and to ask our discharges.[50]

The Commanding Officer and the Adjutant immediately went to Portree and after addressing the Company in the Drill Hall, the men retracted. Three were dismissed and two sergeants were reduced, but there appears to be no evidence that men in regular Highland battalions took any similar type of action, although they must have been aware of what had happened.

Duty apart, two factors interrupted the equilibrium of the military year, change of station and war. It is now almost impossible to imagine the practical and logistic difficulties that must have been involved when a battalion changed station in the nineteenth and early twentieth centuries, and the sheer scale of the military commitment of the Highland battalions worldwide can only put the movements of a modern 'air-portable battalion' completely in the shade.

As a matter of policy, movement of a battalion at home from station to station was carried out on a regular and frequent basis, because ' . . . it has been considered that it is a bad practice to leave troops too long in one quarter'.[51] Due to the state of the roads it was common for movements to include coastal sea voyages in hired transports, and so regiments embarked and disembarked at coastal ports such as Granton and marched through the streets to Edinburgh Castle. Arrivals and departures, particularly of Highland regiments in Scotland, were the subject of much popular and civic interest, and descriptions of the proceedings were nearly always recorded in the Scottish press.[52]

On Monday, 12th May 1893 the 93rd left Edinburgh Castle for Aldershot:

> The Regiment . . . [with] 32 Sergeants, 32 Corporals, 21 Drummers, 386 Privates, 57 Women and 90 Children . . . paraded on the Castle Esplanade at 10.30am and marched via the Mound, Hanover Street and Inverleith Row to Granton . . . The day was bright, clear and sunny and Edinburgh and its beautiful neighbourhood was looking at its very best. Thousands of spectators lined the road to Granton [and] on nearing Granton the 91st Argyllshire Highlanders were passed by the 93rd, both Regiments shouldering arms in salutation of each other.[53]

Playing another regiment in or out of a station and the paying of regimental compliments on the march were important features of trooping and movements, and despite the immense practical problems of a move they appear to have been conducted with considerable decorum and attention to detail. Failure to observe the unwritten rules of manners on the march always provoked comment, as for example when the band of the Black Watch failed to turn out to play the 74th away from Cairo in 1883:

> We had to play ourselves away as they either would not, or could not turn out . . . we would have played them away had they been leaving first.[54]

It took some time for the authorities to appreciate and use the railway system for internal moves. The 92nd first travelled by rail on the Paisley to Glasgow line on 8th October 1844,[55] while on 10th July 1831 the Digest of Services of the 91st recorded: 'The Regiment proceeded this day agreeably to route by steam conveyance for Liverpool'.[56]

Often open carriages were used, but by the 1850s these were obviously unpopular with the soldiers. John Wedderburn of the 42nd describes his Regiment marching in the rain to Woking Station after a month of wet and muddy manoeuvres at Chobham:

> . . . to make matters worse one half of the men had to travel in open trucks, like a flock of sheep, they took it more good humouredly than I would have done and were bleating like sheep to each other for fun.[57]

In spite of the development of the railway system it was still common practice throughout the nineteenth century for a regiment to march between stations. Several days would be spent in preparation and packing, ordering carts, loading and cleaning the barracks before leaving. Then the regiment, usually by divisions, would set off accompanied by the women, children, animals, pets, baggage and carts. Everything they possessed went with them and a regiment on the move represented much of the nomadic way of life of the Army of the nineteenth and early twentieth centuries. When it rained they simply got wet, as John Wedderburn remembers:

> Friday 9th September 1842, Perth. Started early this morning for Crieff, it was raining in torrents and I soon got wet to the skin, as I gave my great coat to one of the soldiers wives who had a little baby in her arms on one of the baggage carts.[58]

In the summer of 1870 the 91st marched from Dover to Aldershot and Private Alfred Guttridge fortunately recorded the event in some detail, illustrating the traditional and time-honoured method of moving station, which by 1870 was beginning to be overtaken by improved road and rail communications.

The Regiment set off from Dover at five on the morning of Saturday 18th June, being played out of the town by the bands of the 97th and 102nd Regiments, and after stopping for some bread and cheese and a pint of beer, reached Canterbury by 11.45am, having covered some twenty miles. On the outskirts of the town, the 91st were met by the band of the 19th Hussars who played them up to Canterbury barracks. Marching did not, however, tire the men out or relieve them of further duty, and Guttridge records:

> When we got in I went to the Canteen with Jim Kelly and got a pint of beer we whent on praid at 4 o'clock the Band played there was a great number of people there to hear our Band after tea I had a walk out in town and I thought it was a very nice place I came into Barracks at Tato our Drummers and Pipers played at Tato whenof to bed at 9.30 had a good nights rest . . .[59]

Sunday was spent in church parade, visiting the Cathedral and another excursion to the canteen, for the Regiment arose at two on the morning of the 20th and marched at 3am accompanied by the band of the Kent Militia, whose

Band Sergeant received 'some money' from the Commanding Officer of the 91st for his trouble. Once more, the early morning halfway house supplied beer and bread and cheese at 6.30am before they set off for Sittingbourne, where they entrained for Chatham. Here they were met and marched to Chatham Barracks by the band of the 3rd Regiment and the band of the Royal Engineers.

The following morning they were up at 3am and marched at 4am for Gravesend: ' . . . that was a short march (11 miles) but it was all up hills . . .'

The arrival of the regiment caused considerable local excitement at Gravesend:

> . . . the 91st Regiment of the Argyleshire Highlanders stayed overnight in the Barracks, having pitched their tents in a field close to the Parade Ground. The novelty of an encampment attracted large enthusiastic crowds to the Barracks, who were entertained by the regiment's Drum and Fife Band and Pipes. The music was very popular with the locals and when the Regiment, complete with Band, resumed its march next day to Aldershot, they were joined by their new supporters who accompanied them for many miles on the journey.[60]

On Wednesday 22nd the 91st were up at midnight and marched at 1.30am; again there was beer, bread and cheese at the halfway house, and then on to Woolwich where they arrived just after 10am. Even after twenty-two miles of marching, Guttridge quickly hung up his things in barracks and sought out old friends with whom 'I enjoyed myself very much'.

The following morning after another very early start, the 91st set off for Kingston via 'Clapon Common' (where there was beer, bread and cheese), and Wandsworth. Reaching Kingston at 9.30am, Guttridge was billeted in a house called the 'Jolly Butcher Beer House'. On Friday 24th June the Regiment were again up at midnight and marched at 1am for Guildford, where they were met by the Militia Band, Guttridge being billeted in the 'Prince Albert'.

On the final day reveille was at 3am, the Regiment left at 4am to the strains of the Militia Band, and at 7.30am they were greeted in Aldershot by the bands of the 42nd, the 67th and the 4th Regiments:

> When we got in Camp the 4th Regiment gave our Regiment a breakfast and there Band gave our Band the same and very much we enjoyed it.[61]

Private Guttridge records some interesting features of marching and movements between stations, the importance of bands on the march, the public interest generated, the etiquette of greeting, reception and leaving barracks, the expected distances per day of some twenty miles, the use of billeting in public houses when barracks were not available, the early morning starts and the basic but alcoholic refreshments to be expected at the halfway house.[62]

Marching in India between stations took on a similar pattern, but over greater distances and often through much more rugged terrain. Regiments were given their route, which contained detailed information on the river crossings and the halting places, and each day an advance party would move ahead to prepare camping grounds and meals. Regiments were always accompanied by camp followers, and the baggage travelled in bullock carts and on camels. The etiquette of bands, greetings and the preparation of camps and meals for the incomers was again an accepted tradition, which was also practised by the Indian Army.

Few people survive today who can remember the event in military life which came to be known simply as 'trooping'. The scenes at Portsmouth and Southampton widely televised in 1982 at the commencement of the Falklands War can only give a hint of the atmosphere and emotion generated by regular departures and arrivals during the 'trooping season', not to mention the considerable amount of work in loading and unloading, added to which departure in the nineteenth and early twentieth centuries meant departure for an extended period of time, with little opportunity of home leave and no chance of a telephone call to keep in touch.

Because of the amount of time that the Highland battalions spent overseas and the variety of foreign stations occupied by them, trooping formed an important part of Highland regimental life. Early troopships were converted men-of-war, but the Admiralty, who were responsible for trooping, developed a system of contracts for carrying troops, particularly with the Peninsular and Orient Steam Navigation Company, the British India Steam Navigation Company and the Bibby Line.[63] Even in the 1850s, however, sailing ships outnumbered steamships in trooping, and standards of safety, comfort and hygiene were very low. Frequently Highland soldiers remark on the shortage of food, rations and water, the filthy conditions on board, sickness, discomfort and especially the mutinous and ill-disciplined nature of the crews.

Returning home from the Cape of Good Hope in 1844 on board the *Sir Charles Napier* with invalids from the 91st, the Royal Artillery and the 27th and the 75th Regiments, Captain Bertie Gordon of the 91st wrote:

> I have the honour to report the arrival off Dartmouth of the invalids from the Cape of Good Hope. I consider it my duty likewise to report that owing to the insufficiency of water and provisions on board the ship, the invalids have been exposed to short allowance of both since 5th June . . . I do not consider the ship in a fit state to proceed to Gravesend owing to the utter absence of all proper control and discipline in the hands of the Master, or the Mates, and other Officers of the ship, one consequence of which is that drunkenness has prevailed to an extent sufficient to endanger the safety of all.[64]

Edward Cuming of the 79th records the voyage of the *Resistance* from Gibraltar to Quebec in 1848:

> The ship was infested with rats, they used to run round the ledge over the berths at night. We could see their sharp eyes piercing down at us, and often, after we were asleep, we were awakened by them jumping down on our beds . . . To keep them out I stuffed my soiled linen into the openings over my berth and when I arrived at Quebec I had not a shirt fit to wear again, the rats had torn them to pieces.[65]

On board Royal Navy ships the Army also came face to face with naval discipline. In 1838 the 93rd trooped to Canada on board HMS *Inconstant*, and Andrew Agnew of the 93rd recorded:

> Naval discipline is much harder than that of the Army—A man noisily drunk is with us shut up in the Black Hole—on board ship he is put in irons and gagged—Boys stand dolefully about on deck to certain hours and in due course receive a sharp caning from the Master at Arms for what appear to be very trivial offences.[66]

Eventually an offending sailor was flogged:

> The wretched man was tied up to the gratings and got a dozen as an example. A Naval dozen is no joke—it has been said to be as good (or rather as bad) as an Army Hundred:- instead of light cats handled by little drummers a much more formidable instrument with heavy knots is wealded with fearful efforts by the bowswain's mates . . . he never spoke but chewed a leadend bullet 'till it was all over.[67]

Often it seems Highland officers were disturbed by naval discipline and the officer/man relationship in the Senior Service, and J.W. Wedderburn of the 42nd wrote of his voyage to Bermuda aboard the 84-gun HMS *Vengeance* in 1847:

> We had a most rascally crew on board, nearly all Irish, the way in which the said crew were treated did not however tend I think to make them better. Almost every morning there was a punishment parade and during our long voyage I am really afraid to say how many men were flogged, not to mention constant whipping inflicted on the rumps of others. The language used Lt. the Honble. Bying to the men was most disgusting and amongst such a young crew, it was not to be wondered at that insubordination was the order of the day. It seemed a rather private dodge to leave hooks and marling spikes in the rigging, especially on that part of the mizzen mast under which the Officers generally walked about . . . a hook was thrown at Mr Newglass a Midshipman [but] . . . it was never found out if it was one of the crew or the 42nd who threw it and Captain Lushington accordingly threatened to flog every 4th man, soldier or sailor . . . Colonel Cameron very wisely forewarned the Captain against such a step . . .[68]

With the men went the women and children of the regiments. In 1822 only six wives per one hundred men were permitted to travel, twelve per one hundred for India and New South Wales, but it is clear that in the Highland regiments, particularly in the 93rd, this figure was often exceeded. When the 93rd sailed from Canada in 1848 they were about 400 strong and had 60 women and 140 children.[69] This practice of exceeding the quota was strongly disapproved of by Lt. Colonel Maule of the 79th, largely for the purely practical reasons that the troopships were too small, badly fitted out and already inadequate for the purposes for which they were intended. Describing his problems to his brother on the departure of the 79th from Gibraltar in 1848, Lauderdale wrote of the *Resistance*, a ship which carried many Highland Regiments all over the world:

> It is like all other troopships, infinitely inferior to transports or freight ships in every

> respect, altho' supposed to be superior. The fact is that Troopships are too small . . . we are shamefully crowded. The tonnage allowed to Troops going to America is 1¾ ton per man. The "Resistance" is 1079 tons and we are 850 souls at least on board. She cannot ever hold the regulation allowance of baggage and to accommodate my men I have been obliged to pay freight on board a merchantman going to Quebec for half our baggage. The unfortunate women and children are packed like slaves in a clipper.[70]

Arriving at Quebec, Maule commented:

> Thanks to my determined opposition to marriages we had only 28 women in all. Had we even had our number, 35, we should have been at our wits end . . .[71]

However, in spite of the regulations and the enforcement of those regulations by individual commanding officers like Maule, the authorities themselves permitted the quotas to be exceeded, and on the return of the 79th from Quebec in 1851 Maule was forced by the DQMG Montreal to troop home women in excess of the authorised figure.[72] This apparent benevolence was in fact of little benefit to the women concerned and in many cases merely resulted in their destitution in a foreign country. As 'extra women' they were not entitled to rations or accommodation in the Regiment, and on arrival in Scotland their husbands marched with their companies and they were abandoned to their own devices. Maule wrote in the autumn of 1851:

> I have two of the husbands of these extra women now in hospital at Stirling and their wives and children are starving in the streets or dependant on the charity of the soldiers.[73]

The discomfort of the ships and sea travel aside, trooping provided a break from ordinary garrison life for the Highland soldier and his family. The 'fortunate' women and the sometimes reluctant men[74] went on board to set sail, amid scenes of lively public interest and often sadness, upon voyages that entailed no small amount of danger. The date of departure could never really be guaranteed in the days of sail and the incoming trooper would usually bring in the relieving regiment. Thus the Regiment *in situ* would double up in barracks for a few days while the ship was re-victualled and scoured with vinegar and chloride of lime.[75]

In Highland regiments the time of leaving a station was the signal for a serious bout of celebratory drinking. On leaving Quebec, Maule wrote of the 79th:

> . . . at 6am on the 4th [August 1851] I marched without a man absent and without a man in liquor and damned few fellows can say that of a march.[76]

However, when the Queen's Own Cameron Highlanders were warned for trooping to Egypt from Gibraltar in 1882, with the prospect of action, Spencer Ewart recorded:

> I am sorry to record that there was a good deal of drunkenness today in the 79th the men being wildely elated at the prospect of active service and escape from the Rock . . . Colour Sergeant Grimmond was reduced and Private Donald Cameron of my company was in [the] Orderly Room too for being drunk and declining to leave off singing the "Cameron Men".[77]

Just prior to or at embarkation, the men were issued with their sea kits and hammocks and taught how to use them.[78] Betting ran heavily at this time, on the day of arrival, the number of days of the voyage or the first sighting of land,[79] and amidst cheering from the quay and the other ships in harbour, the vessel set off. Often a ship would take several days to leave port due to contrary winds, and would be forced to stand off until the wind changed.[80] Then, gradually, the ship settled into a routine. Smoking was not permitted below decks and all washing, usually in salt water, had to be done by 8am in the morning.[81] Men were told off for sentry duties on the liquor and water supplies and over the cows, pigs, sheep and hens that were usually taken on board for fresh milk and meat. Soldiers often assisted in the running of the ship and on steamers they helped with coaling, a process which could last several days and covered everything in a thick layer of black dust. The officers inspected the men's meals as usual and the men paraded each day barefoot, with open-necked shirts, for medical inspection.[82] On Sundays there was a church parade.

The men and the officers would often gather together to provide their own entertainment. Lieutenant J. Wilson of the 42nd records: 'In the afternoon plenty of amusements. The men singing and dancing to two fiddles'.[83] John Wedderburn notes of the 42nd voyage home from Halifax, Nova Scotia in 1852:

> After Dinner the Band played and two of my Company came and sang on the Quarter Deck and they sang right well . . . [The following day] . . . the Band played after Mess also the Pipes and old McLean the Pipe Major danced and played the fiddle like a five year old.[84]

During this voyage Wedderburn found time to write a ship's newspaper.

Where space permitted, platoon exercises were practised, but when the rough weather set in, all parades stopped and most succumbed to seasickness in the chaos below:

> The ship began rolling fearfully and we were holding on by the edges of the tables, when all at once they gave way and sent us all reeling to the other side of the ship . . . You would have seen Soldiers, Tables, Tin pots, Accoutrements all mixed up with Feather Bonnets, Knapsacks and Biscuit rolling from side to side and as the rolling continued the mixture got thicker.[85]

In obviously calmer circumstances Colour Sergeant Joseph Stevens of the 72nd records the routine on board while trooping to India in 1871. At 5.30am all hands turned out and all hammocks were folded and stowed. The hose was turned on for a bath and after the upper deck had been cleaned, breakfast was served out. Then all hands went on deck and the bugle sounded the call 'commence firing', at which the men would light their pipes from a rope fuse. Smoking stopped on the call 'cease firing'. At 10am there was a deck inspection and parade and then the men would settle down with deck and card games, with tobacco as the stakes. At 12 noon came dinner and the issue of rum and porter and lime juice, and at 5pm tea, the evening being spent listening to impromptu musicians and dancing and singing, 'the absence of ladies notwithstanding'.[86]

The large-scale movement of troops and supplies required for the Crimean War resulted in the purchase of troopships by the Government, including the famous *Himalaya*, and while more satisfactory contracts were entered into with the shipping companies, it was not until 1866 the five Government troopships were built, *Crocodile, Euphrates, Jumna, Malabar*[87] and *Serapis.* These ships were in service for thirty years and they were rigged screw ships painted out in white, with a blue riband and yellow funnel. To regiments trooping they became as distinctive as any barracks, and each had her own character and speciality. The *Crocodile*, which ran from England to Alexandria, was popular for her good food. The *Jumna* (Suez to Bombay) was renowned for engine trouble.

Areas of these ships had specific names: the subalterns' quarters 'pandemonium', the cabin deck below the saloon 'the horsebox deck', the unmarried ladies' area the 'dovecote', and the cabins for married ladies and children the 'nursery'.[88]

Despite improved conditions, by 1894 these five ships were worn out and P & O secured the first of the new contracts, building three twin-screw steamers, *Assaye, Plassey* and *Sabraon*, and at the outbreak of the First World War ships from Bibby Line, Union Castle Line and the British India Steam Navigation Company were all requisitioned as troop and hospital ships.

In the main it seems that voyages were not consistently uncomfortable, and the many sights and sounds were a source of constant amazement to the uninitiated. As ships passed they were hailed and news and mail were exchanged where possible. Many voyages provided scenes of extraordinary beauty, which were not lost on the Highland soldier. Leaving Gibraltar after a nostalgic visit, en route for the Crimea in 1854, Lauderdale Maule recorded:

> At 12 we were clear of the Bay—it was a lovely night—Not a cloud obscured the stars—their twinkling light was reflected by the calm sea and the ship sped onwards as if it were on a path of molten silver—the coast lay slumbering under the dark shadows of the lofty lines and the plash of the paddlewheels and the rushing sound of the prow alone broke upon the silence which lingered around—What a night for a cigar! In England those alone who dream of Paradise—the good and the hopeful—have in their sleep visions of nights such as these—they never realise them.[89]

NOTES

1. Colour Sergeant J. W. Stevens. QOHRM 142a 79, p. 17.
2. WO/43/716.
3. Diary of Col. J.W. Wedderburn, 42nd, Bermuda 22.5.1848 and 4.11.1848. BWRM 28/714/1.
4. Diary of Private George Greig 93rd, ASHRM R/144.
5. Ibid. It is interesting to note that this is one of the very few references to internal unrest and near mutiny in a Highland battalion between 1820 and 1920.
6. Diary of Lt. Colonel J. Wheately, 42nd, BWRM.
7. *HLI Chronicle,* Vol. 3, No. 9, April 1903, p. 886.
8. Private Reginald Lobban and Corporal Frank MacFarlane, oral history archive, *op. cit.*
9. General Sir Ian Hamilton, *Listening for the Drums, op. cit.*, p. 69.
10. WO/27/367 79th 10.5.1847.
11. Colonel David Dundas, *Principles of Military Movements Chiefly applied to Infantry illustrated by Manoeuvres of the Prussian Troops and by an outline of the British Campaigns in Germany during the war of 1757,* (London: 1788); and Major General Sir Henry Torrens, *Field Exercises and Evolutions of the Army* (London: 1824). There was obvious and considerable regimental relief when these inspections were over, and a good report would often result in a regimental holiday and the release of men confined to barracks or attending extra duties. At Fort George (Canada) in 1832, for example, the Commanding Officer of the 79th, as a direct result of a good inspection, ordered 'all names to be erased from the defaulters lists at York'. 79th Regimental Standing Orders Book 6.8.1832 QOHRM 144/79.
12. Digest of Services 74th Highlanders Vol. 1 1787-1852. RHFRM D/1/11.
13. Letters of Lt. Col. the Hon. Lauderdale Maule, 79th, 20.12.1847. GD/45/14/634/4 1-98.
14. Diary of General Sir J. Spencer Ewart RH/4/84. Gibraltar 6.1.1882. 8.1.1882. 19.1.1882. 12.3.1882 and 15.4.1882. Diary of Lt. Colonel Adrian Grant Duff, Black Watch. BWRM, and Rules for the Instruction of Recruit Officers, ASHRM 5b 18/16. 16.10.1872.
15. Letters of Private John Tulloch, *op. cit.*
16. Diary of Private A.W. McIntosh, 42nd BWRM, 421(3591(1)-).
17. Royal Warrant 14.11.1845: 'Her Majesty has been graciously pleased to approve of the Seventy-fourth foot resuming the appellation of the Seventy-fourth (Highland) Regiment of foot, and of its being clothed accordingly; that is to wear the tartan trews instead of the Oxford mixture; plaid cap instead of the black chaco; and the plaid scarf as worn by the Seventy-first regiment.
18. John Fordyce was the son of Thomas Fordyce of Ayton, Berwickshire. He served in the 34th, the 94th and the 21st before exchanging into the 74th in 1844. He was killed in action in South Africa in 1851.
19. Sergeant James McKay, *Reminiscences of the Last Kafir War, op. cit.*, p. 125. The Adjutant General only reluctantly agreed to recommend the 'Highland' title in 1845 for the 74th and it is clear that had the recruiting not been successful the title might well have been lost again. Letter, Adjutant General to Lt. Col. Crabbe 74th 13.8.1845. 'His Grace will recommend to Her Majesty that the 74th Regiment be permitted to resume the appellation of 'Highland Regiment', [but] . . . His Grace cannot keep out of view the fact that it is found very difficult to complete the Highland Regiments already on the Establishment of the Army with Highland or even Scotch recruits and that this state of things has rendered it occasionally necessary to extend their recruiting to other parts of the United Kingdom. As however Lieut. Colonel Crabbe holds out sanguine expectations of being able to keep up the establishment of the 74th by means of its local influence in Scotland,

the Commander in Chief yields to the Lieut. Colonel's assurances under that head, but with the direct understanding that should their expectations be disappointed, the expedients resorted to in the cases of other Highland Regiments similarly circumstanced, will be resorted to in the case of the 74th Regiment, that is efficiency of numbers must be maintained from time to time by the other means alluded to if that indispensible object cannot be attained by the exertions of its own recruiting parties.' Digest of Services, 74th Highlanders, Vol. 1, 1787-1852, RHFRM D/1/11.

20. Ibid., 20.3.1849.
21. Ibid.
22. Sergeant James McKay, *Reminiscences of the Last Kafir War, op. cit.*, pp. 64, 69 and 73.
23. Diary of Private A.W. McIntosh 42nd BWRM 421 (3591(1)-).
24. See for example the Standing Orders of the 79th Highlanders 1835, 'Aiding the Civil Power in the Suppression of Riots', QOHRM 143/79.
25. Letters of Lt. Colonel The Hon. Lauderdale Maule, 79th, Glasgow and Paisley 13.2.1837 and 24.4.1837. GD/45/14/634/1.
26. AD/14/38/394 and JC/13/78 of 10.1.1838.
27. Letters of Lt. Colonel the Hon. Lauderdale Maule, 79th, 14.1.1838 GD/45/14/634/1.
28. Ibid., 19.4.1839.
29. Ibid., 8.5.1839.
30. Ibid., 1.7.1839.
31. Ibid., 4.5.1839.
32. Private Donald Cameron 79th RH/4/141.
33. Religious denominations—1830:

Regiment	Protestants	Roman Catholics
42nd	556	5
72nd	555	38
73rd	320	260
74th	425	99
75th	425	356
78th	494	37
79th	489	5
91st	454	113
92nd	685	44
93rd	517	20

WO/17/435 and WO/17/437.

34. Standing Orders of the 93rd Highlanders 1835, ASHRM. R/226.
35. A.J. Semple, 'The Fenian Infiltration of the British Army', *Journal of the Society for Army Historical Research*, Vol. LII, No. 211, Autumn 1977, pp. 133-160.
36. The fate of the 75th caused considerable sadness in the Regiment who were in Malta in 1881 and who would appear to have had little say in what was to happen to them. While accepting the inevitable, they made one last gesture of defiance, marching a coffin representing their Regiment to a grave with full honours on the night of 30th June 1881 and erecting a memorial stone which read:

Here lies the poor old Seventy-Fifth,
But, under God's protection,
They'll rise again in kilt and hose
a glorious resurrection!
For by the transformation power
Of Parliamentary laws,
We go to bed the Seventy-Fifth
And rise the Ninety-Twa's!

Ibid., p. 238.

Fenian considerations aside, Spencer Ewart of the Camerons comments on the damage done to the Regiment by this instant conversion: 'The 75th, a good Regiment, were handicapped (at Tel-el-Kebir) by having just been turned into Highlanders. The Battalion was full of Englishmen and was the subject of much merriment . . .' Diaries of J. Spencer Ewart, Queen's Own Cameron Highlanders, 20.11.1882 RH/4/84.

Rumours of Fenian infiltration continued into the 1880s and appear to have affected regiments other than those who had been in Ireland at the height of the movement. About 1889 there were for example allegations by a Sergeant A.V. Palmer of the 79th Queen's Own Cameron Highlanders that two Fenian soldiers serving with the Camerons had been shot by their comrades at Tel-el-Kebir. The allegations appear to have been without foundation, but caused sufficient concern for Spencer Ewart to be called away from duty to answer questions from the Secretary of State for War. Diary of J. Spencer Ewart, Queen's Own Cameron Highlanders, RH/4/84.

37. Letters of Lt. Col. the Hon. Lauderdale Maule, 79th, Gibraltar 2.1.1847 GD/45/14/634/4 1-98.
38. *79th News*, No. 93, September 1907, p. 7.
39. Lt. Colonel C. Greenhill Gardyne, The Life of A Regiment, *op. cit.*, Vol. 2, p. 49.
40. Diary of Colonel Cuming 79th, *79th News*, January 1935, pp. 79-80.
41. Kenneth J. Logue, *Popular Disturbances in Scotland 1780-1815*, *op. cit.*, p. 58.
42. *Inverness Courier*, 25.7.1827.
43. Eric Richards, *A History of the Highland Clearances*, *op. cit.*, pp. 368-369. This detachment went to the Island by way of Oban and Tiree and arrived on Harris with the Sheriff and other civil officers. They proceeded to Borve where they made five arrests with no resistance. *Inverness Courier*, 24.7.1839 and 7.8.1839.
44. *Inverness Courier*, 4.10.1843.
45. *Ibid.*, 11.2.1846.
46. *Ibid.*, 3.3.1847 and 10.3.1847.
47. *HLI Chronicle*, No. 15, July 1896, p. 712.
48. Lt. Colonel C. Greenhill Gardyne, *The Life of A Regiment*, *op. cit.*, Vol. 2, p. 182, and *Edinburgh Evening Courant*, 3.8.1874 and 5.8.1874.
49. D.W. Crowley, 'The Crofters Party 1885-1892', *Scottish Historical Review*, **UD**18V, pp. 110-126.
50. *Historical Records of the Cameron Highlanders*, *op. cit.*, Vol. 2, p. 77.
51. PP 1850 X c662. Evidence of Fox Maule, p. 20 para. 354.
52. *The Scotsman*, Monday 22.2.1892, p. 7: "DEPARTURE OF THE CAMERON HIGHLANDERS FROM EDINBURGH. After a stay in Edinburgh of four years, the Cameron Highlanders left the Castle on Saturday morning to embark on board the Troopship "Assistance" at Leith, en route for Malta . . . [They] paraded in the Castle yard in full marching order . . . Officers and men wore the white pith helmet recently issued for foreign service. It was a bitterly cold morning, a cutting wind bringing showers of hail, blown from the north east and the men had to stand about without their greatcoats while the calling of the roll and other preliminaries, lasting nearly an hour were gone through. Towards eight o'clock the crowd increased to upwards of a couple of thousands, but the Police blocked the way across the street below the Tolbooth Church and prevented access to the Castlehill and the Esplanade. Lieutenants McEwan and Campbell carrying the Regimental Colours folded upon their staves took their station at the head of the third company with a guard of four men with fixed bayonets . . . Column was formed. The pipes struck up 'The March of the Cameron Men' and the Regiment marched away amid blinding showers of snow dust blown from the battlements overhead.

. . . The Band and Pipes alternately played the Troops along Johnstone Terrace, Castle Terrace and Lothian Road to the station to the strains of such tunes as 'Home Sweet Home', 'Auld Lang Syne' 'Goodbye Sweetheart Goodbye' [and] 'Gadie Rins'."

53. R.H. Burgoyne, *Historical Records of the 93rd Sutherland Highlanders, op. cit.*, p. 342.
54. Joseph Henderson, *HLI Chronicle*, No. 10, April 1895, p. 422.
55. Lt. Colonel C. Greenhill Gardyne, *The Life of a Regiment, op. cit.*, Vol. 2, p. 43.
56. Digest of Services of the 91st or Argyllshire Regiment of Infantry, ASHRM R/17/115/ 9.
57. Diary of J.W. Wedderburn 42nd, 14.7.1853. BWRM 28/714/1.
58. Ibid., 9.9.1842.
59. Papers of Private Alfred Guttridge, 91st Highlanders, ASHRM, kindly lent to the Museum by Private Guttridge's daughter. Guttridge was born in 1845, probably in the Regiment. He may well have been a Bandsman or a Drummer, having been taught the oboe by Band Master Moor of the 13th Regiment at 'Knelly Hall'. In 1872 he married Julia Wallace, a domestic servant at Ardersier Manse, and he retired from the Army to receive an 'out pension' of 1/- a day in 1882. He died in Netley Hospital in 1923.
60. John Milbank Jones, *The History of Milton Barracks Gravesend and its Occupants 1860-1970* (Gravesend: 1985), p. 4.
61. Papers of Private Alfred Guttridge, *op cit.*
62. The march of the 91st Highlanders from Dover to Aldershot 18th-25th June 1870.

18th	Dover to Canterbury	20 miles
19th	Canterbury (Church Parade)	
20th	Canterbury to Sittingbourne	20
	Sittingbourne to Chatham	17 miles by train
21st	Chatham to Gravesend	11
22nd	Gravesend to Woolwich	22
23rd	Woolwich to Kingston	19
24th	Kingston to Guildford	19
25th	Guildford to Aldershot	11
Total miles marching		122

63. Colonel H.C.B. Rodgers, *Troopships and Their History* (London: 1963), p. 73.
64. Letter book of Captain Bertie Gordon, 91st, 25.6.1844 and 26.6.1844. ASHRM R/58.
65. Diary of Colonel Cuming 79th, *79th News*, January 1935, p. 82.
66. Journal of Andrew Agnew of Lochnaw 93rd. GD/154/781. This trooping took place in appalling weather out of season because of the emergency of the Canadian Rebellion.
67. Ibid.
68. Diary of Colonel J.W. Wedderburn, 42nd, 14.2.1847. BWRM 28/714/1.
69. It is important to differentiate between the married establishment, that is the number of men permitted to be married in a regiment and have their wives inside in barracks and receive rations, and the number of those wives permitted to embark overseas with the regiment, the two figures not necessarily being the same. The figures of 6/100 and 12/100 relate to embarkation quotas and these women would be chosen by lot. Standing Orders of the 79th, 1819, pp. 61-56. General Regulations and Orders for the Army, Horse Guards 1.1.1822. General Order of 7.5.1841 $\frac{HG}{54}$ War Office Circular of 9.8.1867. War Office Circular of 1.10.1872. It was, it appears, possible to exceed the allotted figure of wives by presenting them in the returns of embarkation and disembarkation as 'Female Servants', and this category would also have allowed the older female children of the regiment to stay with their families. By 1871 the War Office proforma had amended this category of passengers to read, 'Female servants not soldiers wives'. WO/25/1195 Disembarkation Return 79th Bombay/ Portsmouth 1871.
70. Letters of Lt. Colonel the Hon. Lauderdale Maule 79th, 'on board 'Resistance' Gibraltar 12.6.1848'. GD/45/14/634/4 99-184. The ship hired by Maule was the merchantman barque *Lady Cremorne* which was wrecked off the Canadian Coast. Maule wrote from Quebec, ' . . . [we have] lost a great proportion of our Mess traps

and . . . our private baggage by the wreck of a merchant vessel whose lubberly Master ran her high on Gaspé shore in fine weather and where between a drunken crew, an imbecile captain and a host of lawless wreckers our property was destroyed and plundered'. 24.8.1848. GD/45/14/634/4 99-184.

Many of the irreplaceable books and records of the Regiment seem to have been destroyed at this time in the wreck, and regimental folklore has it that the Cameron Highlanders' silver was lost also, but this was probably not the case. It would seem that the Regiment had little silver in 1848 although Storr and Mortimer were employed as silversmiths. The minutes of a Mess meeting held in Quebec to investigate the losses recorded, 'It was found that much dammage had been sustained in the kitchen utensils and considerable breakage amongst the crockery and glass, that the silver was much stained and that other miscellaneous articles were destroyed. Also that the amount of £50 had been lost'. Quebec 4.9.1848 Minute Book of the Officers' Mess 79th Highlanders, QOHRM 1161.

71. Letters of Lt. Colonel the Hon. Lauderdale Maule, 79th, Quebec 8.8.1848 GD/45/14/634/4 99-184.

72. Letter DQMG Montreal 24.7.1851 GD/45/8/96.

73. Letters of Lt. Colonel the Hon. Lauderdale Maule, 79th, 22.9.1851 GD/45/14/634/6 45-107.

74. J.W. Wedderburn of the 42nd records leaving Leith to set sail for Malta via Deptford: 'Monday 14th November 1842. I got the baggage on board the Leith steamer and placed sentries here and there on shore, but to no purpose, as a Sergeant and six men bolted, they all came back except 3 men'. Diary of Colonel J.W. Wedderburn 42nd, BWRM 28/714/1.

75. WO/25/1167 Embarkation Return, *Louisiana* sailing ship. 79th Dublin 30.7.1857.

76. Letters of Lt. Colonel the Hon. Lauderdale Maule, 79th, 12.8.1851. GD/45/14/634/6 45-107.

77. Diary of J. Spencer Ewart, Queen's Own Cameron Highlanders, Gibraltar 7.7.1882 and 13.7.1882, RH/4/84.

78. A Sea Kit for India in 1857 comprised:

Two canvas smock frocks 3s 3d
One pair of canvas trousers
One neck handkerchief
One pair of shoes
Three pounds of Marine Soap @ 7d
Two pounds of yellow soap @ 7d
Nine balls of pipe clay
One quarter tin pot with hook
One scrubbing brush
Three tins of blacking
One clasp knife
One bag in lieu of haversack
Needles and thread
Three pounds of tobacco @ 2s 8d
Two flannel belts
Two deck shirts @ 2s 6d

The prices were variable and the items were paid for as necessaries out of pay advanced to the men for the purpose. PP 1857-1858 XXXVII c 247.

Diary of Private A.W. McIntosh 42nd, 1858. BWRM 421 (3591(1)-1).

79. Lieutenant J. Wilson, 42nd, Diary of a Voyage to India from England 1857. BWRM.

80. When the 79th left Gibraltar in 1848 they embarked on 7th June, but the west wind kept them in Gibraltar Bay until the 13th, when the wind changed to the east for a short time and they slipped out into the Atlantic. Diary of Lt. William Parke 72nd. QOHRM.

81. Diary of Private A.W. McIntosh, 42nd, BWRM 421 (3591(1)-1).

82. Known as 'toe parade'. Diary of Colonel J.W. Wedderburn, 42nd, 3.5.1852. BWRM 28/714/1.
83. Lieutenant J. Wilson, 42nd, Diary of a Voyage to India from England 1857. BWRM.
84. Diary of Colonel J.W. Wedderburn, 42nd, 10 and 11.6.1852. BWRM 28/714/1.
85. Diary of Private A.W. McIntosh, 42nd, BWRM 421 (3591(1)-1).
86. Reminiscences of Colour Sergeant Joseph W. Stevens, 22nd and 72nd. QOHRM 79/6.
87. R.G. Thomsett, *A Record Voyage in HMS Malabar* (London: 1902).
88. Colonel H.C.B. Rodgers, *Troopships and their History*, *op. cit.*, p135.
89. Letters of Lt. Colonel the Hon. Lauderdale Maule, 79th, GD/45/26/91. Maule never in fact reached the Crimea but died of cholera at Varna on 1st August 1854.

CHAPTER 9

Highland Regimental Music

The Highland soldier's military day was determined by his geographical and physical situation and the time of year. There was in many ways no such thing as 'the typical day', and yet there was throughout the nineteenth and early twentieth centuries a form of routine, a structure, upon which regimental life was built. Like a skeleton holding together different shapes and forms of flesh, this 'routine' was of considerable importance, for wherever these Highland Regiments were in the world, and whatever monotonous or arduous duties they were performing, it enabled them to maintain their traditions (while at the same time being flexible enough to establish new traditions), to retain their individual and Highland identity, to keep discipline and order and in times of stress, to do their job, to do it well and to keep doing it.

Much of the key to the routine of continuity lay in the music of the Highland Regiments. Music marked the timings of the day and the duties and parades; it controlled manoeuvre in battle and was strongly associated too with regimental pride and tradition and with the Regiment as family; it became an integral part of the Mess system and was part of the accepted forms of release and recreation, as well as being associated with the system of discipline. Regimental life without the musicians in the nineteenth and early twentieth centuries would have been unthinkable.

Bands of musicians playing percussion, brass and woodwind instruments have a long historical background, their development in British service being attributed to Turkish, Austrian and Prussian influence.[1] The Drum and Fife are also of ancient origin with long military associations, the drummers in particular being vital in battle, giving signals by set beatings and also having a role of parley with the enemy. In barracks and camp there were in addition set duties and until 1816 Scots Regiments had their own beatings and calls which can be traced to the Scots Brigade in Swedish and Dutch service.[2] The bagpipe, although not an instrument unique to Scotland, in its Scots Highland form was part of Celtic culture, the clan system and the employment of hereditary pipers to chiefs. Unlike the music of the fife and drum and the military band, pipe music was not traditionally learned from staff notation, but by ear or from a series of vocables, or canntaireachd, passed from one player to another. In 1760 Joseph MacDonald wrote his *Compleat Theory of the Scots Highland Bagpipe*, published in 1803, in which he set out three divisions in Highland bagpipe music—Marches, by which he meant Piobaireachd, Jigs and Reels—and he demonstrated the close links between Highland martial traditions and Highland music, stating that the original design of the Highland Bagpipe was to

> . . . animate a sett of Men when approaching an Enemy, [to] Solemnize rural Diversions in Fields, and before walking Companeys . . .[3]

Deeply inspirational and highly evocative in its musical content, Piobaireachd or Ceol Mor includes tunes of considerable antiquity of praise, lament and salute as well as those celebrating battles, or those which were used as 'gathering' tunes for individual clans with their distinctive echo beats.[4]

Wherever Highland soldiers served, either as mercenaries or in British service, pipers appear to have been present.[5] Much of the traditional music of the Highland bagpipe fitted easily into formal military life in British service because of its martial origins, except of course for the fact that it was a great deal older than the systems of drill and manoeuvre set down by Dundas and Torrens, and therefore was not composed to the set paces designed by these systems, and does not appear to have originally included 'quicksteps' or marches as we know them today.[6] The battle music and gathering tunes were however highly appropriate, as were the jigs and reels for dancing, entertainment and enlivening music. Major Mackay Scobie gives a list of tunes used in the 72nd Highlanders taken 'from an old order book', and while I have been unable to trace this book and there is some doubt as to the authenticity of the list, it is nevertheless interesting and appears to show the use of Piobaireachd in Field and Routine calls.[7]

Publication of Ceol Beag, or light music, did not take place until 1818 when *A Preceptor for the Great Highland Bagpipe* was published by Captain Robert Menzies which included tunes in 'Quick step time'. Donald MacDonald published twelve tunes, apparently dance tunes, in his collection of about 1822,[8] and six years later, in 1828, quicksteps appear in his *Collection of Quicksteps, Strathspeys, Reels and Jigs*.[9] It would seem that there were many different styles of playing and that tunes formerly known as dance tunes and some jigs and reels were adapted, where suitable, to fit the necessities of military pace.

The instruments and combinations of instruments used in the Highland Battalions provided a variety of music that was not unique to those designated as 'Highland', as other Scottish Regiments and the Scots Fusilier Guards had pipers too, but it is now often believed, in line with the 'Balmoralised' image, that that was all they had, and this is far from the truth.

Firstly, in 1820, the Highland regimental musicians comprised the Band of Music(k), now known as the Military Band, made up of wind, brass and percussion instruments. Fifteen musicians, including the Master, were permitted in 1821[10] and their number was increased, except in cavalry regiments, to twenty-one in 1846.[11] The figures, in theory, had to be strictly adhered to as the number of musicians was the subject of the half-yearly inspections,[12] and the 75th for example were censured in 1834 for employing NCOs in excess of the permitted figure in their band.[13] However, evasion of the regulations was commonplace in the Highland Regiments,[14] simply by creating 'acting' musicians, by taking the extra men off parade at Inspections or by using the 'boys' of the Regiment, undergoing training as Drummers and Musicians, in the ranks of the Band.

In 1846, 1% of established strength was permitted to be boys who were to be trained as Drummers and Musicians.[15] Boys were particularly recruited as Drummers,[16] but they were also used in the Band as Musicians and their employment had important social repercussions. Boy Musicians, it would appear, were often the sons or orphans of soldiers. As orphans, enlistment provided an alternative to destitution, begging or abandonment in a foreign country, and as sons of serving soldiers they were able to remain in their family in the Regiment, receive a wage and often follow in their fathers' footsteps and obtain some sort of training.

Two families of Highland Regiments provide interesting examples, the Sutherland family and the Sweeney family. James Sutherland (elder) enlisted in the 93rd aged 14 in 1822.[17] He was most probably the son of a soldier in the 93rd. He served twenty years in the Regiment and was Drum Major from 1848 to 1852. James (elder) had three sons, James (younger), William and Thomas Robert. James (younger) rose to the rank of Lance Sergeant in the 79th and served for twenty-four years between 1854 and 1879; William was a Band Sergeant in the Cameron Highlanders and transferred to be Drum Major of the 92nd,[18] and Thomas Robert was a Bandsman in the 79th and transferred to the 36th Regiment to enable him to stay in India in 1871.

James Sutherland (younger) had five sons—Robert, a Bandsman in the 79th, a further son in the Royal Scots and three sons in the Gordon Highlanders—and the known service of this family with kilted Highland Battalions spans at least the years 1822 to 1908.[19]

The Sweeney family has an equally remarkable Regimental career closely linked with Regimental Bands.[20]

Thus the bands were not only an integral part of regimental life, but the men who comprised these bands themselves appear to have formed a special élite, and membership may not only have depended upon musical skill, but also upon regimental and family connections. The two families also show the span of generations and the continuity that was possible between 1820 and 1920; Terence Sweeney was probably serving about 1820 and his grandson, Bandsman Richard Sweeney, who was killed at the Battle of the Aisne on 25th September 1914, when shelling collapsed the cave headquarters of 1st Battalion Queen's Own Cameron Highlanders upon its occupants, was merely part of a line of the family of Sweeney musicians who had served in the Regiment for almost a hundred years. Families such as these formed the heart of a regiment and illustrate clearly that at the centre of a Highland battalion were a remarkable number of families who knew one another and who intermarried through several generations.

Bands of Music were formed in all the kilted and Highland-based regiments, and it is believed that this occurred very shortly after the regiments were raised, although in 1799 the 79th had no Band of Music.[21] Certainly by 1820 all the kilted battalions had bands, whose members were on the strength and paid by

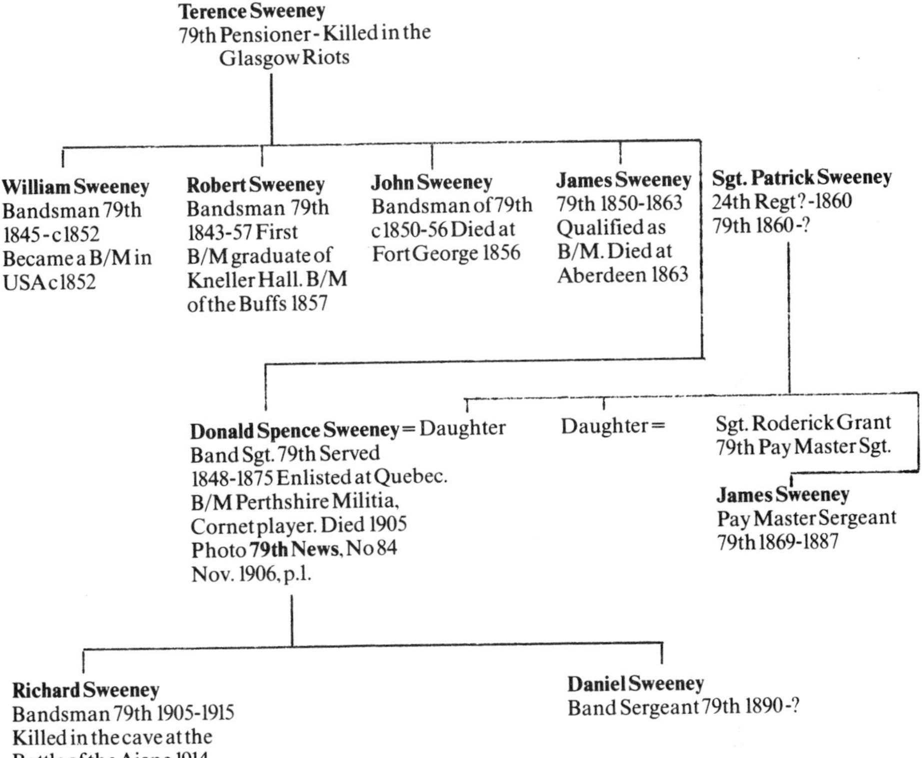

the Army, but whose instruments were purchased by the officers. As a band was considered an important attribute to any regiment, officers contributed heavily to pay for the latest and most modern instruments upon which a greater variety of tunes could be played. Thus the Band of the 72nd acquired keyed bugles in 1824 (if not before), and at the same time the Regiment was investigating the purchase of a 'Royal Patent Basso—Hibernicon' and a 'Hibernion—Tenor—Horn' together with 'the Quick Steps for the Bugle'.[22]

As early as 1810 the 92nd were purchasing 'clarionetts', a 'bassoon', a 'base drum head', a 'tamborrin' and reeds.[23] Unsophisticated though these instruments were, the musical standard appears to have been high by the standards of the day and it continued to improve and develop with the introduction of additional instruments and an expanded repertoire.

The Band of Music had four basic functions, all of which were closely related to regimental life. Firstly formal playing: the Dundas drill system of 1788 placed considerable emphasis on pace and a regular cadence, and Dundas wrote:

> On all occasions of parade, the drums and music add much to the appearance of the troops: but they are improper in manoeuvre . . . They are constantly varying the time of march, they create noise, prevent that equal step which habit can give to troops and tend to destroy that very end they are meant to promote . . . their general use therefore is on occasions of show and parade; at the moment of the charge they may also be allowed as inspiring and directing the attack, and also in column of march.[24]

Torrens, who in 1824 revised and updated the Dundas system, also stated, 'Neither fife nor music must on any account be used'.[25] But he also stated:

> When (at inspection or review) the General is going round the Battalion, the music and drums may play and beat; . . . when marching past the reviewing General . . . the music will begin to play just after the leading Company had made the second wheel . . . and they will continue to play until the rear of the column shall have passed.[26]

Thus the Band of music became an integral part of parades, but not manoeuvres, and they had a formal role in the provision of Inspection music, the march past, during an attack and marching in column of route. It may well have been the case that set tunes were adopted at an early date for the Bands' formal functions, but they were obviously quick to adopt compositions with a good beat, or the popular tunes of the day.[27] 'Orders for the Assistance and Guidance of the Non-Commissioned Officers of the 1st Battalion 79th Regiment' of about 1806 states:

> When the Regiment is marching to the Music, he [the Master of the Band] is never to play any tunes but such as are particularly adapted for that purpose and in which the greatest accuracy of time can be maintained. At other times such as route marching and etc., he may play any good tunes.[28]

Thus, it appears, acceptable, appropriate tunes were adopted for the purposes of regimental march pasts in quick and slow time,[29] while popular tunes were adopted and ultimately accepted as traditional for certain circumstances on the march, tunes which became familiar to the men and were expected by them. Probably the best known of these tunes was the air 'The Girl I left behind me'. All over the world British regiments, including the Highland regiments, left station to this tune, which was usually coupled with 'Auld Lang Syne'. With drafts of the 79th and 93rd, Private A.W. McIntosh of the 42nd remembers leaving Stirling Castle for India in 1858:

> At 3½ O'c pm we paraded in line of march order and marched away at 4 the band playing "The Girl I left behind me". Our spirits were high as we passed through the

> crowded streets of Stirling amid the "God speed you" of the inhabitants who lined the streets and cheered us . . . .[30]

Andrew Agnew of the 93rd, who did not enjoy his service in Canada during the Canadian rebellion, records with considerable relief:

> At one o'clock in the afternoon on the 16th October the Band of the 93rd Highlanders struck up "The Girl I left behind me" and the three companies of the Corps headed to the dockyard . . .[31]

Leaving a foreign station for home would inspire 'Cheer Boys, Cheer', or 'Home Sweet Home',[32] while other Regiments might welcome a Highland Regiment to station with 'Edinburgh Town' or 'My Native Highland Home'.[33] It is interesting that Highland soldiers in their writings could name these tunes and that it was not merely a case of 'any old tune will do', the chosen melody usually being highly appropriate to the situation.

The bands' other formal duties included funerals, when 'The Dead March' from *Saul* would be played,[34] marching the men to Church Parade, and sometimes the Band would play at Retreat.[35]

The other duties of the Band were no less important. In an era without recordings, records, transistors, television, tape recorders or video recorders, the provision of live music took on a special value. While having the Band play to cheer the men may now seem patronising and a little naive, it is clear that the music of the Band was a source of relaxation, entertainment and pride to the Highland soldier. 'Cheering' the soldiers could however also cause some problems as well as amusement. In 1861 the 42nd were at Agra and were attacked by cholera, losing their Pipe Major, James Irvine, and six men. Daily moving camp, a process called 'cholera dodging' on the principle that the disease was transmitted by tiny particles of water in the air, the Band of the 42nd was called upon to play to improve flagging morale:

> We shifted about every second or third day to a new piece of ground, the band was ordered to play on the roadside, but not to play any slow music, nothing but Quadrills, Strathspeys, Reels and Hornpipes, we used to turn out and have some dancing, the Band Sergeant one evening caused the Band to play a song, but before he had got it finished he was a prisoner, but he got off with a caution not to do so again.[36]

The Band also played in the Officers' Mess at Dinner. Originally it would seem that in Highland regiments this was entirely informal entertainment, with the Band probably playing 'God Save the Queen' and a variety of popular and appropriate tunes, which may well have included Scottish airs, but the stiff ritual formality of modern Mess nights was obviously not followed in the 42nd in Halifax, Nova Scotia in 1852:

> A large guest night at Mess. The Band played and were bedevilled by Archie Campbell, who made them play "God Save the Queen" at the wrong time and on being spoken to made them play it a second time.[37]

Gradually, however, the Band procedure at Mess became more formal and the practice developed of writing a set programme of Band music.[38] In 1862 the 91st laid down rules for the Band when playing at Mess[39] and some Highland Regiments also extended or introduced string instruments, an extra 'voluntary' subscription being levied against the officers of the 74th for example in 1890 to pay for their purchase and upkeep.[40]

The Band was closely involved too in certain Highland regimental traditions. As a young subaltern of the 79th, Spencer Ewart, writing from Gibraltar in 1882, records:

> In the evening I witnessed a curious custom which prevailed in the 79th when a man in the Regiment married. Be he Colonel or Drummer he was placed on a table and preceeded by the Drum Major, carrying a domestic broom, and the Band playing "The Rogue's March" was carried round barracks and the Parade ground to married quarters where he was well pelted with soot and flour. Utterly bedraggled and a pittiable object he was then similarly escorted to his own quarters. It was supposed that this ordeal would act as a deterrant to prevent people from contracting marriage. The unfortunate victim in this particular case was Pay Master Sergeant Sweeney.[41]

On the great days of celebration in the Highland regiments the Band was also to the fore, particularly at New Year, on St. Andrew's Night, Waterloo Day, Alma Day and the Anniversary of Tel-el-Kebir. While it was always the custom in Highland regiments to have celebrations on St. Andrew's Day, in the 42nd the Band arose before everybody else in the morning to play a selection of Scottish tunes. John Wedderburn of the 42nd recorded at Stirling Castle in 1852, 'St Andrew's Day—up at 5½ O'ck and found our Band playing away in the dark . . .',[42] and in India this tradition was continued, as Private A.W. McIntosh writes, while the Regiment was on the march between Kamokee and Gogranwalla (sic) in 1860:

> This being St. Andrew's Day the Band rose before rouse and played the following airs through the Camp as usual. "Hurrah for the Highlands"—"Here's a Health Bonnie Scotland to thee"—"Blue Bonnets over the Borders" and "Auld Lang Syne".[43]

The music of the Band was however subject to strict control on Sundays in Highland battalions. In Halifax, Nova Scotia in 1838 Lieutenant Andrew Agnew of the 93rd wrote:

> 11th [Regiment] Band commenced playing regularly on Sundays in Dalhousie Square—Our Colonel objects to the 93rd performing on Sundays.[44]

Standing Orders of the 93rd of 1835 laid down that on Sundays there would be a Parade for Divine Service only:

> There will be no practice of the band, drums or bugles, nor any work performed by the tailors or Regimental tradesmen, nor any settlement of accounts, nor washing

by the women, nor any drills for punishment or instruction, nor any games in barracks.[45]

The final function of the Regimental Band was public entertainment. With increased instrumentation and repertoires, public concerts became increasingly popular in the 1820s and 1830s, and in July of 1837, for example, there was held 'a Grand Promenade in St Andrew's Square [Edinburgh] for the benefit of the distressed operators in the West of Scotland . . . [when] . . . in the centre of the green the fine bands of the 79th Highlanders and the 14th Light Dragoons were situated'.[46] Throughout the same year the Band of the 42nd played regularly in the Assembly Rooms, providing an important link with the civilian population in the realms of what would now be called public relations.[47]

It is interesting that the Bands of the 79th and the 14th Light Dragoons should be apparently playing together in 1838, as it was not until 1858 that a uniform pitch was established for Military Bands:

> . . . to enable the Bands of all corps throughout the Army to play in concert, the General Commanding in Chief is desirous that the instruments of the whole should be of one uniform pitch and that used at the Ancient Philharmonic Concerts has accordingly been selected as the standard or Regulation pitch.[48]

One of the reasons why the Band of the 79th were so 'fine' at this time was the musical ability of their Bandmaster, Herr Adam J. Schott. Herr Schott was a German-born civilian Band Master employed and paid for by the officers of the 79th, which Regiment he had joined sometime before 1837, probably in 1836 when it returned from Canada.[49] These German Band Masters were an interesting feature of the British military bands of the period, and the Highland regiments, anxious to maintain and improve the standards of their Bands of Music, employed several of these men, Prussian musicianship being particularly in fashion at this time.

When the famous Herr Schott moved to the Grenadier Guards in 1844, the officers of the 79th employed Herr Ernest Fromm, 'who had been trained in one of the Prussian Bands',[50] and Fromm remained with the Battalion until 1871 when the 79th returned from India. Despite all efforts to trace him, no evidence has come to light in connection with Herr Fromm, who loyally served the Camerons for thirty-seven years, and the West German authorities are of the opinion that if any records of him still exist they are now in East Germany.

Equally mysterious is Band Master I.I. Bader of the 42nd, again a German civilian. At Dagshai in early 1863 Private A.W. McIntosh writes:

> A Band Master had been engaged for the Band and joined us here, he is a German named I.I. Bader, he has a wife and two children who came along with him.[51]

J.W. Wedderburn of the 42nd also makes reference to Mr. Goldbergh, a Band Master of the 42nd, whose unsatisfactory performance resulted in his being sacked by the officers at Halifax, Nova Scotia in 1852; he too was possibly German.[52]

These Band Masters, while improving the instruction and repertoire of the bands, also, as civilians, shared the dangers of service overseas and Band Master Hartong of the 74th was captured, tortured and killed by the Kaffirs while present with the Regiment at the Cape of Good Hope in 1851. Sergeant James McKay for the 74th records, 'The Bandmaster, a native of Germany, was much esteemed by both Officers and men'.[53]

Many foreign Band Masters did not follow the example of these men and either demanded larger salaries to accompany the Regiment abroad, or simply refused to go, which, as civilians, they were perfectly entitled to do. The Duke of Cambridge, who took a close personal interest in military bands, particularly in the establishment of Kneller Hall, which was opened in 1857, instructed in 1862 that the Army Band Masters trained at Kneller Hall were to take precedence over all civilians,[54] and after 1872 all Band Masters had to obtain a Kneller Hall Diploma: the last of the German Band Masters in the Highland regiments may thus have been Herr Fromm.[55]

These men therefore not only contributed their musical knowledge and expertise, but they were part of the regimental scene and incongruous though it may now appear, German civilians with their wives and families in the midst of the Highland regiments were apparently a totally accepted and respected part of regimental life.

When Musicians were regulated by the General Order of 1803,[56] the authorities insisted that Bandsmen return to the ranks in the event of war, and this old order was invoked in 1854; they did not however return in a combatant role, and on landing in the Crimea Private Robb of the 42nd records that a few days after landing:

> The band, pipes and drums all put their instruments on board ship, and every two had to carry a stretcher . . . They had been taught in Turkey how to dress a wound, roll a bandage, stop blood etc . . .[57]

Bugles were in fact retained and pipes seem to have been kept by some of the men. The Guards managed to keep back some fifes, and on the march to the Alma Private Robb writes:

> The Brigade of Guards had a few small Fifes and they struck up now and then the tune "March to the Battlefield".[58]

In the face of the high-quality French bands of the period, and as the war settled in the trenches of Sebastopol, instruments were returned to those Bandsmen who remained alive, and calls, signals, Tattoo and Reveille were restored.[59] By February 1856 the Bands were fully functioning again and Robb writes of a medal presentation ceremony (which he does not date):

> Here was a treat for lovers of music. The whole of the Bands at the front had been

> taught to play one tune, "Lord Gough's March". I am sure I saw over fifty big drums in the line behind the band. The Bandmaster who conducted them was upon a scaffold giving the time. It was well worth marching the distance to go and hear them . . .[60]

The Bandsmen's secondary duties and dual role were to become permanent and they still are today both Musicians and Medical Orderlies.[61]

The Fifers and Drummers, frequently and confusingly often referred to simply as 'the Drummers', had formal roles in the Highland battalions which were linked particularly with routine timings and discipline, but in addition they also filled parallel roles with the Band of Music in respect of the provision of music and entertainment.

The numbers of Drummers on the establishment varied according to the number of companies and the strength of the battalions, and all the Highland battalions had men on their establishments designated as Drummers and by no means all of these were boys. It becomes clear from a study of the 93rd Descriptive Roll Book that the Drums were used as a training ground for boys before they joined the ranks as Dutymen, as well as for mature Drummers and Musicians for the Band and there was no lack of musical skill amongst their number.[62]

It is not certain what proportion of these 'Drummers' played drums and what proportion (if any in some cases) played fifes, flutes or piccolos.[63] However, there is evidence that the 42nd had six fifes in 1768[64] and that there were still Drummers and Fifers in that Regiment in 1813. After 1813 there are no apparent references to fifes in the 42nd. The 79th had fifes and drums at least until April 1854,[65] the 72nd until sometime after 1885[66] and the 78th until 1868, if not later.[67]

When Drummer John Anderson, aged 15, of the 92nd deserted in Glasgow in 1844 he took with him '. . . two silver mouth pieces belonging to Band Instruments and a Black Sword Belt and plate and a new Fife',[68] but this is one of the few references to fifes in the 92nd,[69] and until further research is done, there appears to be scant reference to fifes in the 93rd.[70] Of the remaining Highland Line and Trews Regiments, the 91st had fifes and drums in 1881[71] and the 73rd in 1863,[72] if not right up to 1881. As a Line Battalion the 75th probably had fifes and drums to that date also, but those of the 74th seem to have lapsed sometime after 1868.[73]

No one therefore, within living memory, can speak of the use of fifes and drums in Highland regiments, and after years of neglect it is only now that a revival of interest in this gentle and beautiful music is being generated, but the Fifers and Drummers were, at one time or another, an important part of the sights and sounds of a Highland battalion.[74] The loss of the fifes is attributable to many causes, most prominent of which were the introduction of a more complex keyed flute, the general fall from fashion of the sound of the fife and the increasing favours bestowed upon the Highland bagpipe.

The Drummers' duties from 1820 onwards included sounding the beatings which marked the structure of the day. In some Highland regiments these were sounded by bagpipes or bugles, but in the 79th in 1820 it would appear the Drummers were used to sound 'Reveille' (2 Drummers) at dawn; 'Rouse' (1 Drummer) at 5, 6 or 7am and one hour later on Sundays; 'Breakfast' (1 Drummer) at 8 or 9am according to the season; ¾ hour warning for morning parade (1 Drummer) at 9.15 or 9.45am; ½ hour warning for morning parade and guard mounting (2 Drummers) at 10 or 10.30am; 'Orders' (1 Drummer) at 2pm; 'Dinner' (?) at 3pm; 'Sergeants Dinner' (1 Drummer) at 3.30pm; 'Drill' (1 Drummer) at 4pm during April to October only, ' . . . when the awkward squads are to turn out and be exercised for one hour and a half by the Sergeant Major'; ½ hour warning for evening Parade (1 Drummer) at 3.30 or 6pm; 'Evening Parade' (?) at 4 or 6.30pm; ¼ hour beating before sunset (1), the 'Retreat' being sounded at sunset by 'the whole Corps of Drummers'. Two Drummers then beat 'Officers Mess Call' followed by the Orderly Drummer sounding, at 7.30 or 8.30pm, the ½ hour call for Taptoo (Tattoo), and 'Taptoo' was sounded by the whole Corps of Drums. Finally, half an hour after Taptoo, 'The Curfew' or 'Setting of the Watch' was beaten by two Drummers and lights were put out.[75]

Secondly, the duties of the Drummers included the administration of corporal punishment, the ceremony of 'drumming out' and the reduction of NCOs to the ranks. Corporal punishment was no everyday occurrence in the Highland regiments, and the 93rd in particular prided themselves on the low numbers of punishments and the fact that no man of the Regiment received corporal punishment for twelve years between 1826 and 1838.[76] During his service in the 42nd between 1858 and 1868 Private A.W. McIntosh only once records the use of corporal punishment in the Regiment:

> Saturday 2nd March 1867. Commanding Officer's Parade for punishment, a District Court Martial was read which had been held on Private I. McKay for "Disgraceful Conduct of a cruel and Felonious Nature in violently assaulting Elizabeth Barr wife of Colour Sergeant John Barr". He was found guilty and sentenced to receive corporal punishmnent of 50 lashes to be administered on his bare back in the usual manner and to be imprisoned with Hard Labour for a period of 365 days, the square was formed two deep and the triangles[77] placed in front of the rear face, he stripped, was tied up and 2 Drummers gave him 25 lashes each . . .".[78]

Donald Cameron writes of a Drumming Out ceremony at the 79th Depot at Dundalk about 1847:

> One day there was a general parade that is every man on duty in the Depot to turn out and a hollow square formed and all facing inwards fixed bayonets and then a prisoner brought into the middle of it by the Guard and the Adjutant reading his former convictions and his present one for stealing was to be drummed out then the Drum Major stripped his coat of its facings then two lines was formed to the gate with a passage between them then the guard of the charge on both sides and behind the prisoner marched along the passage with the drums playing the rogues march when at the gate the prisoner got a shilling from the Sergeant Major and off he went quite happy he was a joiner from Glasgow district did not like the service

> living and knowing that his comrade had some money in his purse or sporran . . . he took a few shillings out and put them in his own . . .[79]

Corporal punishment was abolished altogether in the Army in 1881 and it may well have been that the disciplinary aspect of the Drummers' duties set them apart socially, while they, at the same time, retained an élitist element by virtue of their time keeping and musical responsibilities. In addition, the Drum instruments themselves assumed a symbolic and official status in the conduct of Divine Service and the Presentation of Colours, and, often emblazoned with the Regiment's battle honours, their loss or capture in battle was regarded as a slight on regimental honour.[80]

Closely allied to both the Band and the Drummers were the Buglers, and their interchangeability in a time of military musical transition between the period 1820 and 1920 is a source of considerable confusion. The bugle as as instrument was already in use by the Cavalry,[81] and by the Rifles and Light Infantry by 1820,[82] the latter having gained fashionable popularity as effective independent troops in the Napoleonic Wars. In 1820 all Highland regiments had one company of Light troops for skirmishing, known simply as the Light Company, a hand-picked chosen élite of men whose field manoeuvres were regulated by bugle or whistle, the establishment of Drummers being replaced by Buglers in Light Infantry in 1803.[83]

The man or men who played the bugles were designated Drummers in Highland battalions and their Bugle Calls had by 1820 already become integrated in the daily duty calls; 'Rouse' was for example sounded by the Orderly Drummer as a Bugle Call in the 79th in 1819.[84] Gradually, the Bugle Calls were extended for the Infantry so that in the Highland battalions they not only included field calls but also Regimental and Duty calls. In the 42nd in 1833 each company had its own call, together with calls for 'Fatigue', 'School', 'Rations', 'Drill' etc.[85] Duty calls are still used today, while Field Calls were limited to 'Alarm' and 'Charge' for the Infantry by 1909,[86] although 'Continue or Commence Firing', 'Stand Fast or Cease Fire' and 'Execute Orders Received' still remained in the Manual of 1966.[87]

The Calls had to be carefully learned:

> The Drum Major will be prepared to go through the whole of the Bugle Calls, as now ordered at the termination of each instruction drill—for which purpose, the Officers squad and the Company squads will stand fast until the calls have been gone through. The call will be named by the Adjutant before it is sounded and it will be then repeated by the instructor of each squad to his men.[88]

The calls quickly acquired words, 'Come to the cook house door boys' (Men's meal, 1st Call) being probably the best-known example.[89]

Those who played the drum, fife and bugle were directly responsible to and under the supervision of the Drum Major. Standing Orders of the 42nd of 1833 stated:

> The Drum Major has particular charge of the Drummers and Buglers and he will either instruct them himself, or see that they are taught all the necessary sounds on both instruments . . .[90]

Often chosen for his stature, appearance and bearing, the Drum Major was frequently a formidable figure who held a position of considerable responsibility. He not only taught the Drummers and Buglers, he was also responsible for their welfare:

> As Drummers in general are either boys or very young men and of course inexperienced it particularly behoves the Drum Major to pay the greatest attention to their morals not only to keep them from unguardedly falling into mischief but by teaching them the proper line of conduct.[91]

In addition the Drum Majors acted as Regimental Postmen,[92] a position which they still held during the First World War, they supervised corporal punishment and they led the Band and Drums on parade, using a stick or mace to give signals:

> As the Drum Major is supposed to understand music he will give the signal to play and cease playing at all times when the reports are collecting or marching past in review order . . .[93]

Already therefore a complex and interesting combination of musical sounds forming part of the daily life of Highland regiments was contributed by the Band of Music, the Drums, the Fifes and the Bugles, and there is evidence that in the 91st at least, experiments were carried out combining these elements into one sound:

> Mr Davies, the Instructor of the Band, having been good enough to offer his services in conducting a weekly practice of the Band and Drums united for that purpose, it is ordered that, the Band and Drums shall in future assemble at 9.30 every Saturday morning, at such place as Mr Davies shall appoint for this practice.[94]

The final formal musical sound, the Highland bagpipe, is probably the best known and has the deepest emotional associations with the Highland regiments, but there is evidence to suggest that until the latter half of the nineteenth century, the Pipes did not dominate Highland regimental music and by no means held the prominent position that many Regimental historians would wish.

Until 1854, when an establishment was created in Highland regiments for a Pipe Major and five Pipers,[95] Pipes were tolerated but unofficial. Pipers before 1854 were not separately designated and on paper appear to have been duty men in the battalion, paid and clothed as ordinary soldiers. Their instruments may have been their own or given to them by the officers, who also paid for any special accoutrements they might wear or extra pay they might receive. On formal parades they marched with their companies and it is unlikely that at the half-yearly inspections they appeared as a separate body before 1854 because of their lack of official status and the apparent insistence in these inspection reports that every duty man be armed and accoutred on parade.

There is no doubt however that they were there and that they played for recruiting, in battle, on the line of march, in competitions,[96] at funerals, in entertaining their friends in barracks and the officers in Mess. In addition they assumed some of the official timekeeping duties, playing the duty pipe tunes. This latter function resulted in a complex combination of sounds, calls and tunes to be learned by the men as the various sounds for duty. In the 72nd in 1827 there was a Band of Music, Drums and Fifes and Bugles; in addition, however, for parades a 'warning pipe' was sounded an hour before parade. A quarter of an hour later the NCOs, Band and Drums fell in; half an hour before parade the Drummers sounded the Drummers Call, which was followed by an inspection and the recruits fell out. 'Sergeants Call' was then sounded by the Bugles and the general parade followed, when the Colours may well have been trooped to the music of the Fifes and Drums.[97]

Before 1854 the numbers of Pipers were probably small, although there were no doubt many more men who could play after a fashion and instruments would be handed round when entertainment was called for. Some of these Pipers were musicians of a high calibre and the Highland Regimental Pipers of the period made a substantial contribution to contemporary composition, paticularly in Ceol Beag, while at the same time maintaining the tradition of Ceol Mor.[98]

The sounds of the instrument were however far removed from what is heard today, being louder and lower in pitch, but in spite of the technical difficulties of the individual bore and tone of the instruments, there is considerable evidence that the Pipers played together as well as individually.[99]

Senior amongst the Pipers was the Pipe Major or Piper Major[100] and it would seem that these men were sometimes specially recruited for their musical skill and perhaps their ability to teach less able players already in the regiment. Adam Graham for example was 32 when he was enlisted into the 93rd Sutherland Highlanders in 1822, and when he died at Antigua in 1832 he was 'Piper Major' of the Regiment.[101] Lauderdale Maule of the 79th wrote to his brother in 1847:

> If John McKenzie piper of Taymouth knows of any good looking lad, *skilful* on the Bagpipes *sober and well educated* I'll make him a Sergeant and Piper Major.[102]

The officers of Highland regiments played a considerable part in retaining, encouraging and preserving Highland music in the Highland battalions, and although unofficial, the Pipers must have been brought to the notice of the War Office and Horse Guards, who tolerated the situation, and there appears to be no evidence that the playing of pipes was interfered with in Highland regiments, provided the number of musicians as a whole was not exceeded:

> '. . . it has been repeatedly announced to these Regiments [the Highland Regiments] that there is no desire to discontinue or even to reduce the number of their pipers, pro-

vided the whole number of men, allowed to be employed as musicians, shall not be exceeded and that they are at full liberty to employ ten men as pipers, provided they reduce the number of Drummers from 17 to 10, and the Musicians in the Band to 18, in place of 21, an arrangement which might be adopted without much inconvenience . . .[103]

It appears however that this proposal was unacceptable as the Highland regiments were anxious to retain their numbers of Drummers and Buglers (and where appropriate Fifers) and that they had no intention of reducing their prestigious and often highly accomplished Bands of Music, who at that time seem to have been the primary musical providers, particularly on the march; for although Pipers may have played together and Drummers may have unofficially accompanied Pipers when playing, the concept of the modern Pipe Band of Pipers with Bass, Tenor and Side Drums playing together had not yet been developed, and timekeeping and the beat still remained an important aspect of contemporary drill and marching, all of which required volume, suitable marches and the drum.

The Highland regiments therefore seem to have requested an establishment of ten Pipers, i.e. one per company, but the cost totalling £2191.14.11d[104] was probably unacceptable, and a compromise of five Pipers and a Pipe Major was reached, with the apparent understanding that additional men could be Pipers providing the overall numbers of Musicians was not exceeded.

Once established, the five Pipers in each regiment formed a very special élite, and in a climate of growing Victorian romance regarding the Highland regiments and with the direct interest of the Queen herself, the Pipers began to come to the fore.[105] To boost their numbers men were regularly appointed acting Pipers until an official vacancy occurred.[106] By 1864 a Bass Drummer at least was definitely playing with the Pipers of the 79th,[107] and with the corresponding decline in popularity of the Fife in the Highland regiments where it still survived, an extraordinary musical transition took place, the Drums, although having Bugles, being left without a melody to accompany.

This transition appears to have been slow and individual and personal to each regiment and may well have been influenced by civilian developments of the period. By 1874, in the 91st, the Drummers were being used in concert with the Fifers and with the Pipers at Reveille, Retreat and Tattoo: 'The Drums and Fifes will alternately beat Reveille, Retreat and Tattoo with the Drums and Pipes'.[108]

In the 42nd and 93rd the use of Drummers and Pipers together may well in fact date from a much earlier period, as the Standing Orders of the 42nd of 1833 state:

The pipe-major has the same charge, and is to perform the same duties with respect to the pipers, that the drum-major does towards the drummers and buglers; but the drum-major has charge of the whole on all parades or when at practice together.[109]

Whenever the transition occurred, the establishment of the modern style of

Pipe Band in the Highland battalions provided an exciting and substantial musical sound, capable of playing on the march and of providing an adequate marching beat to rival that of the Band of Music. It appears however that the transition was not without difficulty and that the interplay of personalities and the pride of the individual élite groups of the Band, the Fifers, the Buglers, the Drummers and the Pipers all came into play when it was to be decided who would lead on the line of march, who would play at march pasts and who would play the Regiment home or into barracks. In the 71st (HLI) in India about 1861, Sir Hugh Rose allowed the Pipers to play the Regiment off parade at a formal inspection, a move which apparently caused considerable friction with the Band of Music who claimed the honour,[110] and when the same Regiment marched into Edinburgh Castle after returning from India a soldier recalled:

> . . . the Regimental Band had played the last notes of 'When Johnny Comes Marching Home' . . . [when] a grunt from the drones [of the Pipes] indicated that it was the intention of the Pipes to play us in.[111]

Eventually the friction and lack of uniformity had to be resolved. In 1870, 91st Orders laid down:

> The following will be carried out in future with the music of the Regiment in Marching Past.
> Slow time—Band.
> Quick time (Open column)—Band (struck out) Pipes and Drums.
> (Quarter column)—Pipes and Drums.
> Double time—Band and Drums.
> The Pipes (& Drums) will be prepared to play the Regiment past in open column if required. This will be done in marching past in Brigade. Each Regiment playing its own quick step. When playing at Reveille, Retreat and Tattoo and on the march the Pipes will play alternately with or without drums.[112]

There appears to have been no decision, however, on the important question of who should lead until 1871, when:

> Her Majesty the Queen having directed that the Regiment should *on all* occasions march past to the Pipes, this will take effect from this date. When marching past the Pipes will fall in in front of the Band.[113]

The decision applied to all Highland regiments with established Pipers at that time[114] and continues today, although it may well have been unpopular with the military bandsmen of the period.[115] Firmly established and placed in the position of honour at the head of the Regiment, the concept of Pipers in numbers exceeding five and a Pipe Major and accompanied by Drummers to form a Pipe Band, quickly grew in fashion and popularity, and in 1881 Pipers were sent to the 73rd and 75th, by the 42nd and the 92nd respectively, when these Regiments assumed full Highland status. Fifes or Flutes and Drums survived for a short time in the 91st and the 72nd, but when the Highland Battalions met and combined their Pipes and Drums in massed display, as at

Lucknow in 1911 and at Agra in 1913 and 1914, there was no doubt that the star of the Pipe Bands was indeed in the ascendant.

It is now virtually impossible to hear the kind of sound these pipe bands produced with their lower-pitched pipes, rope-tension drums and 'old fashioned' drumming techniques. Instead of the clipped and clinical music now produced, the sound was much more resonant and rounded, and although the starts and finishes may have been somewhat ragged in modern terms, en masse the sound must have been magnificent.

The practical development of the military piper and the pipe band had interesting and complex repercussions on pipe music, some of which were closely related and interwoven with the Band of Music and the Fifers and Drummers. These musicians do not appear to have considered themselves hidebound by tradition, and there being no 'standard settings' of pipe music, each group felt perfectly free to learn from the other. Although the bagpipe scale is limited and the instrument cannot produce a variation in sound volume, the old fife having in addition no keys, the cross referencing and adaptation of tunes appears to have been common, the Band playing fife tunes, the fifes playing pipe tunes and the Pipers playing fife tunes; all the musicians also adapting popular airs, fiddle, classical, foreign and dance tunes to their own use.[116]

> The Pipers are up to date as usual, and the classic strains of 'Her Golden Hair was Hanging Down Her Back' is now wafted on the breeze from the drones of the mighty warpipe.[117]

The Band, Fifers and Pipers for example all played the 'Belle Isle March', but the tune is known to Pipers as 'The 74th's Slow March'. Pipe Major John Macleod, after hearing the Sardinian Contingent Band in the Crimea play Rossini's ballet music from the opera *William Tell*, adapted a passage from the music and wrote the march 'The Green Hills of Tyrol'.[118]

Nor was original composition neglected, particularly in light music, marches, strathspeys and reels, two of the earliest known contemporary marches which are capable of being dated exactly being 'The 79th's Farewell to Gibraltar' by Pipe Major John MacDonald and 'The 78th's Farewell to Belgaum' by Pipe Major Alexander MacKellar, composed in 1848 and 1849 respectively.[119]

In June 1853, at Chobham Camp, Pipe Major William Ross of the 42nd arranged a selection of tunes which he called 'Long Reveille'.

> Chisholm Castle—Slow time. This tune is played once over and four bars of the first part.
> Fingal's Lament—Slow time. This tune is played twice over and . . . [MS damaged].
> Caledonian Lassies—Quick time. This tune is played and four bars of the first part.
> First two parts of the Athole Highlanders welcome to Loch Katerine.[120]

J.W. Wedderburn makes no mention of this practice and apparent innovation by Pipe Major Ross, but he does imply that Ross received little encouragement from the Commanding Officer:

> Dined at Mess at 7 O'clock. The Band and Pipes played. The first quickstep the Pipes played did not seemingly please Col. Cameron who ordered them never to play it again, poor Ross the Pipe Major was horribly disgusted as it happened to be a first rate tune . . . I at once rose and left the Mess table in a rage.[121]

While Pipe Major Ross did not serve in the Crimea,[122] his 'Long Reveille' seems to have been adapted and extended into what came to be known as 'Crimean Reveille'. It was the practice in Imperial France to hold military parades on the 15th day of every month, and in the spirit of rivalry and no small amount of jealousy of the French Bands, it may not be a coincidence that 'Crimean Reveille' came to be sounded on the 15th day also, the Pipers of the Highland Brigade being capable of producing music without a rival in the French camp. The tunes for 'Crimean Reveille' were 'The Sodger's Return', a song with both Gaelic and English words, 'Granny Duncan', known in the 42nd as 'Johnny Crockle' which is believed to be an old Fife tune, 'Sae will We Yet' ('The Wearing of the Green' played 'diminished'), 'Miss Girdle' or 'The Bowmore Reel', 'Chisholm Castle' or 'Erchless Castle' from 'Long Reveille', and 'Hey Johnny Cope' dating from the 1745 Rebellion.[123]

There was no lack of experiment, improvisation and innovation therefore, and although certain tunes like 'Hey Johnny Cope' were used by most Highland regiments for Reveille, neither the settings nor the tunes seem to have been laid down as obligatory.[124] Thus each regiment had its own way of playing certain tunes, and in the case of 'Highland Laddie' there was a Black Watch way of playing it and a Cameron Highlanders way of playing it.[125]

When Regimental Marches were given official sanction in 1881, and attempts were made to standardise the marches and Duty tunes, it appears that in the 93rd at least in the 1880s, few could remember what the old pre-Crimean tunes were. Writing to R.H. Burgoyne from Maryhill Barracks about 1882, Lt. Colonel Ewan H.D. Macpherson reported:

> I asked the oldest soldiers in the Regt. who are Band Sergeant Kerr . . . & Drum Major Duff . . . what the tunes for parade [were] and they both said Pibroch o' Donald Duh in morning parade and Athole Gathering for the afternoon: but I have still a better authority, a young fellow Mackay a piper enlisted the other day & he is nephew to Mackay who was Pipe Major & went to the Maharaja of Cashmere, he is now retired and living in Aberdeen . . . and he said the three tunes in use in the Regt. in his time were Pibroch of Donald Duh for morning parade, Athole Gathering for afternoon and The Highland Laddie for March Past. Now Mackay joined us about 1850 and left us at Sealcote I think . . .[126]

One of the reasons why pipers were generally encouraged and supported was probably the social implications of the instrument itself. The Highland bagpipe was widely considered in the nineteenth century to be the instrument of a gentleman, closely associated with the Highland revival and acceptable for an officer not only to listen to, but also to play. In 1888 eight officers of the Cameron Highlanders played to a high standard and when the Duke of Cambridge visited the Regiment at Edinburgh Castle, the eight officers joined the fourteen regimental pipers and played round the dinner table. Spencer Ewart records:

> At this period we had eight Officers in the Battalion who could play the Pipes—Leslie, Money, Davidson, Wolridge Gordon, McLeod, Sempill, MacFarlane and myself—and united to the Regimental Pipers we all—22 in number marched round the table in our kilts and played the Duke a 'set'![127]

Ewart and other Highland officers were also responsible for liaising with the Piobaireachd Society, to which many influential Highland officers belonged, to start the first official tuition of Army pipers, ultimately to become the Army School of Piping. The classes which began in 1910 at Cameron Barracks, Inverness under John MacDonald of Inverness were primarily designed for improving Piobaireachd playing, but undoubtedly improved the standard of overall play of those who attended.[128]

In 1914, while the Regular Highland Battalion Bandsmen initially left their instruments in store and went to war as stretcher bearers and runners, the Pipes were taken, although it quickly became apparent that playing in battle was virtually impossible, and it is interesting that Private Lobban and Corporal MacFarlane are both adamant that Pipers could not and did not play in the front trenches or in battle when they were present with the 1st Camerons and the 1st Black Watch, and that romantic and heroic notions of playing on the parapet were a Territorial and New Army phenomenon.[129] Pipers were used as riflemen, runners and stretcher bearers, and although attempts were made to keep some behind the lines, the losses, particularly in the early months of the war, were so heavy that the great pre-war Military Pipe Bands virtually ceased to exist and as a result a great deal of irreplaceable expertise was lost.

Many of the Pipe Majors of the pre-war period were possessed of considerable skill, and men like Pipe Major G.S. McLennan of the 1st Battalion Gordon Highlanders, 1905-1913 and 1918-1919, have become legends in piping history.[130] Such was the power and influence of the Pipe Majors that they often struck a note of awe in the hearts of the young subalterns. Spencer Ewart records that just before the 79th left Gibraltar for Egypt in 1882 he marched a party back to barracks after rifle practice:

> I saw that Pipe Major Grant was very drunk. He made a most horrible noise on his Pipes and as the men were all laughing, I told him when near the Casemate Barracks to leave off playing—which he did. Naturally as a young Subaltern—I held the Pipe Major in great reveration and I was determined to say nothing more and let him walk to barracks if his legs would take him there. However when we got into the most crowded and narrow part of the Gibraltar main street.he suddenly slipped off down a side street and disappeared.[131]

Ewart, deeply hurt when the Pipe Major apparently went unpunished after stating that 'he had been obliged to go down a side street to assist himself', was consoled when he was taken aside by the Adjutant and had it explained to him that punishment was out of the question as the Colonel would never consider allowing the Regiment 'to go on active service without its Pipe Major'.[132]

Thus, while sometimes reprobate characters, the pre-war Pipe Majors also represented the culmination of Highland military musical development from 1820, and from them stemmed much of the modern image of the Highland Regiments, now threatened by financial restrictions and some lack of understanding of their origins, and of the social, emotional and regimental importance of their music.

NOTES

1. Henry George Farmer, 'Turkish influence in Military Music', *Journal of the Society for Army Historical Research*, Vol. 24, 1946, p.177.
2. Henry George Farmer, 'Scots Duty—Old Drum and Fife Calls of Scottish Regiments', *ibid.*, pp. 65-70. Henry George Farmer, 'The Martial Fife', *ibid.*, pp. 66-71. 'Drummers' (Replies), *Journal of the Society for Army Historical Research,* Vol. 20/21, 1941-1942, p. 182. General Order 28.12.1816. 'The Commander in Chief with a view to assimilating the respective "Calls and Beats" throughout the several Regiments of Infantry, is pleased to command that the system of instruction for the Drum and Fife, introduced by Drum Major Potter, of the Coldstream Guards, shall be considered as the established system, and be adopted accordingly'. The old Scotch Reveille was in fact retained as the third part of the amended call in 1816. Infantry Training—The Drummer's Handbook, Army Code No. 71333 File No. D/ACGS (TRG)/13/28/2 1983. One of the conditions which the United Provinces tried to enforce upon the Scots Brigade in Dutch service in 1782 was that the Scots March should no longer be beaten by them. Ed. James Ferguson, *Papers Illustrating the History of the Scots Brigade in the Service of the United Netherlands 1572-1782* (Edinburgh: 1899), Vol. 11, p.401.
3. Joseph MacDonald, *A Compleat theory of the Scots Highland bagpipe*, Edinburgh University Library MS La 111, 804. It is interesting that the only complete tune in this manuscript and the first known written piobaireachd music is entitled 'A March for a Beginner', which is also known as 'The Black Watch's Salute'.
4. Professor Alexander John Haddow, *The History and Structure of Ceol Mor* (Privately printed, 1982).
5. John Mackay, *An Old Scots Brigade—Being the History of Mackay's Regiment*, *op. cit.*, pp. 97 and 224. See also the oil painting 'The Destruction of the Mole, Tangier, 1684' by Stuyp, property of the Earl of Dartmouth in the National Maritime Museum.
6. Dundas gave two timings, 'ordinary or slow march' of 80 paces per minute and 'quick march' of 120 paces per minute, and stated, 'The ordinary or slow march may be eight in a minute; each step 30 inches. It is the pace in parade, common marching in front, and on all occasions where greater celerity is not ordered'. Colonel David Dundas, *Principles of Military Movements chiefly applied to Infantry*, *op. cit.*, p.42. Torrens on the other hand gives four timings: slow time at 75 paces per minute, quick time at 108 paces per minute, wheeling time at 120 paces per minute and double march at 150 paces per minute, stating, 'The slow step hitherto called 'The ordinary march' need only be applied to the purposes of parade, upon some occasions to the march in line, or when required for any special object. The Quick March is the ordinary pace to be applied . . . ' Major General Sir Henry Torrens, *Field Exercises and Evolutions of the Army*, *op. cit.*, p. 72.
7. Major I.H. Mackay Scobie, *Pipers and Pipe Music in a Highland Regiment* (published

by the Ross-shire printing and publishing Company), copy in QOHRM, p. 5. The tunes given are: Daybreak (Reveille)—The MacRae's March; Gathering or Turn Out—Tulloch Ard (The High Hill); Failte (Salute)—Mackenzies Salute; Slow March—Fingals Weeping; Quick step—Castle Donan; Charge—Cabar Feidh; Stimulus (during the engagement)—Battle of Strone; Lament—Mackenzies Lament; Sunset—The Mackenzies March; Tattoo—Head of the High Bridge; Warning before Dinner—Battle of Glenshiel; During Dinner—Battle of Sheriffmuir.

8. Captain Robert Menzies, *A Preceptor for the Great Highland Bagpipe* (Edinburgh: 1818), NLS Mus. Box 9.594. The music in this publication is written one fifth lower than the actual sound. The tunes which he states are to be played in 'Quick step time' are 'Tullochgorom', 'Malbrook', 'A Quick Step' and 'Miss Drummond of Perth'. Donald MacDonald, *A Collection of the ancient martial music of Caledonia called piobaireachd as performed on the great Highland bagpipe* (Edinburgh: Donald MacDonald c.1822). National Library of Scotland/Scotland Glen 298. The tunes included in Donald MacDonald's collection are: Reel of Tulloch; Brose and Butter; Tulloch Gorum; Cock Crowing (Cock of the North); Up and Waur them a', Willie; Monymusk; The Grey Buck; The Amorous Lover; Cripple Malcolm in the Glen (Miss Drummond of Perth); The Warst Carle in a' the Warld; Mrs McLeod of Raasay; Culcairn's Strathspey.
9. Donald MacDonald, *A collection of quicksteps, strathspeys, reels and jigs Arranged for the Highland bagpipe* (Edinburgh: 1828). For details of this and other early publications see, Roderick D. Cannon, *A Bibliography of Bagpipe Music,* (Edinburgh: 1980)
10. WO/3/395/304.
11. WO/3/103/307.
12. See for example WO/27/367, p.4.
13. WO/3/87/389.
14. Henry G. Farmer quotes a letter of 1834 addressed to the Bandmaster of the Royal Artillery Band: 'Dear Bandmaster McKenzie, I would like you to try your drum without the snares being tied to the skin. The band of music of the 93rd Regt. at Canterbury—a good band of twenty four—had a sort of tabor that has no snares—bigger than our drums. The sound mingles with the tones of the music more pleasant, like the soft notes of the kettle-drum... The Master of the Band played the Kent Bugle very well'. Henry George Farmer, 'The Tenor Drum', *Journal of the Society for Army Historical Research*, Vol. 26/27, 1948-1949 (Notes) 907, p. 185.
15. WO/3/103/307.
16. Descriptive Roll Book of the 93rd Highlanders, ASHRM, and Chapter 3.
17. Ibid.
18. For a photograph of Drum Major William Sutherland see, *79th News*, No. 81, September 1905, p. 1.
19. *79th News*, No. 99, September 1908, p. 209.
20. *Ibid.*, p. 210.
21. Rev. Percy Sumner, 'Army Inspection Returns', *Journal of the Society for Army Historical Research*, Vol. 5/6, 1926-1927, pp. 26-27.
22. GD/16/52/36 Nos. 29, 30, 31, 32, and 35. Airlie Muniments, letters to Major Drummond of the 72nd Regiment.
23. GD/1/354/2 Pay ledger of the 92nd Highlanders. An important supplier of musical instruments to the 79th, 92nd and 93rd was the firm of Thomas Glen, 2 North Bank Street, Edinburgh. While Glens were better known as bagpipe makers, their Day Book, dating from 1847, shows a steady supply of instruments and instrument repairs to these Regiments, particularly to the 93rd, including ophicleides, trombones, cornopeans, cymbells (sic), bombardines, sax tubas and bassoons. NLS Acc. 8396/16. Many of these early instruments can be seen in the University of Edinburgh Collection of Historic Musical Instruments, the Reid Concert Hall.

24. Colonel David Dundas, *Principles of Military Movements chiefly applied to Infantry, op. cit.*, pp. 28-29.
25. Major General Sir Henry Torrens, *Field Exercises and Evolutions of the Army, op. cit.*, p. 1.
26. *Ibid.*, p. 310. The march past referred to here is in 'slow time' or what Dundas called 'ordinary time', but the same procedure was followed in 'quick time'.
27. In 1832 an order was issued that no regiment was to use foreign marches at reviews, parades or grand meetings. Farmer Collection, Glasgow University Library, 118/7.
28. GD/174/2315. Maclaine of Lochbuie Papers.
29. The march past of the 73rd was for example until 1881, 'My Love is like a Red Red Rose'. BWRM.
30. Diary of Private A.W. McIntosh 42nd. BWRM 421 (3591(1) -), p.22.
31. GD/154/781. Journal of Lt. Andrew Agnew of Lochnaw 93rd, Halifax N.S. 1838.
32. Diary of Private A.W. McIntosh 42nd. BWRM 421 (3591(2)-) 17.10.1868. The 42nd leaving Cherat, India for Home.
33. Ibid., the 94th welcoming the 42nd to Karachi, 1868.
34. In the 1840s the 92nd are reputed to have followed the Highland custom of standing with their backs to the funeral party as they passed through the barrack gate. Lt. Colonel C. Greenhill Gardyne, *The Life of a Regiment, op. cit.*, Vol. 2, p. 50.
35. As late as 1852 Bands were still not permitted to march Roman Catholic soldiers to and from Church Parade. WO/3/141/398. Count Anatolle Demidoff, *Etapes Maritimes sur Les Cotes D'Espagne* (Florence, 1858: privately printed), p. 187.
36. Diary of Private A.W. McIntosh 42nd. BWRM 421 (3591(1)-), p. 256.
37. Diary of Colonel J.W. Wedderburn 42nd BWRM 28/714/1. Halifax NS. 15.4.1852. The idea of a Subaltern interfering with the Band playing the National Anthem in an Officers' Mess on a Guest Night nowadays would almost certainly result in the Battalion being less one Subaltern the following morning!
38. In 1853 Lt. Colonel the Hon. Lauderdale Maule presented the Band of the 79th with a printing die to head the Band Programmes. Minute Book of the 79th Officers Mess, QOHRM 1161.
39. 91st (1st Battalion Argyll and Sutherland Highlanders) Permanent Order Book 1862-1884. ASHRM Sb 18/16. Dover 4.10.1869.
40. Mess Minute Book of the 74th Highlanders, RHFRM P/8. Peshawar 1890 and Fyzabad 1894.
41. Diaries of General Sir J. Spencer Ewart 79th, RH/4/84/1. Gibraltar 1.3.1882. W.L. Manson suggests that Pipers and not the Band were used for this ceremony in the 92nd and that the practice was relatively common in Scottish Regiments. W.L. Manson, *The Highland Bagpipe* (Wakefield: 1977), p. 141.
42. Diary of Colonel J.W. Wedderburn 42nd. BWRM 28/714/1, Stirling Castle 30.11.1852.
43. Diary of Private A.W. McIntosh 42nd. BWRM 421 (359(1)-) 30.11.1864.
44. GD/154/781. Journal of Lt. Andrew Agnew of Lochnaw 93rd. 20.5.1838.
45. Standing Orders of the 93rd Highlanders, 1835. ASHRM R/226.
46. *Edinburgh Evening Courant*, 20.7.1827.
47. *Ibid.*, 28.1.1837 and 25.3.1837.
48. Horse Guards Circular 23.4.1858 Bands/4 Gen. No. 92/35.
49. Herr Schott moved to the Grenadier Guards in 1844 and later set up business in London in the musical publishing firm of Schott and Sons. Farmer Collection, Glasgow University Library. MS 118.
50. *79th News*, Vol. 4, No. 46, 1.9.1899, p. 13.
51. Diary of Private A.W. McIntosh 42nd. BWRM 421 (3591(1)-) 1863, p. 291.
52. Diary of Colonel J.W. Wedderburn 42nd. BWRM 28/714/1. 13.7.1848 and 19.2.1852. Between 1827 and 1854 Bandmaster Ricks was employed by the officers of the 72nd and it has been suggested that this man too may well have been of German origin.

Lt. Colonel D.J.S. Murray, 'The Evolution of the Regimental Music', *Queen's Own Highlander* (Part 6), No. 68, Summer 1985, p. 22.

53. Sergeant James McKay, 74th, *Reminiscences of the Last Kafir War, op. cit.*, p. 64.
54. Horse Guards Order of 29.8.1862.
55. Henry George Farmer, *Military Music* (privately printed and undated). From the author's collection. p. 53 and Henry George Farmer, 'Foreign Army Bandmasters: their rise and fall', *Journal of the Society for Army Historical Research*, Vol. 26/27 1948-1949, pp. 124-130. While Henry George Farmer must be considered as an important authority on military bands and military music, it is clear from his writings and his papers in Glasgow University that much of his work is unreferenced and some of his references are obscure and difficult to trace. It is my opinion that certain of his propositions must be treated with caution.
56. General Order of 5.8.1803, 'It is His Majesty's Pleasure that, in Regiments having Bands of Musick, not more than one Private Soldier of each Troop or Company shall be permitted to act as Musicians, and that one Non Commissioned Officer shall be allowed to act as Master of the Band. These men are to be drilled and instructed in the Exercise, and in case of actual service, are to fall in with their respective Troops or Companies, completely armed and accoutred'.
57. Writings of Private Alexander Robb 42nd, BWRM.
58. Ibid.
59. Many instruments must have been lost or damaged as for example the 79th who lost their bass drum at this time. *79th News*, Vol. 3, No. 30. 1.3.1897, p. 6. Duty calls appear to have been restored to the Pipers first. "24.11.1854. Camp Balaklava Heights. Memorandum No. 3. A Piper of the 42nd and 79th Regiments alternately will play the rouse pipe (Johnny Cope) every morning at 6 O'clock when the troops will turn out. Should the weather be very wet and inclement and the men not required to turn out into the trenches, the piper will parade at the Brigade Major's tent 10 minutes before 6 when he will receive his orders. The tune when the men are to remain on the alert in their tents will be "Highland Laddie". On the 5th December the general calls and signals and Tattoo and Reveille were restored. Regimental Standing Order Book 79th Highlanders, QOHRM 144/79.
60. Writings of Private Alexander Robb 42nd. BWRM.
61. Corporal Frank MacFarlane of the 1st Battalion Black Watch remembers that when the Battalion left Aldershot in 1914 the Band instruments were put in store and only later followed them to France.
62. Descriptive Roll Book of the 93rd Sutherland Highlanders, op. cit., ASHRM.
63. Some Letters of Service are confusing and unclear on this point. The Letter of Service of the 79th for example permitted 2 Drummers per Company, i.e. 20 Drummers in total, and 2 Pipers in the Grenadier Company. WO/4/149/30. The Letter of Service of the 92nd however permitted 20 Drummers in total and 2 Fifers. Pipers are not mentioned. WO/4/151/207. Neither Fifers nor Pipers are mentioned in the Letter of Service of the 93rd. WO/4/173/481. The creation of an establishment for Pipers in 1854 would imply that the discrepancies went unnoticed, but this does not necessarily suggest that Battalions kept to the establishment of 20 Drummers and 2 Fifers, and there is a theory that while the overall numbers of Drummers remained, there may have been fewer men playing the Drum and more men playing the Fife within that figure. In 1840 the Fifes and Drums of the 78th also included a Triangle. 'Burnley. 20.3.1840. Mr. Horrocks bets Mr. Brydges one bottle of port that there is not a pair of Triangles beating with the Fifes and Drums now playing Tattoo. Lost by Mr. Horrocks'. Betting Book of the Officers Mess 78th Highlanders 1822 to 1907, *op. cit.*, QOHRM.
64. Rev. Percy Sumner, 'Army Inspection Returns', *Journal of the Society for Army Historical Research*, 1926/1927, Vol. 5/6, pp. 26-27. WO/12/5491/5494. The return of the 42nd disembarking after sailing from Bombay to Portsmouth in 1868 raises

some interesting questions as the return includes '14 Drum carriages, 10 Bugles, 10 Drums and sticks, 20 Drummers and Fifers Tunics', but no Fifes. Were the Fifes omitted in error? Did the Drummers play both the Drum and the Bugle or were there 10 men playing Drums and 10 men playing Bugles? If so did they play together as a Drum and Bugle Band or did some of the Drummers play with the Pipers? The Regimental Order Book of the period gives no assistance at all in answering these questions. WO/25/1194.

65. Diary of Colonel J.W. Wedderburn 42nd. BWRM 28/714/2. Southsea 7.4.1854. "Heard the 79th Fifes and Pipers, the latter did not play well".
66. Lt. Colonel D.J.S. Murray, "The Evolution of the Regimental Music" (Part 5), *Queen's Own Highlander*, Vol. 24 No. 67, Winter 1984, p.132.
67. Major H. Davidson, *History and Services of the 78th Highlanders (Ross-shire Buffs)*, (Edinburgh 1901), p.13 and Cameron W. Pulsifer, *The 78th Highlanders in Halifax, 1869-71*, *op. cit.*, p. 63.
68. Register of Deserters 92nd Regiment 1831-1851, p. 37. GHRM.
69. In 1855 the 92nd may well have substituted their old fifes for flutes as the Day Book of Thomas Glen shows:

'The 92nd Regiment.

25.5.1855	1 Ball lapping for flutes	3d.
	Leathers for flutes	6d.
2.6.1855	To 3 Flutes rep.	3/6d.
	2 Bb Flutes new	£1.10/-
8.8.1855	To a set of triangles	10/-
4.9.1855	To a Bb Flute in Ger. silver	16/-
20.9.1855	To 2 Bb Flutes in silver	£2.10/-
	engraving do.	15/- '

There were therefore 8 Flutes at least in the Regiment at this time. Day Book of Thomas Glen. NLS Acc 8396/16. Landing at Gosport from Calcutta on the 20th of May, 1863, the disembarkation return of the 92nd from the *Middlesex* freight ship included, '6 Drums, 6 Bugles, 6 Fifes and cases with slings and Tassles, 4 Fifes left behind'. WO/25/1192.

70. In 1850 the 93rd were buying flutes from Glens also:

'The 93rd Highlanders.

5.8.1850	To 2 Bb Flutes Ivory mounted with 4 keys	
	1 Eb Picola	
	1 F Do.	
17.8.1850	To 5 Bb Flutes @ 2/-	
28.9.1850	To a pr. Triangles	10/- '

Day Book of Thomas Glen. NLS Acc 8396/16.

71. John Milbank Jones, *The History of Milton Barracks Gravesend, op. cit.*, p. 8.
72. Standing Orders of the 73rd Regiment, Cape Town 1850. BWRM. 295/3593. The disembarkation return of the 73rd arriving in Portsmouth from Plymouth in 1863 includes, '5 Drums, 5 Bugles and 5 Fifes'. WO/25/1192.
73. Standing Orders of the 74th Regiment, Belfast 1834. RHFRM D 84, p.7, para. 1. The disembarkation return of the 74th Highlanders arriving at Gibraltar from Dublin on 8.2.1868 includes, '10 Drums, 10 Fifes and cases slings and Tassles'. WO/25/1194. It should be noted however that these returns do not necessarily prove that the instruments were actually played.
74. For interesting information on fifes and drums see, *Drummers Call*, the newsletter of the Corps of Drums Society.
75. Standing Orders of the 79th Highlanders, Dublin 1819. WOHRM 142a/79. Sundays and Thursdays were considered holidays when there was only General Parade at 12 noon, the afternoon being free. During the rest of the week at Morning Parade a 'troop and quick march . . . [was] . . . beat along the line' and the

guard then marched off to duty. Ibid. While it would be easy to assume that all these calls were beaten every day at regular times, there is no guarantee that this was the case as Standing Orders often represented ideals instead of what actually happened.

76. Journal of Lt. Andrew Agnew of Lochnaw 93rd. GD/154/781.
77. The triangles were known in the 74th Highlanders in the 1850s as 'the Adjutant's Wife'. Sergeant James McKay 74th, *Reminiscences of the Last Kafir War, op. cit.*, p. 6.
78. Diary of Private A.W. McIntosh 42nd, BWRM 421 (3591(2)-) p. 149.
79. Account by Private Donald Cameron 79th, RH/4/141. A great deal of subjective material has been written on the subject of Drumming Out, but it would appear in this case that the man was quite happy to go, while at the same time the Regiment would not see one of their number destitute and hence the shilling was given by the Drum Major at the gate.
80. On 9th October 1914, the 2nd Battalion Gordon Highlanders left their Drums at Ostend and they were subsequently taken by the German Army. As a gesture of reconciliation these drums were ceremonially returned from Berlin in 1933, following the personal intervention of Sir Ian Hamilton, and there are some interesting photographs in the Gordon Highlanders Regimental Museum of the formal restoration of the Drums to the Battalion.
81. The Sounds for Duty and Exercise for the Trumpet and Bugle Horns of His Majesty's Regiments and Corps of Cavalry, 1798 GD/364/1/1133. Hope of Luffness Muniments.
82. Arthur Bryant, *Jackets of Green* (London: 1972), pp. 21-40.
83. WO/3/36-81
84. Standing Orders of the 79th Highlanders 1819, p. 42 QOHRM.
85. Bugle Calls of the 42nd 1833 from Standing Orders of the 42nd 1833. BWRM 355-51(42). MacVeigh records that Bugle Calls for Barrack duty were introduced in the 42nd in 1828, James MacVeigh, *Historical Record of the Black Watch, op. cit.*, p.404.
86. *Infantry Bugle Sounds also for Mounted Infantry and Regimental Calls* (London: 1909).
87. *Trumpet and Bugle Calls for the Army* (London 1966) 26/Manuals/3830 Army Code No. 14163.
88. Lt. Colonel Bertie Gordon 91st, Commanding Officer's Rough Order Book, Kamptee 1860. ASHRM R/16. 18.8.1860.
89. *Infantry Bugle Sounds also for Mounted Infantry and Regimental Calls, op. cit.*, There were several sets of words to the calls, not all of them being printable.
90. Standing Orders of the 42nd 1833. BWRM 355-51(42). p. 55.
91. Orders for the Assistance and Guidance of the Non-Commissioned Officers of the 1st Battalion 79th Regiment, c.1814, GD/174/2315, p.9.
92. Ibid., and Standing Orders of the 42nd 1833, BWRM 355-51(42), P.56.
93. Handwritten note by Pay Master, later Lt. Colonel Wheately, 42nd in Standing Orders of the 42nd 1833, BWRM 355-51(42), p. 56.
94. Lt. Colonel Bertie Gordon 91st, Commanding Officers Rough Order Book, Kamptee, 1860. ASHRM R/16. 20.11.1860.
95. War Office Letter of 28.1.1854 WO/3/115/387. 'Sir, I have the General Comg. in Chiefs Command to acquaint you that Her Majesty has been pleased to approve of the addition of one Pipe Major at one shilling and ten pence per diem; and five Pipers at one shilling and a penny each per diem being made to the Regiments specified in the margin. G.A. Wetherall DAG.' The Regiments that were granted an establishment of Pipers at this time were the 42nd, 71st (HLI), 72nd, 74th, 78th, 79th, 92nd, and 93rd. While Pipes were purchased by the Officers of the 91st for the Regiment in 1860, pipers were not permitted on their establishment until 1865, having been ordered off parade at the Inspection of the 91st at Dover in 1850. G.L. Goff, *Historical Records of the 91st Argyllshire Highlanders, op. cit.*, p. 215. From the War Office

records that survive it would appear that the establishment for the five pipers additional to the establishment in Highland regiments was questioned in 1924 when the possibility was discussed of reorganising Lowland battalion pipers. A War Office Memorandum of 9.4.1924 states, 'It is considered that the most satisfactory means is to place the 5 Pipers of Highland Battalions within the establishment, instead of their being additional as at present and to provide that 5 Pipers be included in the establishment of Privates of all Scottish Battalions. Out of the saving thus created of 60 Pipers additional to establishment, it is recommended that 12 Sergeant Pipers should be added to the establishment (i.e. 1 for each Lowland Battalion and Depot), so as to put the Lowland Regiments on the same lines as Highland Regiments'. The net saving was estimated at £1500 p.a. WO/32/5450. The evidence of Lt. Colonel D.J.S. Murray would suggest that 5 Pipers remained additional to establishment in the Queen's Own Cameron Highlanders, if not in other Highland Battalions, in 1944 and until the creation of the 625-man battalion in the 1960s when this unique privilege was simply allowed to lapse.

96. Regimental Pipers competed with considerable success from the earliest days of the known competitions commencing with the Highland Society of London competition at the Falkirk Tryst in 1781. In 1841 an exhibition of Pipers and Dancers began at the Northern Meeting and in 1875 the Highland Society of London awarded a gold medal at the Argyllshire Gathering. These competitions were used by the Highland regiments as an opportunity for both playing and recruiting. W.L. Manson, *The Highland Bagpipe, op. cit.*, pp. 388-392. *The Cabar Feidh Collection, Pipe Music of the Queen's Own Highlanders (Seaforth and Camerons)*, (London: 1984), pp. 282-292. Angus Mackay, *A collection of Ancient Piobaireachd or Highland Pipe Music*, Wakefield: 1972. First published Aberdeen, 1838), pp. 15-20. Regimental competitions are of comparatively recent origin. On 13th and 14th May 1852 the 93rd held a 'Sutherland Gathering' at Weedon, very much on the lines of a modern Highland Games, with races and heavy weight events. There was however no individual pipe playing, but the games did include 'Reel Dancing, Gillie Callum and Highland Fling'. J.A. Ewart, *The Story of a Soldier's Life, op. cit.*, pp. 151-152. In the same year at Stirling Castle J.W. Wedderburn records, 'I went to the bowling green to hear the competition of the Pipers, Highland Games etc. Our old Pipe Major McLean and Ross were the two best, and so near each other, I would have tossed, however the Judges gave the first Prize to Ross (a Pr. of Bagpipes). The 79th Pipe Major had no chance, the dancing was splendid and the broadsword very good'. Diary of Colonel J. W. Wedderburn 42nd, BWRM 28/714/1 24.6.1852. The second 'Sutherland Gathering' took place at Chobham Camp on 8th July 1853, and Games were also held in the Highland Camp in the Crimea in April 1856, when Lt. John C. Stewart wrote, 'We have had lots of racing and Games lately we had Highland Games which lasted two days when the 72nd rather distinguished themselves in carrying off all the best prizes and beating the swell Kilty Regts. to nothing'. Letters of Lt. John C. Stewart 72nd, QOHRM S441. 3.4.1856. Stewart had good reason to be pleased as the winner of the 1st Prize in Piping at this competition went to the Pipe Major of the 72nd, John McDonald. McDonald enlisted in the 15th of Foot in the early 1840s and transferred to the 72nd, becoming a Piper. In 1852 he was a pupil of Mackenzie, the Marquis of Breadalbane's Piper, and he went with the 72nd to the Crimea and India, returning home in 1865 to be Pipe Major of the Stirlingshire Militia. He died in Tiree on 23rd November 1893.

97. Standing Orders of the 72nd Regiment of Duke of Albany's Own Highlanders, Richmond Barracks, Dublin, 1827. QOHRM 676/72

98. Colonel Wedderburn records at the Officers' Mess, Stirling Castle 1852: ' . . . old McLean the Pipe Major played Lord Lovat's Lament most beautifully. I suppose this will be the last time the old fellow will play at Mess and I am very sorry he is leaving the Regt'. Diary of Colonel J.W. Wedderburn 42nd. BWRM 28/714/1.

Stirling Castle 2.11.1852.

99. Lt. Colonel D.J.S. Murray, 'The Evolution of the Regimental Music', (Part 6), *Queen's Own Highlander*, No. 68, Summer 1985, p. 24.
100. The Pipe Major and the Drum Major were given the titles Sergeant Piper and Sergeant Drummer in 1881 and the old titles were not restored until 1928.
101. Descriptive Roll Book of the 93rd Highlanders, *op. cit.*, ASHRM.
102. Letters of Lt. Colonel the Hon. Lauderdale Maule 79th. GD/45/14/634/4 1-98. Gibraltar 6.5.1847. Maule is credited not only with the introduction of the Glengarry in this period, but also with dressing the Pipers in green, a colour later generally adopted (the present pattern of Pipers tunic is in fact 'Archer' green, not the original lighter 'Piper' green). The reason for this may well lie in Maule's interest in converting the 79th to 'Highland Rifles', and the uniform was an entirely unofficial experiment to convince his brother of the viability of his proposals and the attractiveness of the colour. 'A propos et entre nous, if it is proposed to increase the Rifle Corps, get us made Highland Rifles—I have long indulged this hobby it would be the handsomest dress in the Army . . . Look at the dress of the Piper (a model) I sent you and you may judge of the effect of the green with our kilt—It would really be magnificent'. Ibid., GD/45/14/634/4 99-184 Gibraltar, 20.1.1848.
103. Adjutant General to Military Secretary, 12.11.1853. WO/3/321 271-272.
104. Ibid.
105. In 1843 Queen Victoria appointed Angus MacKay as Her first personal Piper; the first military appointment of Sovereign's Piper is believed to have been that of Pipe Major Hardy of the 79th, who is said to have been dismissed for thrashing two English footmen who mocked his Highland accent but who in fact died in Royal service in 1864. Pipe Major William Ross of the 42nd was appointed a Royal Piper in 1854.
106. For example John Kennedy of the 42nd was an Acting Piper in the Regiment sometime before 1860, but was not appointed Piper until 1865. Order Books of the 42nd. BWRM. 27/2270 and 30/2271.
107. *79th News*, Vol. 2 No. 15, 1894, p.4.
108. Permanent Order Book 91st (1st Battalion Argyll and Sutherland Highlanders). ASHRM Sb 18/16. 2.2.1874.
109. Standing Orders of the 42nd. 1833. BWRM 355/51(42), pp. 55-56 and Standing Orders and Regulations for the 93rd Highlanders 1835. ASHRM. R 226, p. 21.
110. *HLI Chronicle*, Vol. 2 No. 8, October 1898, p. 267.
111. *HLI Chronicle*, Vol. 3 No. 9, April 1903, p. 857.
112. Permanent Order Book 91st (1st Battalion Argyll and Sutherland Highlanders). ASHRM Sb 18/16, Aldershot 7.9.1870.
113. Ibid., 4.8.1871.
114. See 42nd Order Book, BWRM 30/2271. Aldershot 10.7.1871. A question must be raised here as to the contemporary procedure in the Guards and also in Lowland regiments with 'unofficial' Pipers.
115. The author, as an Officer with the Scottish Bi-Centennial Tattoo in Washington, USA, in 1976, experienced an interesting legacy of this rivalry. It had been decided that the march off should be the John Denver popular song, 'Take me Home Country Roads', played by the Military Bands, as the Director of Music had decided 'it could not be played on the Pipes'. Immediately Pipe Major John Allan, Queen's Own Highlanders, set about secretly transposing the tune to the Pipes with harmony, and after a surprise rendering on parade, and much to the consternation of the Military Bands, the Pipes and Drums took the honour of the march off.
116. *Drummers Call*, No. 11 December 1980, p. 11. It is interesting that terms used in connection with the structure of Piobaireachd, such as 'doubling' and 'singling' were also used in fife music. Manuscript books of fife tunes thought to belong to a militia unit include such tunes as 'Rule Britannia', 'Lady MacDonald's Reel', 'The

Highland Laddie', 'The Prussian Waltz', 'Lady Mary Ramsay' (strathspey), 'Blakemore' (jig). Five MS books of Fife Music, the property of Miss Maclean of Ardgour, kindly lent to the author by Major Richard Powell, RAOC.

117. *Sutherland News*, Vol. 2, No. 10 October 1895, p. 110.

118. *Piping Times*, Vol. 33 No.9, June 1981. Lt. Colonel D.J.S. Murray, 'What's in a Name', p. 21.

119. There are many such compositions of welcome and farewell. Most pipers today have no idea at all about the origins of these tunes, and all too often titles are shortened or misquoted, 'The 79th's Farewell' losing all the meaning and implications of leaving the Rock and of the Battalion remaining at sea in the Bay of Gibraltar for several days before they could set out across the Atlantic.

120. MS Book of Pipe Music belonging to Pipe Major William Ross 42nd, BWRM 788/91.

121. Diary of Colonel J.W. Wedderburn 42nd. BWRM 28/714/1. Chobham 7.7.1853.

122. 1245 Pipe Major William Ross. Born Knockbain, Ross. Enlisted aged 17 on 1.3.1839 at Inverness. Trade, Piper. Discharged free 11.5.1854. Appointed Piper to the Queen. Died at Windsor Castle 10.6.1891, aged 69.

123. *The Cabar Feidh Collection, Pipe Music of the Queen's Own Highlanders*, *op. cit.*, pp. 244-247.

124. Company Pipe Calls were set down in the 91st in 1877. See Pipe Rules of the 91st, from Permanent Order Book, 91st (1st Battalion Argyll and Sutherland Highlanders), ASHRM Sb 18/16. Belfast 6.7.1877. An interesting volume of 78th Regimental settings was printed in 1901 under the title *Duty Calls and Favourite Tunes of the Seaforth Highlanders* . . . from Pipe Major Ronald Mackenzie's Manuscript Book. Settings played by the 78th Highlanders (Elgin: Seaforth Highlanders, 1901), NLS MHS 167. Mackenzie was Pipe Major the 78th between May 1865 and February 1879 after which he became Pipe Major of the 3rd Seaforth Highlanders until 1892. In 1893 he became Pipe Major of the 3rd Volunteer Battalion Seaforth Highlanders. Some interesting tunes and settings are included in this book which also details duty tunes of the period and notes the procedure at military funerals of playing the first and second bars of 'Lochaber No More' after the first volley, the first, second, third and fourth bars after the second volley and the first part once after the third volley.

125. Evidence of Pipe Major (WO 1) Dippie, Black Watch and Lt. Colonel D.J.S. Murray, Queen's Own Highlanders (Retd.).

126. Letter, Lt. Colonel Ewan H.D. Macpherson to R.H. Burgoyne c.1882. ASHRM.

127. Diary of General Sir J. Spencer Ewart 79th, RH/4/84/1, 12.9.1888.

128. Ibid., RH/3/84/3 11.5.1910 and WO/32/12150. Much of the preservation of Pipe Music and especially Piobaireachd must be credited not only to the Piobaireachd Society, but also to the Army, the Army Class and the Army School of Piping, and while Piobaireachd is presently the subject of a new revival and interest, other developments appear to pose a serious threat to the traditional base of the instrument. Joseph MacDonald writes that Piobaireachd, Jigs and Reels were the sole, traditional and proper music for the Great Highland Bagpipe, but even by 1760 inroads were already being made into its repertoire by the introduction of contemporary Italian pieces and Scotch Airs popular amongst Pipers in the 'Low country' who used 'Pipes with bellows, . . . Thus a passage of Correli . . . or Handel & etc. played with Pipe Cuttings & a Drone must carry a great deal of the Author's meaning in it—& so of Scots Airs Minuets Songs etc.—What a wretched and insipid jargon is this . . . to a judicious ear is obvious. This . . . imitation of other Musick is what gives such a contemptable notion of a Pipe'. Joseph MacDonald, *A Compleat theory of the Scots Highland bagpipe*, *op. cit.*, p. 20. Francis Collinson was concerned with the introduction of 'seconds', i.e. two-part harmony, 'something for which the instrument was never intended', and now accepted as

standard practice in Pipe Bands. Francis Collinson, *The Traditional and National Music of Scotland* (London: 1966), p. 198. Most worrying of all however to the traditional approach is the modern military practice of combined playing by the Military Band and the Pipes and Drums, which does neither justice musically and, carried to its logical conclusion, could, in the long term, retard the development of military piping and result in even fewer of the fine nineteenth-century march, strathspey and reel compositions being played except in solo performance and prevent Military Bands being heard to their best advantage. In 1985 for example the 1st Batttalion Black Watch played an entire Retreat programme of combined playing on the Esplanade of Edinburgh Castle; undoubtedly a sign of things to come.

129. Oral history archive in the possession of the author, *op. cit.*, Compare, however, the records contained in Sir Bruce Seton and Pipe Major John Grant, *Pipes of War* (Wakefield: 1975).

130. For a collection of Pipe Major G.S. McLennan's tunes, see *The Gordon Highlanders Pipe Music Collection*, Vol. 1 (London: 1983).

131. Diary of General Sir Spencer Ewart 79th, RH/4/84/1, 31.7.1882.

131. Ibid., 1.8.1882.

CHAPTER 10

The Regimental Family

As we saw in Chapter 7, another conspicuous part of the routine of Highland regiments was the effort to promote and maintain cleanliness. In barracks, Saturday was the great day of cleaning and inspections, when not only the barracks were cleaned, but the kits and necessaries were laid out in a set order for inspection on the beds.[1] Preparation for these inspections took up a great deal of the soldier's time, but once a set of kit was 'up', that is tailored, with the straps adjusted and trimmed and a good base of blacking and pipe clay and the brasses burnished, the final preparations were minimal, and there developed a pride amongst the men in having the best kit and the best room, which invariably resulted in certain exemptions from the round of inspections. A.G. Greenhill Gardyne of the 1st Battalion Gordon Highlanders recalls in 1891:

> The kits were a marvel, I never saw anything like some of them for neatness . . . So the Colonel was pleased and Ramsay tackled him about exempting the best men from inspection and as a result the best kits need not be shown twice a month says the Orderly room . . .[2]

Considerable skill and technique was required in the cleaning of kit, which was termed 'soldiering', and there is evidence that men with particular skill at burnishing or the application of pipe clay would help others, probably for a small fee, while the older soldiers would always ensure that a recruit on his first guard would be certain to pass the Officer's inspection. Sergeant George P. Miller of the 71st (HLI) at Stirling in 1858 remembers:

> Thus the old soldiers in the room saw to it that the recruit was turned out spick and braw, that he might be a credit to the squad of which he was a member. As the hour of guard mounting drew near he was dressed and thoroughly overhauled, so that even the keen eye of the Adjutant could not detect a speck . . . I well remember once at guard mounting a recruit of the old corps was brought to the front and pointed out as an example how to turn out for the important duty of guard mounting and how the Adjutant with the tail of his eye looked at a squad of old soldiers away in the distance who were watching the recruit. The heart of the recruit beat fast that day and the old soldiers were sky-high with delight . . . Then, having mounted his first guard in these days the Ruck [recruit] was expected to provide the whole guard with tobacco. Just as an apprentice in civil life has to 'pay off' when he attains to the position of journeyman.[3]

Officers relied heavily upon their soldier servants for the preparation of their clothes and the cleanliness of their accoutrements. The position of officers' servants conferred extensive privileges and may well have been sought after. In the 79th servants were allocated to each officer and one was shared by the Sergeant Major and the Quarter Master Sergeant. No front-rank men, and no men from the élite Light and Grenadier Companies were permitted to be servants,[4] but for those who were chosen there were rewards in extra money, exemption from certain parades and the privilege of wearing civilian clothes or the regimental livery.[5] These men also accompanied their masters on shooting expeditions and on leave, and they frequently became close friends, maintaining correspondence long after their service had expired.[6]

Cleanliness was closely associated with regimental pride and individual self-respect, and it would seem that in Highland regiments the insistence on cleanliness was functional, to ensure that a soldier's clothing and equipment were fit for duty and public view, rather than oppressive, and that the concept of cleaning for the sake of cleaning—'bull'—was much more a feature of the inter-war years 1919-1939 when cleaning assumed much of the character of mindless punishment. In the main, Regular soldiers of the pre-First World War Highland regiments were concerned about their appearance, and it is clear from the photographic evidence that a lot of individual effort went into good presentation. Rules can make a man clean but they cannot make him smart unless he wants to be smart. Particularly in the latter half of the nineteenth century and in the early twentieth century, the Highland soldier was not unaware of the romance which surrounded his regiment, and he was also conscious that even an average-looking man presented a good appearance in scarlet tunic, kilt and feather bonnet compared with his drab civilian counterpart.

Now unfashionable, frequently ridiculed and often misunderstood, the cleaning and polishing process was an integral and functional part of Regimental life, particularly in the later Victorian and Edwardian period. Parades and guards with the Bands playing and the Colours flying entailed a lot of work for everybody in the Regiment, but they also provided colour and style, a feature often neglected and unjustly scorned in an age of khaki and camouflage.[7]

As with all British regiments, the social structure of the Highland regiments was firmly based on rank. For officers, rank meant financial commitment, duty and expectations of patronage on the part of subordinates, but for the non-commissioned officers and men the considerations were different.

Even in 1919 the financial rewards for Private soldiers were generally low by industrial standards, while the duties of Warrant Officers and senior NCOs carried considerable responsibility and entailed a great deal of work. It is clear that by modern standards many men were unambitious and preferred to remain, by choice or request, in the rank of Private soldier, a station which appears to have held merit in itself and allowed the individual freedom from responsibility. At the same time, however, the formal rank structure permitted men to visibly improve their status and attain respectability in both military and civilian circles. John Tulloch of the 74th proudly wrote to his brother from

Cannonore in 1855 on being promoted to Sergeant: 'I have a handle to my name and means to keep it'.[8]

Because of the large number of guards undertaken by the Army at home and abroad and the principle that no Private soldier could be trusted on his own initiative to go and do as he was told (evidence would suggest that he could or would not, in spite of being fully aware of the penalties for drinking, absconding, fighting etc.), NCOs and Sergeants were responsible for all the day-to-day supervision of the men, marching parties to the school, the orderly room, the hospital and to and from parades and guards. They were responsible too for the distribution of orders, carefully writing details from the central orders book in the orderly room and passing them on, often verbally, to the men in their squad or company, while the main orders of the Commanding Officer would be read by the Adjutant at the head of the Regiment at general parade. There were however other important but less glamorous duties performed by the NCOs, and in India in the 1860s 91st Orders detailed a Corporal to be told off daily to superintend the milking of the cows, to ensure that the milk was not watered by the native servants.[9]

Invariably there were too many duties and too few NCOs on establishment, and Lance rank[10] was freely used in the Highland regiments both as an incentive to responsibility and as a matter of necessity, a move which generally resulted in the devaluation of the lower ranks. Lauderdale Maule of the 79th complained in Gibraltar in 1847:

> How many Lance Corporals do you think I am compelled to keep up here (and Lance Sergeants in proportion) to give my Non Commissioned Officers 3 nights in bed. Upwards of 40![11]

The system of rank was also flexible and deprivation was an integral part of the system of punishment, thereby avoiding the more severe aspects of military discipline. The most usual cause of deprivation of rank was drunkenness. John Tulloch of the 74th explained:

> . . . the night i cam to Barracks from out post duty i got on the spree with some other Sergeants one of them and myself drank rather heavily and was not able to go to Tattoo parade we were both confined of course and the consequence was that we were both reduced to the ranks . . . there is no use of saying i am vexed or in any way grieved for what has happened that would be of no avail whatever . . . it is possible that i can get on again however i am happy to say that i have not tasted liquor since i got off the spree that was the cause of my reducal . . .[12]

Restoration to a previously held rank was in fact common, illustrating not only the acknowledgement of frailty, but also a certain condonation of the heavy drinking that obviously pervaded the Highland regiments.

Rank was also used as a system of direct reward and encouragement. 91st Orders of the 26th of April 1865 record:

> Corpl. (4007) Willm. W. Cameron is promoted Sergeant in No. 10 Company . . .

> This promotion is due to special service worthily performed as the leader and trainer of that Corps of Pipers, which under many difficulties has been maintained in the Corps, since the Regiment landed in India . . .[13]

Although it was encouraged, in some Highland regiments the ability to read and write was not a prerequisite for promotion, but in general NCOs were encouraged to learn. In 1833 Standing Orders of the 42nd instructed:

> Non commissioned officers are required to attend the Regimental School if not sufficiently well taught in reading, writing and arithmetic . . . Sergeants are expected to learn at least the first four rules of arithmetic.[14]

In an era when written reports, orders, instructions and requests were all-important, it is clear that the ability to read and write soon became a necessity amongst NCOs and Sergeants, although the standard was not necessarily high.

By 1857 the 42nd had set down educational requirements for promotion:

Private to L/Cpl. —	Able to read, write and understand the first four rules of Arithmetic.
L/Cpl. to Cpl. —	As above, with division and Drill without arms. Understand the duties of Orderly, Fatigue and Guard Corporal.
Cpl. to L/Sgt. —	Able to take simple dictation and do proportions and mental arithmetic. Drill with arms. Guard and Escort duties.
L/Sgt. to Sgt. —	Able to take dictation, calculate vulgar fractions and mental arithmetic. Drill a Company and conduct guards and detachments. Fully familiar with standing orders.[15]

In 1860 Bertie Gordon of the 91st, after insisting that all members of the Regiment attend school even for a short time, introduced a competitive examination for the purposes of promotion, allotting vacancies as they occurred, not only to the deserving, but also to those who gained the best marks,[16] and as Army Education developed in the 1860s and '70s, attendance at the Regimental School was virtually made compulsory with promotion depending on the possession of Army Education Certificates.

In practice, however, it was often difficult to sustain the necessary attendance and provide continuous tuition. Lauderdale Maule of the 79th wrote from Gibraltar in 1846:

> . . . we have not a single rank and file in the school because we have not a moment to spare from duties, fatigues and labour on the fortifications. The Band and Drum Boys constitute the sum total of our scholars.[17]

Regimental Orders clearly show that in the Highland regiments, who spent so much of their time on foreign and active service, the school simply had to close down when the regiments were trooping, marching from station to station, or were on internal security or active duty.[18] From the evidence of Private Lobban and Corporal MacFarlane however there is no doubt that by 1914 the Regimental School was a permanent and indeed popular feature of Highland Regimental life, and a First Class Certificate, (which Mr. MacFarlane still holds) was a proud possession.[19]

The system of rank was not only closely linked with education, it also provided a series of positions within the regiment giving employment to men often too old or infirm for the ranks, or men who had served the regiment well over many years. These positions included Hospital Sergeant,[20] Armourer Sergeant, Pay Master Sergeant, Officers' Mess Sergeant, Canteen Sergeant[21] and NCO in charge of the Recreation and Reading Room. All these positions gave opportunities for additional financial remuneration and reward, and it would seem that the small extra charges levied by these men were paid ungrudgingly by Highland soldiers, who were probably fully aware that one day they might qualify for such a post, whereupon they themselves would expect the remuneration also.

It is clear however that Highland soldiers were in no way overawed by rank, and that while certain officers were disliked and were unapproachable, many soldiers of the nineteenth and early twentieth centuries felt free to address their officers man to man, each respecting the security and status of the other's social position. Surgeon William Munro of the 91st and 93rd sums up this interrelationship:

> . . . there existed generally or almost universally, a friendly feeling which extended throughout all ranks, but I think that in Scotch or Highland Regiments there was something more than this. In these there was a friendly intimacy between Officers and men, which by strangers might have been looked upon as familiarity, but which was in reality the evidence of esteem and confidence in each other which knew no fear and was the result, not only of long companionship, but of a feeling of nationality.[22]

This intimate interrelationship of rank allowed some extraordinary scenes to take place in Highland regiments which are not usually associated with the often publicised oppressed nineteenth-century Army. In January 1838, the night before the 93rd were to leave for Canada, the Officers held a Mess party and the young Lieutenant Andrew Agnew of the Grenadier Company, then aged 20, found himself late for dinner:

> I hastily dressed for our last mess party and was hurrying down stairs when from a dark corner out rushed three or four Grenadiers, who in spite of all resistance held me . . . mounted me on the shoulders of one of the party and bore me off in triumph—This was no mutiny! but business had made me forget it was New Year's Day . . . This rough joke was intended as the greatest compliment, implying that the Grenadiers must have the dance with their sweethearts and wives. In vain I

expostulated, in vain remarked that the dinner call had sounded and that I had friends at Mess. I was carried on as steadily as circumstances would permit off to the Grenadiers quarters where I was obliged to make a short speech, drink a glass of whisky and dance at least one reel before I was able to effect an escape . . .[23]

Instances such as this are a marked feature of relations between the ranks in Highland battalions, and amongst those who served in Regular battalions before 1914 and survived the First World War, these feelings of comradeship, nationality and personal respect were very strong.

Personal relationships apart, the formal military code of discipline, embodied in the Mutiny Act, the Articles of War, the Army Discipline and Regulation Act of 1879 and the Army Act, laid down the rules governing the conduct of all soldiers, together with regulations for procedure and the scales of punishment.[24] The rules were explicit and strict and were primarily governed by contemporary penal thought. For many years the most authoritative interpretations of military law were contained in a volume entitled *Observations on the Practice and the Forms of Courts Martial and Courts of Enquiry & etc.* by Lt. General Sir George Charles D'Aguilar, published in 1839, and Highland officers relied heavily on D'Aguilar's work.[25]

Although there appear to be no separate statistics, the most prevalent offences in the Highland regiments would seem to have been desertion and drink-related crimes. The figures, where they exist, must however be considered as misleading because of the lack of precise definition of the crimes, the individual attitudes of commanding officers towards courts martial and the widespread condonation, particularly of the consumption of alcohol to excess that went on in the Highland regiments.

Desertion was *ex facie* a serious offence, frequently coupled with making away with accoutrements or the sale of necessaries. The incidence of desertion was, it seems, often linked with an unpopular commander, an impending move overseas, the station of a regiment and the time of year. By virtue of the fact that the Articles of War were read at the head of the regiments regularly, the men must have been aware that desertion carried a penalty of transportation, stamping or tattooing (it was not really branding in the modern sense) with the letter 'D', corporal punishment or imprisonment, and yet some men persistently deserted and were equally regularly caught until they were transported or imprisoned.

In the twenty years between 1831 and 1851, 339 desertions are recorded as having taken place, an average of approximately seventeen per year, in the 92nd Highlanders,[26] but the numbers are deceptive; many men deserted four if not five times before they were transported and had already been punished or marked with the letter 'D'. In addition sixty-one desertions took place in the period 1831-1834 when the Regiment was in Ireland, prior to leaving for Barbados, and there are only eight recorded desertions in the West Indies. Between February 1844 and July 1846, however, when the 92nd were in Glasgow, Paisley and Edinburgh Castle, 207 desertions are recorded, although many of these men returned. Individual motivation for desertion is difficult to assess, but it is evident that some men had already fallen foul of the disciplinary system prior to desertion and they were prepared to risk the punishments because they had nothing to lose. This particulary applied to desertion in Canada. Lt. Parke of the 72nd recorded at Fredericktown on 7th September 1852;

> Five of our men sentenced to transportation have managed to cut their way out of the strong room and escape, one has been apprehended, the others have got clean off.[27]

In the light of the economic and social background in Scotland and particularly in the Highlands, it might be anticipated that desertions would occur at a notably higher rate in the Highland regiments, but from the figures which are available, it would appear that this was not the case although it seems that Highland desertion figures did peak when the regiments were in Scotland and also when they were in Canada, when desertion meant permanently leaving and crossing the American border. In Canada this desertion in fact became a business:

> The American Companies all through British America endeavour to induce soldiers to desert; a certain set of crimps also eek out their living by taking money to spirit men off . . . Desertion is treated as a much more serious affair than it is in England . . . [and so] . . . the Tattoo rolls are called a second time and [if] anyone is absent a gun is fired from the Fort . . . On hearing this the military police are on the qui vive and any civilian meeting a soldier making off is a [t] liberty to arrest him and claim the reward [of £5]. A most horrible system was brought to our notice at this time—a set of wretches not content with the wages of sin earned by inducing and assisting young soldiers to desert often drunk or half drunk, actually fastened on their victims by lying in wait watching for them on the very routes they had indicated & giving them up to justice.[28]

From the figures that are available in the Enlistment Book of the 42nd, which would appear to be roughly reliable between 1820 and 1870, desertion rates in the 42nd would seem to have been proportionately low.

Desertions 42nd, 1820-1870

Date	No. of men enlisted in that year	No. of men from that enlistment who deserted
1820	29	0
1830	22	1
1840	127	16
1850	6	1
1860	214	33
1870	136	17[29]

The wording of the Roll implies that these men never returned and were not merely returned, punished or transported; but there is of course no guarantee that some of them did not re-enlist in another regiment, which was a common feature of nineteenth-century desertion, and it is clear that detailed statistical and social research requires to be done in this field. It is obvious however that there were heavy temptations to desert in Canada and that a strongly Scots civilian population in some areas, and American labour recruiting agents, were not slow to encourage men to leave the service, rather than leave them to return home, await discharge and pay passage money out. Some men who enlisted, knowing a regiment was in Canada, may well have joined in the first place for the free passage.[30]

Figures extracted from the Standing Order Book of the 79th show that desertions in Canada were usually a joint venture, involving two or three men deserting together on the same day and presumably setting off in a group for the interior or the American border. Few are recorded as being returned, and it can only be a matter of speculation as to whether they survived the bitter Canadian winter and the dangers of the interior, for, of the six men who deserted from Kingston Barracks between Christmas Eve 1830 and 10th March 1831, only one, Private John Campbell, is known to have returned.[31] In total there seem to have been eighteen 'successful' desertions in the 79th in 1831, and it was this very success and permanence, together with a genuine fear of trafficking in labour across the border, that led the authorities to take the far more serious view of desertion referred to by Lieutenant Agnew.[32]

One of the problems in the analysis of desertion statistics is the obvious lack of declaration of deserters by the regiments themselves, and the covering up of the figures in various ways. Lt. Andrew Agnew of the 93rd records:

> Toronto 15.12.1838. Sat on a board (i.e. a board of enquiry). After some examination found that John, the Major's Batman, was drowned . . . The result of this inquest was sufficiently obscure. John was a great character, trusted by his master, much loved by the Officers, a good conduct man with nearly twenty years service; on his being missed desertion was held to be out of the question; and the Major having satisfied himself that he was drowned, after very slight examination of certain persons who proved that he had been last seen on one of the wharfs and found him drowned accordingly.[33]

In fact John was not drowned, and it is clear that the officers knew this perfectly well, but would not record 'deserter' against the name of a good man. This man had deserted and had bought a trading vessel on Lake Michigan. Two years later, haunted by the stigma of desertion, he wrote to the 93rd and declared himself, requesting to pay for his discharge. The authorities however would not accept this, and after a further year he voluntarily walked into the 93rd Guard Room at Drummondville and gave himself up. The Regiment tried to procure him a pardon, but without success, and eventually he was tried by District Court Martial and sentenced to one year's imprisonment. Fortunately, the Colonel of the 93rd was District Commander at the time, and John's sentence was remitted, although he lost all service benefits.[34]

It is clear therefore that in certain cases Highland regiments attempted to remit sentence and punishment of deserters. Concerned about desertion in the

79th, and operating without relish in aid of the civil power at Wigan about 1840, Captain Lauderdale Maule was forced to make an example of three men, never apparently anticipating that they would be transported as a result. In an undated letter he wrote to his brother Fox Maule:

> I find out that the three convicts I spoke of from the 79th Regiment who were to be transported for desertion viz—The two Scotts and Malcolme Ritchie, are on board the Lustitia Hulk at Woolwich. If you can prevent them being sent off in the mean time I'll forward you their papers . . . on their behalf thro' Sir Ronald. Two have never appeared in the defaulters book and the third only twice and then merely for being drunk when off duty—Poor devils—I brought them forward as examples and feel very sorry for them.[35]

One of the reasons for this apparent regimental ambivalence towards desertion was the nineteenth-century lack of latitude in sentencing and penal policy. Until the reform of soldiers' pay and the enhancement of that pay by the issue of certain free items which were formally 'necessaries', the military wage, usually paid in small amounts daily,[36] was never intended as a reward in civilian terms, and therefore its use as a deterrent was limited. After the initial purchase of 'necessaries' most soldiers were already in debt, and while there were forfeitures and fines, there was little point in fining a man who was already in debt, and who was going to incur further debt by way of legitimate stoppages for washing, food and necessaries which would rank first against him.[37]

In addition many officers and men strongly disapproved of imprisonment, which merely allowed a man, in their opinion, to avoid his duty and unburden it on to his more disciplined comrades; while at the same time they seem to have taken little delight in corporal punishment or transportation, although both were undoubtedly used for rough, tough, drunken bad characters whom the Highland regiments, Officers and men, were glad to get rid of. There being a limited middle course in sentencing, particularly extra-regimentally, it would appear that some desertion was, by various means, 'kept in the family'. There is evidence too, by implication, that Highland regiments may have made little attempt to stop men going in certain circumstances. In an undated memorandum of the early 1850s to his brother, Lauderdale Maule wrote:

> The enclosed has reference to two men of the 79th, 2138 Jas. Brodie and 2345 Nail McLean sentenced by Court Martial to be dismissed the service with ignominy. I applied to have them discharged here [Canada] and the men themselves are desirous of hiding their heads in the States and beginning *de novo,* they were convicted of sodomy . . . it is bad policy with regard to the men themselves, who are anxious to expiate themselves were the opportunity given to them.[38]

What happened to these two men is unknown, but the clear inference to be deduced from the memorandum is that the men wanted to go to the United States, the Regiment did not want them, neither party had much to lose, but most important the Commanding Officer understood if he did not sympathise with their situation, and the conclusion can be drawn that if they had managed to desert, little regimental opposition would have been put in their way.

This element of condonation was particularly evident in drinking and drink-related offences in the Highland regiments. Drinking, especially the consumption of spirits as opposed to beer, was, and still is, a serious Scottish problem. In 1834 it was estimated that Scots consumed four gallons per annum per head of population of 'ardent spirits', and Scotland was reputed to be 'the most drunken country on the face of the earth'.[39] Spirits, while cheaper in Scotland and Ireland, were also an integral part of the social and labour system in Scotland; Elizabeth Grant of Rothiemurchus records:

> Amongst the rest [of the servants at Doune House] was a Piper who for the fear of spoiling the delicacy of the touch of his fingers. declined any work unconnected with whisky,[40]

and she records of the timber men employed on the Spey in 1813:

> . . . on collecting, [for work] whisky was always handed round; a lad with a small cask—a quarter anker—on his back, and a horn cup in his hand that held a gill, appeared three times a day among them. They all took their "morning" raw, undiluted and without accompaniment, so they did the gill at parting when the work was done; but the noontide dram was part of a meal.[41]

In the Army in the United Kingdom, NCOs, Drummers and Private men were paid 1d. per day 'Beer Money', instituted in 1800 in lieu of the issue which had previously been in kind.[42] In Gibraltar however in 1847, the ration allowance was still issued in kind, but the men of the 79th preferred the 1d per day and gave away, sold or bartered their allowance.[43] Not that this implied sobriety, for it did not; the men simply used the proceeds of sale or bartered direct for the liquor of their choice; in Gibraltar, Spanish brandy was a favourite. Complaining of alcoholism in the Regiment, Maule wrote:

> In Gibraltar the evil is crying. I have had no less than 4 men with delirium tremens during the last week, one of which a big strong powerful man—dead! raving mad![44]

Maule urged the retention, and where applicable the establishment of canteens, in every barracks to permit some sort of supervision of timings and consumption.[45] Canteens, until 1863 run on a private contractual basis, had the joint function of providing alcohol, and groceries and snacks at a profit to the proprietor.

The canteen itself usually comprised a detached building or an assigned area, divided into a shop, called the 'dry' canteen, sometimes a separate Sergeants' room, a bar counter and a Private soldiers' drinking area with tables and benches, the 'wet' canteen. In theory, by providing facilities for alcohol within the barracks and controlling timings, quality and to some extent prices, many of the problems of alcoholism should have been avoided, but this was far from the case and the Highland soldier took strong exception to separation from alcohol, particularly spirits, taking considerable risks and going to great lengths to obtain it.[46]

In 1832, cholera broke out in the Native Bazaar at Trincomalee, Ceylon and Colonel Martin Lindsay of the 78th immediately took precautions confining the Regiment to the Fort, the canteen being closed although an extra dram was permitted. In spite of the dangers of disease, two soldiers, Privates Henry Ebertson and William McPherson, got out of the Fort at night and swam across the Bay to the town, 'in quest of women . . . and arrack'. Following their escapade fifty-five men of the 78th died of cholera including Ebertson, and although the transmission of cholera was not understood at the time, their search for alcohol was indicative of the desperate measures men were prepared to take despite the dictates of good sense and the regulations.[47]

Allowing the individual soldier to make up his own mind in the full knowledge of the dangers of alcohol and the punishment which followed alcohol-related crimes seems to have been of little use, and officers simply resorted to prevention, by whatever means they could find, and toleration. Colonel Cuming writes of a march of a detachment of the 79th from Castlebar to Ephlin in 1846:

> The following day we marched at daybreak and halted at the village of Frenchpark for breakfast. I allowed the men to fall out for half an hour and gained my first experience of the soldiers love for whisky. When the time had expired I found only two Sergeants present, but with their assistance we turned the men out of shops and public houses in about half an hour. They were nearly all drunk, they could hardly stand; the Sergeants advised an early start in any shape or form, and at length, singing, shouting and tumbling about, they staggered out of the village. I marched in rear looking ruefully at my charge, wondering what Major Ferguson would have said had he met us. Some dropped their bonnets and were too drunk to notice it; the Sergeants and myself were landed with lost property, and were obliged to call a few of the least drunk to our assistance. One man fell down and there was no getting him on his legs again so he had to be left with a Sergeant, who eventually hired a cart and brought him on. Fortunately heavy rain set in and it was astonishing how a good drenching brought them to their senses. This day's march was ever a lesson to me, and afterwards I never neglected any precautions to ensure sobriety.[48]

When dissatisfied with the strength, taste, quality or variety of canteen liquor, the hard drinkers tried to smuggle alcohol of any kind into barracks.[49] It is obvious that Lt. Colonel Duncan McDougall of the 79th in 1832 instituted a serious campaign against drunkenness, and orders issued by him in this respect include:

> . . . a non-commissioned officer will be constantly posted in the Canteen with rolls of the companies and will see that no man drinks more than two wine glasses of spirits or four tumblers of Beer or one glass of spirits and two tumblers of beer in the course of 24 hours.
>
> Quebec. 11.3.1835.
> As it appears that civilian children have been in the habit of bringing spirits into

> barracks, no boy or girl is allowed to enter without the sanction of the Commanding Officer.[50]

While these type of orders were common in Highland regiments, there is in addition strong evidence of condonation of the almost permanent 'happy', if not drunken state, in which many of the men existed, largely because of the social interrelationship between hospitality and alcohol, health and alcohol and manliness and alcohol.[51]

This condonation was evident when J.W. Wedderburn inspected a detachment of the 42nd on a winter's night in Halifax, Nova Scotia in 1851:

> Saw the Decht. but found one man drunk, as he was a very good character, I let him off and said nothing about it, I hope the big wigs won't find out I have done so, or I will catch it I guess.

And again at Gosport in 1853:

> Went the rounds at night . . . Sergt. Wilson was my Sergeant and was drunk and instead of returning to barracks he bolted, so I had to report the blockhead.[52]

Thus, it seems that Wedderburn might not have reported Sergeant Wilson had he not 'bolted', while Colonel Cuming of the 79th writes of officers going in search of drunken soldiers who were in danger of dying of frostbite and exposure in the long cold winters of Quebec:

> Often after Mess we put on our snow shoes and started off in search of men who were absent from Tattoo, and whose convivial habits led us to believe that they might be lost in the [snow] drifts.[53]

Condonation therefore went further than turning the occasional blind eye, and the beer supplied on the march, the free liquor supplied by the officers to the men when the former married, the drinking prior to embarkation, the celebrations at New Year and on St. Andrew's Day and the consumption of alcohol by the officers themselves, were all elements in a complex interrelationship between alcohol and regimental society and discipline. Boredom is often claimed as the cause of so much military drunkenness, but in the Highland regiments it was far from being the sole cause. Alcohol was part of these men's lives, the canteen was their social centre, drinking was a manly pursuit and the crimes related to alcohol consumption, providing they were kept within reasonable bounds, were, it seems, often tolerated and went unpunished.

The social attitudes of the men and society in general were a much more important factor in curbing and controlling drinking and drink-related offences than all the punishments and fines, but even social pressures appear to have been slow to take root in the Highland regiments, a branch of the Army Temperance Association not being formed in the 93rd for example until 1892.[54] Many men were genuinely averse to the 'evils' of drink and were total abstainers, but often abstention was the result of poverty not desire,[55] and temperance was a term open to wide interpretation. The evidence of Corporal Frank MacFarlane and Private Reginald Lobban shows that drinking was an essential part of regimental life before the First World War, but that this drinking was acceptable, and being able to take it was just as important as being able to drink it. Thus although the levels of consumption would be entirely unacceptable by modern standards, we cannot conclude that these soldiers were necessarily dissatisfied, protesting, or in any way lesser men as a result of what would now be labelled heavy drinking, and they certainly did not see themselves in this way.

It must be remembered however that the formal code of discipline was strict and the punishments were hard. Gradually, from 1820 the emphasis and nature of these punishments shifted: in 1829 corporal punishment was limited to 500 lashes at District and Garrison Courts Martial and 300 at Regimental Courts Martial. In 1833 these figures were further reduced to 300 and 200 respectively, together with restrictions on the offences punishable in this manner.[56] In 1840 desertion no longer entailed corporal punishment and in 1846 the total number of lashes which could be awarded by all Courts Martial was reduced to 50.[57] In 1867 such punishment was limited to mutiny and violence to superiors only and in 1868 was further restricted to troops on active service. Finally corporal punishment was abolished in 1881, while the death penalty was, and still is, retained in relation to certain offences on active service.[58]

One case of capital punishment is referred to by Private Lobban of the 1st Camerons in France in the winter of 1914/1915, and while he preferred that this memory should not be recorded on tape, he did relate that the man in question, a member of 1st Camerons, although a first-class soldier in the line, was generally not amenable to military discipline. According to Private Lobban this man wandered off while the Battalion was out of the front line and was apprehended while apparently returning. His execution caused deep unrest in the Battalion, who considered the incident a slight on the honour of the Camerons. Corporal MacFarlane of the 1st Black Watch, who was of course in the same Division, remembers the Cameron Highlander being shot, but emphasises that all Regular soldiers knew exactly what the penalties were for cowardice, neglect of duty or desertion in the face of the enemy:

> It was a Cameron Highlander who was shot poor chap . . . it was hard luck on the lad, we heard he had fallen asleep on outpost duty . . . the sentence was death . . . he was shot at about 8 o'clock of a morning at the back of a black tarred cow shed . . . the firing party, one of them belonging to Dundee, he went practically insane as a result of it.[59]

Civil prisons were used to house military prisoners until the building of military prisons in the 1840s. In Scotland there was a military prison at Greenlaw, just outside Edinburgh, which formerly housed French prisoners of war, now the Scottish Divisional Depot, Glencorse,[60] and later, at Stirling in a converted civil jail, which now stands in ruins.[61] In 1840 transportation to New South Wales ceased and was finally abolished altogether in 1857, resulting in further military prison building and extension wherever there were major British garrisons in the world.[62] Branding was abolished in 1871[63] and fines were introduced for drunkenness in 1868.[64]

The statistics of crime, trials and convictions relating to these punishments are however misleading; the definitions of some crimes changed and often these definitions were ambiguous, resulting in men not being charged. In addition, before 1830 many cases were dealt with summarily by Commanding Officers, but with the restriction of the summary powers of commanding officers, courts martial increased, a statistic that did not necessarily reflect an increase in crime.[65]

But formal punishments do not provide the whole picture; individual regiments established and put into practice a complex scale of minor punishments varying, in the 79th, from the 1st to the 4th degree, being: confinement to quarters, confinement to quarters with disgrace, confinement to the prison or black hole, and corporal punishment or solitary confinement.[66] In addition in 1819, Standing Orders of the 79th identified 'Private and Public' punishments:

> It is therefore directed, that for the punishment of crimes which do not come under a positive Article of War, or are not of very serious regimental nature, private company courts-martial are to be held, composed and regulated as follows. Sergeants or Corporals are not amenable before such court, but are in lieu subject to such reprimand and punishment as by their Captains may be enforced upon them, such as confinement to quarters, reprimand in private, or in front of the Company, or other such reprehension for neglect or irregularity. For the trial of Private Men and Drummers, a court will be composed of a Sergeant, as president, and four Privates who will judge the prisoner, and lay the proceedings in writing before the Captain, who is hereby authorised to carry such sentence into execution, reporting first to the Commanding Officer . . . All extra duties, confinement to barracks, turned coats, fines for the benefit of the messes, and cobbing, are permitted as punishments in private.[67]

The scale of imposition of the various punishments available was, particularly in the first half of the nineteenth century, very much at the discretion of the commanding officers, and this is clearly reflected in the 93rd who took pride in the absence of corporal punishment in the Regiment, although this pride was not applauded by their contemporaries by any means:

> The administration of the 93rd is no doubt unusually mild as Colonel McGregor disaffirms ploughing furrows in men's backs and there has been no corporal punishment in the Regiment for twelve years & his regime certainly answers for there is not a better behaved body of men in the British Army. Officers of other Corps who are a little jealous of the Sutherland Highlanders ask us tauntingly, 'Do you *flog* for selling necessaries?' and on being answered in the negative continue, 'then you've nothing to boast of. Every other Regiment in the service does and

because your Colonel chooses to let blackguards off who ought to be flogged, don't you go and say that your men are better than ours'. This doesn't strike me as sound reasoning . . . I think our Colonel is right.[68]

The twelve-year spell was broken in the 93rd in 1838; Colonel McGregor had left the Regiment, Colonel Spark had not yet arrived and Major Arthur was in command. It is clear that if McGregor had been in command the flogging would not have taken place:

Snow on both banks of the river—A Court Martial in the cabin, some unsubordination having showed itself the Major determined to try corporal punishment, rather unwise I think as his own uncertainty of temper is chiefly the cause of it; no flogging has taken place for twelve years on which the men very fairly pride themselves not a little . . . they eventually received their punishment on deck—a rather disagreeable day . . . a very erroneous one so far as the 93rd are concerned of the uncorruptableness of military discipline.[69]

The contemporary Private soldier's attitude to corporal punishment was complex. Many soldiers approved, knowing that it was the only way of keeping some of the wilder elements in control, safeguarding the orderly and well-disciplined soldier. Sergeant James McKay of the 74th wrote:

Many have spoken for or against this mode of punishment; but the mass of the British Army is composed of such different characters, that I think it necessary to resort to corporal punishment when the offence is great and must be visited with severe chastisement; but great should be the offence that such punishment is awarded for. Let it not be imagined, either by civil or military that the soldier who is flogged returns to his comrades, after the castigation, a dishonoured, disrespected, disreputable character. Not at all; if his moral conduct is of any worth whatever,—and many an upright soldier is flogged,—he returns to his comrades in the barrack room as an injured man, and is pitied, petted and forgiven.[70]

There is substantial evidence too of an entirely informal code of discipline, in the halfway house between discipline and condonation, entailing social rather than physical punishment. Private Donald Cameron of the 79th wrote in 1847:

. . . one day there was a Court Martial for to try some of us for misbehaving on the road the table was set covered with bed covers and one on the floor with one end going in below the table the other for the prisoner to stand on of course there was none of the prisoners in the room while this was preparing. the court then dressed themselves and got in their places the prisoner was sent for when he came he is placed on the end of the cover on the floor and stood there and another man watching the proceedings on the opposite side of the table from the prisoner and when found guilty which always happened but being the first offence there . . . would be a reprieve then he would have to drink the queen's health so there would be a canteen full of water give him so when he was in the act of drinking the man opposite gave a sharp pull to the cover that was under the prisoners feet and over he went on his back with the water about above him then a laugh all round and he was a brother in trouble.[71]

Highland regiments were also early in appreciating the benefits of incentives and praise in discipline, long before the general introduction of the inducements of medals and good conduct pay. Both the 79th and the 93rd instituted Regimental Orders of Merit,[72] with certificates and medals for the deserving men, and it is interesting that these Orders of Merit did not lapse but were specifically forbidden by the War Office, although men already in possession of the Regimental Badge were permitted to continue wearing it.[73] An example of a Certificate given by the 79th reads:

> To a deserving soldier as a token of Long, Faithful and Meritorious Service.
> The Bearer Sergeant WILLIAM BLACK of the 79th Highlanders, was admitted as a member of the First Class Order of Merit instituted in Her Majesty's 79th Highlanders, as a reward for Courage, Loyalty, Sobriety and General Good Conduct.
> Given under my hand and seal of the Regiment this 31st day of December 1837.
> Signed J.C. Young, Major, Commanding 79th Highlanders.[74]

As has already been illustrated, merit was also rewarded by special employment, exemption from parades and inspections, promotion, praise and encouragement, and discipline was by no means the oppressive spectre which many studies portray.

Running parallel to the formal and informal systems of discipline were the accepted forms of release and recreation. While the War Office and Horse Guards insisted on rules and regulations, the Army, at battalion level, appreciated the human factor, the necessity of what might now be called 'winding down' and the social interplay between Officers, Senior Ranks and Private Soldiers. Not all these recreations would be approved of today either socially or morally, but that does not mean to say that they were any less enjoyable, and it would be wrong to condemn certain pastimes, such as smoking, alcohol and promiscuity, without first appreciating how much they were valued and necessary.

Much recreation centred around drinking, but for the men this was of course subject to certain financial restrictions, and while drinking took place outside barracks, it was the canteen that was the attraction for many. The 2nd Battalion Argyll and Sutherland Highlanders' 'wet' canteen at Dalhousie, India in 1894 sold beer, stout and rum, but in order to encourage sobriety, drink was not served unless it was accompanied by food. The hours of opening were 12 noon to 12.45pm, 1.30 to 2 pm and 5.30 to 9.30pm. Men often drank in 'schools' who combined to save or borrow money for drinking or a 'spree', and when the money was finished the 'school' would 'go on the tack' to save for the next session. There appears to have been quite some formality in the system:

> Presently in comes a "school", and after all are seated comfortably round a table, the quart pot passes steadily to and fro for the first hour or so when probably an interruption takes place in the shape of an adjournment for supper, or the "useful man", (there is always a useful man in all schools), goes and fetches sandwiches

round, after which the beer travels faster and faster, the voices become louder and louder, and presently one of the school obliges with a song, which is the signal for a general outbreak of all the budding Sims Reeves. Before closing time there is generally a fight or two, simply to relieve the monotony, and if the belligerents become too noisy or unruly the magic words "four of the picquet" usually lulls the storm . . .[75]

Officers drank in their Mess Room or Quarters, but it was common in Highland regiments, especially at New Year, for all ranks to celebrate, sometimes in each others' Messes, and sometimes all together, an action that was not always understood by other regiments. James Mc Kay of the 74th writes of the Highland celebration of New Year in the Regiment:

> New Years Day was a great festival day in the 74th under [Lt. Colonel Jock] Fordyce. He was an Officer who never indulged in wine at Mess, and was strictly temperate; but on New Years Day the whole Regiment was allowed great liberties and the Colonel also indulged himself and was the most jocular man in the Corps on that day. At night the various companies had singing, dancing and feasting and when the last hour of the old year tolled every man that could blow or beat on a musical instrument had to turn out and join a band at midnight in the square and as soon as the hour had done tolling, the whole struck up the Scottish air, "Here's to the Year that's awa!"[76]

A Colonel of the Buffs observing this scene was heard to remark, ' . . . that Regiment is mad . . .'[77]

Mad they may have been, but the important social and emotional release was a realistic and practical ingredient of Highland regimental life, and while certain officers may have been aloof, distant, strict or disapproving, it was impossible to stand on ceremony when playing pipes on a table being carried round the square of Cairo Citadel Barracks, as Spencer Ewart of the 79th found out:

> As I was escaping from the Citadel I was collared by an inebriated crowd of men of the 75th and was carried on a table round the barrack square. I was also asked to play a tune on the pipes on the table . . . asked for a speech and given some whisky to drink . . .[78]

These occasions may well have been contrary to all the rules of discipline, but they represented the very essence of the spirit of Highland regiments. Here was discipline that permitted legitimate release without loss of respect on either side, a vital but intangible quality now accepted as one of the keystones of morale. This quality in the Highland battalions was to survive even the rigours and trials of the First World War, and to understand it is to appreciate the comradeship that can only exist in the special relationship that men acquire from dangers shared.

At Waldorf, Germany on 31st December 1919 the remnants of the 1st Battalion Queen's Own Cameron Highlanders held their traditional New Year Party. Alistair Jameson wrote:

> We were having a joint dinner with D Coy. on Hogmanay and we asked the CO, 2nd I/C and the Adjutant. We had a most successful dinner and cleared the rooms afterwards when we danced reels until 10 minutes to 12 when we made the Pipe Major play us all up to the big Recreation Hall where the Canteen is and the Battalion was assembled. The CO got a *tremendous* reception and after "Auld Lang Syne" and the usual wishing of Happy New Year, the whole Battalion danced reels until 1.15am. If you got on the platform where the Band was you saw a Foursome composed of the CO and one of the Hd. Quarter Runners and the 2nd I/C and the Drum Major, and the same all over the Hall; Officers, NCOs and Men dancing together, we even danced two-steps and waltzes . . . On New Years Day all the Company Officers dined with their Companies at 4pm, the CO came round them all of course.[79]

The system of Messes also provided circumstances of relaxation and entertainment, which recognised, supported and gave status to rank. It also solved the practical problems of how the members were going to feed themselves, and provided a place where the officers in particular paid for and maintained the necessary furniture, crockery and cutlery to sustain basic comfort. Accounts, records and illustrations would suggest that Officers' Messes in the years to the 1860s were not elaborate affairs in Highland battalions,[80] but were functional establishments where Officers and Sergeants could eat, drink and relax in the company of equals, while at the same time membership, particularly of the Sergeants' Mess, bestowed and required dignity and respectability, great pride being taken in the privilege of belonging.[81]

A further controversial aspect of recreation and release involved women and sexual relations, and while it may now offend present-day feminist principles, it would appear that the nineteenth and early twentieth-century Highland soldier held particular and strong views about women that would now stray even into the realms of illegality.

There seem to have been three categories of the female sex, Mothers, Ladies and Women. The first was respected primarily on religious grounds, the second every man hoped to marry, or was merely admired from a distance by the less fortunate, and the third a soldier hoped to marry if she was 'respectable', or had sexual relations with if she was not. In general Scots men retained and still do retain (that is not a critisism) a much more dominant role, and soldiers, when permitted, married on practical grounds, and the implication was that the woman was very fortunate to be chosen and even more fortunate to be included in the regimental family. Standing Orders of the 2nd Battalion Seaforth Highlanders of 1884 record:

> Every man is responsible for the conduct of his wife. If he is unable to control her he must suffer for his weakness.[82]

Private John Tulloch of the 74th wrote in 1852:

> I intend to save up money and get a wife and won [sic] that can work and get her into barracks and i think we may be happy enough together.

Remaining a bachelor, he wrote again in 1859:

> I was acquaint with a young woman . . . but I never thought of getting tied to her, of course I was a Sergeant at that time, and a Sergeant can get a wife whenever he wants one, the young girls are very parshal to Sergeants . . .[83]

Highland soldiers held Ladies and 'respectable' women in high regard, and were deeply respectful and protective. Every soldier who could, visited the locations where the women were massacred at Cawnpore, experiencing a deep personal desire for retribution. Private McIntosh was however quick to realise that European women in India were not demonstratively appreciative of the Private soldier:

> European women in this country are very saucy in general, I suppose they think they are made of superior clay to the soldier, they pass you with a disdainful toss of the head and their nose turned up in the air; if they deign to look at you their look is one of scorn.[84]

In Ireland in the 1820s it was common for the soldiers to employ girls as barrack maids, there is no indication that these girls were the subject of sexual abuse by the soldiers, and in fact they seem to have been respected and received with simple kindness and generosity. James Anton of the 42nd records:

> . . . it is now customary in some places in Ireland, to have in each room a servant girl, designated a barrack maid . . . Indeed the poor girls have no other means of employment. Here they assist the soldiers wives to wash and dress and keep the rooms clean; for this they generally receive about one shilling a week, and the scraps that otherwise would be thrown to the ash pit become their perquisite; . . . A girl has in addition to her wages, a mess the same as a soldier; and this being more than sufficient to serve an abstemious person, is partly, with any surplus that may be left, taken to her parents.[85]

The limitations on the numbers of married men, and in certain cases a preference for independence, meant that many men took their recreation in casual sexual relations with women, and paying scant attention to cleanliness, precautions or the known dangers, they contracted venereal diseases which are consistently recorded as 'prevalent diseases' in Highland Battalion Inspection Reports and Returns.[86]

In garrison towns many women made their livelihood from this trade and the temptations open to the soldier both at home, and more especially in India, were considerable.[87] In spite of the pressure of Victorian reformers, the work of those anxious to secure the morals of the women concerned and of those wishing to stop the loss of men to the service, the soldiers, and in some cases the officers too, took their pleasures where they could find them. Contracting venereal disease may well have been regarded privately as a symbol of manhood, although many men appear to have hidden the disease from the medical authorities, or attempted a barrack-room cure which usually aggravated rather than remedied the condition and resulted in regular medical inspections.[88]

If a man was serious in his intentions towards a member of the opposite sex and determined upon a long-term relationship, courtship was, in the Victorian era, an elaborate ritual, details of which a man would often decline to record even in his own private diary. Wedderburn's courtship appears to have begun before 1852; he does not refer to the girl by name and when he does mention 'Miss Whaite' in 1852, a Christian name or pet name is never used. When their formal courtship commenced in 1852 Margaret Whaite was 15 years old and Wedderburn 28; their relationship was, it seems, strictly formal, comprising escorted walks, musical evenings at Quarter Master Paton's house, and singing and recitations. At Weedon in 1853 Wedderburn asked her to marry him:

> Took a long walk with Miss Whaite and told her at last my long kept secret and she is now no longer Miss Whaite but my own wee wifie to be, Thank God and I am so happy.[89]

Many NCOs and Private soldiers had equally formal relationships with women, seldom publicised amongst the welter of evidence concerning promiscuity. John Grant, the Paymaster's Clerk of the 42nd, became engaged to Margaret Wilson in 1834 and they maintained a regular, formal and touching correspondence until they were married in 1854.[90] Much formality was, it seems, maintained even in marriage, and in corresponding with his wife in Edinburgh from the Crimea in 1855, Pipe Major Richard Steuart of the 79th commenced his letter, 'My Dear Wife', ending:

> . . . therefore I will conclude dear wife by remaining your affectionate husband till death . . .
> Richd. Steuart
> Pipe Major 79th.[91]

The acquisition of a wife in India, where the number of women was small and wives and children succumbed to disease and the climate, was in some cases virtually a business transaction, often involving very young girls and older soldiers. The high mortality rate amongst adults resulted in many orphan children; the boys were trained to a trade or the Army while the girls awaited marriage or employment as servants. Private A.W. McIntosh of the 42nd records at Agra:

> In connection to the Cathederal there is a school for boys and girls, they are very well looked after, the boys on arriving at a certain age I think 16 are sent to situations and the girls are married, there are several Protestant schools of this sort in the country, but I don't think much of the girls for wives.[92]

Many men not only married girls of 15 and 16, much younger than themselves, but also married 'daughters of the Regiment' as a result of the regulations in force. Adult female children were not permitted to reside in barracks after 15 unless employed as servants or pupil schoolmistresses, and parents anxious to secure their daughter's future and keep her in the regimental family were only too happy to sanction a suitable marriage, although the girl might be young by modern Western standards.[93]

Many men were attracted in their leisure hours by Indian beauty, and while there were brothels, some of which were subject to regimental medical inspection, some men very naturally fell genuinely in love with Indian or Anglo-Indian girls. It would appear that racial intermarriage prior to the Mutiny was socially acceptable for all ranks,[94] but when Privates William Smith and Martin Fahey of the 91st wished to marry Anglo-Indian girls in 1865, Colonel Bertie Gordon required to see and approve the girls first.[95] It is obvious that some men remained in India, transferring from regiment to regiment or buying their discharges, after they had married Indian girls, realising the magnitude of later Victorian social pressures in respect of inter-racial marriage.

There were occasions when men obviously preferred the company of other men to women. It was entirely natural that in an essentially male environment men should turn to one another for companionship, and homosexuality in the Highland regiments was not uncommon.[96] Equality and integration of the sexes being virtually unheard of, men specifically excluded women from certain activities, and in Gibraltar in 1882 Spencer Ewart of the 79th records Lt. Colonel Jock Leith's fondness for what were termed 'Bull picnics' when a 'men only' party set off across the Spanish border for a day's relaxation of eating, drinking, talking and smoking in the countryside.[97]

The Highland soldier's attitute to and relationship with women in his leisure hours was thus complex and intricate and was not necessarily a matter solely of vice and promiscuity. In the masculine world in which these men lived, ladies were respected, but women in general were by no means equal, and were treated accordingly.

Drink, women, courtship and marriage aside, the leisure hours available to the soldier could be filled with an infinite variety of activities. Until the 1840s much of that spare time, of which there appears to have been surprisingly little, was occupied largely at the soldier's own discretion on the principle that supervision was interference. As the nineteenth century progressed, religious, philanthropic and social reformers variously turned their attention to the Army, in some case deciding what was good for the soldier rather than determining what the soldier wanted. Highland soldiers loved to occupy their leisure hours with the things that soldiers had practised for centuries, alcohol, women, gambling,[98] dogfights, cockfights etc.,[99] and many reformers fought uphill battles against traditional attitudes; but while they drank hard and freely associated with women, many Highland soldiers were conservative, traditional, nationally proud and well behaved. Music was part of their culture and playing, singing[100] and dancing came naturally as manly pastimes which did not require enforcement. In addition physical sports as feats of strength, skill and endurance such as quoits, shinty, races, putting the shot and curling[101] were a feature of Highland society, which were in the nineteenth century formalised in Highland Games and from which organised games, tug of war, cricket, fives[102] and football followed naturally. With the growing acknowledgement of the benefits of regular physical exercise for both the individual and the Army,[103] men increasingly began to fill both their leisure hours and some of their working hours with sport. Football was to become a passion in the 1880s and 1890s in the Highland regiments and many men later to be professionals began their playing career in Highland battalion teams.

For the less energetic leisure hours Highland solidiers indulged in an infinite variety of legitimate relaxations such as walking out, visiting places of interest or simply promenading, keeping pets, dogs, monkeys, parrots and caged birds, photography, theatricals, plays, skits and recitals,[104] gardening, knitting, sewing, woodwork and collecting and mounting butterflies.[105]

Entrenched views on education, reading and the possession of books were, in the Highland regiments, difficult to overcome and Lt. Colonel Wheately of the 42nd, then a Private Soldier, records of the Regiment before 1820:

> Neither books nor newspapers were ever seen in a Barrack room. A very few men might at times be seen reading their Bible, but it would hardly do to record the almost general opinion regarding them . . .[106]

In 1828 a regimental library was commenced in the 42nd[107] and several other Highland regiments assembled small library collections, but the very nature of Highland regimental duties militated against carrying collections of books about with the battalions, although the 42nd collection was not sold until 1854.

Men like Archibald McIntosh of the 42nd,[108] George Greig of the 93rd,[109] and Bandsman Barwood of the Black Watch[110] carefully kept diaries, while others occupied their leisure hours in drawing and skilfully colouring portraits of their comrades which they sold for a few pence.[111] Some men wrote letters or dictated to their more able comrades, while others such as Private Greig of the 93rd composed, recorded and adapted poetry and songs.[112] Many men simply enjoyed sitting talking, smoking[113] and story telling, and much of this acted as an initiation for younger soldiers who listened to the tales of their older comrades of real or imagined adventures in distant lands.

An interesting development of the later nineteenth century is the growth of regimental magazines, initiated often by the men themselves as well as the officers and used as a medium of information, entertainment and comment.[114] These men also followed the Victorian fashion of clubs and societies, and in the Highland regiments there were reel clubs, quadrille clubs, cycling clubs, watch clubs[115] and temperance lodges,[116] and the ultimate extension of these societies were the regimental associations formed from serving and retired members of the Highland battalions as friendly societies for social, welfare and employment purposes.

Often the accepted forms of release and recreation in the Highland Regiments involved both officers and men; both partook, apparently without awkwardness, in football, cricket, rowing, dancing, smoking concerts and theatricals. Contrary to the popular idea, many officers were avid readers,[117] while others were accomplished ornithologists and taxidermists,[118] fishermen, shots,[119] polo players, huntsmen[120] and artists. Officers' journals are often beautifully illustrated with sketches, watercolours and illustrations, the most notable of which are those of Colonel A.D. Greenhill Gardyne of the 1st Battalion Gordon Highlanders and those of Brigadier General Henry Robert Kelham of the 74th, whose remarkable journal was sadly destroyed in a fire in the Royal Highland Fusiliers Museum in 1985.

A further accepted form of release was religion, although this was in many cases closely scrutinised and subject to military control. The nineteenth and early twentieth centuries were an age in which although a man might not practise religion, there appears to have been a general belief in Divine Providence and the will of God, a blanket umbrella which could explain misfortune, disease and accident. It was also an age of considerable prejudice, particularly against Roman Catholics. Until 1827 officers were required to take the Oath of Supremacy and Allegiance and receive the sacrament within three months of appointment under the Test Act of 1672.[121] The holding of Mass was not sanctioned in barracks until 1845,[122] and even Presbyterian ministers were not officially admitted to barracks until 1839,[123] although Presbyterian soldiers were no longer compelled to attend Church of England services after 1822.[124] Catholic soldiers' children at the Duke of York's School and the Royal Hibernian School, Dublin, were sent there to preserve them from

> . . . Popery, Beggary and Idleness, and to train them so as to become useful, industrious Protestant subjects.[125]

In the 42nd, 72nd, 78th, 79th, 92nd and 93rd, although the figures are incomplete, there appear to have been low numbers of Catholic soldiers,[126] and the Church of Scotland was the primary faith professed. In Scotland Scottish soldiers were served by Presbyterian chaplains, but abroad these men were rare and Highland regiments, who also had the Gaelic language to consider, either hired and paid their own chaplains, attended Presbyterian civilian churches or established their own Presbyterian or Episcopal congregations, purchasing Regimental Communion Plate.[127]

As a result of the pressure of volunteers and sheer necessity, Presbyterian Army Chaplains were finally permitted on the Army List as 'Assistant Officiating Presbyterian Chaplains' at the time of the Crimean War.[128]

The major upset in Highland battalion religious life was the Disruption of 1843 and the formation of the Free Church of Scotland. From the difficulties in the Highland regiments which resulted from this it is clear that a high proportion of Highland soldiers were active religious participants and were also aware of the religious and political implications. The 93rd were in Canada at the time of the Disruption where, despite the efforts of Lt. Colonel Robert Spark, the Commanding Officer, who was strongly anti-Free Church, half the men of the Regiment joined the breakaway movement. Spark, according to J.S. Ewart, actively issued threats to men joining the Free Kirk and refused to promote William McBean, then an NCO, to Colour Sergeant on the grounds that he was a 'Free Kirker'.[129] Surgeon Munro of the 93rd also refers to 'the injudicious interference with religious feelings' which reflected upon the discipline of the 93rd which led to 'Restlessness, irritability, a tendency to drunkenness and an inclination to offer resistance to authority'.[130]

In the 79th Lauderdale Maule was placed in a particularly difficult position because his brother Fox was a strong supporter of the Free Church. 'Excuse me', he wrote to Fox in 1845, 'but I fear the Free Kirk will be a mill-stone round your neck.'[131] It would appear that Lauderdale himself covertly supported the movement, and he was certainly concerned at the lack of recognition of Presbyterian ministers by the War Office:

> . . . my Parson, a most excellent, simple and single minded specimine of our Kirk and, (but that I would not allow him to sport his opinions to the men) of the Free Kirk . . . He has been most unjustly treated by Mr S. Herbert, your predecessor . . . this poor man has done more than all the other Parsons put together . . . The position of the Presbyterians here (in Gibraltar) is a disgrace to the Government. The national religions of England and Ireland are both represented here by paid Chaplins and we . . . have not a place to worship in.[132]

According to Surgeon Munro, when the 93rd returned from Canada, an attempt was made to force the men who had joined the Free Church to attend Church of Scotland services. They refused, and after the matter had been referred to Horse Guards a decision was given in favour of the men,[133] but this would appear to have been a rare concession as generally there was a considerable lack of flexibility and understanding by the authorities in respect of religious matters and particularly regarding the depth and strength of Scottish and Highland religious opinion, which entailed a strong commitment to Presbyterianism, while certain areas, especially pockets in the Highlands and Islands, were equally committed to Catholicism. In 1825, for example, Bibles and Books of Common Prayer were compulsorily issued to soldiers in Highland regiments, but it appears that only the 92nd had the courage to return the Books of Common Prayer, stating bluntly 'The Books of Common Prayer are not used by men of the Church of Scotland'.[134]

In religion many Highland soldiers and their wives found strength, comfort and solace, but it must also be remembered that their beliefs were the subject of compulsion. Attendance at Church on Sundays was a parade, not only for the officers and men, but also for the women and children, when rolls were carefully returned and censure for absence was administered accordingly:

> . . . all the married soldiers of the Presbyterian persuasion will cause those of their children who are over six years of age to assemble (in fine weather) in the Infant school room at ½ past 8 o'clock on Sunday morning for the purpose of being marched to church by one of the School Assistants.[135]

> The Commanding officer expects that the families of married men will regularly attend Divine Service with the Regiment. A place will be set apart for them and a married non commissioned officer will be warned to march the children to church.[136]

While worship was compulsory, it was a release, although excessive commitment seems to have been viewed with suspicion. Spencer Ewart records:

> A man of the 79th tried to commit suicide; he was one of the religious clique in the Regt.[137]

Thus the system of release and recreation was recognised and in many ways structured. Much of what a soldier did with his spare time was entirely at his own discretion, many used it wisely, some did not, but it must be recognised that the soldiers themselves in Highland battalions were subject to strong social pressures from their contemporaries, and until these attitudes changed it was difficult for the well-intentioned, industrious man to come to the fore. Many men resisted the now accepted idea of making 'productive' use of their spare time on the principle that having done their duty, they were entitled to drink, gamble and associate with women, but considerable efforts were made in the Highland regiments to encourage respectability and 'suitable' leisure activities some of which involved both officers and men, and music, reading, games and religion were by no means neglected.

A final and more elusive aspect of release and recreation is the question of comment and the expression of complaints. It is too often assumed that nineteenth and early twentieth-century soldiers were an oppressed, browbeaten mass, who laboured under duress, unable and afraid to comment on their situation. While there must indeed have been instances in Highland regiments where both officers and men were unjustly treated and were unnecessarily neglected and uncared for, it would appear that they did not pass without comment in one form or another.[138] Often this comment took subtle forms such as Wedderburn's note of the men of the 42nd 'bleating like sheep for fun',[139] when they were put on board open railway trucks at Chobham, or Sergeant George Millar's record of the 71st (HLI) waiting on the dockside at Tilbury after disembarkation from India, when the Battalion stood about for some time, and groups of men began whistling:

> The unmistakeable notes of impatience rang out, the sharp trill of, 'I care for nobody, no not I', 'This is no' my ain Hoose, I ken by the biggin' o't' and 'Tam, hoo lang are we tae bide in this hole' . . .[140]

When made to drill in the hot season, or when forced to attend a church not of their choice, the men of the 93rd clearly expressed their views,[141] and following the First World War, when attempts were made to draft men of the Gordon Highlanders, without their consent, to the Cameron Highlanders for service in India, they refused and set out from Invergordon to march to Aberdeen in protest.[142]

Comment also appeared in subtle forms in regimental magazines, under the heading in the *79th News* for instance of 'Things the folks are saying', or in general articles and editorials.[143] There were in addition channels of formal complaint including for example the Petition of 1846 by 'The Sergeants of the British Army'[144] regarding their loss of benefits as a result of the Good Conduct Warrant of 1845, and it is clear that Highland soldiers addressed their officers with their grievances and problems, that they were listened to and that the efforts of caring officers were appreciated.

On leaving the 42nd on 9th January 1854 at Gosport, J.W. Wedderburn recorded in his diary:

> Bade adieu to everyone and to my Company with great regret, they handed me in a letter which I shall keep and prize . . . as long as I live.[145]

The letter, carefully composed and equally carefully written on Orderly Room paper read:

Haslar Barracks,
Gosport, 6th January 1854.

Sir,

We presume to address you upon a subject which we are almost certain will give you no offence, because the motives that induce us to do so are those of gratitude and respect engendered by a strong desire of letting that gratitude and respect be known.

The circumstances of an Officer leaving the Service, or of a Captain leaving his Company, is certainly an almost monthly occurrence; and many go indeed unregretted, while some carry along with them, not only the esteem but also the affections of all who have ever served under them. That you, Sir, are one of the latter "few" these lines are to bear witness. The civility, the attention, and the kindness which we have experienced from your hands, have, if equaled, never been surpassed by any Captain of any Regiment serving our beloved land. We truly part with you with every demonstration of the most poignant regret and heart felt sorrow!

In leaving us you carry with you our gratitude, our respect and our love which are all the offerings we can give to one who really deserves more. But "Time" will give and recall many years ere *your* name be forgotten amongst us; and as time rolls on, and memory recalls you to our recollections you shall be thought of and spoken of only but with undying respect, not only by the men of the Company which you now leave, but by the men of the 42nd Regiment in general.

Hoping that true happiness, the real aim of our being, shall ever attend you, we have the honour to remain,
Sir,
Your obedient humble servants,
the Non-Commissioned Officers and men of
No 4 Company, of her Majesty's 42nd Royal
Highlanders.[146]

The final aspect of regimental life to be considered is the 'Regimental Family'. It is important to understand that belonging to a Highland regiment was not simply the equivalent of belonging to a club; the implications were, and still are, far greater than that, but viewed by the outsider, the patronage, closeness, obligations and benefits of the members may well seem introverted, petty, patronising and parochial, resulting in considerable misunderstanding, if not jealousy. As in any family the members were not always happy, they did not always get on, they had their black sheep and they did not consistently agree with the head of the family; but belonging held them together in spite of internal difficulties. The result was an unusual and complex system of discipline, interrelationship, obligation, social pressure and welfare, which particularly benefited the long-serving or well-conducted Highland soldier, placing heavy financial pressures upon officers and requiring them to have influence and patronage at their disposal.

An unknown but substantial proportion of Highland soldiers were born into a family already in the Regiment. Their fathers either obtained permission to marry and have a wife 'on the strength',[147] or supported their wives and families, with no little difficulty, 'off the strength' until a vacancy occurred. The child and its mother were the subject of strict control, and it is clear in many cases that this was entirely justified as many of these women were tough to say the least, smoking, drinking and swearing with the best. Standing Orders of the 79th of 1835 noted:

> As the Commanding Officer insists on the soldiers treating the women of the Regiment with the respectful deference which is due from men to the female sex, the men shall have the right to expect that the women will contribute towards the happiness of their husbands and the private comfort of their husbands brother soldiers.[148]

The wives of soldiers washed, cleaned and cooked for the men for a small income and they also sewed, mended and made up shirts. The wives of sergeants washed for the officers,[149] and the wives of officers[150] took an active interest in the welfare and education of NCOs and soldiers' wives and children, holding sewing classes and infant schools. J.S. Ewart's wife and Mrs. Bertie Gordon are included amongst these, and Ewart records, while commanding the 78th in 1868:

> It was the custom of my wife whilst at Aldershot and afterwards at Shorncliffe and

> Dover to hold what she termed "Mothers meetings"; her object in doing so was to instill habits of industry and forethought into the minds of the soldiers wives. At these meetings each woman attended with her work-basket and materials . . . [and] . . . my wife explained to all who required assistance . . . the method of cutting out and making children's clothes.[151]

The wives and children on the strength received free medical benefits, but their housing, protection, feeding and privileges were subject to military discipline, and when they misbehaved they were put out of barracks or fined, and their married quarters were subject to regular inspection. While the men of the 72nd were fighting in Kandahar, Afghanistan in 1880 Regimental Orders recorded:

> The following fines of women at the Depot . . .
> (in India) are published for information.
> Mrs Monaghan wife of Pte. C. Monaghan 8Rs.
> Mrs Hutton wife of Pte. R. Hutton 8Rs
> Mrs Wilson wife of Sgt. T. Wilson 4Rs.
> Mrs Butter wife of Pte. P. Butter 16Rs.
> Mrs Wilson wife of Sgt. T. Wilson 4Rs.
> Mrs Hutton wife Pte. R. Hutton 4Rs.[152]

The children too were strictly regimented from an early age; Spencer Ewart recalls as a child of four embarking with the 78th for Ireland in 1864:

> . . . the Regiment embarked for Ireland on board HMS Himalaya I can just remember this voyage, having some faint and distant recollection of being placed on sentry over a pig to keep me out of mischief.[153]

The children were marched to school and church under a soldier and were often clothed in a uniform of the regimental tartan. Much of the cloth for these children's uniforms was supplied by William Wilsons of Bannockburn. In 1829 Quarter Master Sergeant Miller of the 78th Depot at Edinburgh wrote to Wilsons requesting regimental tartan for 'girls frocks' and 'boys kilts' with Rob Roy tartan for the boys' hose and Blue Bonnets also for the boys,[154] and a similar request was also made by the Quarter Master of the 78th in 1861:

> Gentlemen,
> Mrs Ewart (the Colonel's Lady) is desirous of purchasing some soft Mackenzie Tartan of a description suitable for clothing the children of the Regiment—the boys in kilts and the girls in frocks . . .[155]

The women and children were thus assimilated at an early age into the family within a family, the women being important contributors to the day-to-day work of the Regiment and the children often joining the service, becoming servants in regimental households, pupil schoolmistresses or wives in their turn.

The regimental children were in addition the subject of patronage; Lauderdale Maule of the 79th wrote to his brother Fox from Gibraltar in 1847:

> I have a poor deaf and dumb boy, son of a Private Soldier in the Regiment whom I am anxious to get into some charitable establishment for teaching these unfortunates. Can you help me. I'll send him home free of expense and deliver him anywhere. I enclose a description return. The boy is a good boy and has already learnt [some]thing in our Regtl. School.[156]

But it was the men, particularly the long-serving soldiers, who benefited from the system of the regimental family and patronage. Letters and diaries of Highland officers, especially the more complete collections such as those of Lauderdale Maule, show the wide extent of his patronage, and where an officer had good connections, as Maule indeed had, this patronage worked not only for the regiment as a whole, but also for its less well-connected members, be they Officers, Sergeants or Private men. It was not without good reason therefore that Maule celebrated the elevation of his brother to the post of Secretary of State for War:

> Allah al Allah! the Secretary of State for War is great and the Lieut. Colonel of the 79th is his brother! . . . —Adieu—May your shadow never diminish![157]

For the soldier and his family the Highland regimental family extended beyond the limitations of service. Many hundreds of men may have left the Highland battalions aggrieved, disgruntled, unhappy, unsupported and unprepared for civilian life, but at the same time there is strong evidence to suggest that in many cases it was the system and the general regulations they protested against and not their battalions. Thus veterans gathered, met and visited their old regiments towards which they felt strong affection, an affection which knew no bounds of rank.

On 25th June 1857 the 79th marched to Hyde Park for the Review by the Queen and the presentation of the first Victoria Crosses. Present were many Chelsea Pensioners who had served in the Regiment in the Peninsula and at Waterloo:

> . . . spontaneously and unexpectedly [they] walked or hobbled across the ground to where the Regiment was drawn up. Halting in front of the Colour Party, they knelt down and seized the hem of the Regimental Colour, each Veteran solemnly kissed it after which they all returned to their places.[158]

Thus while Highland soldiers may have been rough and tough, they were equally unafraid of displaying their emotions, and from their feelings of attachment grew the annual gatherings, dinners and the Regimental Associations, with their clubs and branches all over the United Kingdom and the British Empire. Meetings of these Associations were originally formal and military in nature, and when the 74th Regimental Association met in Glasgow in 1894, for example, the members gathered and '. . . the roll was then called and as usual each member answered his name by giving his regimental number of the old corps'.[159]

These Associations reflecting the Highland regimental family not only provided vital financial benefits, but also acted as employment exchanges putting members in contact with employers or giving references where required.[160] Certain jobs came to be specifically reserved for deserving ex-servicemen, and included in these were the jobs for servitors of the Scottish universities.[161]

Employment was also found through the Corps of Commissionaires, founded in 1854 by Captain Sir Edward Walter KCB, of the 8th Hussars,[162] The Railway Companies, the Post Office, the Castle Guides at Edinburgh Castle and the County Police Forces.

It is clear however that there were problems with the employment of ex-servicemen, particularly in relation to drink, and that their employment record was not good. A study of the records of the Corps of Commissionaires for Edinburgh and the East of Scotland shows that of the 504 admissions to the Corps between 1882 and 1920, 223 men were from Highland regiments, priority being given to officers' servants, tradesmen, musicians and men with wives who were prepared to be employed as cleaners and washerwomen. A number of these men were dismissed for drunkenness, but equally many left, obviously finding great difficulty in settling and re-adjusting to civilian conditions, even within the Corps.[163] The records of Dundee Burgh Police also show that a high number of former Highland soldiers enlisted, but again their employment record was not good and many ex-servicemen in the force were disciplined, fined or dismissed for being 'the worse of liquor'.[164]

Clearly Highland solders required additional support in employment, and this they often received through the regimental family and patronage. It became the practice for many ex-soldiers to meet in their club rooms or in specific public houses in Scottish cities and obtain jobs particularly in the building trade,[165] while officers and employers applied to the Regimental Associations for men wanting work.

The Highland regiments too were keenly aware of their ex-members who were too old and infirm to look after themselves, or the orphans of men who were killed, and they contributed heavily in funds to found the Scottish Naval and Military Veterans Residence, Whiteford House, Edinburgh in 1910 and the Queen Victoria School, Dunblane in 1902.

Thus Highland regimental life comprised a complex interplay of duty, music, discipline, release and recreation, obligations and support which centred around the Regimental Family, an entity whose influence remained, even after retirement. The family imposed duties and rules, but it also provided tangible assistance, and pride in belonging was a real and unashamed emotion for its participants.

NOTES

1. Diary of General Sir Spencer Ewart, 79th, RH/4/84/1, 18.2.1882.
2. Diary of A.D. Greenhill Gardyne 75th, RH/4/59/1-8 1891.
3. *HLI Chronicle,* No. 9, January 1895, p. 344.
4. Standing Orders of the 79th Highlanders 1819, QOHRM 142a/79 p. 82.
5. Standing Orders of the 2nd Battalion Seaforth Highlanders 1884, p. 47.
6. Diary and papers of Private H. Ogilvie 1st Battalion Black Watch, BWRM. Private Ogilvie was the soldier servant of Captain Urquhart and Victor Fortune.
7. It is interesting that at the end of the First World War His Majesty the King insisted that the Colours of the Regiments, including the Highland Regiments, be escorted out to France and Belgium and that they be carried as the Regiments marched across the German border. Both Corporal MacFarlane and Private Lobban speak with emotion of the return of their Colours and the remarkable sight of the gleaming 1st Division, with Artillery, Cavalry and Infantry crossing the frontier.
8. Letters of John Tulloch, 74th, *op. cit.*, 23.10.1855.
9. 91st Commanding Officers Rough Order Book. Kamptee India. ASHRM R/16 1860.
10. J. Murray Kendall MBE, FSA, 'The Lancespessade and the History of 'Lance' Rank.' *Journal of the Society for Army Historical Research*, Vol.5/6 1926/1927, pp.81-86.
11. Letters of Lt. Colonel the Hon. Lauderdale Maule 79th, GD/45/14/634/4 1-98 Gibraltar 21.3.1847.
12. Letters of John Tulloch, 74th, *op. cit.*, 28.9.1857.
13. 91st (1st Battalion Argyll and Sutherland Highlanders) Permanent Order Book, ASHRM Sb 18/16, 26.8.1865.
14. Standing Orders of the 42nd 1833. BWRM 255.51 (42), p. 33.
15. 42nd Order Book. BWRM 27/2270. Dover 17.4.1857.
16. 91st Commanding Officers Rough Order Book, Kamptee. ASHRM R/16. 10.9.1860.
17. Letters of Lt. Colonel the Hon. Lauderdale Maule, 79th, GD/45/14/634/3 1-84 Gibraltar 12.12.1846.
18. 91st Commanding Officers Rough Order Book, Kamptee. ASHRM R/16 11.6.1860. 'The Regimental School will reopen after a cessation of two years duration...'
19. Corporal Frank MacFarlane and Private Reginald Lobban. An oral history archive op. cit.
20. For example Hospital Sergeant Robert Jameson 79th: 'I am about to push for an Ensigncy and Quartermastership for my Hospital Sergeant Jameson, in which I shall by next mail request your aid—He is a very good and worthy man'. Letters of Lt. Colonel the Hon. Lauderdale Maule. GD/45/14/634/5 1-56 Quebec 1.2.1849.
21. For example Canteen Sergeant James Knight of the 79th. Knight enlisted in 1854 and served in the Crimea and India; he became Canteen Steward on 16th February 1875, finally leaving the Regiment in 1885. See 'Men who made the 79th', *79th News,* Vol. 2, No. 18, 1895, p.3.
22. Surgeon William Munro, *Reminiscences of Military Service with the 93rd Highlanders, op. cit.,* p. 198.
23. Journal of Lt. Andrew Agnew 93rd, GD/154/781, 1838.
24. For a history of Military Law together with details of offences and punishments, see *Manual of Military Law* (London: HMSO, 1914).
25. Lt. Colonel L. Maule 79th, GD/45/8/96 Memorandum on Habitual Drunkenness c.1851 and Captain R.W. Bennett, 'Military Law in 1839', *Journal of the Society for Army Historical Research,* Vol. XLVIII No. 196 Winter 1970, pp. 225-241.
26. Register of Deserters 92nd Regiment, 1831-1851, GHRM.
27. Diary of Lt. William Parke, 72nd. QOHRM.
28. Journal of Lt. Andrew Agnew of Lochnaw, 93rd. GD/154/781. 1838.
29. Roll of Enlistments, 42nd, 1795-c.1893. BWRM 2285.

30. Sir J.E. Alexander, 14th Regiment, 'On Desertion in Canada', *United Services Magazine*, 1842 Part 2 (London: Henry Colburn, 1842), p. 473. 'It is well known, that for the sake of a free passage to America, and to join friends already in the United States, at little expense, men will enlist at home, and desert from their Corps in Canada at the first favourable opportunity . . . To a person who reflects at all on the subject of desertion I think it will be evident that in national regiments the crime of desertion is likely to be less frequent than in mixed corps. In the former there is more union and sympathy, the one with the other . . . In national corps there is a greater feeling and desire to stand well with those we left at home than in regiments recruited at random in the United Kingdom. 'What will they say in the Gallowgate if they beat us?' said a Glasgow man to his comrades.'
31. Private Campbell deserted on 1st January 1831 and was absent for fifteen days. On his return he was pardoned, probably having drifted off in a haze of alcoholic New Year festivities. Regimental Standing Orders Book 79th Highlanders. QOHRM 144/79.
32. It is interesting to note that much of the desertion in the 79th appears to have stopped when Lt. Colonel McDougall assumed command in June 1832. Ibid.
33. Journal of Lt. Andrew Agnew of Lochnaw, 93rd. GD/154/781.
34. Ibid.
35. Undated letter, Lauderdale Maule to Fox Maule, Wigan, c.1840 GD/45/14/634/6, 45-107. It would appear that military and civilian prisoners were detained primarily aboard hulks in the Thames. Some prisoners would go direct to Australia, while others would go to the hulks in the West Indies and after a selection process would either stay there or go on to Australia. There were in addition hulks off the Cape of Good Hope housing military and civilian prisoners. PP 1831-32 XXXIII c 159.
36. Horse Guards Circular 24.12.1825.
37. See the Warrant of 17.5.1831 establishing rates of pay, necessaries and stoppages.
38. Memorandum by Lt. Colonel the Hon. Lauderdale Maule 79th. GD/48/8/18.
39. PP 1834 VIII c559. Q.1365 p. 121.
40. Elizabeth Grant, *Memoirs of a Highland Lady* (London: John Murray, 1898), p. 22.
41. *Ibid.*, p. 203. I myself recall in the 1970s the collection of rents on Highland and Angus estates, when the Laird, his solicitor and factor toured twice a year at the 'terms', an event which was accompanied by the traditional and obligatory voluminous consumption of whisky, requiring considerable staying power by all concerned, with not a few office hours lost in the recovery period.
42. PP 1830 XVIII c 580.
43. Letters of Lt. Colonel the Hon. Lauderdale Maule, GD/45/14/634/4 1-98. Gibraltar 5.6.1847.
44. Ibid., 21.4.1847.
45. The Select Committee of 1834 took very much the opposite view, which was never in fact put into practice as regards canteens. They recommended 'The abolition of all garrison and barrack canteens, at home and abroad and the substitution of some other and better mode of filling up the leisure hours of men confined within military forts and lines'. PP 1834 VIII c 559 para. viii p. 32.
46. Peter Burroughs suggests that drinking and other crime represented a 'movement of reform from the ranks', and that soldiers 'could and did protest in the negative, unconstructive form open to them against the harassments and monotony of army life and service: they resorted to unruly behaviour, drunkenness and desertion'. While the point may be valid in certain circumstances, it would be wrong to assume that drinking represented some kind of fashionable popular protest by the majority, for it did not; when the Highland regiments drank at marriages, New Year or on embarkation they were celebrating, not protesting, and it is erroneous to apply interpretations according to what either contemporary or modern reformers would like to have seen happen to what *actually* happened. Peter Burroughs, 'Crime and

Punishment in the British Army 1815-1870', *The English Historical Review*, Vol. C No. 396, July 1985, pp. 545-571.

47. Letter Book of Colonel Martin Lindsay 78th, Ceylon 1831-1836 GD/254/697/1. Lindsay of Dowhill Muniments. 4.11.1832.
48. Diary of Colonel Cuming 79th, *79th News*, 1935, p. 79.
49. PP 1834 VIII c.559 p. 432, (In India) . . . 'The soldiers employ their cook boys and sweepers (who are of the lower castes) to procure their liquors. They bribe the natives to procure cheap spirits, often mixed with deleterious matters, as bang (country hemp), datura, opium, which they say induce a degree of delightful exhilaration not to be described during which the power of enjoyment in everything is wonderfully increased'.
50. Regimental Standing Order Book 79th Highlanders, QOHRM 144/79.
51. The question must be asked, 'How drunk was drunk in the nineteenth and early twentieth centuries?' If a man had had a drink, but could still walk straight and did not insist on bursting into song, was he permitted to remain at large? It would seem so. It would appear that there were no excuses for being late for parade etc., but providing that a soldier was present and 'capable', his hangover and how he felt was his own business. Thus it became a point of pride to be able to drink and still appear punctually on parade, sore heads notwithstanding.
52. Diary of Colonel J.W. Wedderburn 42nd, BWRM 28/714/1. 5.12.1851 and 5.9.1853.
53. Diary of Colonel Cumming 79th, *79th News*, April 1935, p. 195.
54. *Sutherland News*, No. 4 1892, p. 12. A temperance society, the 'Assaye Lodge', was formed in the 74th on 16.9.1875. *HLI Chronicle*, Vol. 1, No. 4 Oct. 1893. A Branch of the A.T.A. was opened in the 79th on 2.4.1895 when ' . . . several of the Regiment took the pledge'. *79th News*, Vol. 2 No.19 1895, p.2.
55. Reporting in the *Sutherland News*, an observer of our 'Coffee shop' noted the sale of tea, lemonade, cake and biscuits and that 'being on the steady' implied each man drinking one pint of beer only and that drink was not served without food 'but there are cases when two men have but 4 annas between them, and then a little strategy is needed to obtain their pints; they skirmish around until they find two empty plates, sit down oppisite them, play with the knives and forks and then with the air of men who have just finished a hearty supper, shout for two pints of beer; this move seldom fails'. *Sutherland News*, No. 4 May 1893, p.11.
56. Horse Guards Circular 24.8.1833.
57. Horse Guards Circular 10.9.1846.
58. See, *Manual of Military Law*, 1914, *op. cit.*, p. 378, Army Act 1955 Part II Section 24-27 and Anthony Babington, *For the Sake of Example* (London: 1983).
59. Private Reginald Lobban and Corporal Frank MacFarlane. Oral History archive, *op. cit.*.
60. In 1804 an old mansion at Greenlaw was converted into a depot for French prisoners of war, and in 1813 the buildings were extended to house 6,000 prisoners. At the end of the war until 1845 the site was used as an Ordnance Depot and it was then converted into a military prison, developing a formidable reputation. See for example PP 1850 XXIX c.1241. Report on the discipline and management of the Military Prisons 1849 by Lt. Colonel Jebb. It was the case that these prisons were guarded by soldiers, and whenever a Highland regiment was stationed at Edinburgh Castle a detachment would always be sent to do duty at Greenlaw. See RHP/2700.
61. Between 1875 and 1877 part of Glencorse (Greenlaw) was altered and extended for use as a Brigade Depot and in 1890 the Scottish Military Prison moved to the converted civilian prison at Stirling just below the Castle. While it is now deserted and roofless, it is one of the eeriest places I have ever visited, and it is not beyond the bounds of possibility that Mr. William Boag of the Scottish United Services Museum is quite correct when he asserts that men were known to commit suicide

rather than be sent there. The general term 'glasshouse' used throughout the army for military prisons stems from the building of a prison and detention block at Aldershot in 1855. The three-storey prison was built of wood with a large main roof of glass. A brick building was substituted in 1870. Lt. Col. H.N. Cole, *The Story of Aldershot, op. cit.*, p. 64.

62. Military prisons in 1881 included those at Barbados, Bermuda, Gibraltar, Halifax Nova Scotia and Malta. PP 1882 XXXIII c. 3449.
63. WO/33/22.
64. See Peter Burroughs, 'Crime and Punishment in the British Army', *The English Historical Review*, Vol. c, No. 396, July 1985, p. 559. The fines for drunkenness operated on a scale system. For example in 1872 the fines were
    a) 1st and 2nd acts—admonition or CB.
    b) For every subsequent act
    if within 3 months 7/6d
    if over 3 and within 6 months 5/-
    if over 6 and within 9 months 2/6d.
    if over 9 and within 12 months Company entry.
    if over 12 months to be treated as 1st act.
    c) When four preceding acts commited in 12 months 2/6d to be added to the above amounts.
    General Order No. 28 of 1.3.1872.
65. Horse Guards Circular 24.6.1830. Horse Guards Circular of 22.1.1831 regarding 'Habitual Drunkenness', WO/27/367. Inspection Report of 92nd 1847. GD/45.8.96. Undated memorandum on Habitual Drunkenness.
66. Standing Orders of the 79th 1819. QOHRM 142a/79, pp. 78-79.
67. Ibid., p.77. For interesting detail on a scale of Regimental Punishments, see 'Scale of Punishments Scots Fusilier Guards', GD.172.674, Henderson of Fordell Papers (undated).
68. Journal of Lt. Andrew Agnew of Lochnaw 93rd. GD/154/781, 1838.
69. Ibid., 19.11.1838.
70. Sergeant James McKay 74th, *Reminiscences of the Last Kafir War, op.cit.*, p. 4.
71. Account and diary of Donald Cameron, 79th and 93rd, RH/4/141.
72. Standing Orders of the 79th 1819, p. 74. QOHRM 142a/79.
73. WO/3/133/102 (79th) 1838 and WO/3/455/219 (93rd) 1840.
74. William Black was born in 1779 in Islay. He enlisted in 1807 and was present at Waterloo. He was discharged in 1837 aged 58 and was appointed keeper of the Public Baths at Ayr. He died in 1863. *79th News*, Vol. 9 No. 103, May 1909, pp. 135-36. It was in addition still common practice in the 1850s for the War Office to commend men to their Parish. WO letter 4.9.1854 to the Inverness Parish officers regarding Alexander Maclennan of the 74th *HLI Chronicle*, No.9 January 1895, p. 385. Alexander Maclennan was born in Inverness in 1809 and enlisted at Forres in 1833. He was discharged on 11th July 1854 and he joined the Highland Light Infantry Militia (2nd (Militia) Battalion Queen's Own Cameron Highlanders) where he served as Pipe Major until 1885. He won the Highland Society of London Gold Medal at Inverness in 1860 and was well known as a piping teacher. He died in Falkirk in 1902.
75. *The Thin Red Line*, Vol. 1 No. 8, 1894, p. 116.
76. Sergeant James McKay, 74th, *Reminiscences of the Last Kafir War, op. cit.*, p. 135.
77. *Ibid.*
78. Diary of General Sir J. Spencer Ewart 79th, RH/4/84/1, 1.1.1884.
79. Letters of Lieutenant A.M.M. Jameson, 1st Camerons. NLS MS 10305. 4.1.1919
80. Watercolour of the Officers of the 92nd at Mess c.1840. GHRM.
81. Sergeants' Messes were formally established in the British Army in 1826. In the Officers' Mess it would appear that the only formal meal was dinner with a guest

night once a week and that for other meals officers made their own arrangements usually in groups of two or three. Frequently Officers' Messes were in serious debt in the Highland regiments. In 1849 the debt of the 79th Officers' Mess was £1071.16.9d., which after considerable efforts was reduced to £682.1.3½d. by 1852. Minute Book of the Officers' Mess 1844-1899, 79th. QOHRM 1161. On 26th February 1846 Lt. William Parke of the 72nd recorded, 'A Mess meeting took place today to enquire into the state of the Mess accounts which have got very deeply involved in debts not easily accounted for, arising chiefly from the greatest carelessness'. Diary of Lt. William Parke 72nd. QOHRM.

82. Standing Orders of the 2nd Battalion Seaforth Highlanders Late 78th Highlanders, Lucknow 1884. QOHRM 84/25 p.81.
83. Letters of John Tulloch 74th, *op. cit.,*
84. Diary of Private S.W. McIntosh 42nd. BWRM 421(3591(1)-) 1858, p. 142.
85. James Anton 42nd, *Retrospect of a Military Life, op.cit.*, p. 317.
86. WO/27/367. 78th 1847; WO/17/626 1850, 74th; WO/17/720 1860, 73rd, 74th, 75th, 79th; WO/17/721 1860, 91st; WO/17/627 1850, 92nd, 93rd.
87. The authorities virtually sanctioned the existence of prostitutes by the Contagious Diseases Acts of 1864 and 1866-1869, and by allowing, and providing for, the medical examination of regimental brothels. See Myna Trustram, *Women of the Regiment, op. cit.*, pp. 116-124.
88. 79th Regimental Standing Order Book. Quebec 24.4.1849. QOHRM 144/79.
89. Diary of Colonel J.W. Wedderburn 42nd, BWRM. 28/714/1. Weedon 30.5.1853. Margaret Whaite appears to have been a relative of Quarter Master Paton of the 42nd; the couple married on 27.4.1854. They illustrate the fact that it was not only common for soldiers to marry girls 'in the Regiment' but that officers, who seldom married young, often married their brother officers' relatives.
90. Letters of John Grant 42nd, BWRM File H4(42) sec. G.
91. QOHRM 5092 and *79th News*, 1925, p. 47.
92. Diary of Private A.W. McIntosh, 42nd, 1861. BWRM 3591(1).
93. At Jhansi, India in 1869, for example, James Duff, the 21-year-old Drum Major of the 93rd, married Elizabeth Gibson aged 14, probably an orphan daughter of the Regiment as none of her family was a witness to the marriage certificate. Marriage Certificate of James Duff and Elizabeth Gibson, ASHRM.
94. Diary of Private A.W. McIntosh, 42nd, 1858. BWRM (3591(1)1), p. 73.
95. 91st (1st Battalion Argyll and Sutherland Highlanders) Permanent Order Book. ASHRM Sb 18/16. 8.4.1862 and 11.7.1865.
96. Descriptive Roll Book of the 93rd Highlanders, *op. cit.*, and the letters of Lt. Colonel the Hon. Lauderdale Maule, 79th. GD/48/8/18 and GD/45/14/634-1j 1-84 of 25.12.1846.
97. Diaries of General Sir J. Spencer Ewart, 79th. RH/4/84/1. 5.3.1882.
98. Card games, Crown and Anchor and 'Housie Housie' were very popular although Crown and Anchor was generally forbidden. Card games and gambling provided an interesting example of the differing social roles and behaviour of officers and men. Few soldiers could understand what the officers saw in the apparently very dull game of Bridge as opposed to the popular 'Nap', and interesting comment on this can be found in *79th News*, No. 88 November, 1906, p. 48.
99. Diary of Private A.W. McIntosh, 42nd. BWRM (2591(1)), pp. 276 and 349 and (2), p. 221.
100. Singing was popular with all ranks A.D. Greenhill Gardyne of the 1st Battalion Gordon Highlanders records of the Officers' Mess in Ceylon in 1890, 'The Governor came to dinner in state, it was a success I think. He spoke but I was Vice and could not hear, we had the Pipers to dance reels, sword dance etc., who he seemed to appreciate, and then we sang songs . . .' Diaries of A.D. Greenhill Gardyne, 1st Battalion Gordon Highlanders. RH/4/59/1-8. 21.5.1890. No smoking

concert, or social evening in any Mess or Barrack room appears to have been complete without a song, when some of the more gentle and sentimental side of the character of Highland soldiers came to the fore.

101. Colonel Cuming of the 79th records the rink commenced at Quebec in 1848; "We started a curling rink between the outer walls of the Citadel, but it was too exposed to cold winds and driving snow, so we moved to the Queen's Wharf, put a roof over it, windows in the sides, and curled with more luxury than had ever been known in Canada. In the afternoon a stove was established at the rink; mutton pies and mulled port, both hot, ever ready to cheer the players and lookers-on; the numbers of the latter increasing enormously when the refreshment was produced. The more mulled port was consumed, the louder the visitors applauded; it was indeed a "roaring game" all round". Diary of Colonel Cuming 79th, *79th News*, January 1935, p. 83.
102. A Fives Court was built in the south end of the moat of Edinburgh Castle as early as 1837. WO/44/728.
103. The physical feats of endurance undertaken by Highland soldiers particularly in respect of marching are especially worthy of note and they show that in spite of their hard drinking and unbalanced diet by modern standards, they were extremely tough men. Some of the marches undertaken, particularly in India during the Mutiny Campaign and on the North-West-Frontier, without any sort of mechanical transport, can now only be wondered at, and the Falklands 'yomp', cold, dangerous and difficult though it may have been, bears poor comparison. Even marching between stations in India in the nineteenth and early twentieth centuries, considered a quite normal occurrence to be undertaken without drama or publicity, is now difficult to appreciate in practical and physical terms. These marches were not undertaken by specialist teams selectively trained, but by every man in the battalion. Having seen for myself the route of the Relief of Lucknow and the route of the march from Peshawar to Kohat and into the Tirah of 1897, I could only stand in awe at the nineteenth century Highland soldier's basic physical fitness.
104. A great deal of effort was put into this 'home made' entertainment in which both officers and men shared. The programme of the Regimental Smoking Concert of the Camerons at Malta on 10th November 1894, a typical example of such concerts, read:

    Overture—"Guy Mannering". Band.
    Song—"Come o'er the Stream Charlie". Quarter Master Sergeant Cameron.
    Song—"Playmates in School days were we". Pte. Dawson.
    Comic Song—"The Waiter". Lt. McLachlan (encore, "Ju-ja").
    Exhibition spar—(3 rounds) L/Cpl Boate and Pte. Craine.
    Song—"Sound the Piobaireachd" Lt. McBean.
    Reel—Pipers Grant, McFarlane, McInnes and McIntosh.
    encore, "Highland Fling", Piper McInnes.
    Selection—"Round the Town" Band.
    Comic Song—"The Soldier", Lt. McLachlan.
    Violin Solo—"The Last Rose of Summer", Band Sergeant Alcorn. Encore, "Auld Robin Gray".
    Step Dance—Pte. Walker.

    79th News, Vol. 2 No. 17, 1895, p. 2.

105. Regimental Orders of the 91st record the prizewinning entries of men of the 91st at the central India Exhibition of 1866.

    Private G. Iongens, Model Weighing Machine.
    Private K. Samuell, Picture Frames.
    Private Huggett, Picture Frames and Pen Stands.

91st (1st Battalion Argyll and Sutherland Highlanders) Permanent Order Book. ASHRM Sb 18/16 3.3.1866.

106. Diary of Lt. Colonel Wheately, 42nd. BWRM.
107. James MacVeigh, *Historical Record of the Black Watch* (42nd *Royal Highlanders) 1785-1881, op. cit.*, p. 404. Annotated copy in the SUSM.
108. Diary of Private A.W. McIntosh, 42nd. BWRM 421 (3591(1 and 2).
109. Private George Smollett Greig enlisted in the 93rd on 5.5.1852 aged 18. He was born in Turriff, and his compositions have a definite north-eastern air about them. Much of his poetry shows evidence of the innate romance and sentimentality of the Highland soldier, his love of his homeland and friends, his strong emotional feeling and his love and respect for his ideal girl, who was, it seems, often far away. Diary and Poetry Book of Private G.S. Greig, 93rd. ASHRM R/144.
110. Diary of Bandsman A.V. Barwood 42nd. BWRM.
111. See the portraits of Sergeant Alexander Patterson, 79th, Gibraltar 1841-1845 by a fellow soldier in *79th News*, 1907 No. 92, facing p. 16.
112. Diary and Poetry Book of Private G.S. Greig, 93rd. ASHRM R/144.
113. Pipes and cigars were smoked, not cigarettes, which only became popular in the First World War. Amongst the officers cigars were popular but smoking was officially discouraged. General Order 1845: 'The Commander in Chief has been informed that the practice of smoking by the use of pipes, cigars and cheroots has become prevalent amongst the Officers of the Army, which is not only in itself a species of intoxication occasioned by the fumes of tobacco, but undoubtedly occasions drinking and tippling by those who acquire the habit, and he entreats the Officers Commanding Regiments to prevent smoking in the Mess-Rooms of their several Regiments and in the adjoining apartments and to discourage the practice among the Officers of junior rank'.
114. For example see. *Sutherland News* edited by Private Guy Watson (93rd), The *79th News*, the *HLI Chronicle* 71st and 74th, *The Albany Monthly Record* 72nd, probably the oldest, and *The Tiger and the Sphinx*, Gordon Highlanders. *The Red Hackle* of the Black Watch was not published until 1921.
115. Watch clubs were savings societies for the purpose of the members buying watches which were greatly prized possessions. 91st (1st Battalion Argyll and Sutherland Highlanders) Permanent Order Book, ASHRM Sb 18/16. 30.11. 1869.
116. These Lodges were not Freemasons' Lodges which were forbidden in 1836 in Regiments. WO/3/131/66 and WO/3/100/38. Military Lodges however existed and many soldiers were Freemasons; both Colonel Fordyce and Lt. Carey of the 74th who were killed in the Kafir War were buried with Masonic honours at Grahamstown in 1852. R.F. Gould, *Military Lodges, 1732-1899* (Aldershot: 1899), p. 164.
117. Diary of Lt. Parke, 72nd. QOHRM.
118. The Diaries of Colonel J.W. Wedderburn, 42nd show clearly his keen interest in and knowledge of ornithology. Men of the Regiment often collected specimens for him, which he carefully preserved, stuffed and sent home. Parts of this collection still exist. Diary of Colonel J.W. Wedderburn, 42nd. BWRM 28/714/1 and 2.
119. Diaries of A.D. Greenhill Gardyne, Gordon Highlanders, RH/4/59 1-8, and Henry Robert Kelham, 74th, RHFRM (now destroyed by fire; Kelham frequently contributed to *The Field*, see *HLI Chronicle* Vol. XXXII No. 1 Jan. 1932, pp.8-10).
120. Many Hunts were supported by Highland Officers, most notable of which were the Peshawar Vale (India) and the Calpe Hunt (Gibraltar), Lt. Parke of the 72nd being Secretary and Lauderdale Maule being twice Master of the latter.
121. Lt. Colonel R.M. Grayebrook, 'Test Certificate', *Journal of the Society for Army Historical Research*, Vol. 23/25, 1945-1947. Notes, p. 124.
122. WO/3/103/180.
123. WO/3/133/235.

124. General Regulations and Orders of the Army 1822.
125. (Quoted) A.W. Cockerill, *Sons of the Brave* (Bury St Edmunds: Leo Cooper, 1984), p. 94.
126. MacKerlie (pub. Anon.), *An Account of the Scottish Regiments, op. cit.*, pp. 34-36. It has been suggested to me that Squads in the Highland regiment were divided by religion, and from a study of the Squad Roll Book of Captain F. Burroughs' Company of the 93rd of 1857 this may well have been the case, as all the Catholic soldiers are in Squads 2, 3 and 4 of the Company; however, it is more likely that the division was by area of birth, particular areas of the West and Islands of Scotland retaining a strong loyalty to Catholicism. Squad Roll Book, Captain F. Burroughs, No. 6 Company, 93rd Highlanders 1857. ASHRM SBC 93.
127. See for example the Regimental Communion Plate of the Black Watch and Argyll and Sutherland Highlanders. The 72nd also issued Regimental Church Tokens, *Journal of the Society for Army Historical Research*, Vol. VII-VIII, 1928-1929, Questions, p. 207 and p. 263.
128. Alexander C. Dow, *Ministers to the Soldiers of Scotland* (Edinburgh: 1962), pp.252-271.
129. John Alexander Ewart, *The Story of A Soldier's Life, op. cit.*, p. 145.
130. Surgeon William Munro, *Records of Service and Campaigning in Many Lands, op. cit.*, Vol. 2, p. 21.
131. Letters of Lt. Colonel the Hon. Lauderdale Maule, 79th. GD/45/14/634/3 1-84, 27.5.1845.
132. Ibid., 23.7.1846.
133. Surgeon William Munro, *Records of Service and Campaigning in Many Lands, op. cit.*, p. 22, vol. 2.
134. WO/30/93 . Statement of the Bibles and Books of Common Prayer Sent to the Regiments of the Army 1825-1844.
135. 78th Regimental Order Book, SUSM A/242 72/78. 2.11.1863.
136. Regimental Standing Order Book 79th Highlanders, QOHRM 144/79, 12.11.1856. The Order Book of the 91st also states, '. . . in terms of Queen's Regulations para. 727, the wives of Non commissioned officers and soldiers who do not attend church are to have their names taken . . .' 91st (1st Battalion Argyll and Sutherland Highlanders) Permanent Order Book ASHRM Sb 18/16. See also Forms 12 and 13, 'Divine Service Memorandum of Women's attendance', Standing Orders of the 42nd 1833, BWRM 355-51 (42).
137. Diary of J. Spencer Ewart 79th, RH/4/84/1, 1.8.85. As regards continuing prejudice it is interesting that even in 1914 it still remained unusual for officers in Highland regiments to be of the Roman Catholic faith, Captain D.N.C.C. Miers of the Camerons being a notable exception. In conversation, Colonel G.P. Wood MC of the Argyll and Sutherland Highlanders states that in his experience it was quite common for a Roman Catholic Senior Non Commissioned Officer to be advised to 'reconsider his religion' prior to his being promoted Regimental Sergeant Major of the Regiment, and that it is virtually unknown for a Roman Catholic to be RSM of the Argyll and Sutherland Highlanders. I am obliged to Lt. Colonel Wood for his frankness in this respect.
138. Individual regimental comment must not be confused with the restrictions which existed, and still exist, regarding politics, writing or communicating directly with the press or being linked, associated, or showing sympathy with certain political or subversive organisations, see *Kings Regulations and Orders for the Army, 1912* (London: HMSO, 1912), paras. 449-454.
139. Diary of Colonel J.W. Wedderburn, 42nd BWRM 28/714/1. 14.7.1853.
140. *HLI Chronicle,* Vol. 111 No. 8 1903, p. 821.
141. Diary of Private George Greig, 93rd ASHRM R144. 1859.
142. Incidents of this nature occurred in the Black Watch, the Gordon Highlanders and the Royal Scots Fusiliers in 1919. The difficulty was far from straightforward and

involved not only the question of drafting, but also the national emotional exhaustion and the men's belief in their right to demobilisation. *The Scotsman,* 13.6.1919, *The Edinburgh Evening News,* 17.6.1919 and *The Glasgow Herald,* 18.6.1919. Memoir of the late Captain Alex. D.L. Stewart MC of Achnacone 1891-1919 GHRM.

143. *79th News,* Vol. 2 No. 17 1895, p. 18 (The supply of gas for the men's shaving); *ibid.,* No. 69 October 1903, p. 16 (On the reduction of the numbers of married families); *Ibid.,* No 88 November 1906 (The Sorrows of an Officer's Servant); *Ibid.,* No. 106 November 1909, p. 234 (The Salisbury Plain manoeuvres of 1909 and the uselessness of the mechanical transport which persistently broke down. 'We're here because we're here summed up the situation in a manner which was truly masterly'.)
144. WO/43/787.
145. Diary of Colonel J.W.E. Wedderburn 42nd, BWRM 28/714/2/ 9/1/1854/
146. Ibid.
147. An example of a formal written application to marry can be found in SUSM 42/73 (42) 8571. Private William Clark, 42nd and 79th, 1857-c.1880.
148. Standing Orders of the 79th 1835, p. 148.
149. Standing Orders of the 79th 1819, pp. 51-56.
150. It would appear that very few Highland officers were married below the rank of senior Captain unless they were commissioned from the ranks.
151. J.S. Ewart, *The Story of a Soldier's Life, op. cit.,* p. 290 (Vol. 2). It should be noted that attendance was 'voluntary', but was probably in effect compulsory; Mrs Ewart was after all the Commanding Officer's wife, but the fact remains that she participated and, most important of all, took an interest in the welfare of the regimental wives. It is clear that the rank structure extended to the wives and children in Highland regiments and Mrs Dan Bonnar, wife of Major Dan Bonnar of the 74th (2/HLI), remembers as a young Sergeant's wife arriving in India after the First World War having her linen inspected by the Regimental Sergeant Major's wife who felt perfectly at liberty to walk straight into their quarters unannounced for the purpose. Evidence of Mrs Dan Bonnar in conversation with the author.
152. 72nd Highlanders Regimental Orders During the Afghan Campaign 1878-1880. QOHRM 23/72. 8.9.80.
153. Diary of General Sir J. Spencer Ewart, 79th RH/4/84/1.
154. Papers and Records of Messrs. William Wilson, Bannockburn. SUSM. 4.2.1829.
155. Ibid., 11.9.1861.
156. Letters of Lt. Colonel the Hon. Lauderdale Maule, 79th GD/45/14/634/4 1-98. 4.3.1847.
157. Ibid., GD/45/14/634/5 1-56. 12.4.1849. Maule's patronage was quite remarkable; he pressed his brother alone for positions for Barrack Masters, Adjutants, Quarter Masters, Gate Keepers, Prison Governors, Ministers, Doctors, Sergeants and Soldiers. Colonel Cuming describes him as ' . . . arbitrary, self-willed and often unfair', but it is quite obvious that he was held in high esteem by the men whose gratitude and affection lived on long after he was dead. Open house was maintained at Brechin Castle by both brothers for officers and men of the Regiment; in 1852 Lauderdale wrote in a note to Fox, 'If you see Cruikshanks, the Edinburgh Castle Fort Major, (former Quarter Master of the 79th), whom I asked to call at the "Salutation" for me, just tell him to come on by the train . . . [to Brechin Castle] . . . he is coming here for a few days to recoup his health'. GD/45/14/634/7. Maule, himself often in dire financial straits and having great personal family problems, received and expected no financial return whatever from his work, and it would be entirely wrong to cynically cast aside his genuine efforts to improve the lot of the men of his Regiment because those efforts do not fit in with modern ideas.
158. *Historical Records of the Cameron Highlanders, op. cit.,* Vol. 1, p. 187. *79th News,* No. 86 July 1906, p.1 and *The Times*, 27.6.1857.

159. *HLI Chronicle*, No. 5, Vol. 1 January 1894, p.8. It is interesting that the 71st and the 74th retained their own separate Associations after 1881, keeping the old numbers 71 and 74, re-affirming individual regimental pride, long after these numbers had officially disappeared. The 1st and 2nd Battalions HLI (71st/74th) retained particularly strong individual regimental feelings for many years after 1881 as recorded by Henry R. Kelham. 'I served with the 2nd Bn. HLI (old 74th) for the summers of 1896-97 at Fyzabad then we moved to Cawnpore where I sweated through a third hot weather alleviated by some good pig sticking. At this time I was a Senior Major and in August came an order that I was to proceed to Malta as Second in Command of the 1st Battalion (old 71st). I had a great send off from Cawnpore. Major Becklor (?) RA drove me to the Railway Station in the Artillery Coach loaded with many of my hilarious friends, for it was after a big luncheon and I found the HLI pipes drawn up on the platform to play me farewell as the train moved off. It was a wrench leaving the 2nd Battalion and so many old friends but I had been three summers in the heat of India and looked forward to a change'. Kelham's reception at the 1st Battalion was however cool. The fact was that the CO of the first Battalion . . . could see no good in the 2nd Battalion, nor anyone in it, a narrow minded foolish policy, a relic of ill feeling caused by the abolition of numbers and the affiliation of the Regiments, and by some, kept up for many years . . .' Diary of Henry Robert Kelham, 74th Highlands 1897, Vol VI. RHFRM.
160. *79th News*, No. 97 1908, p. 157.
161. A notable Servitor, Bedellus and Mace Bearer of Edinburgh University was Colour Sergeant W.S. Mitchell of the Black Watch. When he died in 1921 his funeral was attended by the Principal, Sir Alfred Ewan, Professors and Students' Union Representatives. *Red Hackle*, January 1922, p. 27.
162. See *The Corps of Commissionaires*, and *The History of the Corps of Commissionaires* (private publication).
163. The records of the Corps of Commissionaires for Edinburgh and the East of Scotland, Headquarters Edinburgh.
164. The Register of Dundee Burgh Police Force, Tayside Police Headquarters, Dundee.
165. The practice in fact continues today. In Edinburgh the Blue Hackle public house, run by an ex-Cameron Highlander, still acts as a meeting place for men of the Camerons looking for work, as did The Elephant and Bugle in Maryhill Road, Glasgow for men of the HLI.

Conclusion

The Highland soldier's pride in belonging to his Regiment, and the jealous guarding of individual regimental tartans, traditions and music continues today; part of understanding this pride lies in regimental social and domestic history. Too often this apparently mundane aspect is neglected in the face of more glamorous studies in the areas of uniform and battles, and as Hew Strachan has pointed out:

> A regiment's history is not simply a sequence of great deeds from one battle to another, but also the domestic story of a self-contained social institution.[1]

The strength of this pride and tradition in Highland Regiments is also reflected in their survival in the face of the twentieth-century changes which have taken place, not only in the conduct of warfare itself, but also in the structure of the British Army. English County Regiments suffered particularly badly in respect of identity and individuality in the 1960s when many famous names disappeared from the Army List, but the Highland Regiments, in spite of amalgamations, retained and still retain particular social characteristics of family and territorial links coupled with a distinctive uniform.

Historically, the Regiment who fared worst were probably the 74th. In 1881 they were committed to a Lowland Depot and recruiting area, but as the 2nd Battalion Highland Light Infantry they at least retained the word 'Highland' in their name and continued 74th traditions and the use of the old number. Although they lost their old tartan for the Mackenzie tartan, they wore trews, which even in 1881 were as much the mark of a Highland soldier as the kilt. With the adoption of trews by Lowland Regiments generally, however, this distinction was effectively devalued, and although the HLI tried hard to move back into the Highland Brigade, the amalgamation of the 1st and 2nd Battalions in 1947 and the amalgamation with the Royal Scots Fusiliers in 1959 resulted in the intermixing of the traditions of three entirely distinct battalions and the consequent dilution of the individuality of each.

In 1961 another potentially traumatic amalgamation took place in the joining of the 1st Battalion Seaforth Highlanders (72nd/78th) with the 1st Battalion Queen's Own Cameron Highlanders to form one battalion, The Queen's Own Highlanders. The two Battalions were entirely different in their character, and yet by drawing upon the strength of their individual social traditions and by retaining a sound Highland base in recruiting, music and dress, The Queen's Own Highlanders have emerged in their own right as worthy inheritors of the Highland regimental traditions of three famous battalions.

The Black Watch and the Gordon Highlanders have remained intact, although they carry on primarily as the 42nd and the 92nd, a characteristic dating from 1881; while the Argyll and Sutherland Highlanders (91st/93rd), reduced to a single company in 1970, were returned to battalion strength in 1972. The campaign to 'Save the Argylls' is a fine illustration of the strength of 'Highland' feeling in these battalions, and conducted as it was, not only at governmental but at popular level, it showed the position which the Highland soldier still holds in the eyes of the Scottish public.

In an era of financial restrictions what is of greater concern to the Highland Regiments, however, is the rationalisation and centralisation of training depots into the Lowland area for adult soldiers, and into England for junior Scottish soldiers, the standardisation of the hues of tartans by Ordnance and the use of pipers and drummers primarily as riflemen, with their musical duties secondary. While the kilt is worn less frequently, in this age of nuclear, chemical and biological warfare the Highland Regiments may however take heart from the very fact that it has been retained at all, and it would be a brave man, even today, who would propose its abolition. The Army School of Piping continues, fosters and promotes the military traditions of the great Highland bagpipe, but because the public image of a Highland soldier is essentially linked with piping and pipe bands there has been a consequent demise in the popular appeal of the Scottish and Highland soldier playing as a member of a military band, and there is a distinct possibility that these bands may be disbanded regimentally, ending a long tradition of military band music in Highland Regiments.

In conclusion therefore, this study has a direct bearing on the Highland Regiments as they exist today, and their social and domestic history contributes heavily to any understanding of their characteristics and their present survival. In the long term this history may well affect their future, as it is still widely believed that in the event of a national emergency the amalgamated battalions would be broken up and recreated again as individual regiments, and this can only be done if history is understood and traditions are recorded and maintained.

Secondly, the study clearly illustrates the necessity for research into the inner workings of each individual regiment and that comparative studies urgently require to be carried out on the Welsh and Irish Regiments as well as on English Regiments with particular territorial associations.

Thirdly, the unique characteristics of Highland Regiments cannot be said to be founded on one particular aspect, as recruiting, music, location, language, leadership and dress, together with historical, geographical and national considerations have all played their part. Individuals, especially individual commanding officers, were important too, but much of the impetus behind Highland regimental *esprit de corps* came from the men themselves. There were many dissatisfied and badly treated Highland soldiers, but my research has not found this to be the dominant theme which is so often subjectively portrayed today.

Finally it is clear that while statistical and impersonal military studies have their place, they are not the only answer. These studies look simply at a tiny portion of a regiment's history and fail to acknowledge the importance of the individual, the regiment, the regimental family and the soldiers themselves. Behind every man there is a story, and that story goes a long way to explain a man's actions and behaviour. This book has been an attempt to examine some of these stories objectively and factually, and to open up the study of military social history to allow a better, more comprehensive and more realistic appreciation to be made of how and why the Highland Regiments were so unique.

NOTES

1. Hew Strachan, 'The British Army 1815-1856', *Journal of the Society for Army Historical Research*, Vol. LXIII No. 254, Summer 1985, p. 78.

Appendix

Appendix I. The Genealogy of the Kilted and Highland-Based Regiments

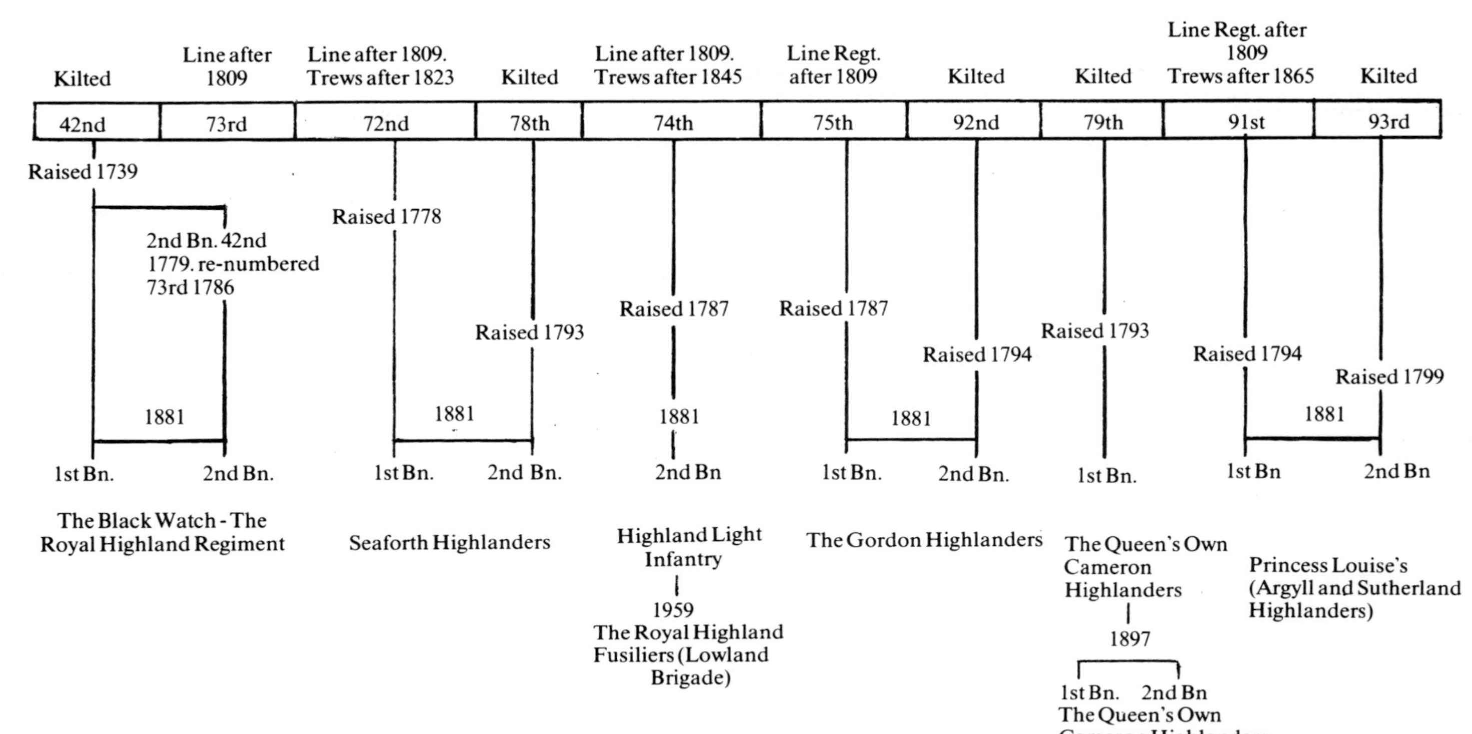

Appendix II. Regimental Locations, 1820-1881 (Kilted Regiments)

Date	42nd	78th	79th	92nd	93rd
1820	Dublin, Kilkenny, Clonmell	Ireland	Channel Islands	Jamaica	Cork, Birr
1821	Rathkeale		Limerick, Dublin		Athlone, Armagh
1822	Limerick				Limerick, Dublin
1823	Buttevant				Barbados
1824					Antigua, St. Louis
1825	Dublin, Gibraltar		Quebec		Dominica
1826		Ceylon			
1827				Edinburgh	
1828			Montreal	Glasgow, Belfast, Dublin	
1829			Kingston		
1830				Kilkenny	
1831			Toronto	Killaloe	
1832	Malta			Limerick	
1833			Quebec		
1834	Ionian Islands			Gibraltar	Canterbury
1835					Weedon, Blackburn, Liverpool
1836	Leith, Glasgow		Glasgow	Malta	Dublin, Newry
1837	Edinburgh		Edinburgh		Belfast, Cork
1838	Dublin	Ireland	Dublin		Toronto
1839	Limerick	Glasgow, Edinburgh	Liverpool, Manchester		
1840	Templemore	Manchester	Wigan, Bolton	Barbados	
1841	Ionian Islands	Ireland	Gibraltar		
1842	Malta*	Bombay			Montreal
1843		Poona, Karachi			Quebec
1844		Sukkor		Glasgow, Edinburgh	
1845		Bombay, Poona			
1846		Kirkee, Belgaum		Ireland	

Appendix II. Regimental Locations, 1820-1881 (Kilted Regiments) (continued)

Date	42nd	78th	79th	92nd	93rd
1847	Bermuda				
1848			Quebec		Stirling, Edinburgh
1849		Aden			Glasgow
1850					Stirling
1851	Canada Halifax		Stirling, Edinburgh	Corfu	
1852	Stirling, Perth Dundee				Weedon
1853	Chobham, Gosport	Poona	Chobham, Portsmouth	Gibraltar	Portsmouth, Chobham
1854	Portsea, Varna, Crimea		Varna Crimea		Varna Crimea
1855				Crimea	
1856	Portsmouth, Dover		Aldershot, Dover	Gibraltar	Aldershot, Dover
1857	Calcutta India	Persia, Bombay	Dublin, Calcutta		
1858		Calcutta, Cawnpore, Lucknow, Bareilly	Lucknow, Bareilly	India	Calcutta, Cawnpore, Lucknow, Bareilly
1859		Fort George	Mean Meer		
1860					
1861		Aldershot	Ferozepore		
1862		Shorncliffe	Nowshera, Peshawar	Gosport	Edinburgh
1864			Rawalpindi	Glasgow	
1865		Gibraltar		Aldershot	
1866			Kirkee	Ireland	
1867		Canada			
1868	Portsmouth, Stirling, Perth, Dundee, Edinburgh	Montreal, Halifax		Jelhundur	
1869	Portsmouth, Aldershot		Delhi, Kamptee		

Appendix II. Regimental Locations, 1820-1881 (Kilted Regiments) (continued)

Date	42nd	78th	79th	92nd	93rd
1870					Aberdeen, Edinburgh
1871	Devonport	Belfast, Londonderry	Parkhurst		
1872					
1873	Devonport, Ashanti	Fort George	Aldershot		Aldershot Woolwich
1874	Portsmouth, Malta	Aldershot			Shorncliffe
1875		Dover	Edinburgh		
1876		Edinburgh	Fort George		Dublin
1877					Curragh
1878	Cyprus, Gibraltar	Ireland	Glasgow	Afghanistan	
1879	Parkhurst	Bombay, Poona	Gibraltar	Kabul	Gibraltar
1880		Afghanistan		Kandahar	
1881	Edinburgh	Sitapur		South Africa	Aldershot

* Reserve Bn. formed

Locations, Highland Regiments, Line and Trews, 1820 - 1881

Date	72nd	73rd	74th	75th	91st
1820	Cape of Good Hope	Ceylon	Nova Scotia	Corfu	Dublin, Enniskillen
1821	London	Weedon		Gibraltar	Glasgow, Paisley
1823	Channel Islands	Hull, Chester, Carlisle, Tynemouth, Edinburgh		Gosport, Windsor Dublin, Birr, Fermoy	
1824	Edinburgh	Castlebar, Athlone	(3 Coys.) - Bermuda		
1825		Naas, Dublin		Dublin, Newry	
1826		Halifax, Huddersfield Bradford		Castlebar, Enniskillen,	
1827	Tower of London	Dublin, Fermoy, Gibraltar		Mullingar, Limerick	
1828	Cape of Good Hope		Bermuda		
1829		Malta		Galway, Fermoy	
1830			Limerick	Cork, Bristol, Canterbury, Cape of Good Hope	
1831			Ennis		Oxford, Weedon, Bolton, Northampton
1832					Ireland, Mullingar
1833					Naas, Fermoy
1834		Ionian Islands	Barbados, Grenada		Limerick, Birr
1835			Antigua, St. Lucia		Dublin, Cork
1836					St. Helena
1837					
1838		Gibraltar, Nova Scotia			
1839					Cape of Good Hope/ St. Helena (to 1842)
1840	South of England				

Locations, Highland Regiments, Line and Trews, 1820-1881 (continued)

Date	72nd	73rd	74th	75th	91st
1841		Canada, Gosport	Montreal, Quebec		Fish River
1842	Manchester, Pres-ton, Blackburn	Woolwich, Bradford, Newport	Halifax		Grahamstown*
1843	Ireland			Plymouth, Newport	Colesburg
1844	Gibraltar	Dublin			
1845		Monte Video	Canterbury, Gosport	Birr	
1846		Cape of Good Hope	Portsmouth, Aberdeen		
1847			Tipperary, Limerick	Dublin	
1848	Barbados				Gosport
1849	Trinidad			Kilkenny, Calcutta	
1850			Fermoy	Umballa	Dover, Portsmouth
1851	Halifax, Nova Scotia		South Africa		Manchester, Preston
1852					Belfast
1853	N.Brunswick, Halifax			Peshawar	Enniskillen, Dublin
1854	Ireland, Malta		Madras	Kohat	
1855	Crimea			Rawalpindi	Greece
1856	Portsmouth				
1857	Channel Islands, Shorncliffe, Bombay			Delhi, Lucknow	Corfu
1858	India	India	Bellary		India, Kamptee
1859	Mhow, Poona				
1860					Dover
1861		Plymouth			

Locations, Highland Regiments, Line and Trews, 1820-1881 (continued)

Date	72nd	73rd	74th	75th	91st
1862				Devonport	Jubbulpore
1863			Edinburgh	Aldershot	
1864			Aldershot		
1865		Limerick			
1866	Edinburgh	Hong Kong, Japan		Ireland	Dum Dum, Calcutta
1867	Aldershot		Dover, Dublin	Gibraltar	
1868	Manchester, Ireland		Gibraltar		Kamptee, Dover
1869		Ceylon			
1870					Aldershot
1871	Bombay, Umballa			South Africa	Fort George, Aberdeen
1872			Malta		
1873	Peshawar				Edinburgh
1874		Cawnpore			Newry
1875	Nowshera, Cherat			Ireland	Curragh
1876		Sabathu			
1877	Sailkot		Penang, Singapore, Malaca	Guernsey Alderney	Enniskillen, Belfast
1878	Afghanistan	Lucknow	Hong Kong	Aldershot	Dublin
1879	Kabul		Singapore		Aldershot
1880	Kandahar		Glasgow		South Africa Durban/Mauritius/
1881	Mean Meer, Lucknow	Portsmouth	Aldershot	Malta	St. Helena

* Reserve Bn. raised 1842, disbanded 1855.

Regimental Locations, Kilted Regiments, 1881-1920

	The Black Watch		Seaforth Highlanders		Gordon Highlanders	
Date	1st Bn (42nd)	2nd Bn (73rd)	1st Bn (72nd)	2nd Bn (78th)	1st Bn (75th)	2nd Bn (92nd)
1881	Edinburgh	Portsmouth	India	Lucknow	Malta	South Africa
1882	Egypt		Aden, Egypt, Parkhurst		Egypt	Edinburgh
1883		Aldershot				Devonport
1884	Soudan				Soudan	
1885		Curragh/ Belfast	Windsor, Aldershot	Bareilly	Malta	Guernsey
1886	Malta	Dublin	Edinburgh			
1887						Belfast
1888		Belfast	Glasgow	Hazara NWF	Ceylon	
1889	Gibraltar		Dublin, Fermoy		Rawalpindi	
1890		Limerick	Tipperary			
1891				Hazara NWF		Curragh
1892					Umballa, Subathu	
1893	Egypt, Mauritius/S. Africa	Glasgow		Ferozepore		
1894		Edinburgh			Rawalpindi Lahore	Glasgow
1895			Aldershot	Chitral	Chitral, Rawalpindi	
1896	Ambala, Sabathu	York				Aldershot
1897			Malta, Crete	Dover	Tirah, Deolali	
1898	Sitapur, Benares	Aldershot	Egypt, Sudan		Edinburgh	Umballa, Solon
1899		S. Africa	Cairo	Ft. George, South Africa	South Africa	South Africa
1900						
1901	Kamptee S. Africa					
1902	Edinburgh	Ambala			Glasgow	Sailkot
1903			Nasirabad	Dublin		Thobba
1904	Ft. George	Peshawar		Aldershot	Cork	Peshawar
1905			Nowshera			
1906	Curragh			Edinburgh		
1907		Sialkot	Murree Hills		Aldershot	
1908			Bazar Valley			Calcutta
1909	Limerick		NWF Peshawar		Ft. George	
1910			Bareilly		Colchester	Cawnpore
1911	Edinburgh	Delhi	Delhi			Delhi
1912		Calcutta	Agra	Shorncliffe		Cairo
1913	Aldershot					
1914	Flanders	Bareilly, Flanders	Flanders	Flanders	Plymouth, Flanders	Flanders
1915		Mesopotamia	Mesopotamia			
1916						
1917			Baghdad			Italy
1918		Palestine	Egypt	Fort George		
1919	Aldershot, Allahabad	Glasgow	Fort George	Meerut	Germany Cromarty	Aberdeen
1920		Cologne/ Upper Silesia			Ireland, Catterick, Constantinople	Dublin, Glasgow

Regimental Locations, Kilted Regiments, 1881-1920 (continued)

	Cameron Highlanders		Argyll and Sutherland Highlanders	
Date	1st Bn (79th)		1st Bn (91st)	2nd Bn (93rd)
1881	Gibraltar, Egypt		Cape Town	Aldershot
1882				Glasgow
1883				
1884	Khartoum Sudan		Zululand	Portsmouth
1885			Ceylon	Parkhurst
1886				Cork
1887	Devonport			
1888	Edinburgh		Hong Kong	Curragh
1889				
1890				Aldershot
1891				Ambala
1892			Edinburgh	Dagshai
1893				
1894			Aldershot	
1895	Gibraltar			Nowshera
1896		2nd Bn.	Glasgow	
1897	Cairo	Fort George		Tochi Valley
1898	Sudan	Aldershot	Dublin	Bareilly
1899		Gibraltar	South Africa	
1900	South Africa			Ranikhet
1901				Delhi
1902	Fort George	Crete/Malta/Cyprus	Johannesburg	Calcutta, Poona
1903		Malta	Longmore	
1904	Dublin	South Africa		
1905			Chatham	
1906				
1907	Tidworth			South Africa
1908		Hong Kong		
1909	Aldershot	China, Bangalore	Malta	
1910				Glasgow
1911		Delhi		
1912			India	Fort George
1913	Edinburgh	Poona		
1914	Flanders	Flanders	Flanders	Flanders
1915		Macedonia	Salonica	
1916		Struma Valley		
1917				
1918		Bulgaria, Georgia		
1919	Germany, Inverness, Rawalpindi	Inverness, Aldershot	Glasgow	Stirling, Glasgow
1920		Queenstown/Cork	India	Aldershot, Belfast

Locations of Depots to 1881 - Kilted Battalions (1825 Depot Coys. Formed)

Date	42nd	78th	79th	92nd	93rd	
1825	Edinburgh	Dublin	Cork,Glasgow			
1826			Belfast, Newry, Cavan	Glasgow	Perth	**Note;** When the Service Companies were at home the Depots were amalgamated with them, however many Depot locations still remain uncertain.
1827			Belfast	Edinburgh	Glasgow	
1828			Birr		Liverpool?	
1829	Paisley	Edinburgh	Burnley			
1830	Edinburgh	Aberdeen	Stirling	Kilkenny	Brecon	
1831			Aberdeen		Hamilton	
1832			Perth		Ayr, Ft. George	
1833			Dundee		Aberdeen	
1834			Stirling	Londonderry	Canterbury	
1835			Aberdeen	Greenlaw/Ft. George	Weedon	
1836			Edinburgh, Paisley	Perth/ Londonderry		
1837			Edinburgh	Armagh	Armagh, Cork	
1838	Dublin	Cork	Dublin	Nenagh Limerick	Fermoy, Buttevant	
1839		Glasgow	Manchester	Birr	Cork, Stirling	
1840	Limerick	Edinburgh		Glasgow	Aberdeen	
1841	Stirling	Burnley, Bolton	Paisley, Aberdeen	Fort George	Dundee	
1842	Aberdeen	Dublin		Dundee	Carlisle	
1843		Canterbury				
1844			Stirling, Naas	Carlisle	Templemore, Birr	
1845				With service coys.	Newbridge	
1846			Castlebar		Naas	
1847			Boyle		Newbridge, Glasgow	
1848					Aberdeen, Stirling	
1849			Nenagh			
1850			Kinsale, Preston			
1851			Berwick, Stirling			
1852	Aberdeen		Edinburgh	Carlon		
1853	Gosport		Bury, Preston, Portsmouth	Galway		
1854			Winchester	Naas		2nd Depot Malta
1855	Stirling		Aberdeen	Belfast	Dundee	
1856				Edinburgh	Dover	
1857	Aberdeen		Edinburgh?	Fort George	Chatham	
1858		Aberdeen		Stirling		
1858	Stirling					
1860						
1861	22 D.Bn. Stirling	23 D.Bn. Aberdeen	22 D.Bn Stirling	Perth	23 D.Bn. Aberdeen	
1862						
1863				22 D.Bn. Stirling		
1864						
1865	15 D.Bn. Aberdeen	15 D.Bn. Aberdeen	15 D.Bn. Aberdeen	?	15 D.Bn. Aberdeen	

Locations of Depots to 1881 - Kilted Battalions (1825 Depot Coys. Formed) (continued)

Date	42nd	78th	79th	92nd	93rd
1866		Stirling			Stirling 15 D.Bn. Aberdeen
1867	Stirling	15 D.Bn. Aberdeen			
1868	?		Fort George	15 D.Bn Aberdeen	
1869	?		Stirling		Perth
1870	Aldershot	Aberdeen	Aldershot	Aberdeen	Aberdeen
1871		with 93rd Aberdeen	with 42nd Aldershot	with 93rd Aberdeen	
1872	Devonport	Belfast	with 103rd Parkhurst		Edinburgh
1873	Perth	Fort George	Perth	Aberdeen	Aberdeen
1874					
1875					
1876					
1877					
1878					
1879					
1880					
1881	Perth	Fort George	Fort George	Aberdeen	Stirling

Locations of Depots to 1881, Highland Battalions (Trews)

Date	72nd	73rd	74th	75th	91st
1825					Isle of Wight
1826			Edinburgh		
1827			Perth		Berwick
1828					
1829					
1830	Fort George	Kinsale	Limerick	Sheerness	Londonderry Portsmouth
1832					
1833					
1834					
1835					
1836					Dublin?
1837					Paisley
1838					Dundee, Aberdeen, Naas
1839					
1840					
1841					Mullingar, Templemore
1842					Parkhurst
1843					
1844					
1845	Cork		Canterbury, Gosport		

Locations of Depots to 1881, Highland Battalions (Trews) (continued)

Date	72nd	73rd	74th	75th	91st
1846	Templemore	Cork	Portsmouth, Aberdeen		
1847	Nenagh	Clare	Tipperary, Dublin		Gosport
1848		Newbridge			
1849	Sheerness	Fermoy			
1850		Templemore		Chatham	
1851	Bristol	Naas	Aberdeen		
1852	Guernsey	Londonderry			
1853	Clare	Jersey			
1854		Bristol			Chatham
1855	Limerick	Jersey			Aldershot
1856	Edinburgh	Jersey			Berwick
1857	Fort George	Colchester			Preston
1858	Aberdeen	Jersey			Pembroke
1859					
1860		Chatham			Chatham
1861	23 D.Bn. Aberdeen	2 D.Bn. Chatham	23 D. Bn. Aberdeen	3 D. Bn. Chatham	3 D. Bn. Chatham
1862					
1863		21 D. Bn. Chichester	Perth		
1864		4 D. Bn. Colchester			
1865	Stirling	?	?	?	9 D. Bn. Preston
1866					15 D. Bn. Aberdeen
1867		12 D. Bn. Shorncliffe	Fort George	12 D. Bn. Shorncliffe	Stirling
1868					Fort George
1869	?		Stirling		?
1870	Buttevant	Bradford	Dover	Devonport	Dover
1871	Cork	With 35th Newcastle	With 91st Aldershot	With 57th Devonport	Aldershot
1872	With 91st Ft. George	With 35th Sheffield	With 42nd Devonport	With 57th Limerick	Fort George
1873		Edinburgh		With 57th Kinsale	
1874			Hamilton	39 Bde Depot Weymouth	
1875					
1876					
1877			Hamilton		
1878					
1879					
1880					
1881	Fort George	Stirling	Hamilton	Aberdeen	Stirling

Bibliography

Archival Sources

Scottish Record Office: Edinburgh

GD/1/354/2	Pay Ledger of the 92nd Highlanders c.1810.
GD/1/530/3	Letters of John Murray MD, FRCS, 1820-c.1837.
GD/16	Airlie Muniments.
GD/16/52/36 Nos. 29, 30, 31,32 and 35.	Letters to Major Drummond of the 72nd Regiment, 1824.
GD/45	Dalhousie Muniments.
GD/45/8	Papers of Lt. Colonel the Hon. Lauderdale Maule.
GD/45/14/634	Letters of Lieutenant Colonel the Hon. Lauderdale Maule, 1836-1853.
GD/45/26/91	Journal of Lieutenant Colonel the Hon. Lauderdale Maule 1854.
GD/112	Breadalbane Papers (Military).
GD/112/52	Proposals concerning the Highlands.
GD/139	Sutherland of Forse Muniments.
GD/139/450	Letter from Robert McBeath 78th Highlanders to George Sinclair of Brabster, 13.9.1828.
GD/154	Agnew of Lochnaw Papers.
GD/154/745	Letters of Lt. Andrew Agnew of Lochnaw 93rd Highlanders.
GD/172	Henderson of Fordell Papers.
GD/172/674	Scale of Punishments Scots Fusilier Guards c.1830.
GD/174	Maclaine of Lochbuie Papers.
GD/174/1708/11	George W. MacQuarie 42nd Account.
GD/174/2315	Orders for the Assistance and Guidance of the Non-Commisioned Officers of the 1st Battalion 79th Regiment, c.1806.
GD/189	Murray of Polmaise Papers.
GD/189/2/867	Letter by Miss Murray to Captain J. Murray of Polmaise, Grenadier Guards 10.1.1855.
GD/189/2/1081 (4)	Letter, General Sir J. Spencer Ewart to Murray of Polmaise 20.12.1914.
GD/225	Leith Hall Muniments.
GD/225/39/8	Diary of Captain A.S. Leith Hay 93rd 1844-1846.
GD/225/Box 41	Report on Barracks 1833.
GD/225/Box 42	Report of Lt. Colonel Alexander S. Leith Hay 93rd.
GD/225/Box 42 BI XI	'Instructions for keeping the Records of Soldiers Services' 25.11.1829.
GD/225/Box 42/BI XI	Warrant Regulating the Provision of Clothing, Necessaries, Great Coats, Accoutrements and Appointments of Corps of Infantry 21.6.1828.
GD/244	Buccleuch Muniments.
GD/244 Box 24	Estimate of clothing and Accountrements for an officer of the 79th Highlanders c.1845.
GD/254	Lindsay of Dowhill Papers.
GD/254/697/1	Letter Book of Colonel Martin Lindsay 78th Highlanders Ceylon 1831-1836.
GD/364	Hope of Luffness Muniments.
GD/364/1/1133	The Sounds for Duty and Exercise for the Trumpet and Bugle Horns of His Majesty's Regiments and Corps of Cavalry, 1798.
RH 2/4/207	HO Correspondence (Suppl).
RH 2/4/71 F.238v.	

Archival Sources (contd.)

Scottish Record Office: Edinburgh

RH/4/59/1-8	Diaries of A.D. Greenhill Gardyne, 1st Battalion Gordon Highlanders.
RH/4/84	Diaries of General Sir J. Spencer Ewart, 79th and Queen's Own Cameron Highlanders.
RH/4/141	Account by Donald Cameron, 79th and 93rd Highlanders.
RH/4/141	Notebook of Robert Sinclair 93rd Highlanders.

AD (Lord Advocate's Department)

AD/14/13/9	Precognition, the Kildonan Riots, Declaration of John Bannerman 3.2.1813.
AD/14/38/394	Papers regarding the trial of James Wilson, collier, 1837.
JC/13/78 of 10.1.1838	Lord Advocate v James Wilson, collier.
MW/1/78	HM Office of Works file on Edinburgh Castle.
MW/1/155	Correspondence regarding bathroom facilities at Edinburgh Castle.
MW/1/183	Commission of Works files on Edinburgh Castle.
RHP/2700	Plan of the Ordnance Depot and Lands at Greenlaw, 1836.
RHP/35483	Plan of the Canteen, Fort George c.1870.

Public Record Office: London

WO/3	Correspondence. Commander in Chief. War Office out letters.
WO/3/72/391	Instruction in respect of Regimental Records of Service.
WO/3/100/38	Masonic Lodges. 1843
WO/3/103/180	Holding of Mass in Barracks 1845.
WO/3/103/266-267	Correspondence regarding Drummers, Pipers and Musicians in the 79th. 20.12.1845.
WO/3/103/307	Establishment of boy musicians. 1846.
WO/3/115/387	Establishment of Pipers in Highland Regiments. 28.1.1854.
WO/3/131/66	Masonic Lodges. 1836.
WO/3/133/102	Abolition of the Order of Merit. 79th Highlanders 1838.
WO/3/133/235	Admission of Presbyterian Ministers to Barracks 1839.
WO/3/321/271-272	Correspondence regarding the establishment of Pipers in Highland Regiments. Adjutant General to Military Secretary. 12.11.1853.
WO/3/395/304	Establishment for Bands, 1821.
WO/3/455/219	Abolition of the Order of Merit. 93rd Highlanders 1840.
WO/4/149/30	Letter of Service of the 79th Regiment.
WO/4/151/207	Letter of Service of the 92nd (100th) Regiment.
WO/4/173/481	Letter of Service of the 93rd Regiment.
WO/4/729-130	St. Helena. Transfer from H.E.I.C. to the Crown 1833-1842.
WO/12	Muster Books and Pay Lists.
WO/17	Monthly Returns.
WO/25	Registers various.
WO/25/1137	Vol. 6-156 Papers relating to the Investigations into the services of soldiers discharged and of soldiers serving1828-1833.
WO/25/1167	Embarkation Return. 79th Dublin 30.7.1857.
WO/25/1192	Disembarkation return of the 73rd arriving at Portsmouth from Plymouth 1863.
WO/25/1194	Disembarkation Return of the 74th Highlanders arriving at Gibraltar from Dublin, 8.2.1868.
WO/25/1194	Disembarkation Return of the 42nd arriving at Portsmouth from Bombay 14.3.1868.
WO/25/1195	Disembarkation Return of the 79th, Bombay/Portsmouth 1871.
WO/27	Inspection Reports.

Archival Sources (contd.)

Public Record Office: London

WO/30/93	Statement of the Bibles and Books of Common Prayer sent to the Regiments of the Army 1825-1844.
WO/32/5450	Papers regarding the establishment of Pipers in Lowland Regiments c.1924.
WO/32/12150	War Office file regarding the training of Army Pipers in Piobaireachd c.1909.
WO/33/6A	Report of the Barracks and Hospitals Improvement Commission. Interim Reports on Barracks and Hospitals. 1858.
WO/33/7	Report of the Barracks and Hospitals Improvement Commision. Interim Reports on Barracks and Hospitals, 1859.
WO/33/8	Report of the Barracks and Hospitals Improvement Commission. Interim Reports on the Barracks and Hospitals 1859.
WO/33/22	Papers regarding the abolition of branding 1871.
WO/33/26	Papers on the Ashanti War: Wolsey to Cardwell 18.12.1873.
WO/43/422	1827-57 (54039) Edinburgh Inhabitants Objection to the billeting of troops.
WO/43/542	WO Memorandum 1831 regarding Soldier Settlers in the Colonies.
WO/43/666	Liability of Soldiers to maintain their families.
WO/43/716	Papers regarding soldier's gardens in the West Indies c.1840.
WO/43/787	Petition of 1846 by the Sergeants of the British Army.
WO/43/871	Clothing and Accoutrements. 1854/55.
WO/44/139	Papers regarding the drainage system, Gibraltar 1832.
WO/44/546	Plan of Barrack room interior Forton Barracks c.1820.
WO/44/549	Plan of Men's and women's privies Portsmouth 1829.
WO/44/549	Plan of the Canteen at Cambridge Barracks Portsmouth 1829.
WO/44/551	Plan of Cast Iron Barrack fittings c.1827.
WO/44/560	Bedstead design by Lt. Hall. 1838-1844.
WO/44/596	Plan of the Canteen at Port Louis 1829-1834.
WO/44/597	Installation of Gas lighting at Halifax Citadel N.S. 1844.
WO/81/69	Judge Advocate's Records.
WO/91/13	Courts Martial Reports.
WO/93/18	Trials of Officers 1806-1904.
WO/97	Soldiers Records.
WO/97/1020	Papers of James Ross 93rd.
WO/97/3354	Enlistment and Attestation Forms of Pipe Major John McDonald 42nd.
WO/284/64	Garrison Order Book, Gibraltar.

National Library of Scotland

Acc. No. 8396/1 (Glen Collection): MS Book of Pipe Music probably belonging to Piper James Hogg 25th King's Own Scottish Borderers Meerut India 1886.
Acc. No. 8396/4 (Glen Collection): MS Book of Pipe Music c.1880 (author unknown).
Acc No. 8396/16: Day Book of Thomas Glen, 2 North Bank Street, Edinburgh. 1847.
NLS. MS/10305: Letters of Sydney B. Jameson, HQ 1st Army and his son Alistair Jameson, 7th and 2nd Seaforth Highlanders and 1st Cameron Highlanders.
MacDonald, Donald. 'A Collection of the ancient martial music of Caledonia called Piobaireachd as performed on the great Highland Bagpipe'. Edinburgh: Donald MacDonald, c.1822. (Glen 298)
NLS MHS 167: Duty Calls and Favourite Tunes of the Seaforth Highlanders · · · from Pipe Major Ronald Mackenzie's Manuscript Book. Settings played by the 78th Highlanders. Elgin: Seaforth Highlanders, 1901.
NLS Mus. Box 9.594: Menzies, Captain Robert, 'A Preceptor for the great Highland Bagpipe'. Edinburgh: Oliver and Boyd, 1818.

Archival Sources (contd.)

National Library of Scotland (contd.)

NLS 313: Sutherland Estate Papers. NLS 313/2236, 2259 and 3478.
NLS MS/2234: Diary of F.W. Traill Burroughs 93rd Highlanders.
NLS Map Division: a) Malta: OS 1929 Sheet IV and V, War Office Geographical Section General Staff No. 3852. b) Lower Egypt in 4 sheets. Compiled at the Intelligence Branch, War Office from the original French survey in 1818-1882. Int. Dept. No. 104-107. Map L.35.32.

Central Library, Edinburgh

Scottish Naval and Military Academy 1/U 548/B29327. Major Charles Downes, Letter to the subscribers of the Scottish Naval and Military Academy 1832.
Scottish Naval and Military Academy 1/U 548/B29246. Second letter of Major Charles Downes to the subscribers of the Scottish Naval and Military Academy.

Scottish United Services Museum Archives, Edinburgh Castle.

Formal written application to marry by Private William Clark 42nd and 79th. 1857—c.1880. 42/73 (42) 8571.
Rules of the Military Academy, Edinburgh.
Regimental Order Book 78th Highlanders 1857-1866. A242 72/78.
Standing Orders of the 74th Highlanders 1850.
Letters and Papers of William Wilson and Son, Tartan Manufacturers, Bannockburn.

Argyll and Sutherland Highlanders Regimental Archives, Stirling Castle (91st and 93rd)
(Items are listed in chronological order)

Digest of the Services of the 91st or Argyllshire Regiment of Infantry 1794-1860 R/17/115/9
The Descriptive Roll Book of the 93rd Sutherland Highlanders 1799-1831.
91st Highlanders. Register of Soldiers who have died while serving in the Regiment from 1812 to 1881. R/94.
Alexr. Murray 93rd, Soldiers Small Book 1827.
Regimental Order Book Left Wing 93rd Highlanders, Morne Bruce Dominica 1830-1832. Sb/17.
Standing Orders of the 93rd Highlanders 1835. R/226.
Letter Book of Captain Bertie Gordon 91st South Africa 1843-1846. R/58
Squad Roll Book of Captain F. Burroughs No. 6 Company 93rd Highlanders 1857. SBC/93.
Private George Greig 93rd Highlanders. Diary and Poetry Book. R/144.
Commanding Officer's Rough Order Book 91st Highlanders Kamptee, India 1860. R/16.
91st (1st Battalion Argyll and Sutherland Highlanders) Permanent Order Book 1862-1884.
Marriage Certificate of Drum Major James Duff 93rd Highlanders to Elizabeth Gibson, Jhansi, India. 22.6.1869.
Papers of Private Alfred Guttridge 91st Highlanders. 1870.
Undated letter c.1882 to Lt. Colonel Ewan H.D. Macpherson to R.H. Burgoyne.
Scrap Book History of the 91st Highlanders presented to the Officers Mess 1st Battalion Argyll and Sutherland Highlanders by Lt. Colonel H.G. Robley 17.7.1883. R/50.
Diary of George A. McL. Sceales, B Coy. 1st Battalion Argyll and Sutherland Highlanders Oct. 1899-1903. R/264.
An Officer's notebook, probably belonging to Lt. Hunter, Argyll and Sutherland Highlanders regarding trooping to and service in South Africa 1900. Sb.5.
Colonel R.B. Urmston. 'A District Command', unpublished paper, c.1909.
Diary of Lt. Robert Lindsay Mackay MC, 11th and 1/8th Argyll and Sutherland Highlanders Sept. 1916-Jan. 1919.

The Black Watch Regimental Archives, Balhousie Castle, Perth (42nd and 73rd)

Roll of Enlistments of the 42nd 1795-1873. 2285.
Wheately, Lt. Colonel John, 42nd. Diary.

Archival Sources (contd.)

The Black Watch Regimental Archives, Balhousie Castle, Perth (42nd and 73rd) (contd.)

Standing Orders of the 42nd, 1833. 355-51 (42).
Agent's account of Ensign Pitcairn 42nd Highlanders 19.10.1835. 395 File HS—P-Q.
Letter of Sergeant John Grant 42nd. c.1844. File H4 (42) Sec. G.
Diary of Colonel J.W. Wedderburn 28/714/1 and 2.
Standing Orders of the 73rd Regiment, Cape Town 1850. 295/3593.
Order Book of the 42nd. 1854-1860. 27/2270.
Order Book of the 42nd, 1864-1886. 30/2271.
Lt. J. Wilson 42nd, Diary of a Voyage to India from England 1857.
Diary of Private A.W. McIntosh 42nd. 421(3591 (1) and (2)).
Robb, Private Alexander, 'Reminiscences of a Veteran' 933/Ac. No. 4440.
MS Book of Pipe Music belonging to Pipe Major William Ross 42nd. 788/91.
Diary of Bandsman A.V. Barwood, 1st Battalion Black Watch. 1883.
Diary of Lt. Colonel Adrian Grant Duff, Black Watch 1888-1914. BWRM.
Recruiting poster of the Black Watch c.1890.
Diary and papers of Private H. Ogilvie, 1st Battalion Black Watch.

Gordon Highlanders Regimental Archives, Aberdeen (75th and 92nd)

Journal by Private Soldier in the Ranks of the 92nd Gordon Highlanders 1794-1805. (The writer is believed to be Private Nicoll.)
Returns and States 92nd Regiment 1799-1805. Return of Men of HM 92nd Regmt. of Foot Rejected by Staff Surgeon Peak—Kilkenny 25th February 1802.
Register of Deserters 92nd Regiment.
75th Regiment, Delhi and Lucknow Prize Roll.
MS Account of the 1st Battalion Gordon Highlanders in the Le Cateau area August 1914 by 2/Lt. Hon. S. Frazer, later Lord Saltoun.
Memoir of Captain Alex. D.L. Stewart MC of Achnacone.
Letter of Lord Saltoun to Ian Stewart of Achnacone 1978.

Queen's Own Highlanders Regimental Archives, Cameron Barracks, Inverness (72nd/78th and 79th)

Recruiting Handbill of the 79th.
Account of Alan Cameron. 79th Highlanders.
Standing Orders for the 79th Regiment of Foot (or Cameron Highlanders), 1st May 1819. 142a/79.
Standing Orders 1821: 78th, or Ross-shire Highland Regiment, Dublin.
Betting Book of the Officers Mess 78th Highlanders 1822-1907. (London: privately printed, 1909).
Report of Sergeant Cameron 79th Highlanders 18.7.1822. MS/646.
Record of Donations of Plate 72nd Regiment, 1823.
Standing Orders of the 72nd Regiment or Duke of Albany's Own Highlanders. Richmond Barracks, Dublin, 1827. 676/72.
Regimental Standing Order Book. 79th Highlanders 144/79.
Standing Orders of the 79th Highlanders 1835. 143/79.
Standing Orders of the 78th Highlanders 1847. 839/78.
Reminiscences of Colour Sergeant Joseph Wylie Stevens 22nd and 72nd. M. 79/6. 1865-c.1890.
Minute Book of the Officers Mess 79th Highlanders 1844-1899. MS/1161.
Diary of Lt. William Parke 72nd. 1845.
Mess Rules adopted by the Officers of the 79th Highlanders, Quebec 1st May 1849. MS/149/79.
Letters of John C. Stewart 72nd Highlanders 1849-1858. S/439.
Letter of Pipe Major Richard Steuart 79th Highlanders to his wife, 24.2.1855. 5092.
Standing Orders of the 72nd Highlanders Peshawar 1873. Privately printed.
Military Forces Localisation. Bill of Quantities for Erection of a Brigade Depot at Inverness, North Britain, July 1877.
72nd Highlanders Regimental Orders During the Afghan Campaign 1879-1880. 23/72.

Archival Sources (contd.)

Queen's Own Highlanders Regimental Archives, Cameron Barracks, Inverness (72nd/78th and 79th)

Record Book of Plate, Books, Pictures etc., presented to or acquired by the Sergeants Mess 72nd Duke of Albany's Own Highlanders, now 1st Battalion Seaforth Highlanders. Compiled by G.W. Anderson.
Standing Orders of the 2nd Battalion Seaforth Highlanders, late 78th Highlanders, Lucknow 1884. 84/25.
War Diary and MS Notes of Colonel Craig Brown, Queen's Own Cameron Highlanders. 1914.

Royal Highland Fusiliers (21st/71st and 74th) Regimental Archives

Digest of Services 74th Highlanders Vol. 1 1787-1852. D/1/11.
Standing Orders of the 74th Regiment, Belfast 1834. D/84.
Diaries and Notes on Ornithology and Sport of Henry Robert Kelham 74th Highlanders 1875-1910.
Mess Minute Book of the 74th Highlanders, 1890. P/8.
Handbill advertising the sale of an Officer's stable of the 74th Regiment. Byzabad India, c.1890. Contained in Photograph Album and Scrap Book of the 74th Regiment. N/44.
Standing Orders of the 74th HLI, Jersey 1904.

Edinburgh University Library Archives and Collections

'Comparative view of the Pay of Officers in the French and British Service 1835'. Edinburgh University Library Special Collections P/384.
MacDonald, Joseph, 'A Compleat theory of the Scots Highland bagpipe'. MS La 111, 804.
University of Edinburgh Collection of Historic Musical Instruments. The Reid Concert Hall, Edinburgh.

Glasgow University Archives

The Farmer Collection MS 118.
The McLagan Collection. 'Selection from the King's Regulations in Gaelic', Glasgow University MS 1042/11. 'An Address to the Soldiers of the 42nd Regmt', Glasgow University MS 1042/135(A).

Oral History Archives

Major Dan Bonar 2/HLI (74th).
Private Reginald Lobban, 1st Battalion Queen's Own Cameron Highlanders. Tape recordings in possession of D.M. Henderson.
Corporal Frank MacFarlane 1st Battalion Black Watch. Tape recordings in possession of D.M. Henderson.

Private Sources

Five MS Books of Fife Music belonging to a Highland Militia Unit, c.1813. Property of Miss Maclean of Ardgower.
The Records and Archives of the Corps of Commissionaires for Edinburgh and the East of Scotland, Headquarters, Edinburgh.
Register of Dundee Burgh Police Force, Tayside Police Headquarters, Dundee.
Letters, papers and uniforms of the Mackay family regarding Henry Mackay and John Mackay of the 79th Highlanders. Lent by the surviving members of the Mackay family, New Zealand and United States of America.
Diary of Colonel A. Stirling 2nd Battalion Argyll and Sutherland Highlanders 1914. Property of Colonel J. Stirling (Retd.).
Letter of Sergeant John Tulloch 74th. 1855-1859. Property of Mr. L. Tulloch, Ballyclare, Co. Antrim.

Archival Sources (contd.)

Private Sources (contd.)

MS Book of Pipe Music belonging to Piper A. Thomson, G. Company, 1st Battalion Argyll and Sutherland Highlanders, Hong Kong 1888. The Army School of Piping, Edinburgh Castle.

Register and Papers in the Archives of Queen Victoria School, Dunblane.

Parliamentary Papers

PP 1802-03 IV c.45	Reports of the Select Committee on the Survey of the Central Highlands of Scotland. Mr. Telford's survey and Report on the Coasts and Central Highlands of Scotland.
PP 1822 XIX c.565	A Return of the Manner in which £40,000—voted in the Ordnance Estimates for 1821 for stores—was Expended.
PP 1822 XIX c.570	Army Return of Public Servants in the Army who have become defaulters in their Accompts with the War Office 1810-1822.
PP 1824 XVI c.15	Estimates of the Office of Ordnance.
PP 1824 XVI c.60	Abstract of the Accounts of the Several Commissaries.
PP 1825 XVIII c.35	Ordnance Estimates. Commissariat Department.
PP 1826 XX c.60	Estimates for the Office of Ordnance (Gibraltar).
PP 1828 XVII c.28	Estimates of the Office of Ordnance.
PP 1828 XVII c.56	Account of Extraordinary Expenses of the Army.
PP 1829 XVI c.17	Estimates of the Ordnance Department. Military Store Branch.
PP 1830 XVIII c.130	Abstracts of Commissaries Accounts (Jamaica).
PP 1830 XVIII c.210	Return of the numbers of contracts now existing for supplies for the Ordnance Department.
PP 1830 XVIII c.580	A Return of the Rates of Pay and Allowances to the Officers and men of the Army in the years 1792-1829.
PP 1830-31 VI c.268	Abstracts of the Accounts of the Several Commissaries, upon the Colonies for 1829. Commissariat Accounts Quebec.
PP 1831-32 XXXIII c.159	Report on Convict Hulks.
PP 1833 VII c.650	Report from the Select Committee on Army and Navy Appointments.
PP 1834 VIII c.559	Report from the Select Committee on Inquiry into Drunkenness.
PP 1835 XXXVIII c.171	Reports of Officers on the State of the Disembodied Militia of the United Kingdom.
PP 1835 VI c.473	Report from the Select Committee on Colonial Military Expenditure.
PP 1836 XXII c.59	Report from His Majesty's Commissioners for Inquiry into the System of Military Punishments in the Army.
PP 1837-38 XL c.596	Statistical Report on the Sickness, Mortality and Invalidity Among the Troops in the West Indies.
PP 1849 XXXII c.120	Return of Non Commissioned Officers, Royal Military College Cadets and Private Gentlemen who have obtained Commissions without purchase.
PP 1849 XXXII c.360	Account of the total charge for Military and Naval Half-Pay, and Pensions, and civil, Superannuation, and compensation Allowances, in each year, 1828 to 1848, both inclusive, compared with the whole Expenditure for the effective Establishments, and other National Expenses.
PP 1849 XXXII c.532	Memorandum of the Points upon which Candidates are to be examined before they are recommended for Commissions.
PP 1850 X c.662	The Report of the Committee on Army and Ordnance Expenditures.
PP 1850 XXIX c.1241	Report on the discipline and management of the Military Prisons 1849 by Lt. Colonel Jebb.
PP 1854-55 XII c.317	Report from the Select Committee on Sandhurst Royal Military College.

Archival Sources (contd.)

Parliamentary Papers (contd.)

PP 1857 IX c.101	Return showing what are the present subjects of Examination on entering the Army.
PP 1857-58 XXXVII c.127	Notice and Memorandum Recently issued, together with a copy of the Regulations for the future Admission of Candidates into the Junior Department: - Regulations for the Admission to, and for the Studies of Officers at the Staff College, and for other matters connected therewith.
PP 1857-58 XXXVII c.498	Report of the Commission Appointed to Enquire into the Purchase and Sale of Commissions in the Army.
PP 1857-58 XXXVII c.499	Number of General Courts Martial held on Officers during the last Five Years both at Home and Abroad.
PP 1861 XV c.2762	Report of the Commissioners Appointed to Inquire into the Present System of Recruiting in the Army.
PP 1861 XVI c.2839	General Report of the Commission appointed for improving the Sanitary Condition of Barracks and Hospitals.
PP 1862 XXXIII c.3051	Army Medical Department Statistical Report. 1860.
PP 1867 XV c.3752	Report of the Commissioners Appointed to Inquire into the Recruiting for the Army.
PP 1870 XLII c.57	Memorandum of the Inspector General of Recruiting.
PP 1872 XXXVII c.171	Return of the number of English, Scotch and Irish Commissioned Officers.
PP 1872 XXXVII c.315	Return of the Number of English, Scotch, and Irish Non-Commissioned Officers, Corporals and Privates in each Regiment.
PP 1872 XXXVII c.493	Memorandum and Report on the Organisation of the Various Military Land Forces.
PP 1872 XXXVII c.575	Army Estimates.
PP 1873 XVIII c.712	Final Report of the Committee on the Organisation of the Various Military Land Forces of the Country.
PP 1877 XVIII c.1654	Report of the Committee to Enquire into certain Questions that have arisen with respect to the Militia and the Present Brigade Depot System.
PP 1877 XVIII c.1655	Report of the Inspector General of Recruiting.
PP 1877 XVIII c.1677	Report of the Committee on Boy Enlistment.
PP 1881 XX c.2793	Report of the Committee on the Formation of Territorial Regiments.
PP 1881 XX c.2832	Annual Report of the Inspector General of Recruiting.
PP 1882 XXXIII c.3449	Report on the Discipline and Management of Military Prisons 1881.
PP 1886 XIII c.4677	Annual Report of the Inspector General of Recruiting.
PP 1890 XIX c.5953	Annual Report of the Inspector General of Recruiting.
PP 1892 XIX c.6582	Report of the Committee to consider the Terms and Conditions of Service in the Army (The Wantage Committee).
PP 1903 X c.1421	Report of the Committee to Enquire into the Nature of the Expenses Incurred by Officers of the Army and to suggest Measures for bringing Commissions within Reach of Men of Moderate Means.
PP 1904 XL c.1789	Report of His Majesty's Commissioners appointed to inquire into the Military preparations and other matters connected with the war in South Africa.
PP 1920 XXVIII c.119	Estimates.

Hansard

1766 Vol. XVI Speech of William Pitt, p.98.

Archival Sources (contd.)

Statutes

Act of Attainder 1746 2 Geo 19 c XXVI.
Act for Disarming the Highlands 1746 2 Geo 19 c XXXIX.
Vesting Act 1747 2 Geo 20 x XLI.
Heritable Jurisdictions Act 1747 2 Geo 20 c XLIII
Act for the Annexation and Administration of Forfeited Estates 1752 2 Geo 25 c XLI.
The Mutiny Act 1837.
The Crofters Act 1886, 49 and 50. Vict c 29.
The Military Service Act 1916.

Army Orders/War Office Circulars/Royal Warrants

G.O. of 5.8.1803 — Order Relative to Musicians and Bands of Music in Regiments.
G.O. of 28.12.1816 — Adoption of Drum Major Potter's system for Calls and Beats of the Drum and Fife.
Warrant of 1821 — Line Regiments Regulation Prices of Commissions
General Regulations and Orders of the Army of 1822. London: William Clowes (SUSM)

Regulations for sale of Retired Full and Half Pay Commissions. 25.4.1825.
H.G. Circular 24.12.1825 — Regulations regarding daily payment of soldiers.
Warrant of 21.6.1828 — Warrant Regulating the Provision of Clothing, Necessaries, Great Coats, Accoutrements and Appointments for Corps of Infantry (see SRO GD/225/Box 42/Bl.xi).
H.G. Circular of 24.6.1830 — Restrictions on the summary powers of Commanding Officers.
H.G. Circular of 22.1.1831 — Habitual Drunkenness.
Warrant of 17.5.1831 — Rates of Pay, Necessaries and Stoppages.
H.G. Circular of 24.8.1833 — Restrictions on Corporal Punishment.
H.G. Order of 1.1.1836 — '. . . an account of the services of every Regiment in the British Army shall be published . . .'.
Royal Warrant 14.11.1845 — Warrant granting the 74th the title '74th '(Highland)' Regiment of Foot'.
H.G. Circular of 10.8.1846 — Restrictions on Corporal Punishment.
WO Circular 14.5.1850 — Introduction of examinations for promotion from Ensign to Lieutenant and Captain.
Warrant 6.6.1854 — Provision of Clothing by Colonel of Regiments.
HG Order 9.9.1856 — Depot Battalions.
WO Circular 194 of 28.12.1857. — The experimental use of Pensioners in Recruiting.
G.O. 71 of 3.2.1858 — Levy Money (Infantry).
H.G. Circular of 23.4.1858 — Bands/4 Gen. No. 92/35. Establishment of a uniform pitch in British Military Bands.
WO Circular 573 of 27.3.1860 — Regulations regarding Gas Supply to Barracks.
GO Horse Guards 23.5.1860 No. 752 — Syllabus of training, lectures and examinations Staff College.
WO Circular 606 of 11.7.1860 — Whitewashing—Foreign barracks.

Archival Sources (contd.)

Army Orders/War Office Circulars/Royal Warrants (contd.)

WO Circular 767 of 26.6.1862	Barrack coal allowance.
H.G. Order of 29.8.1862	Army Bandmasters to take precedence over all civilians.
WO Circular 788 of 28.10.1862	Supply of Toilet Paper by Barrack Masters.
WO Circular 828 of 13.7. 1863	Scales of cooking utensils.
H.G. General Order 828 of 13.7.1862.	Provision of Sergeant Cooks on establishment.
WO Circular of 1.1.1869	Whitewashing of barracks.
Royal Warrant 20.7.1871	Abolition of Purchase.
G.O. No. 28 of 1.3.1872	Scale of fines for drunkenness.
G.O. of 1.7.1880 No. 93	General Order forbidding the use of barrack room kit boxes.
Army Order 186 of 1906	Militia extended training.

SECONDARY SOURCE MATERIAL

Printed Books

Adam, R.J. (ed.), *Papers on Sutherland Estate Management 1802-1816*, vols. 1 and 2 (Edinburgh: Scottish History Society, T. & A. Constable Ltd., 1972).
Alexander, Ziggi and Dewjee, Audrey (eds.), *Wonderful Adventures of Mrs Seacole* (Bristol: Falling Wall Press, 1984).
Anton, James, 42nd, *Retrospect of a Military Life* (Edinburgh: H.H. Lizars and Fraser and Co., 1841).

Army Lists, 1820-1920

Babington, Anthony, *For the Sake of Example* (London: Leo Cooper, 1983).
Baird, William, *General Wauchope* (Edinburgh & London: Oliphant Anderson and Ferrier, 1907).
Bamfield, Veronica, *On the Strength, the Story of the British Army Wife* (London: Charles Knight & Co. Ltd., 1974).
Barnes, Major R.M., *The Uniforms and History of the Scottish Regiments* (London: Sphere Books, 1972).
Barnett, Correlli, *Britain and Her Army* (London: Allen Lane, The Penguin Press, 1970).
Barthorp, Michael, *War on the Nile* (Poole: Blandford Press, 1984).
Binney, Harris and Winnington, *Lost Houses of Scotland* (London: Save Britain's Heritage, 1980).
Blair, Daniel, MD (ed John Davy MD, FRS), *Some Account of the last Yellow Fever Epidemic of British Guiana* (Inspector General of Army Hospitals, 1850).
Bond, Brian, *The Victorian Army and the Staff College 1854-1914* (London: Eyre Methuen, 1972).
Bruce, Anthony, *The Purchase System in the British Army 1660-1871* (London: Royal Historical Society, 1980).
Bryant, Arthur, *Jackets of Green* (London: Collins, 1972).
Bulloch, J.M. *The Gordon Highlanders: The History of their Origin together with a Transcript of their First Official Muster* (Banffshire Field Club, 1913).
Burgoyne, R.H. *Historical Records of the 93rd Sutherland Highlanders* (London: Richard Bentley and Son, 1883). Copy in the Argyll and Sutherland Highlanders Regimental Museum, Stirling Castle has been annotated by E.S. Wood.
Burke, Sir Bernard, *Dictionary of the Landed Gentry* (London: Harrison, 1858).
Dictionary of the Peerage and Baronetage (London: Harrison, 1876).
History of the Landed Gentry (London: Harrison, 1879).

Archival Sources (contd.)

Secondary Source Material (contd.)

Burke's Landed Gentry (London: Harrison, 1937). 15th Edition.
Burt, Captain, *Letters from a Gentleman in the North of Scotland to his Friend in London* (London: Rest Fenner, 1818).
The Cabar Feidh Collection, Pipe Music of the Queen's Own Highlanders (Seaforth and Camerons) (London: Patersons Publications Ltd., 1984).
Campbell, R.H. and Dow, J.B.A, *Source Book of Scottish Economic and Social History* (Oxford: Basil Blackwell, 1968).
Cannon, Roderick D., *A Bibliography of Bagpipe Music* (Edinburgh: John Donald Publishers Ltd., 1980).
Childers, E.S.E., *The Life of Childers* (London: MacMillan & Co., 1901).
Cockerill, A.W., *Sons of the Brave* (Bury St. Edmunds: Leo Cooper, 1984).
Cole, Lt. Colonel H.N., OBE, TD, *The Story of Aldershot* (Aldershot: Gale and Polden, 1951).
Collinson, Francis, *The Traditional and National Music of Scotland* (London: Routledge and Kegan Paul, 1966).
Comrie, John D., *History of Scottish Medicine* (London: William Blackwood, 1932).
The Corps of Commissionaires. Handbook of the Corps of Commissionaires. (privately printed).
The History of the Corps of Commissionaires (privately printed).
Davidson, Major H., *History and Services of the 78th Highlanders* (*Ross-shire Buffs*) (Edinburgh: W. and A.K. Johnston, 1901).
Debrett's Illustrated Peerage, Baronetage, Knightage and House of Commons (London: Doan and Son, 1866).
Demidoff, Count Anatolle, *Etapes Maritimes sur les Côtes D'Espagne* (Florence: 1858, privately printed).
Dictionary of National Biography (Oxford University Press, 1930).
Dow, Alexander C., *Ministers to the Soldiers of Scotland* (Edinburgh: Oliver and Boyd, 1962).
Drew, *Commissioned Officers in the Medical Services of the British Army 1660-1960* (London: Wellcome, 1968).
Drummond-Norrie, William, *Loyal Lochaber* (Glasgow: Morison Brothers, 1898).
Duff, David (ed.), *Queen Victoria's Highland Journals* (Exeter: Webb and Bower, 1980).
Dundas, Colonel David, *Principles of Military Movements Chiefly applied to Infantry illustrated by Manoeuvres of the Prussian Troops and by an outline of the British Campaigns in Germany during the war of 1757* (London: T. Cadell, 1788).
Dunn-Pattison, R.P., *History of the 91st Argyllshire Highlanders* (Edinburgh: William Blackwood and Sons, 1910).
The Edinburgh Almanac or Universal Scots and Imperial Register for 1826 (Edinburgh: Oliver and Boyd, 1825).
Ewart, Lt. General John Alexander, *The Story of a Soldier's Life* (London: Simpson Low, 1881).
Ewing, Juliana Horatia, *The Story of a Short Life* (London: The Society for Promoting Christian Knowledge, 1900).
Fabb, John and Carman, W.Y., *The Victorian and Edwardian Army from Old Photographs* (London: Prunell Book Services Ltd., (undated)).
Fairrie, Lt. Colonel A.A., *A History of the Queen's Own Highlanders* (Inverness: RHQ Queen's Own Highlanders, 1983).
Farmer, Henry George, *Military Music* (Privately printed and undated).
Ferguson, James (ed.), *Papers Illustrating the History of the Scots Brigade in the service of the United Netherlands 1572-1782*, 2 Vols. (Edinburgh, University Press, 1899).
Ferguson, Thomas, *Scottish Social Welfare 1864-1914* (Edinburgh: S. Livingstone Ltd. 1958).
Forbes, Archibald, *The Black Watch* (London: Cassell, 1896).
Forbes-Mitchell, William, *Reminiscences of the Great Mutiny* (London: Macmillan and Co Ltd., 1910).
Fortesque, The Hon. J.W., *A History of the British Army* (London: Macmillan and Co. Ltd., 1910).
Forty, George and Anne, *They also Served* (Speldhurst, Kent: Midas Books, 1979).
Gleichen, Major General Lord Edward, *A Guardsman's Memoirs* (London: Blackwood, 1932).
Glover, Michael (ed.), *A Gentleman Volunteer—Letters of John Hennell from the Peninsular War 1812-1813* (London: Heinemann, 1979).

Archival Sources (contd.)

Secondary Source Material (contd.)

Goff, G.L., *Historical Records of the 91st Argyllshire Highlanders* (London: Richard Bentley, 1891).

Gordon-Alexander, W., Lt. Colonel 93rd Highlanders, *Recollections of a Highland Subaltern* (London: Edward Arnold, 1898).

The Gordon Highlanders Pipe Music Collection, vol. 1 (London: Paterson's Publications, 1983).

Gould, R.F., *Military Lodges, 1732-1899* (Aldershot: Gale and Polden, 1899).

Grant, Elizabeth, *Memoirs of a Highland Lady* (London: John Murray, 1898).

Greenhill Gardyne, Lt. Colonel A.D., *The Life of a Regiment*, vol. III (London: Leo Cooper, 1972).

Greenhill Gardyne, Lt. Colonel C., *The Life of a Regiment*, vols. I and II (London: The Medici Society Ltd., 1929).

Grierson, Major General J.M, *Records of the Scottish Volunteer Force 1859-1908* (Edinburgh: William Blackwood, 1909).

Gunn, Adam and Mackay, John (eds.), *Sutherland and Reay Country* (Glasgow: *Celtic Monthly*, John Mackay, 1897).

Haddow, Professor Alexander John, *The History and Structure of Ceol Mor* (privately printed, 1982).

Hamilton, General Sir Ian, *Listening for the Drums* (London: Faber and Faber, 1944).

The Soul and Body of an Army (London: Edward Arnold, 1921).

Hamilton, Ian B.M., *The Happy Warrior* (London: Cassell, 1966).

Harries-Jenkins, Gwyn, *The Army in Victorian Society* (London: Routledge and Kegan Paul, 1977).

Harrow School Register 1801-1893 (London: Longmans, 1894).

Historical Records of the Queen's Own Cameron Highlanders, Vols. I-IV (Edinburgh: William Blackwood and Sons, 1909).

Infantry Bugle Sounds also for Mounted Infantry and Regimental Calls (London: Henry Potter & Co., 1909).

Infantry Training—The Drummer's Handbook. Army Code No. 71333 File No. D/ACGS(TRG)/13/28/2 1983.

James, Lawrence, *1854-1856 Crimea—The War with Russia from Contemporary Photographs* (Thame, Oxfordshire: Hayes Kennedy, 1981).

Jones, John Milbank, *The History of Milton Barracks Gravesend and its occupants 1860-1970* (Gravesend: W.E. Lewis and Sons Ltd., 1985).

Keltie, J.S. (ed.), *History of the Scottish Highlands, Clans and Regiments* (Edinburgh: A Fullarton and Coy., 1881).

The King's Regulations and Orders for the Army 1912 (London: HMSO, 1912).

Leask and McCance, *The Regimental Records of the Royal Scots* (Dublin: Alex. Thom and Co. Ltd., 1915).

Linklater, E. and A., *The Black Watch* (London: Barrie and Jenkins, 1977).

Logue, Kenneth J., *Popular Disturbances in Scotland 1780-1815* (Edinburgh: John Donald Publishers Ltd., 1979).

MacDonald, Donald, *A collection of the ancient martial music of Caledonia called piobaireachd as performed on the great Highland bagpipe* (Edinburgh: Donald MacDonald c.1822). (Copy in the National Library of Scotland, Glen 298.)

A collection of quicksteps, strathspeys, reels and jigs Arranged for the Highland bagpipe (Edinburgh: Donald MacDonald & Son, 1828).

Mackay, Angus, *A Collection of Ancient Piobaireachd or Highland Pipe Music* (Wakefield: E.P. Publishing Ltd., 1972) (first published Aberdeen, 1838).

McKay, James, 74th Highlanders, *Reminiscences of the last Kafir War* (Grahamstown: Richards Glanville & Co., 1871).

Mackay, John, *An Old Scots Brigade—Being the History of Mackay's Regiment* (Edinburgh: William Blackwood, 1885).

Mackay, Scobie, Major I.H., *Pipers and Pipe Music in a Highland Regiment* (Ross-shire printing and publishing Company). Copy in the QOHRM.

Mackenzie, Sir G. Stewart, Bart., *A General View of the Agriculture of the Counties of Ross and*

Archival Sources (contd.)

Secondary Source Material (contd.)

Cromarty with Observations on the means of their improvement (London: Constable and Co., 1810).

MacKerlie (published Anon.)., *An Account of the Scottish Regiments with the Statistics of Each, from 1808 to March 1861* (Edinburgh: William Nimmo, 1862).

MacLeod, Donald, *Donald McLeod's Gloomy Memories* (Glasgow: Archibald Sinclair, 1892).

MacVeigh, James, *Historical Record of the 42nd Royal Highlanders (Royal Highland Regiment, the Black Watch)* (Edinburgh: Thomas Jack). Edited and annotated by Major I.H. Mackay Scobie. Copy in SUSM, Edinburgh Castle.

Malcolm, Lt. Colonel G.I., *History of the Argyll and Sutherland Highlanders* (Stirling: Learmonth, 1972).

Mason, W.L., *The Highland Bagpipe* (Wakefield: E.P. Publishing, 1977).

Manual of Military Law (London: HMSO, 1914).

Middleton, Colonel A.H. (compiler), *Records of the Stirlingshire, Dumbarton, Clackmannan and Kinross Militia, Highland Borderers Light Infantry* (Stirling: E. Mackay, 1904).

Mitchell, B.R. and Deane, Phyllis, *Abstract of British Historical Statistics* (Cambridge: University Press, 1971).

Mockler Ferryman, Major A.F., *The Annals of Sandhurst* (London: Heinemann, 1900).

Munro, Surgeon William, *Reminiscences of Military Service with the 93rd Highlanders* (London: Hurst and Blackett, 1883).

Records of Service and Campaigning in Many Lands (London: Hurst and Blackett, 1887), 2 vols.

New Statistical Account (Edinburgh: William Blackwood & Sons, 1845).

Niven, David, *The Moon's a Balloon* (London: Coronet Books, 1973).

Oatts, Lt. Colonel L.B., DSO, *'Proud Heritage'—The Story of the Highland Light Infantry* (Edinburgh: Thomas Nelson, 1952).

An Officer, *Fifteen Years of Army Reform* (Edinburgh: William Blackwood, 1884).

Officers of the Black Watch 1725-1952 (Perth: Thomas Hunter, 1952).

Operations of the Tochi Field Force 1897-98 (Quetta, Pakistan: Nisa Traders, 7 Jinnah Cloth Market, Quetta, 1978).

Paget, Julian, *The Story of the Guards* (London: Osprey, 1976).

Palmer, Roy (ed.), *The Rambling Soldier* (Bungay, Suffolk: Peacock, 1977).

Paul, Sir James Balfour (ed.), *The Scots Peerage*, Vols. I—IX (Edinburgh: David Douglas, 1914).

Prebble, John, *Mutiny* (London: Secker and Warburg, 1975).

Pulsifier, Cameron W., *British Regiments in Halifax* (Parks, Canada, 1980).

The 78th Highlanders in Halifax 1869-71, The experiences of a Highland Regiment in a Garrison Town, vol. 1 (Parks, Canada, 1983).

The Queen's Empire, Part 6, *The Houses of the Queen and Her People* (London: Cassell and Co. (c. 1897)).

Queen's Regulations and Orders for the Army, July 1844, 1858.

Register of the Privy Council of Scotland II AD 1569-1578, ed. John Hill Burton (Edinburgh: HM General Register House, 1878).

Richards, Eric, *A History of the Highland Clearances* (London and Canberra: Croom Helm, 1982).

Richards, Frank, *Old Soldier Sahib* (London: Anthony Mott, 1983).

Richardson, General F.M., RAMC, *Fighting Spirit* (London: Leo Cooper, 1978).

Richardson J.S. and Root, Margaret E., *Official Guide, Stirling Castle* (Edinburgh: HMSO, 1978).

Rodgers, Colonel H.C.B., *Troopships and Their History* (London: Service and Co. Ltd., 1963).

Royle, Trevor, *Death Before Dishonour, The True Story of Fighting Mac* (Edinburgh: Mainstream Publishing, 1982).

Sage, Rev. Donald A.M., *Memorabilia Domestica; or Parish Life in the North of Scotland* (Edinburgh: Albyn Press, 1975).

The 5th Earl of Selkirk, *Observations of the Present State of the Highlands of Scotland with a view of the causes and probable consequences of emigration* (London, 1805).

Seton, Sir Bruce and Grant, Pipe Major John, *Pipes of War* (Wakefield: E.P. Publishing Ltd., 1975).

Archival Sources (contd.)

Secondary Source Material (contd.)

Skelly, Alan Ramsay, *The Victorian Army at Home* (London: Croom Helm, 1977).
Smout, T.C., *A History of the Scottish People 1560-1830* (London: Fontana, 1973).
Smyth, Brigadier Sir John, VC, *Sandhurst* (London: Weidenfeld and Nicholson, 1961).
Spiers, Edward M., *The Army and Society* (London: Longman, 1980).
Stanley, George F.G., *Canada's Soldiers 1604-1954* (Toronto: Macmillan and Coy. of Canada, 1954).
Stewart, Colonel David of Garth, *Sketches of the Character, Manners and Present State of the Highlands of Scotland with details of the Military Services of the Highland Regiments*, Vols. 1 and 2 (Edinburgh: Constable and Co., 1822).
Stewart, John of Ardvorlich, *The Camerons* (Stirling: Clan Cameron Association, 1974).
Swifte, Lt. Colonel L.B., *Victoria Barracks Sydney* (Sydney: National Library of Australia, 1974).
The Thin Red Line Almanac (Edinburgh: W. and A.K. Johnston Ltd., 1980).
Thomasson, Katherine and Buist, Francis, *Battles of the '45* (London: Book Club Associates, 1962).
Thomsett, R.G., *A Record Voyage in HMS Malabar* (London: Digby, Long & Co., 1902).
Thomson, William P.L., *The Little General and the Rousay Crofters* (Edinburgh: John Donald Publishers Ltd., 1981).
Torrens, Major General Sir Henry, *Field Exercises and Evolutions of the Army* (London: William Clowes, 1824).
Trumpet and Bugle Calls for the Army (London: HMSO, 1966). 26/Manuals/3830 Army Code No. 14163.
Trustram, Myna, *Women of the Regiment* (Cambridge: Cambridge University Press, 1984).
Walton, Colonel Clifford, CB, *History of the British Standing Army 1660-1700* (London: Harrison and Sons, 1884).
Wauchope, Major General A.G. (ed.), *A History of the Black Watch in the Great War* (London: Medici Society, 1926).
Wellington College Register 1854-1973 (The Old Wellingtonian Society, 1975). 9th Edition.
Wood, Evelyn, *From Midshipman to Field Marshal* (London: Methuen & Co., 1906), 2 vols.
Woodham-Smith, Cecil, *Florence Nightingale* (London: Constable, 1950).

Articles

Alexander, Sir J.E., 14th Regiment, 'On Desertion in Canada', *United Services Magazine*, 1842, Part 2 (London: Henry Colburn 1842), p. 473.
Anon., 'Drummers' (Replies), *Journal of the Society for Army Historical Research*, Vol. 20/21, 1941-1942, p. 182.
Bennett, Captain R.W., 'Military Law in 1839', *Journal of the Society for Army Historical Research*, Vol. XLVIII, No. 196, Winter 1970, pp. 225-241.
Burroughs, Peter, 'Crime and Punishment in the British Army 1815-1870', *The English Historical Review*, Vol. C, No. 396, July 1985, pp. 545-571.
Crouch, John, 'Majuba', *Soldiers of the Queen*, Journal of the Victorian Military Society No. 26, September 1981, p. 30.
Crowley, D.W., 'The Crofters Party 1885-1892', *Scottish Historical Review*, xxxv, pp. 110-126.
'Diary of Colonel E. Cuming 79th Highlanders', *The 79th News*, January 1935, pp. 78-84; April 1935, pp. 194-200; July 1935, p. 245.
Fairrie, Lt. Colonel A.A, 'Erracht's Regiment' (in 8 parts), *The Queen's Own Highlander*—Regimental magazine of the Queen's Own Highlanders (Seaforth and Camerons), May 1976-Winter 1980.
'100 years of the Local Regiment' (in 5 parts), *The Queen's Own Highlander*—Regimental Magazine of the Queen's Own Highlanders (Seaforth and Camerons), 1982-83.
'The Story of Fort George', *Queen's Own Highlander*, Vol. 24, No. 67, Winter 1984.
Farmer, Henry George, 'The Tenor Drum', *Journal of the Society for Army Historical Research*, Vol. 26/27, 1948-1949 (Notes), 907, p. 185.
'Foreign Army Bandmasters: their rise and fall', *Journal of the Society for Army Historical Research*, Vol. 26/27, 1948-1949, pp. 124-130.

Archival Sources (contd.)

Secondary Source Material (contd.)

'Scots Duty—Old Drum and Fife Calls of Scottish Regiments', *Journal of the Society for Army Historical Research*, Vols. 23/24/25, 1945-1947, pp. 65-70.

'Turkish influence in Military Music', *Journal of the Society for Army Historical Research*, Vols. 23/24/25, 1945-1947, p. 177.

'The Martial Fife', *Journal of the Society for Army Historical Research*, Vols. 23/24/25, 1945-1947, pp. 66-71.

Grayebrook, Lt. Colonel R.M., 'Test Certificate', *Journal of the Society for Army Historical Research*, Vols. 23/24/25, 1945-1947, Notes, p. 124.

Henderson, Diana M. (ed.), 'Private Reginald Lobban, 1st Battalion Queen's Own Cameron Highlanders', *Queen's Own Highlander*, vol. 24, No. 66, Summer 1984, pp. 29-32, and vol. 24, No. 67, Winter 1984, pp. 137-140.

'A Cunliffe Re-discovered—The 79th Highlanders in 1854', *Journal of the Society for Army Historical Research*, Vol. LX, No. 244, Winter 1982, pp. 191-195.

Johnston, S.H.F.,'The Scots Army in the Reign of Anne', *Transactions of the Royal Historical Society*, 1953.

Jones, R.M., 'Cox and Co.—Army Agents', *Journal of the Society for Army Historical Research*, No. 164, December 1962, pp. 178-186 and XVIV No. 180, December 1966, pp. 195-204.

Kendall, J. Murray, MBE, FSA, 'The Lancespessade and the History of 'Lance' Rank', *Journal of the Society for Army Historical Research*, Vol. 5/6, 1926/1927, pp. 81-86.

Mackay Scobie, Major I.H., 'The Scottish Tartan Manufacturers and Bonnet Makers', *Journal of the Society for Army Historical Research*, Vol. 20/21, 1941/1942, pp. 64-70.

'Unpublished Letters of John Cheetham McLeod, A Scotsman in the Crimean War', *The Red Hackle*, No. 210, August 1984, p. 870; No. 211, December 1984, pp. 12-14.

Murray, Lt. Colonel David J.S., 'What's in a Name', *Piping Times*, Vol. 33, No. 9, June 1981.

'The Evolution of the Regimental Music', *Queen's Own Highlander*, Vol. 24, No. 67, Winter 1984, p. 133, and No. 68, Summer 1985, p. 22.

Pereira, Major H.P.E., 'Colonel Eyre Crabbe of the 74th, with some observations on D. Cunliffe as a Military Painter', *Journal of the Society for Army Historical Research*, Winter 1955, Vol. XXXIII, No. 136.

Razzell, P.E., 'Social Origins of Officers in the Indian and British Home Army 1758-1962', *British Journal of Sociology*, Vol. XIV, Sept. 1963, pp. 248-160.

Rogers, Byron, 'Still waiting for Napoleon', *Sunday Telegraph Magazine*, No. 375, December 18th, 1983, pp. 36-38.

Semple, A.J., 'The Fenian Infiltration of the British Army', *Journal of the Society for Army Historical Research*, Vol. LII, No. 211, Autumn 1977, pp. 133-160.

Strachan, Hew, 'The British Army 1815-1856', *Journal of the Society for Army Historical Research*, Vol LXIII, No. 254, Summer 1985, p. 78.

Sumner, Rev. Percy, 'Army Inspection Returns', *Journal of the Society for Army Historical Research*, Vol. 5/6, 1926-1927, pp. 26-27.

Turner, J.D., 'Army Agency', *Journal of the Society for Army Historical Research*, Vol. XII, 1934, pp. 27-46.

Periodicals, Newspapers and Journals consulted:

Albany Monthly Record, Regimental Journal of the 72nd Highlanders.

The Argyllshire Highlanders Regimental News, Regimental Magazine of the 1st Battalion Argyll and Sutherland Highlanders, 91st.

Journal of the Society for Army Historical Research.

British Journal of Sociology.

Caledonian Mercury.

Drummers Call, The Newsletter of the Corps of Drums Society.

Edinburgh Evening Courant.

Edinburgh Evening News.

The English Historical Review.

The Gentleman's Monthly Magazine of Fashion and Costumes de Paris.

The Glasgow Herald.

Archival Sources (contd.)

Secondary Source Material (contd.)

The HLI Chronicle. The Regimental Journal of the Highland Light Infantry, 71st and 74th.
Inverness Courier.
Piping Times.
The Red Hackle. The Chronicle of the Black Watch (Royal Highland Regiment), the Affiliated Regiments and the Black Watch Association.
Transactions of the Royal Historical Society.
The 79th News. Regimental Magazine of the Queen's Own Cameron Highlanders.
The Scotsman.
Scottish Historical Review.
Soldiers of the Queen. Journal of the Victorian Military Society.
Sunday Telegraph Magazine.
Sutherland News. Regimental paper of the 2nd Battalion Argyll and Sutherland Highlanders.
The Thin Red Line. Regimental paper of the 2nd Battalion Argyll and Sutherland Highlanders.
The Tiger and the Sphinx. The Regimental Journal of the Gordon Highlanders.
The Times.
The Queen's Own Highlander. The Regimental Magazine of the Queen's Own Highlanders (Seaforth and Camerons) Incorporating Cabar Feidh and *The 79th News.*
United Services Magazine.
The Wykehamist. Journal of Winchester School.

Unpublished Theses and Papers

Bond, B.J., 'The Introduction and Operation of Short Service and Localisation in the British Army 1868-1892', London University M.A. Thesis, 1962.
Carpenter, Stanley Dean, 'Patterns of Recruitment of the Highland Regiments of the British Army, 1756-1815', M.Litt Thesis, St Andrews, 1977.
Fraser, Kenneth B, 'The Knock Note-Book of 1731-1733. A Relic of the New Independent Companies'. Private research papers.
Lobban, R.D., 'The Migration of Highlanders into Lowland Scotland (1750-1890) with particular reference to Greenock', Edinburgh University Ph.D thesis (1969-1970).
McLean, Marianne, 'Peopling Glengarry County—The Scottish Origins of a Canadian Community'. Papers presented to the Canadian Historical Association, June 1982.
Moses, N.H., 'Edward Cardwell's abolition of the purchase system in the British Army 1868-1874; a study in administrative and legislative processes', London University Ph.D. thesis, 1969.
Senior, E.L., 'An Imperial Garrison in its Colonial Setting; British Regulars in Montreal 1832-1854', Ph.D. Thesis, McGil University, Canada, 1976.
Spiers, E.M., 'The reform of the Front Line Forces of the Regular Army in the United Kingdom 1895-1914', Edinburgh University Ph.D. thesis, 1977.
Strachan, H.F.A., 'The Post-Crimean origins of Reform in the British Army', Cambridge University D.Phil. thesis, 1977.
Sweetman, J., 'The Effect of the Crimean War upon the Administration of the British Army, 1852-1856', King's College, University of London Ph.D., 1971-72.

Legal Actions

Brevet Colonel William Eagleson Gordon VC *v* John Leng and Co. Ltd. (the Proprietors of the *People's Journal.*) 1919 Session Cases, p. 415.

Index